Humanitarian Governance and the British Antislavery World System

Humanitarian Governance and the British Antislavery World System

Maeve Ryan

Yale

UNIVERSITY PRESS
New Haven & London

Yale University Press books may be purchased in quantity
for educational, business, or promotional use. For information,
please e-mail sales.press@yale.edu (U.S. office)
or sales@yaleup.co.uk (U.K. office).

Set in Bulmer type by Westchester Publishing Services.
Printed in the United States of America.

ISBN 978-0-300-25139-5 (hardcover : alk. paper)
Library of Congress Control Number: 2021944807
A catalogue record for this book is available from the British Library.

This paper meets the requirements of ANSI/NISO Z39.48-1992
(Permanence of Paper).

10   9   8   7   6   5   4   3   2   1

For Matt, Ted, and Sam

Contents

Acknowledgments

SINCE I STARTED THIS PROJECT, I have accumulated so many debts of gratitude, personal and professional, that it is a daunting task to try to capture them all in a few short pages. I fear I will not be able to do justice to the kindness, patience, friendship, and wisdom of the many wonderful people who have taught, inspired, and supported me throughout. To each, I say thank you. The weaknesses, errors, and oversights of this work are mine alone.

I am very grateful for the support of the Trinity College Dublin Ussher Fellowship and the Irish Research Council for the Humanities and Social Sciences (now Irish Research Council) for enabling me to conduct my doctoral research. I am also very grateful to the Leverhulme Trust for supporting my postdoctoral research through an Early Career Fellowship that opened up many new and exciting avenues, and gave me the space to develop my thinking, grow my research networks, and build new areas of expertise. Thank you also to the Grace Lawless Lee Fund for facilitating archival research in Freetown, Sierra Leone.

A huge thank you must go to my PhD supervisor, Patrick Geoghegan, for his encouragement to undertake doctoral research in the first place, and for his guidance, inspiration, and enthusiasm. I was lucky to be part of a cohort of wonderfully supportive fellow PhD students at Trinity College Dublin, including Sean O'Reilly, Daniel Steinbach, Sarah Frank, Eamon Darcy, and Stephen Carroll, and to be a member of the research community of the Centre for War Studies: Trinity College Dublin, led by John Horne. Many thanks also to Jane Ohlmeyer for mentorship and encouragement during my time at Trinity and since.

I have benefitted from the advice and kindness of librarians and archivists at repositories across three continents, including the Public Archives of Sierra Leone, the British Library, the National Archives of the

United Kingdom, Southampton University Library, Hull History Centre, the National Library of Scotland, Durham University Library, Duke University Library, the National Archives of Cuba, the Department of Archives at the Bahamas, and the Bodleian Library. A very sincere thank you also to Anne-Marie Callan and Karen Miller for offering wonderful hospitality in Freetown, and to Manuel Barcia for making me so welcome in Havana and giving invaluable assistance in navigating the archives. For permission to reproduce material first published in my article "'A Moral Millstone'? British Humanitarian Governance and the Policy of Liberated African Apprenticeship, 1808–1848," *Slavery and Abolition* 37, no. 2 (2016): 399–422, I thank Taylor & Francis and Gad Heuman, the journal editor. For permission to reproduce material from my chapter "British Antislavery Diplomacy and Liberated African Rights as an International Issue," in *Liberated Africans and the Abolition of the Slave Trade*, edited by Henry Lovejoy and Richard Anderson (University of Rochester Press, 2020), 215–37, I would like to thank the University of Rochester Press and the editors.

The volume *Liberated Africans and the Abolition of the Slave Trade* grew from a conference held at the University of York in July 2017. I am immensely grateful to the conference organisers for inviting me to contribute to this thought-provoking and inspiring meeting, and to the network of scholars from whose expertise and generosity I have benefitted so much: Paul Lovejoy, Henry Lovejoy, Chris Saunders, Dale Graden, Daniel Domingues da Silva, Walter Hawthorne, Érika Melek Delgado, Laura Rosanne Adderley, Katrina Keefer, Olatunji Ojo, José Curto, Nielson Bezerra, Daniella Cavalheiro, Maciel Henrique Carneiro da Silva, Maria Clara Carneiro Sampaio, Vanessa Oliveira, Andrew Pearson, Sean Kelley, Sharla Fett, Robert Murray, Philip Misevich, Martin Klein, Bruno Véras, Abubacar Fofana León, Allen Howard, Inés Roldán de Montaud, Tim Soriano, and Randy Sparks. A particular thank you to Daryle Williams for his generosity and kindness in sharing some very valuable source material, as well as useful guidance about many aspects of the history of liberated Africans in Brazil and much-needed help with some Portuguese translations. Thank you too to Suzanne Schwarz, who acted as external examiner on my PhD and who has offered very kind support to my work since then.

To Richard Anderson, Matthew Hopper, Manuel Barcia, Kyle Prochnow, Christine Whyte, Kevin Bales, Bronwen Everill, and Matthew Dziennik: thank you for the many fascinating conversations we have had and the frequent, very generous exchanges of source material and archival suggestions. I am so fortunate to have met you, and I look forward to many opportunities to collaborate in the future and put the world to rights over conference buffet sandwiches and archive café lunches.

To the anonymous reviewers of this monograph, I am very grateful to you for sharing thoughtful and insightful comments and suggestions. Likewise, many thanks to the participants at seminars and conferences over the years—including at Cambridge, Canterbury, Leeds, Liverpool, Oxford, San Diego, Madrid, Berlin, Geneva, Toronto, and Chicago—and to anonymous reviewers for *Slavery and Abolition, Journal of Colonialism and Colonial History,* and *Gender and History* for engaging with and enriching my work. Many colleagues in the wider fields of African history, imperial history, and slavery studies have kindly shared their time and expertise over the years, including Nemata Blyden, Marina Carter, Padraic Scanlan, Dawn Hewitt, Zoe Laidlaw, Beatriz Mamigonian, Leo Spitzer, Silke Strickrodt, Richard Huzzey, David Lambert, Tim Lockley, Melissa Bennett, and William Mulligan.

Many thanks to Jaya Chatterjee for your confidence in this project and excellent editorial input, and to Eva Skewes, Phillip King, Beverly Michaels, and the team at Yale University Press for all your help and guidance. It has been a pleasure to work with you on this book.

The seeds of this project began a long time ago, while I was a Masters student at Cambridge, where I was privileged to study under the guidance of Brendan Simms. Since then, I have enjoyed collaborating with Brendan on a number of academic projects. For his mentorship, kindness, generosity, friendship, and belief in me, I am truly thankful.

I was fortunate to spend the first year of my Leverhulme Trust Early Career Fellowship at the University of Leicester, where the powerhouse team of the Carceral Archipelago project led by Clare Anderson took me under their wing. A particular thank you to Clare for your support and encouragement. You are one of the most inspiring role models I have ever known. And thank you to Eureka Henrich, Katy Roscoe, and Richard Butler for listening patiently and offering sage advice as I figured out the arguments of this book.

To my superb colleagues and friends at the Department of War Studies, King's College London: you have supported and encouraged me as this project developed through pandemics, pregnancies, and much else besides. To John Bew: "thank you" seems very inadequate for all you've done for me as a mentor and friend. But thank you. And thank you to Jess Carden, Andrew Ehrhardt, Flavia Gasbarri, Hillary Briffa, Alessio Patalano, Nicola Leveringhaus, Nick Kaderbhai, and Charlie Laderman, who together have built the Centre for Grand Strategy into a vibrant research community. A big thank you also to Matt Moran, Barbara Zanchetta, Rebekka Friedman, Mike Goodman, Shiraz Maher, Jules Gaspard, Tim Stevens, Mervyn and Lola Frost, Rudra Chaudhuri, Jack McDonald, Inga Trauthig, Mike Rainsborough, Susanne Krieg, John Fogarty, Abby Bradley, Khushboo Puri, and the whole Professional Services team.

The final word must be to thank my family and friends for their support, cheerleading, proofreading, and high levels of (apparent) interest in the complex histories of humanitarianism and empire. To Liz, Sarah, Laura, and Tom: it is a really lucky thing to have four siblings who are also the best friends I could wish for. I would particularly like to thank my parents, Siobhan and Peter, for inspiring in me a deep love of history and a passionate sense of curiosity, and for all of the hard work and the sacrifices you have made for us over the years—and particularly for our education. I count myself very lucky to have such parents and friends. To David and Sue: you have always looked after me with patience, understanding, perfectly timed cups of tea, and specially sourced furniture—even a desk with an ocean view. Many, many thanks for putting up with my constant working. To Cyril Clements: I wish you were still here so that I could thank you in person. Without you, this book would never have happened. A huge thank you must also go to my extended family of friends for offering encouragement and help in so many ways. In particular, Rachel McGovern,

Alice Aldridge, Menah Raven-Ellison, Dave Hanney, Tarik Begić, and Catarina Vaz Afonso went above and beyond the call of duty. To Ann and Conor Hanly: thank you for always being so welcoming on the many occasions I have arrived on your doorstep with a teetering stack of books and papers.

This work is dedicated with love to my husband, Matt. Your support, love, patience, and encouragement have made this possible. And to Ted and Sam, whose cheeky smiles are the light of every day and whose shared fascination with the keyboard of my computer has certainly resulted in some strange typos somewhere in this book.

Humanitarian Governance and the British Antislavery World System

Introduction

It shall be lawful for His Majesty, His Heirs and Successors, and such Officers, Civil or Military, as shall, by any general or special Order of the King in Council, be from Time to Time appointed and empowered to receive, protect, and provide for such Natives of Africa as shall be so condemned, either to enter and enlist the same, or any of them, into His Majesty's Land or Sea Service, as Soldiers, Seamen, or Marines, or to bind the same, or any of them, whether of full Age or not, as Apprentices, for any Term not exceeding Fourteen Years. . . .

Any Indenture of Apprenticeship . . . shall be of the same Force and Effect as if the party thereby bound as an Apprentice had himself or herself, when of full Age upon good Consideration, duly executed the same. . . .

Every such Native of Africa who shall be so enlisted or entered as aforesaid into any of His Majesty's Land or Sea Forces as a Soldier, Seaman, or Marine, shall be considered, treated, and dealt with in all Respects as if he had voluntarily so enlisted or entered himself.

—Article VII, "An Act for the Abolition of the Slave Trade," 1807

THE HMS *DERWENT* ARRIVED in Freetown harbour in March 1808, escorting two captured American ships: the *Eliza* and the *Baltimore*. On board were 167 enslaved people: 58 men, 14 women, 41 girls, 51 boys, and 3 infants. As African people sold into the transatlantic slave trade, they followed in the wake of millions who had passed before them—captured or born into slavery, sold and resold, marched in shackles to the coastal barracoons, forced into the fetid, airless slave ships that plied the West African coast, and transported to the plantations of the Americas, never again to see the continent of Africa. Over three million more would follow this path after 1808.[1] What made the "*Derwent* captives" unusual was that their journey was interrupted—and for a very particular reason. They were not simply captives, but "recaptives." No longer bound for the Americas, these "liberated Africans" were instead bound to the British empire: one of the first groups of survivors of the Atlantic slave trade to be brought to a British colony under the newly operational Slave Trade Abolition Act of 1807.[2]

For Thomas Ludlam, the acting governor of Sierra Leone, their presence presented a problem. No specific instructions had yet arrived from London about what to do with enslaved people found aboard captured slave ships, and no court had yet been created to manage the legal proceedings. Ludlam had only the text of the Abolition Act to guide him. Twenty-six of its twenty-seven articles were of no use in this regard—their focus was on creating a mechanism for stopping, searching, and seizing illegal slave ships, for prosecuting the resultant criminal actions in the British courts, and for ensuring the captors received bounty money to reward their efforts. Only one article related to the ships' human cargoes. It conferred responsibility on the British Crown to "receive, protect, and provide for" the survivors. It was intended to be a heavy-handed kind of protection; the liberated people were not at liberty to decline it. Along with the slave ship and any inanimate cargo, these involuntary passengers were to be rendered "Prizes of War" and forfeited to the Crown, which would either enlist them into the armed forces for life, or bind them into indentures of up to fourteen years. The act offered no alternative "disposal" for those obviously excluded from these two options through age, infirmity, or otherwise. Although the act stated clearly that liberated people should never be "treated or dealt with as Slaves," the freedom into which they had been delivered—as they would learn—was not intended to mean anything more than freedom from being legally owned as chattel. Former slaves were expected to repay the debt of their salvation.[3]

Connaught Hospital in present-day Freetown stands on the site of what was once the Liberated African Yard, the receiving depot where for over half a century, slave-ship survivors were initially brought. A visitor to that site can still observe the inscription marked in the keystone of the original gate: "Royal Hospital and Asylum for Africans rescued from Slavery by British Valour and Philanthropy." Perhaps the *Derwent* captives" were perplexed when they learned that they had been "rescued" from slavery— or that as a group, they would come to be known as liberated Africans. It would be difficult to construe their experiences on arrival at Freetown as deliverance from the incarceration, coercion, and violence of their enslavement to date.[4] Under Acting Governor Ludlam's authority, they were herded into a cattle pen behind the fort, where they were named, numbered, and auctioned off. The strongest men and boys were enlisted. Most of the remaining people were sold as apprentices for a fee of twenty dollars each. Thirty were retained by the Sierra Leone Company (of whom Ludlam was also an employee), where they were put on rations and formed into a Corps of Labourers. Each day they were sent out to labour under the superintendence of overseers armed with whips. Perhaps a third of them managed to escape and fled to a nearby Temne village upriver from Freetown. At least twenty of those apprenticed to private individuals also fled their masters. Several were recaptured. They were imprisoned in the town's gaol and put to work in chain gangs.[5] The distinction between their former state of enslavement and this particular brand of freedom must have seemed very slight indeed.

William Wilberforce, Zachary Macaulay, and the other framers of the Abolition Act of 1807 expected that the British slave trade suppression effort would harvest the labour of some enslaved people. In particular, they looked forward to the arrival of some indentured labourers to shore up the prospects of the precarious colony of Sierra Leone, a private venture in which several leading abolitionists were shareholders. They expected too that as the slave trade was swiftly crushed by the Royal Navy, some slave ships would also be recaptured on the far side of the Atlantic, yielding useful additions to the workforces of the British West Indies islands. But the abolitionists did not anticipate for how long the suppression effort would continue, or how many survivors it would produce. In total, between 1808 and 1863, at least 180,969 enslaved people were captured aboard 1,994 slave ships of the transatlantic slave trade and resettled in locations across the Atlantic world, from Freetown to Cape Colony, Luanda to Havana, Charleston to

New Providence, St. Helena, Ascension Island, Liberia, and beyond; the
true figure might be 200,000 or more. Additionally, at least 22,000 others
disembarked in ports from East Africa to India and the Persian Gulf between 1808 and 1896.[6] Nowhere, not even the labour-hungry colony of
Sierra Leone, was prepared for this volume of arrivals. No new infrastructure was initially planned or budgeted for. The Collector of the Customs
at each site was given responsibility for sheltering, feeding, and distributing liberated Africans.[7] The procedures were ad hoc and the results extremely variable, and frequently delivered tragic results. After 1810, when
the Colonial Office eventually acknowledged that the number of arrivals
was overwhelming the resources of the colony of Sierra Leone, a "Superintendent of Captured Negroes" was appointed and a separate parliamentary vote was granted for "the subsistence of the Captured Negroes" at
Freetown—the first move to formalise a bureaucratic infrastructure.[8]

In most of the British colonies that received liberated Africans, the
subsection of the colonial government responsible for them became known
as the Liberated African Department or Liberated African Establishment.
By far the largest, most expensive, and longest-lived of these administrations was that at Sierra Leone, where the number of arrivals is estimated at
99,752. The Sierra Leonean administration existed under various names
and iterations from 1808 until 1891, twenty-four years after the termination
of the transatlantic slave trade. A small number of pensioners continued to
be supported from the colonial budget until their deaths, with the final such
payment made in 1922.[9] Establishments also emerged in the vicinity of
Vice-Admiralty courts at Cape Colony, at various locations in the British
Caribbean including the Bahamas, Antigua, Dominica, Barbados, Jamaica,
and Tortola, and much later, at Jamestown in St. Helena. At least 150,000
liberated Africans fell under the jurisdictions of these British Atlantic establishments. Many liberated people were resettled near an establishment;
others were trans-shipped—and not always voluntarily—to secondary sites,
including the Gambia and various locations in the British Caribbean. Slave
ships captured in the Indian Ocean were, for the most part, brought to Port
Louis (Mauritius), Aden, Port Elizabeth, or Bombay, at gruelling distances
of between 1,300 and 2,800 miles from the places of interception; up to

35 percent of those who survived the voyages died shortly after formal liberation.[10]

Under the terms of a series of bilateral slave trade suppression treaties that Britain signed with other powers after 1817, administrative structures later emerged at Havana (Cuba), Rio de Janeiro (Brazil), Paramaribo (Dutch Suriname), and the Portuguese colony of Luanda (Angola)—many of which continued to oversee and interfere in the lives of liberated Africans and their children until late into the nineteenth century. The United States ran its own rather limited naval suppression campaign, capturing 68 slave ships and 6,346 enslaved Africans, of whom many were held in federal detention camps in Charleston and Key West in 1858 and 1860. An estimated 5,761 survivors were deported to the American colony of Liberia.[11] Between them, Brazil, Portugal, Spain, France, Argentina, and Haiti were responsible for the "disposal" of at least 43,000 liberated people. In total, liberated African status was conferred on at least 180,969 individuals in the Atlantic world over the course of sixty years, and possibly as many as 200,000 or more. This constituted the third-largest stream of coerced migrants in the nineteenth century.[12]

The story of the liberated Africans straddles a period of profound change in the history of the European empires and in the ideological assumptions and claims that underlay them. The Abolition Act of 1807 was crafted within an imperial polity that still regarded slave labour as essential to the economics of empire. By the time of the adjudication of the last slave cargo at Sierra Leone in 1863, chattel slavery had been illegal in much of the British empire for almost thirty years. In its place, new forms of unfree labour had been substituted: systems of indenture and apprenticeship that drew explicitly on models first crafted to incorporate liberated African labour into the political economy of empire. For Britons throughout this period, the liberated Africans lay at the intersection of atonement and opportunity; of exploitative chauvinism and pious newfound guilt for culpability in the slave trade. Scattered across a whole ocean, most liberated people had little in common with each other, yet their fates were in many ways bound together by the dual discourses of compassion and control that evolved around them. They were a contested group of people: argued over as resources, as labour units to be distributed, as expenses on a balance sheet, as objects of paternalistic concern and contempt, as potential Christian converts and proselytisers of a British "civilising" mission, and as instruments in diplomatic confrontations. Throughout, the liberated people found ways to disrupt and resist. They refused to be a blank canvas onto which imperialist goals, ambitions, and fantasies could be imprinted. As such, they presented successive governments and generations of abolitionists with a complex series of moral, political, ideological, and practical challenges. As the Brazilian historian Beatriz Mamigonian noted more than twenty years ago, the history of the liberated Africans "has the potential to be one connecting thread linking the history of the abolition of the slave trade, the history of the transition from slave to free labour in the Americas, and the history of African experience on both sides of the Atlantic" if only we can draw this complex, interwoven, and highly fragmented historiography into a clear, "mosaic-like but meaningful" frame.[13]

This book is in part a response to Mamigonian's call. Drawing together research across the diverse sites of implementation, this study seeks to deepen our understanding of the conceptual origins and implications of liberated African policy, and its consequences across the Atlantic world from 1808 to 1867 and beyond. In particular, it demonstrates the significant role the liberated African resettlement and integration experiments played in the particularly carceral origins of imperial humanitarianism, in the emergence of discourses and practices of a new phenomenon of "humanitarian governance," and in the consolidation of a British "antislavery world system."[14]

Sierra Leone looms large in this story, and is therefore the central case study of this book. But this is also a story of the liberated African establishments as a whole. An important contention of this book is that these sites should be viewed together within one frame, because it was here—in this "archipelago" of establishments—that discourses and practices of nineteenth-century British imperial humanitarian governance were first articulated, implemented, and worked through. Although diverse, disconnected, and in most operational senses discrete entities, these establishments all had essentially the same purpose: to implement the disposal terms of the abolition legislation, adapting its professedly humanitarian overarching purpose to suit local interests and to serve the purposes of empire more broadly. Each evolved into a power structure that administered self-professed benevolence through observation and control, sought to mediate the liberated Africans' first contact with, and assimilation into "civilised" society, and attempted to reconstitute the enslaved African as a free but subservient, useful, Christianised British subject. The overt justification was sympathy, philanthropy, and benevolence, and the policy of liberated African resettlement was infused with a distinctly humanitarian register of governance. Yet to echo Ann Laura Stoler, such sentiments "required inequalities of position and possibility," and were "basic to the founding and funding of imperial enterprises."[15] The history of the liberated African establishments demonstrates that the origins of humanitarian governance lie in the often hypocritical and exploitative logic of empire, and specifically in an anxious post-Enlightenment desire to salve the national conscience over Britain's leading role in the slave trade while preserving white power over black labour.

What may be perhaps most intriguing for historians of humanitarianism and empire is less the fact that this dimension of slave trade abolition policy originated in fundamentally self-serving motivations, or that it created a system geared to generate profit from vulnerable people and to consolidate imperial power. Such outcomes are unlikely to surprise those who study nineteenth-century slavery and abolition. Rather, it is that these first early experiments in the implementation and governance of a stated humanitarian goal (blended from the outset with a discourse of "civilising" social engineering) went on to materially shape the structures, systems, and organisational discourse of colonial governance more broadly. What began as a convenient expedient—cloaked by abolitionists in the language but not the substance of rescue and salvation—was the beginning of a process whereby humanitarian discourses, dispositions, justifications, and rationalities began to infuse and shape the exercise of colonial governance across the wider British empire after 1814.

Perhaps most important of all, what the liberated African establishments demonstrate is that the imperial point of origin of what can be usefully termed "humanitarian governance" is also the point of origin of systematised state-level humanitarian action as a whole—a set of undertakings that has both domestic and international manifestations, including the provision of political refuge to non-nationals, the consensual deployment of state aid, and the non-consensual deployment of military force in humanitarian intervention. In terms of both frequency and complexity, state-level humanitarian action has expanded hugely over the past two centuries from a series of tentative, mainly Western-centred experiments into a central (albeit not uncontested) feature of modern international political discourse and, for many, an important ingredient of global stability and order.

    This book sets out to make three main arguments. The first is that the system that evolved to manage the administration and disposal of liberated Africans at Sierra Leone represents the earliest elaboration of humanitarian governance in the history of the modern world. Indeed, the Liberated African Department at Sierra Leone was a point of origin for systematised humanitarian state action more broadly. It blended in one institution both the "emergency" and "alchemical" (or "developmental") varieties of humanitarian engagement identified by Michael Barnett in his groundbreaking two-century history of humanitarianism and power, *Empire of Humanity*.[16] A key objective of this book is to build upon Barnett's work and to move toward a better understanding of the origins and practice of humanitarian governance in the age of imperialism by showing how in the earliest incarnations of such governance at scale, primarily in Sierra Leone, both emergency and developmental forms of intervention coexisted and coevolved within a colonial, labour-management context explicitly predicated and defended on the basis of its ultimate profitability and utility to the British empire. The book situates the making and remaking of liberated African policy across the first seven decades of the nineteenth century within the intricate framework of relations between the British empire and its evolving self-image as a humanitarian state actor; between the hard exercise of power in the pursuit of self-interest and the evolution of an ideology and practice aimed at providing relief and refuge, as well as imposing developmental "civilisation" on distant others.

It would seem prudent before going any further to offer a few defini-
tions. The term "humanitarian" is used with care here, and with due regard for the differences in connotation for present-day readers compared
with its nineteenth-century proponents and detractors. In the present day,
the word "humanitarian" is broadly understood to imply a concern for
others, including distant strangers, and a desire to advocate or act to improve and protect human welfare. Such action can but does not necessarily mean a commitment to universal human rights.[17] Although many
mid-nineteenth-century abolitionists would not have described themselves
as humanitarians—the term was commonly used contemptuously, reflecting a level of "compassion fatigue" in the wake of decades of public activ-
ism on a variety of fashionable global causes—nevertheless some elements
of the modern-day understanding of the term are discernible in nineteenth-
century usage.[18] Where present-day understandings of "humanitarian" do
resonate strongly with the ideologies and interventions of early nineteenth-
century abolitionism is in a characteristic willingness to deploy power
without consent in order to implement what practitioners believe to be protections and improvements in the lives of the victimised and vulnerable.
For this reason, and in this sense, the term is used throughout this book.

Humanitarianism is difficult to define—or more particularly, to con-
dense into a single definition that satisfactorily bridges the two hundred
years since the phenomenon emerged in a recognisable form. A popular
present-day understanding of the term would probably include mention
of its origins in compassion and a shared sense of humanity, and of the
apolitical, impartial provision of relief to populations affected by conflict,
scarcity, and natural disasters. Yet this "emergency" branch, with its singular focus on the provision of relief to people in immediate danger, is
only one dimension of what humanitarianism has been historically, and
what it seeks to be.[19] It is a definition that has been shaped profoundly by
the politics and interests of the International Committee of the Red Cross,
and is traceable to the transformative experience of Henry Dunant on the
battlefield of Solferino in 1859. Alongside the emergency branch, scholars
of the history of humanitarianism have identified at least one other distinct
type: the "alchemical," or "developmental." This branch is concerned

with tackling the root causes of human suffering and, as such, engages readily with the politics of addressing systemic issues and crafting long-term solutions. If the emergency branch of humanitarianism is regarded to have a "battlefield father" in Solferino, the developmental or alchemical branch is generally traced back to an "antislavery mother," and the self-appointment of western abolitionists as the benevolent agents of a civilising imperialism.[20]

The term "humanitarianism" refers to more than simply compassion or concern, although these are central ingredients. Following Barnett, "humanitarianism" for the purposes of this book should be understood in terms of the characteristics that defined it as a new phenomenon in the early nineteenth century as against earlier forms of compassion and community- or identity-based charity. It signifies a series of interventions and activities beyond borders, justified by invoking a duty of care towards distant strangers that is grounded in a higher, transcendental (often, though not necessarily, religious) moral purpose, and involving an intent to expend significant organisational and governance effort and resources to improve the welfare and safety of those who are unable to help themselves. Yet— and this has been an enduring tension at the heart of humanitarianism from the abolition campaign to the present day—any act of intervention, however well intended, is an exercise of power, driven by an intent to control, and made possible by inequality.[21] It is no coincidence that humanitarianism had its birth in the context of empire. An emergence of "western concern for distant strangers," and specifically the desire to remake the world in the image of one's own moral code, was a product of colonial encounters, a way of thinking that was born in the context of the violent and exploitative expansion of western empires, and of a wholesale assumption on the part of white imperialists of the inferiority of other peoples.[22]

British abolitionist humanitarianism did not exist separately from the imperative to exploit and profit from the power imbalance between white Britons and the "uncivilised" world—indeed, the capacity to derive immense direct and indirect profits was, as the following chapters will show, a central element of early abolitionist strategy. From the moment of seizure of the slave ships, every step in the process of administering the captures was conceived of around this imperative. For this reason, from its earliest incarnation, Britain's "archipelago" of liberated African establishments cannot be divorced from the wider pursuit of imperial commerce, culturally imperialist projects of "civilisation" and "improvement," and the global propagation of Christianity. They should be viewed as part of a wider process whereby British imperialist humanitarianism contributed to the transformation of labour relations along the coast of Africa and facilitated the growth of forced labour throughout the continent, and in so doing, provided the most important pretext for the subsequent European partition.

For this reason, there is significant complexity in trying to understand or measure the relative "humanitarianism" of the liberated African establishments, and to interrogate what humanitarianism can even mean in a context so loaded with racial and imperialist discourses, and so very much geared from the outset towards highly constrained forms of postenslavement freedom that left its objects chronically vulnerable to abuse and interminable exploitation. On one hand, in its two primary functional spaces of surveillance and labour management—the Liberated African Yard and the purpose-built villages—the Liberated African Department of Sierra Leone blended within one organisational framework both emergency and developmental forms of humanitarianism. This represents a distinct and important elaboration of the concept of humanitarian action. Indeed, it became after 1815—at least on paper—something quite ambitious: a support structure for large numbers of non-voluntary migrants, which incorporated a system of food rationing related to the health of the individual, and the provision of allotments of agricultural land, family housing, regular supplies of clothing, child and adult education including agricultural and technical training, access to medical treatment, and recourse to a judicial system, primarily at government expense. For a not insignificant number, their status as liberated Africans opened up a series of opportunities for social mobility in Freetown and beyond. Famously, some came to be leading merchants and traders, and their descendants came to dominate the economic and political life of the colony later in the century.[23] Some others had the opportunity to return to their homes—either by negotiation with the colonial authorities or by escaping on their own initiative to the nearby Temne and Mende territories—or to migrate elsewhere in West Africa or beyond.[24]

It is important not to overstate the point, but it is fair to say that many liberated Africans brought to Freetown exercised a wider range of options and had significantly greater opportunities for eventual autonomy than those at many other locations, such as Cuba, Brazil, Cape Colony, the British West Indies, or indeed at Bombay, Aden, and the other establishments of the Indian Ocean world. It is also important to point out that although labour conditions and opportunities for liberated Africans in the slaveholding export economies of other British colonial territories were often bleaker than at Sierra Leone, a series of policy reforms enforcing time constraints on apprenticeship from the 1820s prevented most of those liberated in British colonial territories (and their children) from lingering under the interminable, slave-like condition of many Africans whose "liberation" was administered at Havana, Rio de Janeiro, and the southern United States ports of Charleston and Savannah.[25] The welfare of liberated Africans was certainly never particularly high on the political agenda in metropolitan Britain, but the issue could and did provoke some governmental, parliamentary, and public discussion and debate on humanitarian grounds, and a series of structured inquiries from the 1810s to the 1840s kept periodic account of the state of the various establishments and their functionality and fitness for purpose.

The challenge is to hold all of this in mind while still taking account of the basically coercive paternalism underlying the system. Both before and after the liberated Africans were released from the yards and into the disposal pathways that had been chosen for them, the establishments offered for many of their charges perhaps the very worst of both worlds. Some—perhaps many—liberated Africans at Sierra Leone eventually enjoyed the "province of freedom" which was so celebrated by the historian John Peterson.[26] Yet many did not. The Liberated African Department at Freetown operated a series of powerfully coercive spaces of confinement, discipline, and surveillance; and yet simultaneously, in failing to provide meaningful safeguards for the welfare and safety of the liberated Africans it disposed of, exhibited a complacency, wilful negligence, and cynical instrumentalism that facilitated the abuse and re-enslavement of an unknown number of people. As a structure of post-intervention governance, it was outwardly organised and rationalised around distinctly humanitarian registers, and yet was still, in essence, one final "middle passage," designed to funnel the putatively liberated people not towards full freedom, but along what Clare Anderson has termed the "continuum of labour exploitation."[27]

The concept of humanitarian governance follows from the close relationship between humanitarianism and empire, and reflects the central place the history of humanitarianism occupies in the history of imperial relations.[28] Humanitarian governance in the British empire should be understood more in terms of discourse and stated aims than measurable "humanitarian" outcomes. Throughout this book, it is used to refer to the framing of imperial and colonial governance in the language of a higher moral purpose, the pursuit of declared humanitarian goals through the exercise of state power, and the design of strategies of intervention explicitly justified on the basis of human need and articulated in a "moral vernacular." In *Colonization and the Origins of Humanitarian Governance,* Fae Dussart and Alan Lester make a convincing case that the early nineteenth century marked the incorporation of humanitarian principles into the apparatus of governance—the elaboration of "a new art of governance." The point of origin they identify is the introduction of slavery amelioration policies in the Caribbean in the 1820s. This, they argue, was the moment at which "'humanely' governed British imperial expansion and indigenous devastation established an intriguingly ambivalent foundation for subsequent humanitarian registers of government." By the 1830s, following a series of "transimperial governmental experiments in violently colonised settler colonial spaces," it was a commonplace of public life that indigenous "improvement" was the proper sphere of governmental activity.[29]

Yet it is possible to discern the seeds of a complex and ambivalent elaboration of the concept of humanitarian governance at least a decade prior to this, and primarily in West Africa rather than the Caribbean. This trend was driven by a series of actors who—not unlike George Arthur and others identified by Lester and Dussart—infused a certain register of humanitarian governmentality in projects of autocratic, conservative-humanitarian imperialist "improvement" that developed "in antagonism to, rather than in complementarity with, democratic humanist ideas of the universal rights of man."[30]

In turn, the liberated African establishments both drew on and informed quite unrelated social engineering experiments within the settler empire. Discourses and locally evolving practices of "humane" governance at Sierra Leone helped to shape British conceptions of the role of the metropolitan imperial state in defining and safeguarding post-enslavement rights and the rights of displaced indigenous populations from southern Africa to the Antipodes, Canada to the Caribbean, and in the provision of refuge at the peripheries of empire.[31] These discourses of refuge and protection are then discernible in later elaborations of the concepts of imperial "development," benevolent guardianship, and imperial trusteeship. The liberated African establishment not only transformed the governance of the colony of Sierra Leone, but formed part of a new way of understanding of what colonial governance could be for, because it opened up a new, embryonic form of—and rationale for—imperial expansion in West Africa: developmental imperialism.

In its present-day form, humanitarian governance has achieved truly global reach. Now regarded as the manifestation of nothing less than a transnational humanitarian order, it rests upon a complex "interlocking set of norms, informal institutions, laws and discourses that legitimate and compel various kinds of interventions to protect the world's most vulnerable populations; a surfeit of conventions and treaties that are designed to secure the fundamental rights of all peoples," and "a metropolis of states, international organisations, [and] non-governmental organisations."[32] The endeavour is framed and legitimated by discourses of compassion, responsibility, and a universal human concern, which help define how the norms, laws, actors, and institutions of international humanitarianism interact with the problems they define as requiring intervention. These discourses also serve to perpetuate the core foundational assumption that there is such a thing as an international community, which has obligations to intervene in order to defend, rescue, and rehabilitate its weakest and most unfortunate members. The modern international humanitarian order has generated what Barnett terms "a machine of intervention" in the form of humanitarian governance: a system of transnational governance geared towards tackling the most severe forms of human suffering through emergency relief, public health interventions, development work, and defence of the ideal of universal human rights. This is a system which

> aspires to not only regulate what already exists—saving lives from immediate death, but also to transform what currently exists, including cultures, institutions, and social relations, in order to reduce vulnerabilities, improve human capabilities, and give individuals the capacity to live their lives as they (re) imagine them.[33]

Perhaps unavoidably, then, the modern world's international humanitarian governance "machine of intervention" rests upon the same inequalities of position, power, and possibility which formed the basis for humanitarian action in the age of imperialism. From disaster relief to post-conflict reconstruction, developmental and civil society projects, human rights interventions and democracy promotion, the humanitarian record of the twentieth and twenty-first centuries is littered with examples of interventions designed without reference to the needs and wishes of target populations, and sometimes even in explicit opposition to those needs and wishes. Humanitarian governance endeavours typically blend both compassion and control. They are founded in paternalistic, often implicitly or explicitly racialised assumptions about the decision-making capacity of the target population, and their proponents must be comfortable with exercising some degree of domination by withholding at least some degree of consent. "Everywhere we look," Barnett observes, the humanitarian community is "committed to the protection of people from unfavourable conditions, from others, and from themselves."[34] This evaluation could just as easily have been made of Wilberforce, Macaulay, and the African Institution in the earliest years of abolition, and about the systems of hard power and coercion that intertwined with the practices of Christianising, "civilising" compassion they believed it their right to impose on the formerly enslaved.

   As will be by now hopefully clear, throughout this book, the terms "humanitarian" and "humanitarian governance" are not invoked as a projection of some imagined pious or selfless intent onto the initiatives of the various British colonial governments. Nor are they intended to read entirely benign, altruistic, or benevolent purposes into the actions of colonial administrators, private interests, and wider British or foreign opinion. A central theme of this book is that imperialist chauvinism, self-aggrandising opportunism, and racist ideas of white superiority were baked into humanitarian antislavery at the most fundamental level. The kinds of "civilising" antislavery humanitarianism discussed in this book were inseparable from projects of empire, from racist assumptions about the capacity of black Africans, and about the right of white Europeans to mould the world in their own image. This book starts from the assumption that moral or humanitarian considerations were a form of rational self-interest in their own right, and that, taken together, the objectives pursued by the abolitionists and the humanitarians that followed in their wake were driven by an ordering imperative by which Britain conceptualised the world it sought to make. Antislavery formed the ideological core of an imagined future moral or humanitarian order that would complement the political and economic forms of order around which understandings of state security, stability, and prosperity were organised.

   This is the book's second core argument: that the articulation and pursuit of professedly humane models of governance were important expressions of a larger vision of global order that functioned to soften and legitimate the more obviously self-interested forms of order sought by the British state and the private commercial actors whose interests its formal and informal imperialism served increasingly over the course of the nineteenth century. This vision of order was more than a set of humanitarian or antislavery values.[35] It was an imagined future that was expected to follow the successful projection of British power, when the morally uncomfortable problems of slavery and reliance on slave-grown produce would have been solved by new labour regimes in which free black men and women manifested characteristics associated with "Britishness" through so-called habits of industry that served the political economy of empire, and in which "fear of want had replaced the dread of the lash."[36] Taken together with economic and political orders, it amounted to a vision of order that could serve both the moral expectations of an antislavery public and the material expectations of security and prosperity that defined imperial power and state success in the age of empires. It was in the pursuit of this vision of humanitarian order that we can discern the shift from older forms of compassion and concern to something distinctly new: the age of humanitarian imperialism in the long nineteenth century. Put another way, the emergence of a domestic British mandate for empire-building—with all of the inequalities and inflicted hierarchies that enabled economically and politically motivated imperialist adventures across borders—provided both the resources and the mindsets that gave rise to modern state-led humanitarianism by creating the context in which ideas of antislavery morality infused both ideas of good governance and assumptions about the acceptability of applying British state coercion to achieve forms of international order that served British interests.[37]

The book's third main argument flows from this: that British humanitarian governance, and the multifaceted visions of order that it served, functioned in both imperial and foreign policy terms as an important and underappreciated dimension of what can usefully be termed an "antislavery world system" of power projection. This argument builds upon an idea articulated in Richard Huzzey's *Freedom Burning* (2012). Huzzey traces the shifting emphasis of nineteenth-century antislavery "from a question of imperial morality to a cause for moral imperialism," and identifies how Britain deployed an aggressive and morally contradictory world system towards the objectives of a newly "antislavery state." He demonstrates how the British state transformed itself into a complex apparatus of international slave trade suppression by authorising various arms of state power to act towards antislavery ends, and by developing a complex (and often quite incoherent) set of tools, strategies, and tactics—or an "antislavery world system"—to deploy those powers. Drawing on John Darwin's concept of the British empire as a chaotic and pluralistic assemblage of world power that was "varied in local tactics but united by strategic considerations and linked in subtle, myriad ways," Huzzey points to the heterogeneous and often conflicting actors and interests who made up this system: from the Admiralty and the Royal Navy squadrons to the clerks and writers of the Foreign Office's Slave Trade Department; from the judges of the Vice-Admiralty and Mixed Commission courts to the vast intelligence-gathering network of consuls, ambassadors, ministers, and traders scattered around the globe funnelling between themselves and back to London a constant stream of empirical data, rumour, personal observations, opinions, warnings, and suggestions. Particularly as the apparatus of the antislavery state moved into its second and third decades and beyond—and, as Roger Anstey has observed, as the central place of abolitionism on both humanitarian and commercial grounds was internalised by successive generations of diplomats and bureaucrats as "a good and proper concern of policy . . . which did not require to be argued afresh as one generation of officials succeeded another"—an organisational culture emerged within the British antislavery state in which perceived antislavery zeal was a pathway to gaining the approval of superiors and a reputation for effectiveness as a public servant.[38]

Huzzey's model of the antislavery state and its "world system" emphasises the foreign policy dimensions of British action as orchestrated by the Foreign Office. Projects of humanitarian governance such as that at Sierra Leone, which fell under the purview of the Colonial Office, are not included. This is understandable, since Huzzey's focus is on the immediate stated goals of that system: to bring all maritime states into line with Britain's newfound zeal to suppress the transoceanic slave trades, as a first step towards the much longer-term, significantly less urgent objective of eliminating plantation slavery by removing its supply. Yet let us consider for a moment one of Britain's core purposes in projecting externally the power of the "antislavery state": to achieve a stable, secure, and prosperous (for Britain) global transition from enslaved to "free" labour. Of course, as is abundantly clear from the moral and legal chicanery of British delegalisation of Indian slavery in the mid-nineteenth century, and in colonial policies around "domestic slavery" in post-partition sub-Saharan Africa, the degree of real-terms freedom implied by the term "free labour" was not really the point. If the British antislavery state can be reduced to one essential quality that characterised it from its inception to the end of the nine-teenth century, it was its skillful adaptation of the mandate given by broad public opinion against the institution of slavery into a consciously far nar-rower strategic emphasis on suppressing slave trading; the narrowing of fo-cus, in other words, from a mission of antislavery writ large to a set of specific "abolitionist" or anti-slave-trade goals.

However, although the British antislavery state's often aggressive sys-tem of intervention shied away from direct interference in the domestic slavery of other powers, and indeed in the spectrum of coerced labour prac-tices prevalent in many of its own colonial territories, the narrative of the ultimate profitability and importance of replacing slavery with free labour was woven deeply into discourses of empire and formed a foundational as-sumption of nineteenth-century British conceptions of future interna-tional order. Although the precise pathway and pace of change from the suppression of slave trading to the ultimate termination of global slavery was the subject of fierce debate, what united antislavery-minded Britons of all stripes was the sense of being global leaders in an epochal shift from slavery to free labour. The essential purpose of the antislavery world system was to give form and expression to this—and to deploy force where necessary to achieve these goals.

It is important therefore to incorporate into this picture the experi-ments in large-scale post-emancipation labour management piloted by the liberated African establishments at Sierra Leone and other Atlantic-world sites. They came to play at least four important roles in support of the Brit-ish antislavery world system. The first was that they supplied a variety of colonies with significant amounts of military manpower. As Secretary at War Viscount Palmerston told the House of Commons in 1815: "as some-thing must be done with the captured negroes, it was a favourable destina-tion for them to be put on something like the level of a British soldier."[39] Through lifetime enlistments, liberated people served as a partial replace-ment for the slave regiments that were outlawed after 1807. The precise number of liberated African men, women, and children enlisted for the military and the navy between 1808 and 1867 is not known, although for the land forces it was sufficiently high that a recruiter remarked in 1837 that "the whole of our African corps, and a great part of the West India Regiments that serve in the West Indies, are supplied from the liberated Africans at Sierra Leone."[40]

Another important function the liberated African establishments came to serve within the antislavery system was as a series of testing grounds for ideas of how to orchestrate a stable post-slavery labour transition through term-limited non-voluntary indentures, or "apprenticeships." "Apprenticeship"—which itself echoed the provisions of previous abolitionist experiments, such as Pennsylvania's "Act for the Gradual Abolition of Slavery" in 1780—went on to form the basis of the post-1833 labour-management process in the sugar islands of the West Indies and elsewhere. Related to this was the third function: the liberated African population at Sierra Leone offered British abolitionists and colonial officials an unprecedented opportunity to attempt to prove the foundational claims of early nineteenth-century British abolitionism that free labour would prove more profitable than slave labour, and that after the slave trade ended, West Africa would be transformed into a series of major plantation export economies. Founded in 1787 as the "Province of Freedom," and re-founded in 1792 by a new joint-stock company, Sierra Leone was the only colony in the British empire built on an expressly antislavery mandate. When the suppression effort resulted in a huge, unplanned injection of involuntary migrants, the colonial government did not adapt immediately, but when it did, in the period after 1814, one governor in particular saw an opportunity to blend the practical functions of the Liberated African Department with a programme of experiments in social engineering.

As chapter 2 will explore, under Lieutenant-Governor Charles Mac-Carthy, a series of purpose-built agricultural villages in the mountainous hinterland of the colony provided a laboratory for a series of experiments in indigenous "improvement" under the banner of a wider antislavery global mission, and acted as the material basis for various imagined projects of imperialist expansionism in West Africa. In a vision as hubristic as it was paternalistic, MacCarthy looked to create a form of governmentality in Sierra Leone that was less about translating the imperatives of the abolition campaign into quick profits for the colony, and more focused on shaping a new type of imperial subject and a new type of imperial frontier.[41] These "model village" experiments in humanitarian governance predated other forms of experimental social engineering projects of empire, for example in the Kat River settlement of southern Africa, the indigenous resettlement experiment at Flinders Island off Van Diemen's Land, and the post-emancipation "free villages" of Jamaica, to name three.

Finally, the governance structures implemented to manage and harness the labour of liberated Africans in the Atlantic and Indian Ocean worlds also served some useful purposes in terms of framing foreign policy and Britain's place in the world. In their expense, complexity, and longevity, they acted—at least in British eyes—as a source of "moral capital" and legitimacy for claims to virtuous commitment to costly, long-term antislavery and free labour policies.[42] The establishments were often framed as sites of "refuge" or "asylum," which reflects a trend in metropolitan Britain after 1750 whereby the state was increasingly understood to have a duty to accept and protect persecuted peoples.[43] Particularly in the wake of the French wars and the loss of the American colonies, a "wholesale shift" is discernible in British cultural assumptions, whereby broad normative claims on behalf of refugees wove into the broader tapestry of an emergent proud humanitarian abolitionist national self-image. The state came to be seen as having a moral mandate to assist those fleeing—or, to a much lesser extent, rescued from—unjust governance and exploitation. In the late eighteenth century, the category of *refugee* referred specifically to the French Huguenots, but by the mid-nineteenth century, the term had widened to be applicable in theory to anyone seeking asylum from injustice and oppression, regardless of their race, class, politics, or religion. This could include candidates as diverse as Hungarian patriots, North American fugitive slaves, and French democratic-socialist exiles.

In practice, life as a refugee in Britain and its territorial empire was often characterised by poverty, precarity, and day-to-day xenophobic hostility. But in the imaginations of the British public, refugee status meant being conferred with the material support and physical protection required to live a dignified, independent existence. Like the campaign to abolish the slave trade, Britain's provision of political refuge was "a foundational act of an increasingly triumphant" or perhaps triumphalist liberal ideology. The rapid expansion of Britain's territorial empire provided the catalyst, and the space, to transform this "morality tale" into a national, and then an imperial, raison d'être.[44] The liberated African establishments represented an interesting elaboration of the concept of refuge, demonstrating the role the imperial state could play as a provider of "asylum" on a systematised rather than entirely ad hoc basis.

The framing of the British Atlantic-world establishments as sites of rescue and refuge gained additional significance when the liberated African question assumed a foreign policy dimension. British experience of managing sites of surveillance, experimentation, and information collection provided an evidence base that informed the demands Britain placed on other powers in constructing the bilateral antislavery treaty network after 1817. From the early 1820s onwards, British diplomats corresponded with the governments of Spain, Brazil, Portugal, and others regarding their treatment of liberated Africans, and by the 1830s, began negotiations to transfer all liberated people to British colonies in the West Indies. Over several decades, the comparative treatment of liberated Africans by Britain and its treaty partners formed a yardstick against which British diplomats, consuls, naval officers, and bureaucrats sought to evaluate the antislavery zeal of treaty partners and gauge the scope and necessity for the military and naval power of the antislavery world system to flex its muscle. This role found its most dramatic expression in a series of flagrantly illegal land operations and naval incursions into Brazilian territorial waters in the early 1850s.

This book is organised into seven chapters. The first four chapters investigate the origins and evolution of liberated African policy and practice in the Atlantic world. Chapters 1 and 2 focus on the making and remaking of British liberated African policy, primarily for and within Sierra Leone, between 1802 and the 1820s. Together, these chapters show how a structured, systematised, and relatively well-funded model of refuge-provision and governance emerged for a time in that colony—an unplanned, embryonic experiment in humanitarian governance constructed around the dual imperative to provide refuge and to extract advantage. First, these chapters explore humanitarian governance's distinctly un-humanitarian intentions and precedents; and then show how actors within the colony reshaped Colonial Office views of both the needs of, and the opportunities made possible by, the ever growing liberated African population.

Chapters 3, 4, and 5 situate the discourses of humanitarian governance associated with the Liberated African Department of Sierra Leone within the wider scope of British interests and relations in the Atlantic world. They consider the distinct domestic and foreign policy dimensions of the liberated African question, and seek to demonstrate its importance to the evolution of a British antislavery "world system." Chapters 3 and 4 focus on sites of liberated African resettlement in British territories and consider the establishments' different responses to their purportedly humanitarian mandate. Chapter 5 explores British interference in the slavery politics and practices of other powers including Spain, Portugal, Brazil, the Netherlands, and the United States. It shows how the question of *emancipado* rights formed the basis of the first sustained piece of international diplomatic humanitarian advocacy, and the first engagement between Britain and another power on the subject of the humane governance of vulnerable populations.

The final two chapters demonstrate the role liberated Africans played in the evolution of humanitarian governance across the "archipelago" of Atlantic-world resettlement sites, and the impact of interventionist experiments on the lives of these people. While the same purportedly humanitarian purpose laid the basis for each liberated African establishment, in practice each became the site of a different articulation of that purpose— in part because of adaptations by and for local interests, but in no small part because of the efforts of liberated people to resist or negotiate the forms of constraint imposed upon them. Chapters 6 and 7 explore liberation and disposal as lived experience, primarily in the colony of Sierra Leone; as encounters between the survivors of the slave trade and the interventionist imperial power that undertook in law to "receive, protect, and provide for" them through apprenticing and enlisting them.[45] These chapters assess how two key legislative provisions were interpreted, implemented, and developed over the period 1808–1863; how liberated Africans experienced and responded to them; how they resisted and mediated efforts to assimilate, instrumentalise, and exploit them; and how those responses shaped the evolution of both practical policymaking and policy framers' perceptions of the justice, effectiveness, and future potential of their approach.

These two thematic chapters make no claims to be comprehensive studies of all aspects of the apprenticeship and enlistment of men, women, and children throughout the Atlantic world. They focus on policy and practice—primarily in the colony of Sierra Leone—and ask three questions: First, what can we know about how liberated people experienced and responded to the systems of governance created to harness their labour and assimilate them into colonial life? Second, did their experiences and responses—and the perception by British colonial officials and observers of their experiences and responses—provoke metropolitan debate and reform, either towards more just and "humane" forms of governance or towards more "pragmatic" or efficient forms of exploitation? Finally, in what ways did the disposal policies support the "emergency" and "developmental" purposes of the Liberated African Department? To what extent did critiques and ongoing reform of the policies reflect and reinforce (or not) evolving discourses of humanitarian responsibility and the duty of the British empire to provide refuge to slave trade survivors? As these two chapters seek to demonstrate, the experience of being "disposed of" constituted for the liberated people in many ways another "middle passage." While British administrators and colonial bureaucrats engaged in protracted debates that contested the very character of humanitarian governance and its balance between the provision of refuge and the extraction of value, tens of thousands of African men, women, and children moved through the carceral transit zone of the Liberated African Yard and into the disposal routes selected for them—sequential steps in a process of serial displacement that merely underscored the profound difficulty of regaining full freedom after even the briefest period of enslavement.[46]

The story of the liberated Africans offers important clues about what the earliest proponents of abolition were actually trying to achieve. They were not seeking to rescue and rehabilitate people who had been enslaved, but rather to disrupt the slave trading ecosystem as a means to prevent the future enslavement of other Africans, and to prove by almost any means necessary the economic viability of "free" labour. The liberated Africans were the afterthought of an intervention that was not intended to save them. But they were far from being passive recipients of British experiments in social engineering, and far from being mere cyphers in Britain's efforts to rationalise its empire in humane and benevolent terms. In their story lie the origins of international humanitarian governance.

ONE

"Management Without Responsibility"
The Sierra Leone Connection

IN LATE JULY 1807, four months after the Abolition Act passed the House of Commons and almost two months after it became law, a parliamentary bill to transfer the colony of Sierra Leone to the formal control of the Crown passed the House of Commons on its third reading. Five months later, on 1 January 1808, the Sierra Leone Company flag was hauled down in Freetown and the Union Flag hoisted in its place. Histories of this period frequently mention in the same breath the formal relationship between the Abolition Act and the colony of Sierra Leone: that at around the same time as the Abolition Bill was making its way through Parliament, the Crown assumed sovereignty over the "province of freedom."[1] Yet the designation of Sierra Leone as a Crown Colony was not an intrinsic element or inevitable consequence of Britain's legislative abolition of the slave trade. These should be seen as two separate events, deliberately related to one another by the design of a number of individuals financially interested in the precise manner in which the suppression campaign would be pursued, and with what consequences. Far from being passed over in a few words, the relationship should be interrogated—as should the centrality of liberated African labour to the project—because this relationship was in many ways representative of the tension between "costly moral action" and the aggressive pursuit of self-interest that was to characterise the implementation of British abolition policy across the Atlantic basin.[2] The origin of liberated African policy—and with it, the first major state experiment with humanitarian governance—lay in the identification of abolition as a potential route to rescuing the fortunes of an ailing colony and the fortunes of those who had invested in it. For the abolitionists of the Sierra Leone Company, 1807 was not supposed to be a new dawn of a humanitarian anti-slavery, but rather the beginning of the second phase of their experiment. The liberated African policy they wrote for the British government was crafted to manage that transition—no more, no less.[3]

The Sierra Leone Connection

The Abolition Act of 1807 was only the first in a series of legal devices needed to turn Britain from the world's leading slave trading nation to its would-be anti-trafficking police force. The act was clear about its goal, but imprecise on how this would be achieved. A naval enforcement strategy was explicitly indicated, but the act gave no details of where the naval squadron would patrol, with which Vice-Admiralty courts it would cooperate, or precisely how the enlistment and apprenticeship of the freed slaves would be administered. In order to be enforceable, it required further elucidation. Two Orders in Council were issued on 16 March 1808: the first outlining more specific regulations for the administration and disposal of liberated Africans by enlistment and apprenticeship; the second expressly signalling the desire of His Majesty's government that "when it can be done conveniently," as many slave ships as possible should be brought to Sierra Leone for adjudication. There, on 2 May 1807, a Court of Vice-Admiralty had been established—almost three months before the transfer bill passed the House of Commons and eight months before the colony became Crown territory—conferred with a prize jurisdiction limited to the prosecution of captured slaves, the ships in which they were taken, and all other goods found on board.[4] In this way, well before it was transferred to the Crown, Freetown was marked out to become the West African base of anti-slave-trade naval operations, and as the primary landing and adjudication site for interdicted slave ships and their enslaved passengers.

Yet the transfer was not a foregone conclusion. The precarious and unprofitable nature of the colony was more than apparent; by 1802, it had become virtually reliant upon an annual parliamentary grant. In that year, the Sierra Leone Company's directors had begun to petition the government to take over the colony and allow them to wrap up their affairs. As a group, the shareholders carried an important degree of political leverage with successive governments during this period. There were also some practical arguments in favour of acquiring a deep-water port on the West African coast. Nevertheless, doubts were expressed within government about the wisdom of accepting the increased responsibility and expense, and a naval officer, Captain Benjamin Hallowell, was sent out to report on the current state and future prospects of Sierra Leone. Hallowell's report so alarmed the Chancellor of the Exchequer that, far from approving the transfer request, he insisted on a full parliamentary investigation to determine whether any further funds should be voted to support the colony. A committee was duly formed. Its membership included Henry Thornton, who was a cousin of William Wilberforce and the chairman of the Sierra Leone Company's board of directors. This committee gathered evidence and testimonies of some key figures who refuted Hallowell's conclusions and argued that the Crown should indeed assume control of the colony, primarily to avoid the expense of uprooting the existing settlers and resettling them elsewhere in the empire. The argument was sufficient to persuade the prime minister, William Pitt, to move for the grants to be paid for another two years, along with an additional four thousand pounds for fortifications.[5] After some objections, Parliament assented to these grants, but the matter of the transfer was not pursued.

By the time the transfer bill was introduced to Parliament in early 1807, the Sierra Leone Company had received over £109,000 from the Treasury. Opponents grumbled that a transfer was out of the question, and that the total of the parliamentary grants voted to the company to date "ought now to be refunded," as John Dent argued, since Parliament should not "be made to pay for the fanciful notions of any set of men." William Eden agreed that "the object of the company had in a great measure failed," but felt that the real question was what "the cheapest mode" would be of maintaining the Nova Scotian and Maroon settlers, whose safety remained the responsibility of government. He felt that it would be cheaper "to maintain them where they were than to remove them to any other place," and "he rested his assent to the bill on that ground, for he did not expect much

from the project of civilization." John Fuller argued that "he always conceived the sums of money advanced by government to the Sierra Leone
company as done entirely with a view to conciliate the support of a certain
description of gentlemen within these walls." It was surely "impossible for
the committee of finance to overlook so flagrant a waste of the public
money," without demanding reimbursement by "the wealthy bankers and
merchants who composed [the Sierra Leone] company."[6]

Few voices were raised in enthusiastic support of the motion. Those
who supported the transfer did so on the grounds that the Sierra Leone
Company had taken responsibility for the maintenance of the Nova Scotian and Maroon settlers, and that it would be unfair to request reimbursement of monies paid by Parliament. Lord Henry Petty argued that the
British government was "bound to continue its protection to the black inhabitants of Sierra Leone, whom it would be the most cruel injustice to
abandon, after the fidelity and attachment they had manifested to the British government." Henry Thornton gave an impassioned defence of the
progress the colony had made. From difficult beginnings—made more
challenging by the wars with France—the colony had matured. There
now "existed a body of colonists on the coast of Africa, speaking the English language, attached to the English people, advancing in civilization
and morals, and increasing in numbers, from whom, undoubtedly, and
from whose children, this country might hope to derive substantial advantages." "In whatever sense [the colony] might be said to have failed," it
"had afforded proof of the practicability of civilizing Africa."[7]

The passage of the transfer bill in July 1807 was a hard-fought victory for Henry Thornton and his Sierra Leone Company allies, including Zachary Macaulay, William Wilberforce, Thomas Babington, and
others from the elite group of abolitionists sometimes referred to as the
"Saints." Once they were finally freed of direct responsibility for the expensive and time-consuming colony, they turned their sights to other
interests and personal ambitions in West Africa. Several took on leading
roles in the newly constituted, professedly non-commercial African Institution. Most notable among them was Zachary Macaulay, a former
governor of Sierra Leone, who exchanged his more recent role as Sierra
Leone Company secretary for the position of honorary secretary for

the African Institution and set about building personal commercial links with Freetown. He bought a ship and in 1808, in partnership with his nephew, commenced trading as Macaulay and Babington, a firm that swiftly built a powerful monopoly over the colony's trade. On matters relating to West Africa, Macaulay had the ear of the secretary of state for war and the colonies, Lord Castlereagh, and played an important role in designing the terms of the Abolition Act.[8] After the transfer, Castlereagh—who had little interest in the recent acquisition—continued to accept Macaulay's counsel, including his suggestion that Sierra Leone become the seat of a Vice-Admiralty Court. Macaulay then went on to direct the recruitment of colonial officials and members of staff for the court, including members of his own family. He drafted a set of instructions for the capture of slave ships, which were then circulated to the naval commanders on the West African coast. Macaulay also wrote numerous memoranda on the administration of the colony and even for a time administered its finances. He summarised his influence in an 1807 letter to the then acting governor of Sierra Leone, Thomas Ludlam, describing how the "Government will be disposed to adopt almost any plan which we may propose to them, with respect to Africa, provided we will but save them the trouble of thinking."[9]

In the first decade of its operation, the suppression campaign in the vicinity of Sierra Leone reaped vast sums of money for its practitioners. It is important to recognise that the abolitionists explicitly intended it to be so: abolition was supposed to be not just a pious atonement for the sins of the slave trade, but a prudent and profitable measure as well. From the outset, the argument was that by stamping out slave trading, Britain would open up vast new markets for its manufactures, and that the cost of the intervention would be offset by the significant profits that would accrue. The elite abolitionists of the African Institution assumed that since the economies and peoples of the African continent had been so hollowed out by the scourge of slave trading, their political economy was a primitive tabula rasa onto which more "civilised," Western capitalism could be imprinted with ease. Once slave trading was crushed, so the thinking went, "legitimate trade" would fill the void and the coastal peoples of West Africa would be convinced that it was more profitable to put their people

Table 1. Enslaved People Liberated and "Disposed of" at
Sierra Leone, 1808–1833

Year	Men	Women	Boys	Girls	Total
1808	39	12	16	11	78
1809	86	57	80	57	280
1810	471	195	281	140	1,087
1811	246	121	114	64	545
1812	1,265	377	408	180	2,230
1813	227	57	117	45	446
1814	1,029	278	437	159	1,903
1815	583	277	253	183	1,296
1816	1,197	548	477	323	2,545
1817	246	101	143	113	603
1818	360	152	160	53	725
1819	237	124	177	137	675
1820	145	63	133	81	422
1821	550	197	194	191	1,132
1822	1,424	572	437	415	2,848
1823	265	117	128	106	616
1824	655	217	193	82	1,147
1825	786	306	580	321	1,993
1826	1,504	730	697	544	3,475
1827	1,136	646	533	543	2,858
1828	1,390	700	792	563	3,445
1829	1,684	1,327	960	886	4,857
1830	1,338	775	799	596	3,508
1831	855	200	501	266	1,822
1832	871	149	402	120	1,542
1833	437	102	256	184	979
Total	19,026	8,400	9,268	6,363	43,057

Source: National Archives of the United Kingdom, CO 267/127

Note: Most clerks in this period used fourteen as the dividing line between child and adult, usually estimating age based on the individual's height rather than their own account of their age.

to work producing export crops and commodities—ideally, though not necessarily, as free labourers—than it was to sell them to Europeans. Many trading interests did indeed flourish as commodity exporters from the West African coast in the decades after abolition. In the more immediate term, Wilberforce, Macaulay, and their African Institution colleagues crafted the terms of the Abolition Act in such a way as to load the naval suppression process with heavy financial incentives. Each slave ship "prize" was liable for resale, along with its cargo of trade goods and foodstuffs, which injected both cash and goods into Freetown's economy. A whole series of ancillary services thrived to service the processing of prize claims, including surveying, contracting, auctioning, and refitting and provisioning.[10] The result was that the arrival in the harbour of a captured slave ship was greeted with excited anticipation.

Policies and attitudes relating to the management of liberated Africans throughout the British Atlantic in these early years were essentially a by-product of this broader system of value creation. Since the Abolition Act rewarded naval officers with "head money" for every slave-ship survivor brought ashore, each liberated African represented a profitable prize for the captors. Those who were not then snapped up by the enlistment officers became a charge on the colonial authorities, who had a mandate to "dispose" of them as units of labour, usually for a fee, to the many would-be apprentice masters hungry for an inexpensive, bonded workforce. The liberated African establishments were thus in their first incarnations little more than temporary expedients designed to funnel the liberated Africans as quickly and cheaply as possible through to their ultimate masters, as part of a system whose primary focus was on monetising the suppression effort. Within a decade, Zachary Macaulay had amassed a personal fortune of over one hundred thousand pounds, primarily through managing the provisioning contracts for the greatly enlarged army and navy presences, through handling the asset sales and prize bounty transactions associated with the Vice-Admiralty Court, and through provisioning the liberated Africans held in the custody of the colonial government at the King's Yard (later known as the Queen's Yard or Liberated African Yard).[11] The transatlantic slave trade had perfected at scale a system of turning African people into merchandise: "bodies animated only by others' calculated investment in their physical capacities."[12] The colonial experiment founded on the explicit mission to end this trade operated on more or less the same set of assumptions—as did its post-1807 reincarnation as a hub for Britain's anti-slave-trade interventions in West Africa. Years later, the pro-slavery pamphleteer James MacQueen recalled the ease with which Macaulay and Babington had swooped in to capitalise upon the immense profits to be made from the slave trade suppression campaign. He condemned the influential men of the African Institution who had "interested themselves" financially in the colony. They had, MacQueen argued, only sought a Vice-Admiralty Court there so as to acquire captured slaves, who as "apprentice" labourers would be "the readiest and most rational way of obtaining labourers to cultivate the soil."[13]

"It Is as I Suspected"

MacQueen was not the first person to level this critique. In spite of how effectively Macaulay and his former colleagues dominated metropolitan policymaking for Sierra Leone in the first decade after the passage of the Abolition Act, the very first Crown Colony governor arrived in West Africa in July 1808 spoiling for a fight specifically on the subject of the liberated Africans, and on the ways in which officers of the colonial government had colluded to deny them true freedom. Although Macaulay and Wilberforce had handpicked Sierra Leone's new governor—Thomas Perronet Thompson, the son of a family friend of William Wilberforce—the young man did not live up to their expectation that he would be an amenable and malleable tool of the African Institution's continued influence in West Africa. Even before he left England, Thompson had already clashed with Zachary Macaulay on the labour practices of the Sierra Leone Company. He deplored the company's practice of "redeeming" enslaved Africans from nearby villages and "apprenticing" them in the colony as bonded labourers to repay the cost of their redemption. "Macaulay . . . said it was ransoming and I said it was buying," he later recalled.[14] Thompson was perplexed at how eagerly Macaulay appeared to favour this brand of coerced labour. "Macaulay and I had a battle about it," Thompson confided to his fiancée, Nancy Barker. He was appalled that the professedly antislavery colony had cooperated with local political economies of slavery and slave trading, and he rejected the argument that this was a necessary evil that would serve antislavery's deeper purposes.

When he arrived in Sierra Leone and learned how Ludlam had managed the first 167 liberated Africans of the *Eliza* and the *Baltimore,* Thompson believed that his suspicions had been confirmed. He was particularly incensed to discover the escaped apprentices in irons in the town's gaol. Thompson condemned Ludlam's apprenticeships as illegal, not simply because their adjudications had not been prosecuted in the correct fashion, but because payments had been made. For Thompson, the twenty-dollar apprentice fee levied meant that the *"natives ha[d] been bought for money."* The difference between apprenticeship and slavery had been, both in theory and in practice, reduced to one of mere terminology: the "apprentices" were slaves, their "indentures" were sales, and other "redemptions" of slaves from the Sierra Leone hinterland were purchases. "It is as I suspected," he wrote to Nancy. "These apprenticeships have . . . introduced actual slavery."[15]

The new governor hastily declared all apprenticeships prior to his governorship null and void, ordered the twenty-one apprentices released, and threatened Ludlam with prosecution under the Abolition Act. To those liberated Africans who had run away from their masters, Thompson offered regular work for wages under the circumstances that "they should go to no masters but what they liked." He later reported that they had agreed and had declared their willingness to work as free labourers on the land and assist in the defence of the colony; since their release, they had kept their word.[16] Then, in an increasingly feverish and paranoid state of mind, perceiving enemies and conspiracies everywhere around him, Thompson set about trying to identify and dismantle the intricate system of compromises the Sierra Leone Company had made with local slaving interests and the unsettling lack of conceptual clarity between slavery and apprenticeship in the labour infrastructure of the colony.

Thompson's governorship lasted nineteen months. In that time, some 1,200 Africans were liberated at Sierra Leone. Although Thompson remained bitterly critical of the concept of apprenticeship, several hundred of these arrivals were distributed under indenture—a policy he defended on the grounds that there was no financial provision for an alternative. He reported to London that a culture was developing within the colony whereby settlers flouted the ease with which they could effectively own and trade in slaves, ill-treating them with impunity, and freely using the language of ownership. He relayed to Castlereagh the story of an eight-year-old girl he encountered who bore burn marks on her back and other evidence of harsh treatment from her European master. When Thompson challenged the master, the man claimed "a right to do as he pleases with his own," arguing that "Africans" were prone to misbehaving when treated well, and insisting that the girl belonged to him because he had paid for her: "I redeemed her." The broader effect of this form of apprenticeship was, Thompson argued, to stimulate the regional slave trade. The slave traders of the region mocked the African Institution's "apprentices and [its] act of abolition," because essentially, all it had achieved was an alteration in price.[17]

In place of apprenticeship, Thompson proposed a scheme of settling the liberated Africans in outlying agricultural villages. The advantage of this supposed innovation, as he outlined in some of his many despatches to the secretary of state, was that it would solve the problem of resettling the liberated Africans safely and without fear of re-enslavement. It would also create a rural peasantry to provide foodstuffs for Freetown, which remained primarily a trading centre and a reservoir of skilled craftsmen dependent upon the public works. Thompson's plan merely reflected the self-directed movements and resettlement patterns of the ever increasing liberated African population, patterns he could likely have done little to influence; nonetheless, it represents the first recognition on the part of a colonial governor of the need to plan ahead—in terms both of town planning and resource allocation—for a population which would only grow in proportion to the success of the West Africa Squadron's efforts.[18] For the colonists, Thompson published a series of announcements in the *Sierra Leone Gazette* voiding the apprenticeships of the *Derwent* liberated Africans, reminding settlers of the prohibition of slavery within the colony, and attempting to dispel the apparently widespread belief that Sierra Leone inhabitants had the right to purchase slaves.[19]

Over time, Thompson's lengthy reports to the secretary of state became highly emotional attacks on the hypocrisy of the elite abolitionists of the African Institution. He professed real shock at the discovery that their former Sierra Leone Company employees and current colonial appointees would connive at the virtual enslavement of the liberated Africans.[20] At first, he placed the blame on the servants of the Sierra Leone Company who were based in the colony, and he merely chided the absent directors for being so easily misled by the unscrupulous activities of their employees. Wilberforce responded with a restraining letter to Thompson in October 1808, arguing that liberated African apprenticeship was the agreed policy of government and had been specifically included in the Abolition Bill to give it a better chance of passing both houses of Parliament.[21] Thompson was supposed to be swayed by the pragmatism of this argument; instead, the suggestion that an apprenticeship clause had been included in the bill as a sweetener for pro-slavery Members of Parliament and potential investors in the new Sierra Leone Crown Colony reinforced his opinion of the innately cynical nature of British elite abolitionism. He now regarded his family friend and former mentor with "more pity than it were perhaps good for him to know." "Mr W. has thought that *a little slavery* might be connived at," he wrote to his fiancée, "*a little breaking* of a few Acts of Parliament, so long as the slaves were made good Christians in return for it, and *that* is the Delilah which has seduced him." "Messers Wilberforce Thornton and Co have at last become slave traders with a vengeance in their old age."[22]

Thompson's voluminous correspondence was met with only silence from the secretary of state. Meanwhile, the young governor began to receive indications that he had made powerful enemies in London and in Sierra Leone who were consolidating a position against him and seeking his recall. In response, he wrote with even more abandon. The close linkages between the defunct Sierra Leone Company and the new African Institution now assumed a more sinister, even "dangerous" appearance in his mind:

The Sierra Leone interest is the leaven which sets all in motion. At the African Institution they impudently declare

that they have no concern either with commerce or with missions; they step into their coaches and presto—they are the
Sierra Leone Company—*hey pass* and they are the Society
for Missions to Africa and to the East; another transformation makes them the Society for the Suppression of Vice, a
fourth carries them to the India House, and a fifth lands them
in the House of Commons.

The transfer of the colony to the Crown was, Thompson pressed, the most
sinister development of all. "What appear[ed] to be their defeat [was] in
fact their triumph," for they had now achieved "management without responsibility."[23]

"Indolence Is a Disease Which It Is
the Business of Civilization to Cure"

Thompson's friendship with Wilberforce did not survive the conflict;
nor indeed did his governorship. The well-connected targets of his attacks
closed ranks. He was recalled to London in early 1809 and relieved of his
post. Although it is easy to be distracted by the personal nature of his vit-
riolic clash with his former friends in the African Institution, his specific
criticisms of liberated African disposal policy are worthy of note: that the
policy was inappropriate to the circumstances and needs of many arrivals,
in particular the very young and the sick; that it was ineffective in addressing the needs of high numbers of people; and most of all, that it was simply
unethical to enrich the colony and its elite backers through the profits of
the unfree labour of "rescued" slaves. What Thompson failed to understand, as Padraic Scanlan's work has shown, was that the relationship that
had been negotiated across the previous decade between the Sierra Leone
Company and the wider regional political economy was a relationship in
which the survival of the colony relied upon its tacit acceptance of regional
slavery, slave-produced goods, and by extension, the slave trade. In his letters to Thompson, Wilberforce evidently wished to bring the young governor around to his understanding of the long-term benefits of short-term
moral compromise by implying that such compromise had been, for the

abolitionists, a journey of mature reflection and pained acceptance. Yes, he admitted, the disposal provisions for liberated Africans were "on the very face of them, grossly objectionable," but he defended himself and his African Institution brethren, claiming that they had been "forced into adopting" these measures "by some overruling necessity." He bewailed—but avoided detailing specifically—"the difficulties which forced us into acquiescing in the system of apprenticing."[24]

There is considerable disingenuity in Wilberforce's suggestion that the treatment of liberated Africans was conceived very unwillingly for purely practical reasons, partly to minimise costs and prevent a logistical problem and partly as a concession to pro-slavery interests determined to prevent any experiment in meaningful black freedom. Well before the passage of the Abolition Act, Macaulay, Wilberforce, and others actively sought out new opportunities for importing Africans into the colony of Sierra Leone for defined periods of unfree labour as a solution to one of the major challenges that had faced the colony since its inception. From the outset, they rationalised such programmes of coerced labour as an "improving" intervention, an opportunity for the "uncivilised" to be schooled in the Protestant ethic of work. The abolitionists' belief in the need to apprentice enslaved people had a long pedigree in the former "province of freedom." In 1804, Macaulay wrote to the then governor, Ludlam, stating that while he opposed the purchase of Temne, Susu, Mende, and other local slaves by the Maroons, Nova Scotians, and European settlers within Freetown, yet he believed that "redeeming" and indenturing enslaved Africans from the surrounding regions was the best method of supplying labour to the flagging colony. "While the slave trade lasted," he wrote,

> I certainly felt very averse to giving any direct encouragement to the purchasing of slaves, with a view to the benefit of their labour for a certain given period; but I always looked forward to the event of the Abolition, as removing many objections to that system. Indeed I have always been of the opinion that the slave trade being abolished, the most likely means of promoting civilisation in that country would be by indenting the natives

for a time not exceeding seven years, or till they attained the
age of 21, under regulations which should be well-defined and
rigidly enforced.

William Dawes, a contemporary of Macaulay and Ludlam who also served
three times as governor of Sierra Leone between 1792 and 1803, went further, admitting to Thompson in 1808 (or so Thompson claimed) that he
had always considered some form of slavery to be necessary in Sierra
Leone and that he still felt it so.[25]

The elite abolitionists were, more broadly, always keen to emphasise publicly their extremely gradualist attitude to ending the institution
of slavery, and their profound horror at the idea of transforming an enslaved person into an autonomous agent in one single act of liberation. In
an 1805 debate on the abolition of the slave trade, Wilberforce argued
forcefully against the accusation that he was planning the eventual emancipation of the West Indies' slaves rather than simply the abolition of the
slave trade. Wilberforce professed such an objective to be "mad." Enslaved individuals could not be "fit" to receive sudden freedom, he argued, and it would be "madness to attempt to give it to them." Mere days
after the Abolition Bill passed the House of Commons in 1807, Wilberforce again put forward his belief that all enslaved people must be trained
gradually for freedom. Similarly, Lord Holland argued that the aim of
emancipation was "the subordination of the Emancipated," and in a pamphlet the same year, Wilberforce argued that "True liberty," was "the
child of reason and law, the parent of order and happiness," a plant for
which "the soil and climate must be prepared." "A certain previous course
of discipline is necessary. They must be trained and educated for this
most perfect state of manly maturity."[26] Wilberforce later suggested a personal ambivalence on the question of liberated African apprenticeship,
implying that the choice of coercive disposal terms had simply been "the
least objectionable way of rescuing slaves," but Lord Brougham, reflecting
in 1823 on the suppression campaign to date, dismissed the idea that there
had ever been any uncertainty amongst abolitionists on the question of
imposing constraints on liberated Africans through apprenticeship and
enlistments:

> No rational person ever thought of at once conferring upon that
> ill-fated race that freedom which would have been . . . con-
> verted into a curse rather than a boon; but no one once doubted
> that the principal good of the abolition was to be its improving
> the negro's condition, and gradually raising his character to the
> level at which he might become fit to enjoy personal freedom.[27]

In a similar vein, the abolitionist James Stephen wrote to Lord Liverpool
in 1811 that "Africans or new negroes, as they are called, neither being intelligent enough to protect their own freedom, nor able immediately to work
for their own subsistence . . . it was necessary in respect of them, to give,
for their own sakes, the power of enlisting or apprenticing."[28]

Indeed "liberation" was not intended to deliver the newly arrived,
usually destitute slave trade survivors into a significantly different material
condition. The antislavery humanitarianism of the elite abolitionists was
an ideology incubated in the context of aristocratic privilege and evangelical moral panic, combined with a deeply held belief in the moral necessity
of hard work; even a glorification of poverty and deprivation as valuable
cleansing experiences. Fundamentally, for them, the abolitionist cause was
a reform not of a primarily social evil, but of vice and sin—a breach of di-
vine law that forced the possessor of one soul to be held as the property of
another. As Eltis has observed, an overweening concern with freeing the
African spirit from bondage to sin made evangelicals appear rather less fas-
tidious about the secular concepts of bondage and freedom.[29] Gruesome
and horrifying representations of the Middle Passage functioned as effective emotive devices during the public campaigns, yet the bodily sufferings
of the slave were not the primary concern of abolitionists such as Granville
Sharp, William Wilberforce, Thomas Clarkson, and Zachary Macaulay.
These men did not consider poverty or deprivation as represented in the
Gospel to be an ordeal to be avoided or an evil to be cured; quite the opposite.[30] "The peace of mind, which Religion offers to all ranks indiscrim-
inately," Wilberforce explained,

> affords more true satisfaction than all the expensive pleasures
> which are beyond the poor man's reach . . . The poor have the

advantage . . . that if their superiors enjoy more abundant comforts, they are also exposed to many temptations from which
the inferior classes are happily exempted.[31]

To this view, it was not the business of Britain to elevate the liberated Africans from poverty, rather to stimulate in them the "Protestant ethic
of the dignity of labour—the moral necessity of work."[32] While the purchase of shares in the Sierra Leone Company was constructed as an ethical, morally cleansing form of investment, still "these pious men" did not
have a specific ambition to actually help or rehabilitate emancipated slaves.[33]
To truly liberate enslaved Africans and allow them to prosper autonomously
as free peasants in a manner of their own choosing would have been to demonstrate the independent capability of former slaves. If Africans liberated
from the holds of slave ships were ready for full, immediate liberation, why
not the Africans who had disembarked in the West Indies? The emancipation of the slaves in the British empire was still decades away. Slavery
was still legal; indeed, for many, its continuance was considered desirable,
or at least unavoidable. The slaves intercepted on the high seas and delivered to Freetown represented the interruption of an outcome that was still
in essence considered justified—if not always morally, then certainly economically—by a large proportion of the British population.

Conceptually, the "liberated African" existed between the issue of
abolition and the issue of slavery. The "Saints" were very keen to distance
themselves from any overt acknowledgement of the independent capacity
of enslaved people, and not purely for pragmatic reasons. Previous experience of colonial management influenced these views: the early settlers of
the Sierra Leone colony persistently refused to subordinate themselves to
the economic objectives of the company. These settlers' "false and absurd
notions . . . concerning their rights as freedmen" were as upsetting as their
"inadequate or enthusiastic notions of Christianity." Indeed, Wilberforce
complained to Henry Dundas in 1800 that their "crude notions . . . about
their own rights" made them the "worst possible subjects . . . As thorough
Jacobins as if they had been trained and educated in Paris."[34] Freedom for
liberated slaves was a safer concept when positioned as the final stage of a

process of assimilation, one that would include rejection of traditional African cultural practices for British, a preference for regular wage labour over subsistence farming or petty trading, Christian observance over traditional beliefs, and a sustained pursuit of consumer comforts. It was not an invitation to select an independent way of life, but rather to accept British commercial priorities as "values," Christianisation and literacy as moral improvement, and above all, a rigid sense of social stratification: apprentice below master, master below colonial authority. Central to the abolitionists' worldview was a belief that the great tradition of English liberty—a white heritage—could and should be extended to black subjects, but only in a carefully controlled sense.[35]

Once the Abolition Act was in place, elite abolitionist attention moved away from the specifics of domestic enforcement to the business of securing from the great powers of Europe a multilateral slave trade suppression treaty. For over a decade, leading abolitionists did not engage in any meaningful way with the terms under which liberated Africans were administered at Sierra Leone or elsewhere, nor consider the idea of seeking the consent of liberated Africans for the disposal pathway selected for them.[36] The assumption was implicit in the African Institution's view that liberated Africans would integrate easily into Sierra Leone's heterogeneous cultural environment hundreds or thousands of miles from their homelands and families, would marry (or remarry) and would learn the English language to overcome the practical difficulties of Freetown's more than one hundred spoken languages. The abolitionists did not concern themselves much with the details of that transition, but with what came next: the opportunity for missionaries to have regular access to an ever growing population of would-be converts, in whom could be inculcated solid, hardworking British Protestant "habits of industry." "Indolence," declared the Committee of the African Institution in 1807, "is a common characteristic of all uncivilized people . . . But indolence is a disease which it is the business of civilization to cure."[37]

It is evident that the personal views of Zachary Macaulay and the Sierra Leone Company and African Institution directors played a key role in shaping liberated African disposal policy in 1807 and 1808. To echo David Eltis, to take note of the degree to which Macaulay and Babington profited financially from the period of Macaulay's greatest personal influence over the colony of Sierra Leone and the disposal of many thousands of liberated Africans "is to make an important ideological point rather than to be cynical."[38] Combining both significant personal influence and the substantial weight of elite abolitionists' moral authority, Macaulay was instrumental in creating the terms of an operational policy that functioned by seizing enslaved people, co-opting their labour as apprentices or soldiers, and locating them in a place where he and his associates held significant financial interests, including in the highly lucrative provisioning systems required to keep the whole system functioning.

The disposal pathways designed by these elite abolitionists were adapted from practices incubated and developed much earlier in the very different contexts of metropolitan Britain and the American colonies. Liberated African disposal policy as framed in the Abolition Act took its inspiration from indentured servitude, coercive enlistment or impressment, and child apprenticeship as a means of removing pauper children from the responsibility of government. These were old solutions repurposed for a new kind of social problem, one created by the abolitionist intervention against the slave trade, and by the determination to prosecute that intervention in ways that—as Lester and Dussart observed about humanitarian governance in the context of violent mass dispossession in the settler colonial empire—sought to "have it all": an exploitative relationship that preserved absolute dominance over the formerly enslaved, yet with the clean conscience of the humane and benevolent.[39] In prosecuting the suppression campaign by designating the slave ships "prize" and utilising the established mechanism of the Vice-Admiralty courts to process captures and reward captors, these were solutions that would also be—for at least some of the policies' architects—highly lucrative. With no apparent sense of irony, the self-consciously pious men of the African Institution supplemented their narrative of national atonement for the sin of slave trading with an explicit expectation that the liberated Africans should repay part of the cost of the intervention by providing the British Crown Colony with years of free labour and a lifetime of subservient religious, social, and cultural conformity. Similar logic would be deployed after 1833 to support a comparable policy of "apprenticeship"-based post-slavery economic transition in the Caribbean and elsewhere.

Although Governor Thomas Perronet Thompson represented himself as the antithesis of Macaulay and his associates, his actions throughout his governorship belie the idea that he entirely rejected the concept of coercively instrumentalising the labour of formerly enslaved people. Rather, he opposed the specific uses to which the Sierra Leone Company had put the "blank slate" of the liberated Africans.[40] Nevertheless, he was the first of several prominent colonial administrators to suggest that there were moral limits to the power of the state over the lives of individual liberated Africans; that the state had what might be termed humanitarian responsibilities to fulfil, and—crucially—that the rationality of humane, antislavery governance could be one and the same thing as the rationality of expansionist colonial power; indeed, that one could be fuel to the other. One of Thompson's more successful and long-lasting successors, the energetic imperialist Lieutenant-Governor Charles MacCarthy, expanded this interpretation of the opportunities and responsibilities the liberated African population represented. As the following chapter will explore, through the increasingly sophisticated and expensive apparatus of the "Captured Negro Department," later the Liberated African Department, MacCarthy oversaw the development of an early incarnation of humanitarian governance that merged emergency and developmental forms of intervention within a colonial, labour-management context explicitly predicated and defended on the basis of its ultimate profitability and utility to the British empire—an experiment that was sustained for decades in spite of delivering very little in the way of direct commercial or geopolitical advantage to the imperial state. What is particularly interesting about these first two decades of experimental and evolving governance in Sierra Leone is the contingent and almost accidental way in which the British state found itself having a conversation about the welfare needs and autonomy of the liberated African population—a population the original framers of the Abolition Act never thought of as anything other than contraband to be counted, valued, and distributed, and whose freedom was supposed to be characterised by being, in real terms, no more free.

"With a View to Their Own Welfare"

The Liberated African Department of Sierra Leone

AS THE GEARS OF FREETOWN'S colonial economy turned excitedly around the flurries of profit and possibility created by the abolition industry in its early years, enslaved people often lingered days and weeks aboard ships at anchor in Freetown harbour, awaiting the decisions of the Vice-Admiralty Court. Epidemics of dysentery, ophthalmia, and smallpox were common. Packed into low, filthy, and poorly ventilated decks, many people also suffered from physical injuries sustained since embarkation: limbs were trapped between crudely constructed planks, and the weight of tightly packed bodies inflicted crushing injuries on the smaller children.[1] When they were finally allowed to come ashore, the earliest arrivals are recorded as having been "dumped" in the city gaol or other convenient repositories. The Colonial Surgeon, James Higgins, reported in August 1811 on his discovery of "more than a hundred of the negroes captured in Prizes afflicted with various diseases (chiefly . . . of the worst description)." They had been "placed in an old building formerly a barracks [and] had been neglected with respect to medical treatment." He described their "habitation" as "extremely offensive." Many died within weeks of arrival in the colony; many more were left with permanent physical disabilities or lingering psychological trauma.[2]

Medical facilities available in the first few years of abolition fell far short of what was required either to treat the illnesses and injuries they were confronted with or to handle the volume of patients requiring help. In the absence of a dedicated staff or support infrastructure, the colonial government absolved itself of formal responsibility towards the many liberated

Africans not considered able-bodied and available for employment. From 1808 to 1813, the "system" of liberated African management was little more than a series of ad hoc expedients, designed to utilise liberated African labour for the benefit of the colony and dispense with the remainder as quickly and inexpensively as possible.

Both the practical and moral insufficiencies of this situation quickly became apparent to those in the colony. More than 6,000 liberated Africans arrived between 1811 and 1815, at least half of whom remained in the vicinity of Freetown.[3] As early as 1811, liberated Africans constituted over three-fifths of the population of Sierra Leone and its mountainous hinterland, including the surrounding Temne villages. Once ejected from the custody of the colonial government, many settled in the colony or in new settlements springing up nearby. However, not all were able to find employment or shelter. Vagrant recaptives were reported to have roamed the colony, foraging for basic subsistence. Missionaries deplored the ongoing state of poverty and ill health of many new arrivals, and they reported high rates of mortality, claiming that some liberated people were left to die of starvation on the streets of Freetown. Significant numbers of liberated Africans reportedly vanished—either escaping upcountry or, it was feared, falling victim to the slave trading kidnappers who loitered in the colony's back streets.[4] Those who were distributed to private homes found themselves labouring out of the sight of the colonial government as part of a murky not-quite-free subclass of "apprentices," which also included Africans brought in from the nearby regions ostensibly to learn new skills, and those who had been "redeemed" from slavery in the nearby Mende and Temne communities.

Although the two governors who succeeded Thomas Perronet Thompson both raised the issue of the increasingly unsustainable liberated African population in their reports to the Colonial Office, the matter was not accorded much attention. The British Parliament passed a modified Abolition Act in 1811—by which date at least 1,200 enslaved people had been adjudicated free by the Sierra Leone Vice-Admiralty Court—the terms of which only tightened the naval enforcement mechanisms of the 1807 legislation; it did nothing to alter the management of the liberated people.

Nevertheless, from 1814 onwards, the system underwent a profound transformation. Under the auspices of the new Captured Negro Department—renamed in 1822 the Liberated African Department—the colonial government undertook a new approach to the liberated African question: a programme of systematised resettlement and labour management in the colony.[5] By the mid-1820s, this department had morphed into a sophisticated (and expensive) governance structure, organised around a blend of proselytising and "civilising" objectives and discourses, that reached across most aspects of government and was integrated deeply into the fabric of colonial life. This chapter examines the shifts that took place in the department's approach to governing liberated Africans, linking these changes to the differing conceptions held by successive administrators regarding the purpose and mandate of that department, and positioning the evolution of Sierra Leone's experiments in "humanitarian" social engineering within their wider economic and imperial contexts.

"To Remedy These Evils"

Thomas Perronet Thompson's two immediate successors were both far more amenable than Thompson had been to the moral compromises and ideological nuances inherent in implementing abolition policy as it had been originally written. Captain Edward H. Columbine—a naval captain and friend of William Wilberforce—was sent out to the colony with strict orders to cut expenditure, regardless of any public distress caused. Upon his arrival in early 1810, he commandeered from the Royal African Corps the lower storeroom of a warehouse at Falconbridge Point—"an old wooden building in very bad repair," in his own words—as a shelter for newly landed liberated Africans, to be guarded by soldiers from the corps. During his short administration, he attempted to return as much as possible to the apprenticeship-enlistment model, promoting "voluntary" enlistment of able-bodied men and apprenticing as many as he could of the remainder, although a poor relationship with the commander of the Royal African Corps frustrated his plans. Those not enlisted or apprenticed were given

some rations, and sometimes seeds and tools, and left to their own initiative. Columbine reported to his superiors in London that he intended to
hold weekly Saturday musters to monitor apprentice welfare, although it
is not clear when or whether this happened.[6]

Columbine's rival and eventual successor, the aggressively ambitious
Lieutenant-Colonel Charles W. Maxwell, also arrived determined to reduce
the burden created by the liberated Africans on the colony's accounts. However, unlike Columbine, he saw that this ever growing population might
also represent an opportunity to tighten his personal control over the colony and surrounding area, and subordinate its settler population—the "old
vile scum," as he termed them.[7] The liberated Africans were "the most useful and creditable part of the population" because they were blank slates,
in his view: a mass of people whose identity and autonomy had been erased
through enslavement, and whose loyalty and attachment to the colony could
be ensured because they had no means of leaving, nor of resisting the terms
of their labour. Much more than Columbine had, Maxwell viewed the liberated people as a resource at his personal disposal. Liberated African men
might be recruited directly from the Vice-Admiralty Court into a new company of the Royal African Corps, which among other things, could act in
a police capacity for the colony. Others—adults and children—could be
held under indenture by the colonial government rather than by private individuals, and employed on the public works, building roads and other
infrastructure to develop and expand the colony. To this end, Maxwell even
tried to establish a new village and an experimental plantation on the site of
what had been Zachary Macaulay's farm. The "captured Negroes and government apprentices" were not "free agents," Maxwell was clear: they were
"persons regularly condemned as lawful prize to H[is] M[ajesty]." They
were "at the absolute disposal of the Crown."[8] However, Maxwell was frustrated in some of his more ambitious plans to maintain the liberated Africans as a readily available labour corps in the longer term. From 1811, the
British Parliament consented to provide a small additional sum to support
"the subsistence of the Captured Negroes," but the secretary of state rebuffed Maxwell's attempts to establish a centrally managed rice-rationing

programme to support those outside the receiving depots, or to use liberated African settlers to push out the physical boundaries of the colony.
Bathurst gave permission for money to be spent maintaining those least
able to support themselves, but cautioned that "the numbers of Persons so
supplied" must be "reduce[d]" to "within the narrowest limits."[9] No financial support was provided to help establish new settlements.

In 1816, the Reverend Edward Bickersteth travelled to West Africa
to report on the state of the Church Missionary Society (CMS) missions at
the Rio Pongas, River Dembia, and Freetown, and to make recommendations for the future of the society in West Africa.[10] Maxwell's successor,
Governor Charles MacCarthy, saw an opportunity. MacCarthy's assumption of the governorship coincided with the conclusion of the French
wars—a shift from belligerent status that narrowed the effective jurisdiction of the 1807 Abolition Act and brought a series of high-profile legal challenges in the High Court of Admiralty that significantly reined in the
availability of easy prize money and slowed the inflow of seized ships and
cargo into Sierra Leone's economy. The conclusion of the wars also col-
lapsed demand for African military recruits. With Freetown's slave trade
suppression industry thus in a slump, the tone of governance approaches
towards the liberated Africans underwent an abrupt shift. Like Maxwell,
MacCarthy recognised in the growing population the potential to transform the colony and in so doing, to fulfil his own rather grandiose personal
ambitions. Just as Maxwell had, MacCarthy saw the strategic benefit of
utilising the liberated Africans to—quite literally—carve out new outposts
of cultivated, "civilised" colonial territory in the densely forested mountainous peninsula and the swampy coastal lowlands.

To this end, MacCarthy set about reorganising the relationship between the colonial government and the liberated people. To London, he
expressed shock at the paucity of resources to accommodate this rapidly
growing population, and he proposed to remedy this by formalising the
scattered villages around Freetown and drawing them into a centrally controlled administrative system. MacCarthy envisaged each parish as a permanent community of liberated African families tending individual
agricultural plots for subsistence and sale, worshipping at the local church

and sending the children of their Christian marriages to receive practical and religious education in the colony schools or in England. Key to this system, as he imagined it, was a staff of village superintendents to monitor the "progress of civilisation" and to ensure order in each settlement. What had previously stood in the way of this idea becoming reality was sufficient personnel. The missionaries of the CMS represented a potential solution.

MacCarthy took the opportunity to impress upon the Reverend Bickersteth that Freetown's liberated African population was just the mission field that the CMS was looking for—thousands of disrupted lives to which the missionaries could have regular, unrestricted access, without the dangers of ministering unprotected in the slave rivers. MacCarthy proposed that the society should close the Susu mission and send missionaries to act as superintendents and schoolteachers for each of seven newly created parishes. The missionary superintendent would represent in one individual the secular, religious, and judicial authority of the district, to whom the liberated Africans would look for guidance and example:

> It is by [the superintendents] that the morals and manners of this new establishment will be formed; it will yield like wax to any impression they choose to give it: their responsibility is great; they will no doubt, under Divine Providence, act wisely. They will, by their example,—
> "Allure to brighter worlds and lead the way";
> and in this world they will teach the people to be industrious, to be honest, and to be happy.[11]

MacCarthy made explicit the real and total power that the CMS missionaries would hold as representatives of central government at parish level:

> It is nearly impossible for a Clergyman *residing* in the mountains with Captured Negroes to do much good, unless to that character he unites that of Magistrate & Superintendent:—by the authority of the two latter offices he can keep the uncivilized in due order and reward the industry of the well behaved.[12]

Bickersteth was easily won over. In Sierra Leone, he declared in his report to the society:

> there is a most extended field for every exertion. Recaptured ne-
> groes are continually brought in, who are in the most deplor-
> able and wretched condition—naked, ignorant, weak, diseased;
> and in every form of wretchedness that can be imagined . . .
> Many of [the liberated Africans], alas! soon fall victims to the
> hard treatment which they had received on board the slave-
> ships: and many, if not most of the others, remain, for want of
> European assistance, in a deplorable state of ignorance, indo-
> lence, idolatry, licentiousness, and sin. To remedy these evils
> it appears to be of the first importance, without delay to com-
> municate that religious instruction, which, when truly received,
> will effectually arrest the progress of evil.[13]

Bickersteth's assessment reveals clear differences between how the CMS envisaged the practical implementation of the plan, and how Mac-Carthy imagined it. To Bickersteth and the CMS, the secular duties of the superintendent would be the access point for his "real" work of evangelis-ing the liberated Africans. For MacCarthy, the villages' lack of Christian-ity was less of a concern than the fact that "none of them [had] raised a sufficient crop of Rice or Cassava" for their own subsistence that year.[14] Al-though to the Colonial Office and CMS, MacCarthy presented his plans as the perfect synthesis of fiscal economy and proselytising opportunism, in reality he took as little heed of both as he could manage. MacCarthy's interest in Christianity was primarily as a tool to give cohesion to the dis-parate groups of liberated Africans. Missionary involvement was primar-ily, as MacCarthy saw it, a means of securing the committed personnel required to impose and administer a system that secular colonial gover-nance structures did not have the resources to manage alone. The tempo-ral needs of the liberated Africans could be addressed through the spiritual ambitions—and material resources—of the Church Missionary Society.

Meanwhile, the colony would reap the benefits of a regularised and stable labour force, and the governor would have realised his vision: to consolidate Sierra Leone as a foothold of British cultural values and imperial power on the West African coast.[15] The newly constituted liberated African villages were intended to be physical manifestations of that vision. MacCarthy shared with the British elite abolitionists of the Clapham Sect a strong appreciation for aesthetic order and "habits of industry." He requisitioned from Britain such items as weathercocks, church bells, and tower clocks (alongside "vast stores" of shoes, shoe brushes, blacking balls, and ladies' bonnets, amongst other things), and issued numerous directives that the rural villages be built in the image of English hamlets; regular streets with numbered houses and fences between properties, a marketplace, and a church at the heart of the community. Land for housing was allocated to new arrivals not on the basis of its fertility but according to how its buildings would appear in relation to the rest of the village.[16]

In 1816, the CMS sent out four missionaries, followed by two schoolteachers in 1817 and thirteen more recruits in 1822. During this period, 12,765 liberated Africans were brought ashore at Freetown. Of these, 11,123 remained in the colony.[17] Through the newly instituted Captured Negro Department, MacCarthy set about putting his vision into practice. The newly liberated Africans who had not been hospitalised or selected for apprenticeship, the public works, or military enlistment were held under guard at the yard long enough to be registered, renamed, and assigned a village. They were then escorted to their new homes, where they were supplied with clothing and various basic household items, such as pots, pails, tin dishes, drinking pots, spoons, mats, blankets, and, for each of the men, a bill hook, cutlass, and hoe. MacCarthy and Joseph Reffell of the Captured Negro Department later reported that liberated Africans tended to recover their health and cheer faster when located in villages with others of their "countryfolk"; thus the policy became to house new arrivals with such countrymen until such time as the women had been married and the men had cleared the plot of land allocated to them, built themselves a house, and begun to reap a mature food crop. In the meantime, they were provided with daily rations of rice, salt, and palm oil, with "those who are greatly emaciated" receiving an additional daily portion of fresh beef and vegetables.[18] Altogether, between 1816 and 1830, thirteen of these "model" villages were formally instituted on the Freetown peninsula—Regent, Waterloo, Wilberforce, Kissy, Gloucester, Hastings, Charlotte, Aberdeen, Bathurst, Wellington, Leopold, Kent, and York—as well as the two villages of Dublin and Ricketts on the Banana Islands off the southern tip of the peninsula, and another village on the tiny Isles-de-Los to the north.

The total government expenditure recorded for Sierra Leone's liberated Africans in the period 1812–1825 was £410,118, a figure better understood when compared with the total expenditure for the colony during the same period: £745,819. From an outlay of £10,849 in 1815 to a peak of £59,629 in 1823, the average annual expenditure for liberated Africans under MacCarthy and the CMS was £40,482.[19] A sizable proportion of this was spent on clothes and food rations for the new arrivals, most of whom continued to be fully supported for at least a year, many longer. The other main financial outlay was the cost of constructing and maintaining the physical infrastructure of village and town administration—the carpentry, masonry, shingle-making, and smithing required for the colony's parish churches, official residences, and schoolhouses in every village— as well as new school buildings for Freetown, a hospital, and buildings for the fast-growing bureaucracy of what was renamed in 1822 the Liberated African Department. The Commissioners of Inquiry reported in 1827 that of the four hundred different types of "stores" being supplied from Britain for the Liberated African Department, "about one hundred and twenty" were "tools and implements for the use of the mechanics." The home government, once so unwilling to accept the expense of responsibility, demonstrated little ability or willingness to rein in MacCarthy's enthusiastic spending. With an impressive ability to charm money from the Treasury, he continued to spend with practically unchecked abandon until his death in 1824. For its part, the CMS estimated that it spent £70,000 on the Sierra Leone mission between 1804 and 1824.[20]

Retreat and Fragmentation

The partnership between the Colonial Office and the CMS was never a particularly happy one. The missionary superintendence scheme never achieved the religious, practical, and humanitarian ends imagined by its planners, at least not to the degree of productive, pastoral perfection envisaged by MacCarthy, and certainly never to the level of Christian order and conspicuous virtue demanded by the missionaries. As one missionary, Gustav Nyländer, explained to Bickersteth in 1819, "neither I nor any of our missionaries, placed as superintendents to a Captured Negro Town, are in our right sphere as missionaries." The latter role required them to "devote their time and talents to their ministry; but here we are encumbered with everything connected to our situations as *Superintendents of public works, clearing* and *repairing Roads, imprisoning* and *punishing—settling disputes* and *quarrels* between people."[21] The Reverend C. F. L. Haensel, the first principal of Fourah Bay College, later commented that village superintendence had been a distraction: "secularizing the minds of the society's servants and drawing them off from fishing for men's souls to fishing for the governor's applause."[22] Most of all, the missionaries became frustrated with their inability to impose wholesale upon liberated Africans the kinds of religious, cultural, and social behaviours they believed indicative of moral progress and civilisation. As would be the case in Sturge Town and the other "free villages" of Jamaica after emancipation, the missionaries had resolved to "civilise" Africans through a teacher-pupil dynamic in which black societies would submit to the leadership of white men and women.[23] Thus they had great difficulty recognising and incorporating the pre-existing cultures of the people into the tapestry of their imagined communities and into their own worldview.

The cultural change and assimilation that did appear to take place was not passive indoctrination but adaptation and negotiation led by the liberated Africans themselves, who demonstrated a keen sense of how to utilise the resources of the Liberated African Department to their own best advantage. As David Northrup has shown, liberated people were active participants in religious instruction and village leadership, and often wielded "more authority and influence over the congregations than did the European missionaries who were officially in charge."[24] The result was that alongside recognisably British and European cultural practices and behaviours, many African cultural forms also persisted both openly and covertly in the villages. Burial customs, including drinking and late night drumming and dancing, continued regardless of missionaries' entreaties—one of many examples of how respect for ritualistic traditions persisted in parallel with villagers' outward demonstrations of Christian observation. Many denominations flourished in the colony, frequently blending forms of Christianity with a variety of other religious beliefs and practices. Overall, the newcomers exhibited an independence of spirit that belied the home government's perception of the liberated Africans as "so utterly ignorant and helpless that it is absolutely necessary, with a view to their own welfare, to treat them in some measure as children."[25] Resisting pressure from the superintendents to settle in "hygienic seclusion" on assigned family units, many chose to remain with their country people indefinitely. Groups frequently departed the villages to form their own settlements. Some moved away to find land more suited to growing crops; others left to escape the watchful eye and interference of government and missionary. Many returned to Freetown to seek their fortunes in petty trade.[26] The liberated Africans did not, in MacCarthy's words, "yield like wax," forming orderly rural communities arranged under the ticking clock of the parish church tower. The stores left rotting in Freetown, totally useless in the Sierra Leonean climate, were a testament to the chimerical nature of this vision.

A yellow fever epidemic in 1823 carried off twelve of the twenty-eight Europeans active in the mission. By 1826, of the seventy-nine missionaries, wives, and schoolmasters sent to Sierra Leone since 1804, only fourteen remained in service—the majority of the others were dead. The CMS agreed to maintain parish ministers in the parishes of Sierra Leone and to retain overall charge of Freetown's schools, but handed back superintendence of the villages, including the village schools, to the Liberated African Department.[27] In 1824, MacCarthy was killed in conflict with the Asante at the Gold Coast. In the twenty-six years that followed his death, the colonial government passed through twenty-seven different administrations.

Just as the liberated Africans had been the object of MacCarthy's personal ambitions, they became the battleground for his successors' local power struggles and contests for approval from London. Following reports in 1826 that "the whole system [was] defective," the colonial secretary sent a well-known explorer of Africa, Lieutenant-Colonel Dixon Denham, to assume the post of General Superintendent of the Liberated African Department.[28] Denham's principal task would be to "repress" amongst liberated Africans their "vicious habit" of moving freely about the colony and settling in large numbers in the vicinity of Freetown. He was also tasked with ensuring that new arrivals were given land capable of producing a saleable crop "so that they may be enabled to maintain themselves without expense to this country."[29] However when Denham arrived in Sierra Leone, he found that the colony's governor, Sir Neil Campbell, had his own plans for the liberated population.

As the officer appointed to escort Napoleon to Elba, Campbell had been blamed widely for the emperor's escape—a past that haunted him with an "anxious, zealous—I may add *fidgetty*—disposition."[30] He had little time for discourses of "improvement" and investment, nor for the idea that the colonial government was responsible for the recovery, rehabilitation, and development of communities of slave trade survivors. Caught up in a feverish determination to reform the colony of the "feckless extravagance" of the MacCarthy years, Campbell stripped back the Liberated African Department's mandate to absolute basics through the Plan of January 1st.[31] Food rations to liberated Africans in the villages were replaced with daily cash payments of 3d., and the period of support was reduced to three months for women of marriageable age and six months for men (with an option to extend this period for those liberated Africans landed with "weakly constitutions"). The residential liberated African schools were broken up and the children distributed as apprentices to "old settlers" until they reached fifteen years of age, when they would no longer be supported in any way. Until that time, they were expected to work two days a week for the village manager and four days for their "adopted parent."[32] In theory, the children were also still supposed to attend school every day, but in practice, most "adopted parents" refused to release them from labour in order to attend classes, and the liberated African schools effectively disappeared. Campbell also sent soldiers to close down the hospital at Leicester Mountain.

Dixon Denham reported regularly to the Colonial Office in 1827 and 1828, mostly through private letters to Under-Secretary Robert Hay, which were highly critical of Campbell's attitude to the liberated Africans. The letters must be read in the light of Denham's dislike for Campbell and the power struggle between them for control over the Liberated African Department. Even taking this into account, Denham's reports reflect a completely different vision of the colonial government's practical and moral responsibilities. From the outset, Denham wrote in paternalistic terms of the "natural" abilities and inclinations of the liberated Africans: that so many had thrived so well in the colony with so little governmental support was a testament to "the very interesting class of persons Great Britain has taken under her protection." He reported to Hay that the "industrious African" was "a creature not so rare as you may have been led to imagine," and observed the strong taste for consumer articles within the liberated African community and a manifest willingness to work hard to earn and save to obtain these. The suggestion that London should give up the colony of Sierra Leone—which was at that time a common refrain of the anti-abolition, pro–West India, pro-slavery lobby—was "a most extraordinary idea."[33]

Like MacCarthy, Denham saw the expensive and complex system of the Liberated African Department as an important long-term investment. Many of the series of "wasteful indulgences" Campbell sought to cut were, to Denham's mind, essential services that helped new arrivals to establish themselves as participating members of colonial society. He criticised how Campbell's military mind focused fervently on cutting costs to please London and not on tailoring measures towards local circumstance. He deplored in particular the short-sightedness of distributing the children, and how within a few months the schools were all but empty and the number of young prostitutes in the Freetown area had increased dramatically, many of them eleven and twelve years old. In a few years, he predicted, the English language would be "totally lost in the villages," and with it "all love and respect for those to whom they owe their deliverance."[34]

Within a few months, Denham did prevail upon Campbell to reverse his policy on the schooling of liberated African children. Although he reported that the damage done was severe and would be long-lasting, Denham began the process of gathering as many as possible of the children who had been distributed and relocating them back into the residential schools.[35] Campbell still continued to be obstructive in many other areas, and it was only upon the governor's death in August 1827 that Denham was able to implement his own policy approach. Shortly afterwards, he was appointed lieutenant-governor. Along with reconstructing the school system, Denham set about reconstituting the system of local policing, dismantled by Campbell.[36] He also reformed the system of distributing liberated African women as wives, and the practice of allowing army and navy recruitment directly from the Liberated African Yard. In both areas, he reported to Hay, he introduced systems to ensure that engagements were entered into voluntarily and in full comprehension of the consequences.[37]

Under Denham's brief governorship, the administration of liberated Africans assumed an outward character and framing discourse reminiscent of MacCarthy's. Indeed, throughout his tenure in the Liberated African Department and as lieutenant-governor, Denham referred to the liberated Africans in terms of a personal connection characterised by heavy paternalism; terms very similar to those used by MacCarthy. "Africans" had, he declared sweepingly, "natural good propensities." Any dishonourable conduct was the fault of the poor example that had been set by the white men sent to Sierra Leone. As Denham told Hay, "the liberated Africans are my children and I shall not neglect their welfare."[38] Denham argued persistently for a system planned around longer-term investment in his "children"—a self-confident population entirely capable of flourishing and prospering.

"This Most Complicated Department"

Governor Denham's reform programme ended prematurely when he died after only one month in office. His successor, Lumley, also died within weeks of his appointment. Within a year, almost all of the reform measures

were forgotten. The Liberated African Department continued to grow—
indeed by the 1830s, it had evolved into a complex support- and surveillance-
oriented machine that effectively acted as the bureaucracy of local
governance for much of the colony. But from June 1828 until 1837, the colonial government passed through ten different governorships, more than
half of them acting. Governor Richard Doherty survived his three-year
posting from 1837 to 1840, but after the death in office of his successor, Governor John Jeremie, in April 1841, few of the subsequent post-holders remained in office for more than a year or two. None lasted long enough to
comprehend fully the scale of the department's functions or to take control of its activities.[39] By 1841, the department had long outgrown the basic
accommodation and maintenance function set out by the initial parliamentary grants. In that year, it listed over 200 people on its payroll, of whom
twenty-four were officers and senior management. Many employees were
themselves liberated Africans or the children of liberated African parents.[40]
In 1838, one acting superintendent called it "this most complicated Department, which I beg leave to observe is the most varied and difficult in
the colony."[41]

    In 1843, influenced by a highly critical royal commission report into
the state of the colony, and in the dual expectation that the slave trade was
on a terminal decline and that Africans liberated in Sierra Leone could be
persuaded to emigrate to the West Indies, Colonial Secretary Lord Stanley ordered that the Liberated African Department be reduced "to the lowest point consistent with the maintenance of order and promotion of
education among those liberated Africans already settled in the colony."
He professed to be at a loss to understand why "the crowds of petty func-
tionaries of various denominations, who are attached to each village" should
continue to be employed.[42] Richard Doherty, a former governor of the colony, told the commission that "'the complex and cumbrous machinery' of
the Liberated African Department is a phrase very commonly used in the
colony by many who know nothing of the subject, and who never stay to
enquire how far such epithets continue to be applicable." It was "a phrase
without meaning" because the department was "in effect the government
of the country districts." Those individuals, known as magistrates in other

contexts, in Sierra Leone "bear the name of managers, and in addition to their magisterial duties, perform the kinder, more paternal offices of watching, advising, and directing persons but lately reclaimed from the savage state; settling their differences, preventing their offences, and encouraging their good efforts." "To abolish their office would merely be to withdraw this superintendence . . . without any diminution of expense."[43] Stanley was not swayed. Departmental officer numbers were cut to just three: the general superintendent (a role filled by the governor), one cash and store keeper, and one writer. Primary responsibility for the welfare and disposal of the liberated Africans was transferred back to the Collector of Customs. Auxiliary staff numbers were cut to just thirty-six in total for the whole colony.[44] The supply of stores was to be reduced if possible to "the amount necessary for about 500 persons."[45] The following year, the Liberated African Hospital at Kissy was transferred to the colonial government and redesignated a Colonial Hospital.[46]

Stanley's reductions reflected a false optimism about the decline of the transatlantic trade. In fact, the 1840s and 1850s saw a fresh burst of slaving activity, sustained by Brazilian and Cuban market demands. It was not until March 1863 that the final slave-carrying ship adjudicated at Freetown was condemned by the Vice-Admiralty Court. The navy continued to interdict smaller slave-carrying vessels on the West African coast until 1864. Officer numbers of the Liberated African Department crept up again during these years, but were again reduced in 1874, when all but the clerk in charge and one messenger were discharged.[47] By the early 1890s, the now-tiny establishment remained responsible only for the support of a few pensioners and hospital inpatients, and the maintenance of liberated African children at Charlotte school. In 1891, the department was finally wound up, the school at Charlotte closed down, and responsibility for the support of the hospitalised and indigent was transferred to the colony's poor fund. A small number of pensioners continued to be supported from the colonial budget until 1922.[48]

Stanley's gutting of the Liberated African Department reflected more than simply a desire for efficiency and economy. For him, the only useful functions the department might serve were "the maintenance of order and promotion of education," and even then, only for liberated Africans already settled in the colony. He sought to end the in-colony provision of emergency shelter, food, clothing, and medical support to recent arrivals by diverting as many of them as possible to the plantations of the West Indies.[49] By contrast, Governor Doherty had emphasised the department's "kinder, more paternal offices"—language that reflected a different vision of state responsibility and the opportunities that humanitarian imperialism might represent. In a similar vein, Governors MacCarthy and Denham had emphasised the complex material and social needs of the new arrivals and the irresponsibility of coercing all liberated Africans into indentured servitude or military service simply to get them off the government books. They each—and for their own reasons—counselled the need for long-term investment of appropriate financial resources on the part of the metropolitan state in order to reap the rich potential rewards of assimilating the liberated people as fully contributing subjects of the imperial system. Like Thompson before them, both MacCarthy and Denham sought to frame—in their reports to the Colonial Office, at least—the nature of the governance relationship as a consensual one, and to emphasise their personal connection with the wishes and experiences of the liberated African communities. Also like Thompson, they both critiqued on ethical grounds the policies of predecessors who had neglected the basic welfare needs of the liberated people, and by extension, the negligence of metropolitan governments who failed to accept that the duty of care went beyond the act of seizing the slave ships. The ambition of men like MacCarthy and Denham was to preside over the transformation of the liberated Africans into a distinctly new kind of subject population. By contrast, Governors Campbell, Maxwell, Columbine, and others (including Lord Stanley) shared a detached, pragmatic, and instrumental tone in relation to liberated Africans, essentially constructing them as a mass of black bodies dehumanised by enslavement and available to be processed and disposed of as cheaply and efficiently as possible.

Ultimately, these differences in approach reflected how different actors understood the position of the liberated Africans relative to the grand narrative of the British state's antislavery crusade. For the elite abolitionists of the African Institution, focused primarily on the growth of their former colony and the success of the wider international suppression campaign, the liberated African population was a useful by-product of the abolitionist intervention. Following this lead, under the likes of Lieutenant-Governor Campbell, the sites within Freetown were the prime focus of government energy: the Liberated African Yard, the Liberated African Hospital, and the public works. At these sites, the role of government was to meet the immediate, "emergency" needs of new arrivals—providing as economically as possible very basic foodstuffs, shelter, clothing, medical assistance, and protection from re-enslavement, and extracting labour value where possible through compulsory labour on public works until such time as the people were moved out of the yard and sent off to create value for apprentice masters or for the armed forces. Armed guards and overseers posted at the yard lent this site a carceral character, forcibly isolating liberated Africans from the population until such time as the colonial authorities wished to release them. That liberated Africans sent out on public works were reportedly "worked in gangs with the convicts of the place," sometimes chained together and always under threat of corporal punishment, suggests a heavy degree of crossover between the categories of "convicted" and "liberated," and implies that the sense in which abolitionists first intended the term "recaptive" to be meant still held power: these were not emancipated people. They had merely been recaptured.[50]

By comparison, under MacCarthy and Denham, the yard was the preparation ground for the second and more important "developmental" phase of government intervention: life in the model village. MacCarthy's experimental village system served a number of pragmatic colonialist purposes: it was a means of absorbing large inflows of people, of directing and distributing labour throughout the colony, of expanding the colony's borders and firming up its claim to the Freetown peninsula, of raising food crops to decrease the colony's reliance on slave-grown regional imports, and of attracting metropolitan interest and investment through the ideological mission of "civilising" Africa through the plantation of model societies. But the anticipated stability of this system relied upon the manufacture of a domestic context characterised by land ownership, social order, formalised marriage and child education, strict gender roles, and above all, religious observance. The idea was that the transplanted populations within these carefully designed spaces would absorb and manifest British cultural values and behaviours under tight supervision and constant "tutelage" based on both positive and negative and incentives, first by CMS missionaries and then by the lay superintendents of the Liberated African Department.

"A Suitable Asylum"

The concept of the experimental model village built around such ethnocentric and patriarchal assumptions was not unique to Sierra Leone. Similar schemes were attempted over the following decades, both in metropolitan Britain and in its empire. Examples include the "free villages" of Jamaica in the late 1830s and 1840s, the Owenite communities in Britain from 1821 to 1845, and the ultimately disastrous Tasmanian Aboriginal resettlement programme attempted at Bruny Island and later Wybalenna on Flinders Island in the 1830s and 1840s.[51] The Baptist missionary William Knibb delivered a speech to the World Antislavery Convention of 1840 at Exeter Hall in which he captured the intent of the Jamaican villages: sanctuaries where "tyranny could not reach [the former slaves], and the power of the oppressor could not be felt" there. As freeholders, the formerly enslaved could live "in their proper places" with the Bible occupying a central place in their homes. In language much reminiscent of the assumptions and expectations of MacCarthy and the CMS missionaries at Sierra Leone two decades previously, Knibb's reports pointed to the pleasing, ordered aesthetic of the villages and the geographically anchored lifestyles of their inhabitants as indicators of moral progress: the Jamaican village of Kettering in 1844 was

> laid out in four hundred building lots . . . Regular streets intersect each other, and neat cottages are rising on every hand. My own dwelling house stands in the centre, with a neat chapel and school-room adjoining, and already nearly two hundred of the members of my church have here fixed their abode.[52]

Like the Anglicans in Sierra Leone, the Baptist missionaries in Jamaica believed their superintendence of these experiments to be central to the survival of the freedpeople. In the process, they rejected the idea that formerly enslaved people could have raised their own crops, built their own homes, and carved out stable and prosperous paths autonomously. The nature of missionary interference and management is captured in James Mursell Phillippo's *Jamaica: Its Past and Present State,* published in 1843:

> The land required for the formation of these village establishments had, in most cases, been first purchased by the missionaries, who also surveyed and laid out the allotments, superintended the construction of the roads and streets, directed the settlers in the building of their cottages, and cultivation of their grounds, supplied them with the deeds of conveyance, formed societies among them for the improvement of agricultural operations, gave them a relish for the comforts and conveniences of civilised life, and improved their domestic economy. They endeavoured at the same time, by every means in their power, to convince these simple-minded people that their *own* prosperity, as well as that of the island at large, depended on their willingness to work for moderate wages as labourers on the plantations of the former slave-masters.[53]

As at Sierra Leone, the Jamaican free-village system was grounded in several assumptions: that the most important measure of the inhabitants' "improvement" was their service as regularised, waged labourers in the white-dominated colonial political economy; that in order to flourish and prosper, formerly enslaved populations should be held within a physical space purpose-built to inculcate particular habits and behaviours through targeted developmental interventions; and that the developmental interventions must be directed by a resident white authority figure to whom the villagers would look for paternal guidance and discipline. The physical space of the model village loomed large in the frame: its aesthetic order or disorder, and the gender dynamics upon which this order was built, were considered the essential litmus tests at any given moment of the moral progress of the experiment.

Similar assumptions underpinned attempts at the relocation, "conciliation," and eventually "amelioration" programmes to which the surviving Aboriginal peoples of Tasmania were subjected, first at Bruny Island, off Hobart, and later at the remote and desolate Flinders Island in the Bass Straight during the governorship of George Arthur in the 1830s and 1840s.[54] These oft-cited experiments in humane governance arose, as at Jamaica, in response to the violence of the powerful and well-organised settler colonial class. By the late 1820s, the settlers outnumbered the surviving Aboriginal people of Tasmania by approximately twenty to one, and were engaged in a programme of extermination. Although Arthur oversaw the allocation of some 1,899,332 acres of Aboriginal land to European settlers in the first seven years of his governorship—a 1,433 percent increase over the total acreage expropriated in the eighteen years prior to his tenure— nevertheless he expressed great personal turmoil at the results, and at the impossibility of ensuring the security and economic prosperity of the rising settler population while also preventing the mass murder of the entire original population of the island. In 1829, Arthur advertised among the Hobart settlers for a superintendent to govern a settlement of nineteen survivors of the South-East Tribe at the former ration station on Bruny Island, off the Hobart coast. This superintendent would be expected to lead an experiment to determine whether "Van Diemen's Land Aborigines could be redeemed and 'reclaimed' for Christianity within a new, colonial environment." The successful applicant, George Augustus Robinson, drew not only on ideas of indigenous protection, amelioration, and developmental humanitarianism, but on an Anglican missionary-influenced evangelical religious discourse more broadly. The proposed settlement, he argued, should be built upon two pillars: "civilisation," enacted through the construction of model villages, and religiously infused "instruction." He cited as inspiration an East India Company model of Christian education originally designed for children of company soldiers.[55]

The Bruny Island settlement attempted under Robinson's superintendence was not considered a success. Nevertheless, Robinson was subsequently tasked with relocating the main island's Aboriginal population far to the north, to Flinders Island. Some two hundred Aboriginal people were assembled for transport to Flinders in 1835, on the promise that the move was a temporary measure, and that they would be granted an extensive reservation and hunting ground upon their return to the mainland. By 1847, only forty-seven were left alive.

The "model" Aboriginal Establishment created at Flinders Island was built on the site of a convict settlement and a military encampment—an unconscious echo of how militarism and convictism had infused the first experiments in humanitarian governance at Sierra Leone decades earlier. It was also an inauspicious physical embodiment of how the Flinders establishment would fuse and confuse the ideas of protection and incarceration for its unhappy inmates. In negotiating the transfer to the island, Robinson had given clear guarantees to the Aborigines that their culture and traditions would be respected and safeguarded, including their right to hunt and to organise the patterns of their daily lives according to their own wishes and practices. In reality, he intended to use the establishment to prove that the people desired British "civilisation" and that they would transform under his tutelage into a quiescent subaltern class, ready to submit to the dominance of the white settler class on the main island.

Upon arrival at Flinders, Robinson immediately set about erasing the Aborigines' preferred modes of living, beginning by renaming each person, just as the liberated Africans were renamed, and housing them in purpose-built huts designed for the close surveillance of nuclear family units, sited between the chapel and the commandant's house. The men were expected to abandon hunting for agriculture, and to spend their time clearing and enclosing land, tending sheep, cultivating gardens, and building roads, and in addition to attend "improving" evening school classes. They were to cut their hair and commit to formally recognised marriages. The children were isolated from the adults, separated according to gender, and subjected to a long daily routine of schooling and religious worship. The women were placed under the control of a female overseer, who inspected them physically every morning, examined their huts, and supervised a rigid daily routine of cooking, sewing, washing, and religious instruction. On Sunday mornings before chapel and hymn-singing, all were lined up outside their huts to be inspected by Robinson—the men in trousers and buttoned-up tail coats and the women in gingham petticoats with hand-kerchiefs tied around their heads. When the people resisted the imposition of Robinson's white colonial fantasy of order and civilisation, his attempts at retaliation echoed coercive strategies attempted by the CMS missionaries at Sierra Leone: denying rations, conspicuously awarding favours, encouraging spying, and appointing several of the men as paid constables and overseers over their own people.[56]

Yet unlike Sierra Leone, Flinders was a small, isolated island with severely limited natural resources. Dependent upon insufficient rations and poor medical care, many inmates succumbed to malnutrition, chronic illness, and despondency. Major Thomas Ryan, commandant at Launceston, visited the settlement in 1836 and "tremble[d] for the consequences" of what he found. The establishment at Flinders was "an artificial society" where "the race of Tasmania, like the last of the Mohicans, will pine away and be extinct in a quarter of a century." In March 1842, Robinson's eldest son wrote of the few survivors: "the island has been a charnel house for them." Regardless, in his report to the colonial secretary, Arthur praised the experiment as respectful, peaceful, and humane. The Aborigines had gone to Flinders "with their own free will and consent. They have been removed from danger, and placed in safety in a suitable asylum . . . where they are brought under moral and religious inculcation."[57] By Robinson's own account, the "tribes knew" what to expect in being relocated to Flinders, and recognised that the purpose of the move was to render them "secure from the attack of the depraved portion of the white population and where they would enjoy uninterrupted tranquillity in the society of their kindred and friends, their wants and necessities were to be amply supplied."[58] Robinson comforted himself that "the sad mortality which has happened among them since their removal is a cause for regret, but after all it is the will of providence, and better they died here where they are kindly treated than shot at and inhumanly destroyed by the depraved portion of the white community."[59]

Common to the three "model village" experiments attempted at Sierra Leone, Jamaica, and Flinders Island was the assumption that problems created by colonialism and imperialist expansion could be solved by more perfect, more utopian forms of imperialist expansion. Implicit in this was the belief that the violence inherent in empire could never be effectively challenged or prevented by either metropolitan or colonial governments, and that a proper function of imperial governance was to carve out from spaces unwanted by white settlers a series of secure "refuges"—or in Arthur's terminology, "asylums"—reserved for colonised and contained populations. Indeed, one of the villages in Jamaica, originally called Wilberforce, was even renamed "Refuge."

Yet liberated Africans, emancipated people, and transplanted Aboriginal survivors were not seen as refugees in the same sense that European political exiles were, or even as fugitive slaves in the cast of George Harris from Harriet Beecher Stowe's *Uncle Tom's Cabin*.[60] In part, this distinction reflects a racist hierarchy that valued the lighter-skinned European, often a Christian, over the darker-skinned other. Yet it is also about the different narrative of injustice associated with the suffering of these populations and the centrality of a heroic narrative to the refugee ideal. Political exiles and fugitive slaves had acquired a self-initiated narrative of freedom that enabled the British public to "lionise" them as "personifications of liberal virtue." Other ingredients essential to the narrative of the ideal refugee included a strong ethic of work, a reputation for steadfast industriousness, moral righteousness, and proud independence from reliance on others' charity. These characteristics had enabled the European refugee to enact a daring escape from his (generally, rather than her) home country, and would form the basis of his participation in British society. By contrast, it was suffering and rescue rather than heroism or romantic struggle that dominated the narrative of how liberated Africans, emancipated people, and transplanted Aborigines were understood. The "heroes," if there were any, were their protectors: the missionaries, military and naval officers, and colonial bureaucrats who endured thankless postings in harsh climates in order to preside over the rescued peoples' deliverance from peril. The freedom of rescued populations was not perceived to be the result of their own agency, resilience, and ingenuity, and so they had not "earned" the respect accorded to other types of refugees.[61] The focus therefore was on the site of refuge rather than the refugee; on the physical site in which benevolence took place, and, importantly, in which "habits of industry" and the Protestant ethic of work could be inculcated in a manner that would make these populations worthy of the munificence of British intervention.

"It must be recollected," Sir Robert Inglis mused to the House of Commons in 1845, that the liberated Africans brought to Sierra Leone "were taken upon the high seas with as little regard to their own will as they were taken from the interior of Africa to the coast." Indeed, the entire intervention was exercised as a "benevolent despotism," because "the slaves themselves had no voice in selecting the direction in which they should go when taken under the charge of an English officer." In the process of diverting this "living cargo" to Sierra Leone, the slaves were "as little entitled to the description of free agents as when still in the hold of the slave ship."[62] Inglis's critique reflects a tension inherent in unilateral humanitarian action in general, and abolition policy specifically: that intervenors can tend to assume that the objects of intervention are voiceless and passive; that in the case of the suppression of the slave trade, it was acceptable that they be transported without their consent to a location of their captors' choosing and "disposed" of by the authorities there.[63]

The embryonic experiment in humanitarian governance that took form in Sierra Leone under MacCarthy's governorship reflected, in terms of discourse, a tension between the concept of refuge and duty on the one hand, and the imperative to exploit and render profitable on the other. While elements of the experiment and its supporting discourses lingered on after MacCarthy's death, utopian metropolitan visions for the transformative "civilising" potential of the system at Sierra Leone took a steep nosedive after 1827. In 1842, Zachary Macaulay's son, the former Sierra Leone Mixed Commission Court judge Henry William Macaulay, argued vehemently to a parliamentary select committee that welfare support for liberated Africans at Sierra Leone should be slashed to one week's provisions only, after which time they should be ejected from the yard and sent to the labour-hungry West Indies. When questioned as to whether liberated Africans should at least be given a choice to remain at Sierra Leone, he replied "certainly not"; "the Act of Parliament does not even contemplate such an option being given." Macaulay was briskly matter-of-fact on the subject: the current, long-established method of dealing with liberated Africans was that "the negro [was] taken to Sierra Leone, and located there, without his opinion or wishes being consulted." To Macaulay it was obvious that "in the same way, he might be transported to the West Indies." Again, he referred to the Act of 1807: "The Act never contemplates any option whatever being exercised by the persons seized, because it allows of their being drafted into the army and navy, without any reference to their own will . . . It leaves no option with the party bound."[64] At the more extreme end of this approach were the views of Commissioner Moody, one of two commissioners sent to Tortola in the early 1820s to report on the condition and future potential of the Africans liberated there. In sentiments reminiscent of the expressions of Zachary Macaulay between 1804 and 1808, Moody argued in 1826 that it was simply not acceptable that Africans should be allowed to refuse to labour, and to accept a simpler material life as a consequence. "The liberated African . . . must be *forced* to experience the advantages resulting from the enjoyment of the wealth to be *created by his own labour.*"[65] Zachary Macaulay and his colleagues had tried and failed to realise such visions in post-1808 Sierra Leone, to a significant extent because of sustained resistance from the liberated Africans themselves. Instead they lived to see an entirely different discourse of antislavery governance and humanitarian imperialist social experimentation take root. By the early 1840s, in a fog of disillusionment and racially charged disgust with the economic cost of emancipation and the perceived failure of the free-labour experiment in the West Indies, the debate had come full circle.

THREE

Seeking Freedom in a Slave Society

Cape Colony and the British West Indies

IN 1821, THE SLAVE SHIP *Emilia* was seized on the high seas and escorted by its Royal Navy captors to the port of Rio de Janeiro, where it became the first case adjudicated at a Mixed Commission Court. On board were 392 West Africans, including 90 women, 191 men, 10 girls, and 101 boys. They would be the first of many thousands of slave-ship captives declared liberated by antislavery courts in the territories of powers signatory to bilateral abolition treaties with Britain between 1821 and 1867.[1] From this moment on, Britain's involvement with the governance of liberated Africans began to assume a foreign policy dimension. This new, external, Atlantic (and later, Indian Ocean) element of the suppression campaign was an initiative led by the Foreign Office, focused primarily in the Americas. It involved ongoing diplomacy with Spain, Brazil, Portugal, the Netherlands, and the United States to secure or execute bilateral right-of-search treaties, to navigate disputes regarding seized slave ships, and to resettle tens of thousands of liberated Africans. It was executed by the Foreign Office's Slave Trade and Consular and Commercial departments, the Courts of Mixed Commission, and the Royal Navy: a network of bureaucrats, lawyers, informants, consuls, naval officers, and diplomats scattered across thousands of miles whose efforts combined into a haphazard "antislavery world system." "Varied in local tactics but united in a series of core strategic objectives," these diverse actors and interests were the engine for what Foreign Secretary Lord Aberdeen once called the "new and vast branch of international relations" that was the British slave trade suppression effort.[2] The system collected and funnelled back to the Slave Trade Department of the Foreign Office vast quantities of documentary evidence, trade intelligence, personal observation, and opinion on all subjects touching upon slavery and the slave trade. This included, after 1821, material relating to the treatment of the Africans liberated under treaty arrangements with Spain, Portugal, and later the Netherlands, Brazil, and others.

Up to 1821, the management of liberated Africans had been a matter of domestic imperial policy, overseen by the Colonial Office. The liberated African establishment at Sierra Leone remained the largest in the Atlantic world, but significant numbers of liberated people were also resettled in the British West Indies and Cape Colony. After 1824, several thousand individuals would be transferred from Sierra Leone to new settlements at the Gambia River and (to a much lesser extent) Ascension Island. For a time, Fernando Po (modern-day Bioko) also housed a liberated African establishment. From the 1840s onwards, many thousands would likewise be transferred from the new establishment on the mid-Atlantic island of St Helena to the plantations of the British West Indies and to Cape Colony, where their labour was in demand following the legal ending of slavery in 1838 across much of the empire. Together—and after the 1820s in particular—the British liberated African establishments of the Atlantic world came to function as parallel, frequently interlinked sites in which the same purportedly humanitarian purpose found radically different articulations, influenced in no small part by networked, trans-imperial actors shaping local-level discourses and practices.[3] Much like those at Sierra Leone, the establishments that evolved at Cape Colony and the British West Indies sought to harness the labour of liberated Africans in order to meet local needs, and to integrate notionally free African people into each colonial society in ways that did not threaten the established order, including its racial hierarchy.

However, unlike at Sierra Leone, slavery still defined the labour markets in these colonies and in many ways shaped the kinds of freedom made possible for the survivors of the slave trade. As we saw in the previous chapter, underlying the discourse of governance applied to liberated Africans at Sierra Leone was a tension between providing refuge and extracting profit: a tension between a deeply paternalistic developmental imperialism and an entirely unsentimental, exploitative kind of pragmatism. This tension finds echoes in the discourses of governance that emerged at British liberated African establishments across the Atlantic world, at Cape Colony and the West Indies, and later at the Gambia River and the island of St Helena. In configurations unique to each location, the imperatives of humane governance formed the overt justification for each establishment, but local circumstances and interests dictated the way formal abolition policy was interpreted and shaped into practices that sought to define the post-enslavement lives of many thousands of people. From 1808, Freetown had been an important testing ground for ideas of how to achieve a stable post-slavery labour transition—perhaps most importantly because the establishment facilitated early experimentation with term-limited non-voluntary indenture periods, or "apprenticeship" contracts. After 1833, similar ideas would be applied to the British Caribbean and other former slavery-based colonial economies as a way of containing and controlling the labour of formerly enslaved people, with the justification that it was both prudent and just for the British empire to extract advantage from its various antislavery interventions. Yet it is clear that the ethical complexities of this position were not uncontested within the assemblage of government offices, interests, and personalities that comprised the "imperial government" and its peripheral administrations.[4] Contemporaries grappled with the question: Was Britain, the great antislavery state, entitled to "make a profit of our humanity"?[5]

Previous chapters explored the making and remaking of abolition policy, and how its implementation in the colony of Sierra Leone facilitated unprecedented experiments in professedly humane forms of governance for vulnerable, post-intervention populations. We shall now widen the lens to look at the other sites of liberated African resettlement in the Atlantic world. The following two chapters will focus on those in British territories—primarily the West Indies, Cape Colony, the Gambia, and St Helena—and consider the establishments' different responses to their purportedly humanitarian mandate. Chapter 5 will then consider the post-liberation experiences of formerly enslaved persons in Cuba, Brazil, and other non-British Atlantic-world territories and colonies, their significance to an evolving international rights-based diplomacy, and their importance to Britain's projection of power through a global antislavery system.

Cape Colony

Between 1808 and 1816, the first of two waves of liberated Africans—some 2,100 individuals—passed through the Court of Vice-Admiralty at Cape Colony and were disposed of by the Collector of Customs. Unlike at other sites, this liberated African population comprised survivors of both the Atlantic and Indian Ocean slave trades.[6] Most were placed under indenture to private individuals, far outnumbering those who were enlisted. A census in 1823 registered 1,118 male and 652 female liberated Africans in the colony. A commission of enquiry in 1826 found 1,875 liberated Africans still accounted for: 1,490 as apprentices, 151 employed by the colonial government, 111 enlisted into the army, and 123 recruited by the navy. After 1839, when Britain assumed unilaterally the right to capture Portuguese slave ships south of the equator, a second wave of liberated Africans began to arrive at the Cape. It is believed that between three thousand and four thousand were brought to Cape Colony in this second wave between 1839 and the closure of the Atlantic slave trade in the mid-1860s.[7]

Slave trade survivors in the first wave found themselves thrust into a colony in legal flux. A Dutch slave colony captured by Britain in 1795, lost to the Batavian Republic in 1803 under the Treaty of Amiens, and then recaptured as recently as 1806, the Cape was technically under military occupation for the first seven years of the abolition period. As with other colonial territories seized during the decades of war with France, the Cape in the early years provided little more than "a thin veneer of British legal and administrative practice stretched over an entrenched and alien system of governance" in which local interests held considerable power to evade both the letter and the spirit of legal obligations towards liberated Africans.[8] Arrivals in the first wave (1808–1816) were subject to terms of indenture of fourteen years, and often longer, as colonists found creative ways to

compel apprentices and their children to remain in slave-like bondage
well beyond the end of their indenture contracts, or to conceal from apprentices their entitlement to full freedom when their terms expired. From
the outset, these liberated Africans at Cape Colony shared the labour market with slaves, receiving the same clothing and food and working at identical occupations under both public and private indentures.[9] They were
known as "prize negroes" or even "prize slaves," broad terms that covered
not simply Africans liberated after due process by the Vice-Admiralty
Court, but also those smuggled into the colony after the legal prohibition
on slave trading in 1808. Usage of the term "prize negro" in this way is an
interesting reflection on how Africans liberated by the Vice-Admiralty
Court were seen by the population of the colony—as, quite literally,
"prize," in the strictest sense of the 1807 Abolition Act. Declared forfeit,
they were pounced upon eagerly and, in the mix of other forced indentured labour at the Cape, quickly lost sight of by the Collector of Customs. Slippage from the term "prize negro" to "prize slave" indicates a
significant degree of (probably wilful) conceptual vagueness around the
precise legal status and rights or entitlements of slave trade survivors.[10]
Furthermore, when the Commission of Eastern Inquiry published its report in 1823 into governance at the Cape, they noted the presence of liberated Africans at the prison of Robben Island, apprenticed into servitude
there and labouring alongside convicted inmates, enslaved people, "free
blacks," eight "near-destitute lunatics," two "women of colour of advanced
years," and some Europeans awaiting banishment or transportation—a
microcosm of the empire's overlapping incarceratory regimes and exclu-
sionary ideologies, and the interchangeable identities of marginality,
bondage, and unfreedom they produced.[11]

The legal status of liberated Africans at the Cape was in theory distinct from that of slaves. However, in practice, the virtually unassailable
control colonial authorities allowed to private indenture holders meant that
most, perhaps all, liberated Africans of the first wave never successfully asserted the rights associated with their legal status, nor established a group
identity that would force colonial society to differentiate them from others
deemed "prize." There was no suggestion by the colonial government of

allowing liberated people to form autonomous village settlements, or to exercise any other form of independence from white control. To the colonists, the liberated people were a cheap and controllable source of labour. They could be treated as slaves, and hired out in lucrative third-party contracts, without any significant government oversight or legally enforceable rights.[12] While it is certainly possible to overstate the opportunities for personal autonomy and social mobility for liberated Africans within Sierra Leone's "Province of Freedom," with the effect of erasing and silencing the experiences of those excluded from the emergent Krio elite, it is still important to note the stark contrast between the spectrum of potential post-liberation outcomes for those brought to Freetown and those at Cape Colony. As Christopher Saunders has observed, no liberated African at the Cape ever became a successful entrepreneur. Throughout the period after 1807, liberated Africans laboured alongside slaves and indentured Khoisan in a poorly differentiated colonial subclass.

The Emancipation Act of 1833 did nothing to improve their relative status, although the Masters and Servants Ordinance of 1840 at least provided a process by which apprentices could submit to magistrates their complaints of ill-treatment, and shortened the terms of indenture from fourteen to three years.[13] In the early 1840s, 1,410 liberated Africans were sent to Cape Colony from the receiving depot on the island of St Helena after Cape colonists paid three thousand pounds to "import" them.[14] While for this second wave of Cape Colony "prize negroes," the conditions of indenture appear to have improved substantially (with some brutal exceptions), liberated Africans remained a much sought-after commodity at the Cape right until the termination of the transoceanic slave trades.[15]

It would be inaccurate to attribute to all colonial settlers and administrators the very worst and most exploitative pro-slavery attitudes and violent propensities, for there were those who supported first the amelioration and later the abolition of slavery, and as the various commissions documented, those who as indenture holders honoured the obligations of the apprenticeship contracts and went on to facilitate the integration of time-expired apprentices into colonial society as free people. Nevertheless, the evidence overwhelmingly suggests that the majority of white (and also some free black) colonists who took on apprentices acted to harness and exploit their labour to the fullest extent possible, and resented any efforts by the colonial government to monitor or assert special rights and protections for liberated Africans and their children. Of course, it will surprise no historian of slave systems that European imperial labour integration programmes for formerly enslaved people would privilege and enrich white settlers, nor that they would facilitate endemic abuse and exploitation of Africans. Yet it is interesting to compare how different liberated African establishments of the Atlantic world interpreted their claimed humanitarian mandate, and to examine how colonial bureaucrats responded at different times and in different contexts to the custodial role in which they were placed, with its attendant responsibilities of observing, documenting, and corresponding with the Colonial Office in London regarding the welfare of slave trade survivors. In effect, these responsibilities positioned individual colonial administrators as intermediaries between the antislavery legislation and policies of the metropolitan government on the one hand, and on the other, the private citizens and commercial interests of the slaveholding colonies. This produced a spectrum of responses, which illuminate a variety of different power relations.

At one end of the spectrum is the case of Charles Blair and William Wilberforce Bird, Collector and Comptroller of Customs respectively, who ran the Customs Department at the Cape from 1808 to 1826 as a "private fiefdom" and who saw in their absolute control over the liberated people and the assignment of their labour "rampant opportunities for personal gain."[16] Prompted by a complaint to the Treasury by a disgruntled Cape colonist, the Commissioners of Eastern Enquiry who arrived at the Cape in July 1823 began to probe allegations that Blair had been trading "prize negroes" like chattel for fifteen years. Although their report shied away from direct indictment of Blair and Wilberforce Bird, the accumulated evidence strongly implicated Blair as the lynchpin of a system of abuse, exploitation, and corruption that reached across the elites of colonial society, through which the accused had "distributed Prize Negroes in return for services rendered to them, or for payment of debts due to them."[17] The testimonies gathered—including those of William Cousins and Samboo, two of Blair's own liberated African apprentices who alleged sustained physical abuse and ill-treatment—revealed how for well over a decade, Blair handed out liberated Africans as presents to his family, friends, and creditors, and to himself. At least fifty-four individual liberated people were revealed to have been apprenticed to his household and estate, although the total number whose labour Blair coerced throughout the period of his domination of the Customs Department was almost certainly higher.[18] At the sale of Blair's personal estate of Stellenberg, one deponent testified, Blair had attempted to sell the liberated Africans with the property. He allegedly offered a verbal promise that the estate came with long-term or permanent bonded labour: "he would pledge his word and honour that the Prize Negroes should not be removed after the expiration of their term," a labour force calculated to add at least 20 percent to the value of the estate.[19] Other deponents gave evidence that Blair and Wilberforce Bird facilitated a system of informal transfers of indentures and verbal "gentleman's agreements" by which they commoditised the liberated Africans.[20]

In spite of the substantial weight of detailed circumstantial evidence and the testimonies of many colonists amassed against them, Blair and Wilberforce Bird successfully wriggled free from the net of official scrutiny.[21] The informality of Blair's networked system was key: when it came to the investigation, Commissioners Bigge and Colebrooke could find little hard evidence of wrongdoing. Writing in his own defence, Blair drew heavily on the idea that a strict sense of moral duty animated him in his role as intermediary between the state and the liberated African: "the Order in Council [of March 1808] instructs the Collector to apprentice Prize Negroes to good and humane masters; and the Collector has so done to the best of his judgment." He had, he claimed, sought simply to place the liberated Africans with masters and mistresses "whom he consider[ed] most likely to benefit the apprentices and act kindly towards them." In language drenched in the kind of stern-but-fair paternalistic duty that played well to metropolitan antislavery imperialist audiences, Blair portrayed himself as the agent of the antislavery state, guided in his actions solely by his legal obligation to "apprentice Prize Negroes to"—and he repeated the language of the Orders in Council—"*good and humane* masters." He had "left certain

Prize Negroes" on his Stellenberg estate at the time of its sale out of concern for their own interests, he claimed, because they had been employed there "for some years," and "they were much attached" to the place because their wives and children lived there.[22]

On the subject of the alleged abuse and exploitation of William Cousins, Blair flipped the accusations. He had brought Cousins to England, he claimed, where he had had him "instructed and baptized." Returning to the Cape, he had employed Cousins as a waged labourer before dismissing him for "becoming drunken." Cousins's charges of abuse were all the more "improbable and aggravating," Blair asserted, because "the boy" [Cousins] had originally "been landed from the ship in a dying state, rejected as an apprentice by every one, and received and nurtured by Mr. Blair from humane motives, as though he was an individual of his own family." On the charge that he had illegally removed Malamo, another liberated African child apprentice, from a colonist named Corbitt, Blair again invoked language of paternalistic, humane governmentality: "the discharge of [his] duties" was his only goal, he pled, and "the protection and comfort of the Negro" was the ultimate focus of those duties—so much so, that he again had offered refuge within his own personal domestic sphere. "Abandoned by his master," as Blair claimed Malamo had been, "I judged it most favourable to the future comfort and improvement" of the child "to take him for the remainder of his term into my own family."[23]

Blair was performing the language expected of the custodian of "prize negro" welfare and the man acting as intermediary between metropole and colony, protecting above all else Britain's reputation as a sincerely antislavery state delivering meaningful post-enslavement freedom to the objects of its naval interventions.[24] It does not seem that this language of nurture, compassion, and duty actually convinced the commissioners, whose report rings of deep disapproval short of full censure. "The power of apprenticing a Prize Negro . . . or of reapprenticing him afterwards to another master," they judged, "was intended to be conferred on the Collector of Customs *for the benefit of the Negro alone.*" Blair and Wilberforce Bird had exercised this right "less with a view to the advantage of the Negro . . . than to the maintenance and augmentation of [their] patronage."

The instances are numerous and of daily occurrence in which Prize Negroes who are perfectly competent to support themselves are reapprenticed by the Collector and Comptroller, and become a source of profit in the hands of poor masters, who derive considerable profit, if not their principal subsistence, from hiring out the Negroes to other persons.

Yet when confronted by Blair's professions of compassionate dedication, and in the absence of hard evidence of "corrupt motives," the way was clear for the commissioners to stop short of recommending Blair's dismissal, or even the removal from his service of the liberated Africans who had come forth at great personal risk to themselves to bear witness to the violence Blair inflicted upon them and their families. In the final conclusion, the commissioners allowed Blair and Wilberforce Bird the benefit of the doubt, going no further than to present the system of abuses as an insufficiency; as a regrettable failure to deliver for liberated people the true, humane intent of the Orders in Council:

We certainly perceive that [Blair] and [Wilberforce Bird] have either misunderstood or overlooked the meaning of the sixth clause of the Instructions of His Majesty in Council, respecting the reassignment of Prize Negroes, and that they have thus unnecessarily increased their patronage or their own accommodation, without sufficiently keeping in view the advantage of the Negroes.[25]

Blair's capacity to so successfully and profitably abuse his position depended upon more than just force of personality. For much of the period in which he had controlled the liberated African establishment, Cape Colony provided a context in which shared values and racialised social hierarchies allowed the unlawful exploitation of liberated Africans to continue with scarcely a murmur of significant dissent. The Collector of Customs acted in this case not as an amplifier of metropolitan antislavery values or government policy, but as a paid agent of enslaver interests.

"The Sierra Leone of the Northern Caribbean"

At around the same time in the mid-1820s, on the opposite side of the Atlantic, an intriguingly different set of governance behaviours emerged at the Bahamas. The Bahamas was one of several British Caribbean colonies in which slave trade survivors had been resettled since 1808, having been conferred with liberated African status by Caribbean-based British Vice-Admiralty courts (and later Mixed Commission courts), primarily at Antigua, Tortola, the Bahamas, and Havana. In all, over the sixty-year period of the Atlantic suppression campaign, at least 40,000 liberated Africans were resettled in the British West Indies—the majority of them transferred from other locations, primarily Sierra Leone, St Helena, Cuba, and Brazil, and mostly in the years after the legal emancipation of the empire's enslaved populations, although a sizable population also arrived before 1833.[26]

In theory, these liberated people were legally subject to the same policies of disposal as those at Sierra Leone and Cape Colony.[27] In practice, much depended on the type of colonial economy into which they were brought: whether one dominated by large plantations, such as at Trinidad and Jamaica, or smaller peripheral islands such as the Bahamas, whose mixed economies could include some small-scale plantation agriculture alongside subsistence agriculture, salt raking, fishing, wrecking, and trading and shop-keeping within the larger towns and ports, and whose enslaved populations experienced quite different labour terms to the enslaved of the large plantations. In these smaller, marginal, non-plantation colonies, local populations often did not clamour for liberated African labour, but rather viewed the unanticipated new arrivals with suspicion and misgiving. In both contexts, the perceived "Africanness" of the new arrivals created much anxiety among British authorities, panicked to the point of absurdity about the prospect of introducing "the contagion of savage life" into majority Caribbean-born post-enslaved populations.[28]

As we have seen, in Sierra Leone, the inflow of slave trade survivors quite literally transformed the colony. The Liberated African Yard loomed large at the heart of Freetown, at a site still visible to this day, and was the physical space of varying levels of carcerality around which was organised a vast and complex economy, bureaucracy, and set of discourses of humanitarian governance.[29] Beyond the yard (in both a spatial and an experiential sense), the villages planted all over the Freetown peninsula represented outposts of colonial activity conceptualised as part of a vigorous attempt at imperial expansion and consolidation. These two primary functional spaces that emerged for the surveillance and management of liberated African labour—the yard and the villages—were spaces in which, alongside the simple labour-management imperative set out in the abolition legislation, both emergency and developmental forms of humanitarian engagement also coevolved within one organisational framework. It was an unintended innovation that represented a new and important elaboration of the concept of humanitarian action by the imperial state at its periphery.

By contrast, in the Bahamas and other colonies of the British West Indies, the emphasis was on absorbing the liberated Africans into the labouring population as quickly and smoothly as possible, whether as apprentices or, to a lesser extent, as enlisted soldiers.[30] Little innovation was required to create transitory spaces for the relatively small and (by comparison with Sierra Leone) relatively infrequent groups of liberated Africans arriving in the first decades of abolition. The basic requirement to feed slave-ship survivors, and to surveille and shelter them (by compulsion, if necessary) could be met reasonably easily and inexpensively through the existing physical infrastructure of maritime trade and imperial bureaucracy. The yards and outbuildings of the various Collectors of Customs could function as holding sites, as military recruitment venues, and later as auction yards for would-be apprentice-holders.[31] Failing that, warehouses, military barracks, and even prisons could be used.

Some similarities exist between how the Bahamas and Cape Colony responded to the liberated African arrivals: both colonial economies were constructed around slavery, both subjected liberated people to arduous labour outside the terms of their "disposal," and both allowed indenture holders to hire out their apprentices through a "truck" system, just as slaveholders hired out enslaved people.[32] Yet there existed a marked difference in terms of how the white colonial population at the Bahamas regarded the presence of liberated people within their communities. Bahamian colonists saw liberated Africans as destabilising influences, augmenting the free black population, whom an 1816 petition described as "a species of Population of little use and already too numerous." The petitioners complained bitterly about a group of liberated people in Nassau seeking to exercise autonomy and govern their own labour, calling them "the most worthless and troublesome class of black people" in the town.[33] The colonial assembly and council even went so far as to question the constitutionality of the Abolition Act, arguing that since the liberated Africans were "not 'liege subjects' of the Crown, they had no natural right to a resource" in any part of the empire. "Any act of parliament that bestowed rights among liberated Africans in the West Indies 'without the consent and against the wishes and interest of the colonies' was a violation of [the white colonists'] constitutional privileges."[34]

By 1825, the fourteen-year indentures of the first liberated Africans at the Bahamas had begun to expire. Groups on the island of New Providence took the initiative to form a series of squatter settlements, and to provide for themselves a variety of community services through "friendly" or "benefit" societies. Charles Poitier, the Collector of Customs, saw some advantage in the government formalising such settlements, with a view to resettling both time-expired and future liberated African arrivals there.[35] In a decision quite unlike anything his counterpart in Cape Colony might have taken, Poitier purchased from public funds—and possibly without the consent of the acting governor—a tract of four hundred acres of land to parcel out for resale to the liberated Africans. Selling plots for ten shillings apiece, repayable in instalments, in a village seven miles southwest of Nassau that was initially known as Head Quarters and later renamed Carmichael, Poitier sought to reshape the community of liberated Africans— literally and figuratively—into something colonial authorities regarded as ordered.[36] Himself a slaveholder, Poitier expressed some sympathy for the extreme "jealousy" and hostility the prosperity of the free liberated Africans provoked in the white population. They were "hostile to the advancement of [the liberated Africans] in the scale of political rights," he explained to the foreign secretary, Lord Bathurst. "As a considerable slave owner myself," he confessed, "their ideas are brought home to my own feelings." It could not be expected of these people who had invested "property . . . under the sanction of law, in slaves . . . [to] view with complacency, His Majesty's well clad free Africans coming into our market, bending under the horse loads of provisions, the produce of their voluntary labour, industry and keen desire of acquiring property."[37]

Five years later, following Poitier's death, Governor James Carmichael-Smyth took the Head Quarters initiative a step further. In 1830, he wrote to the Colonial Office of his concern at the loss of Poitier's "protecting and fostering hand . . . which would have guided and supported [the liberated people's] steps until they could walk alone." In paternalistic language much reminiscent of Governor MacCarthy at Sierra Leone fifteen years previously, Carmichael-Smyth wrote of the "tolerably industrious" nature of most liberated Africans in the village, but the risk that they would become "idle, profligate, and dissolute, instead of being formed into useful and industrious members of the community" because of the "want of instruction and the absence of all control." He was seeking funds of £400 for the construction of a schoolhouse and teacher's residence, and £150 per annum "for the salary of a Teacher or Instructor for the indented Africans and their children."[38] This was a request that went far beyond the limited disposal terms set out in the abolition legislation, and one the Bahamian Assembly had already refused to grant.

Reading between the lines of his correspondence on the matter, Carmichael-Smyth seems to have relished the ire this initiative would provoke among colonial elites. An abolitionist, Carmichael-Smyth was the presumed author of a polemic tract that first appeared in 1830 in the *Dublin Morning Post,* and later reappeared under the title *West Indian Slave-Holders' Lust of Cruelty, the Same Now as Ever.*[39] He would later assume the governorship of British Guiana and gain a reputation for defending the rights of the enslaved; in particular, for seeking to prohibit the flogging of enslaved women. In the liberated Africans of Head Quarters, and in the idea of liberated African villages more broadly, Carmichael-Smyth saw an opportunity to use his government's custodial responsibilities to force a wholly unwelcome interpretation of the abolition legislation upon the white enslaver classes. Apparently taking his cue from the Sierra Leone model, during his governorship he established three more villages—Adelaide, Highborne Cay, and Gambier—as well as an "African Hospital" at Fort Charlotte. He reported to the Colonial Office, again in language reminiscent of the developmental imperialists in Freetown, on the pride the liberated people took in maintaining the villages: "cottages are neat and clean and there is an appearance of cheerfulness and industry about the whole African settlement which is gratifying to watch." Such was his keenness on the proposal for a school at Head Quarters, when the Colonial Office approved the request but delayed in making the money available, Carmichael-Smyth advanced one thousand pounds from his own funds and pushed the project through. "The interest I took in the affairs of these free Africans could not but be known and talked of in a small community like this, and produced a sour sulky feeling amongst a number of the ignorant & prejudiced white Inhabitants," he reported to Goderich in 1832.[40] Writing in *West Indian Slave-Holders' Lust of Cruelty* a year earlier, Carmichael-Smyth had been more explicit regarding his views of white Bahamian slaveholders: their behaviour was "disgraceful, inhuman, and unmanly." It was a product of the unnatural power they wielded over the enslaved, a power that rendered them inexorably "tyrannical" and instilled in them "a positive love of cruelty."[41] To the liberated African (male), on the other hand, Carmichael-Smyth attributed a kind of universal humanity—or more precisely, a kind of universal manliness based on rational self-interest and a solid work ethic. "The real truth is . . . that the African, like every other Man, will exert himself or not exert himself in the exact proportion as he finds his own interests affected."[42]

Laura Rosanne Adderley has called the Bahamas "the Sierra Leone of the Northern Caribbean." It is an interesting comparison. While the Bahamian villages certainly did not attract the same missionary attention or secular social engineering ambition as the Sierra Leone villages had over the previous decade, the analogy draws attention to the expanded scope of the liberated African establishment at the Bahamas—compared with islands such as Trinidad, for example. For a time, the colonial government at the Bahamas assumed not just "emergency" but "developmental" responsibility over liberated Africans, with the attendant expense and resource requirements this entailed. In total, between June 1831 and December 1838, around 4,200 more liberated Africans arrived in the Bahamas, primarily the survivors of Portuguese slave ships. An African Board, comprised of government officials and "liberal local inhabitants" was established to manage this new inflow and "to look after the welfare and interests of the liberated Africans," particularly those not yet apprenticed and those whose apprenticeships had expired. The majority of newly liberated people in these years were settled in villages on the island of New Providence, although some were still distributed as agricultural labourers on private indentures in the outlying islands of the Bahamian archipelago, as many earlier arrivals had been.[43]

For a brief period, the management of the villages of Adelaide and Head Quarters, or Carmichael from the 1830s, echoed aspects of the experiments of Sierra Leone. Those liberated people not sent to the African Hospital were transferred to one of these villages. There they were supplied with suits of clothing, tools, and utensils, and were expected to build or assist with the building of their houses. Alongside tending subsistence plots, the men were employed (presumably not voluntarily) on the public works, building and repairing roads and public buildings. Village superintendents were appointed in 1833 "to protect and control the Africans." Their formal duties blended the religious and the secular; an amalgam of lay missionary, schoolteacher, colonial administrator, constable, and ethnographer. They were expected to hold services at the newly built chapels, teach both adults and children, source and distribute rations, and act as constable, even to the extent of pursuing and apprehending suspected criminals. The eye of the superintendent was to be everywhere: the African Board expected detailed journals to be kept on all subjects, from the names, numbers, and individual progress of church attendees to the welfare of child apprentices and the behaviour and associations of the adults. Above all, they were to "encourage industry and good behaviour."[44]

With relatively high numbers of liberated African arrivals and a sufficient amount of available land, the Bahamas was the British Caribbean colony most likely to produce such village settlements. The Head

Quarters model of government-sponsored community creation was not attempted in other colonies in quite the same form. After 1831, several captured Portuguese slave ships were landed at the Bahamas so as to spare the passengers the ordeal of another transatlantic voyage back to the Anglo-Portuguese Mixed Commission at Freetown, and to avoid, in the governor's words, the "moral certainty of a considerable mortality amongst them." Given the pending legal case against the slave-ship owners, the new arrivals were not to be apprenticed, but rather left, under the supervision of one overseer, to their own independent living. "After a certain length of time, partly by cultivating the ground and partly by fishing," the governor judged that "they will be able to take care of themselves."[45]

The primary intent behind the villages, particularly after 1831, was to keep the liberated Africans separate from the rest of the island's population: to create "sanitary enclave[s] in which the Africans would be acclimatized and trained to be useful and untroublesome members of society but kept apart from the rest of the black [population] (and from predatory whites)."[46] On that, Governor Carmichael-Smyth and local elites could at least agree, albeit for different reasons. However, these visions of segregation and deferential submission were never realised. Many of the village settlers resisted the secluded, subsistence agricultural life imposed upon them. Particularly from the mid-1830s onwards as the settlements became overcrowded and under-resourced, younger inhabitants often left and moved closer to the markets and opportunities of Nassau. Those who stayed asserted the territories of the villages as their own. They utilised the anti-slavery sympathies of the governor to insist upon their own interpretation of their rights as liberated people, and to disrupt not only white colonists' understandings of the place of liberated people in the social order, but the order itself. One example of this is in the village of Carmichael.

In theory, the village superintendent was the ultimate authority figure for the community, the voice and instrument of the colonial government. In practice, village superintendents had to navigate three constituencies: the African settlers, the white population, and the colonial governor, and their incompatible expectations regarding the "balance of force and conciliation" that should be used to govern the villages. By 1832, Carmichael village had expanded far beyond the initial four-hundred-acre purchase, as escaped slaves saw an opportunity to join a free population already numbering over five hundred people. In that year, the village superintendent, Thomas Rigby, appears to have colluded with a white slaveholder named Johnson who attempted to abduct an escaped slave woman taking refuge in the village. Johnson was met by an armed group of liberated African villagers who refused him entry without "a paper of authority from the governor."[47] Prior to this, in July 1831, Rigby had clashed with the survivors of the Portuguese slave ship, the *Rosa*, who resisted labouring to his demand. When he ordered them flogged, a delegation of seven villagers walked seven miles to Nassau to complain in person to Governor Carmichael-Smyth. In the event, the governor sided with the villagers, and Rigby was eventually dismissed. His replacement, John Minns, the son of an emancipated African woman and her white English immigrant husband, was given a wider set of powers and appointed as Protector of Liberated Africans. Under the superintendence of Minns and his successor, a "Female School of Industry" was established, with a resident female teacher. Regulations were put in place to limit the ability of "unwelcome white visitors" from entering the village. Penalties of up to twenty pounds were put in place by the colonial secretary for anyone attempting to "seduce, entice, or carry away, harbour or conceal any liberated African."[48]

The Johnson altercation is suggestive of how the liberated Africans utilised their relationship with Carmichael-Smyth to resist and reject the property claims and assumed supremacy of the white slaveholding classes, while yet being seen to accept both the legitimacy of the colonial government and the imperial subjecthood that had been forced upon them. The liberated people had not chased the slaveholder Johnson out of town in 1832, nor assaulted him. The armed group of villagers simply staked a claim to the territory of the village and refused to let him cross their borders without authority—a territorial claim that was reinforced, in a way, by the governor's subsequent designation of spaces exclusively for the refuge of liberated Africans. In denying the slaveholder access to the community, the liberated Africans successfully asserted a kind of quasi-sovereignty over their village. They did not reject the legal superstructure by which slaveholders exercised property claims over enslaved persons under colonial law, but they demanded that such claims could only be conferred with legitimacy by the written instruction of the governor. This incident suggests a degree of consent on the part of the liberated Africans in these years to be governed within and by the institutions of colonial and imperial governance, on the condition that they had recourse to an authority figure in whom they had at least some degree of trust.

"To Make a Profit of Our Humanity": The Colonial Office Minute of 1835

Carmichael-Smyth left the Bahamas in 1833 for British Guiana. In February 1835, the governorship of the Bahamas was assumed by William Macbean George Colebrooke, the former Commissioner of Eastern Inquiry at the Cape, Mauritius, and Ceylon, who had conducted the investigation into Charles Blair's abuse of the liberated African disposal system at Cape Colony in the mid-1820s. Upon his arrival, Colebrooke learned that the strong preference of the Colonial Office was to uproot and transfer liberated Africans recently settled in the Bahamas to Trinidad—or at the very least, to transfer as many female liberated Africans as possible in order to help address the gender imbalance at Trinidad. Colebrooke protested against this decision on a number of grounds. "No colony is so favourable [as the Bahamas] as an asylum for the Africans," he told Colonial Secretary Lord Aberdeen.[49] The Bahamas offered "unappropriated land, fisheries [and] demand for labour," as well as a salubrious climate, "superior means of education," and an "intelligen[t]" and hardworking labouring population to learn from. The colony's blended disposal practices were already offering liberated Africans the best possible start; Colebrooke compared the success of the villages to "the success which [he had personally observed] has attended similar settlements in the poorest lands of South Africa." Those liberated people who were resettled on Eleuthera, a neighbouring island to New Providence, who supported themselves "on their own exertions [were] the most industrious and useful class of labourers in the Colony." In particular, Colebrooke emphasised the inhumanity of breaking up and transferring the liberated African communities; they had formed family connections and a thriving community, and it would cause them immense distress to be removed from their home. In what comes across as a carefully worded rebuke, Colebrooke reminded the Colonial Office of "the absence [in the Bahamas] of that temptation which exists at Trinidad to use [the liberated Africans] as articles of commerce and thereby to forget that their welfare is the primary object" of the whole antislavery intervention.[50]

Colebrooke's arrival in the Bahamas coincided with a very important moment in the evolution of British antislavery—a moment in which the imperial state was being forced at last to make hard choices about precisely what its long-standing signature "ethical" foreign and imperial policy was actually for. The Slavery Abolition Act of 1833 had abolished slavery as an institution in most of the British empire from 1 August 1834, with the exceptions of St Helena, Ceylon, and the territories governed by the East India Company under the oversight of the Board of Control.[51] In addition to a compensation fund of twenty million pounds, slaveholders had been promised a transition period of between four and six years, in which time the formerly enslaved would be bound to continue labouring as "apprentices" in their previous employments under conditions of more or less similar coercion. By May 1835, damning reports circulated within metropolitan Britain of widespread abuse of the system by planters seeking to prolong and deepen the coercive terms of apprenticeship. The various factions of the antislavery movement, including Thomas Fowell Buxton's "moderate" Anti-Slavery Society and the more radical followers of Joseph Sturge in the newly founded Central Negro Emancipation Committee, forced onto the parliamentary agenda and into public consciousness the question of the lingering moral debt Britain still owed to the "formerly" enslaved.[52] Yet many within British antislavery circles fretted about the pace of execution of the labour transition. One of the abolitionists' central promises was finally being put to the test: the promise that free labour would prove more profitable than slave labour. Should this prove not to be the case, and if the emancipation experiment in the sugar colonies were to fail, the fear was that this would be an enormous boon to the pro-slavery position in the United States and worldwide, and a terminal blow to the cause of global antislavery. It was imperative that the sugar economies of the British West Indies somehow flourish under "free" labour.[53]

Up to this point, those engaging in British discourses and practices of humane imperial governance had made the most of a comfortably vague ethical place between pragmatic self-interest and self-proclaimed compassionate virtue. For the most part, it had been possible to defend the more coercive elements of the liberated African disposal process as the necessary constraints required to resettle and incorporate a migrant population into pre-existing colonial societies. The uncompensated value reaped from liberated African labour (as soldiers, seamen, apprentices, seamstresses, washerwomen, domestic servants, clerks, lumberjacks, builders, water-carriers, agricultural labourers, prostitutes, salt-rakers, boatmen, and more) could be fudged as a fortunate reward for a benevolent nation engaging in a historic act of altruistic self-denial, and leading the world on its epochal transition from slavery to free labour.

The crises of the sugar plantations made this argument harder to sustain. The new bilateral slave trade suppression treaty with Spain, which came into effect in 1835, mandated the transfer to British Caribbean colonies of all Africans liberated at Cuba since 1833—an assumption of responsibility by Britain that reflected a sharp about-turn on the part of the Colonial and Foreign Offices, and that cannot be understood independently of the fears of labour shortages in British plantation colonies.[54] An important expectation on the part of British government in amending the Anglo-Spanish treaty in this way, and at the time they did so, was that the Africans liberated by the Havana Mixed Commission Court would be sent to Trinidad and other labour-starved plantation colonies; a standing arrangement to that effect was agreed upon with Governor George Hill of Trinidad.

Colebrooke's interest in the liberated Africans of Cuba had been piqued by his stopover at Havana on his way to assume the governorship of the Bahamas in 1835, when he had "had an opportunity of witnessing the condition of the liberated Africans there." He wrote to the Colonial Office to suggest that "a considerable number of them might be favourably (for themselves at least) settled in the Bahamas," and "announced his readiness to undertake the charge of them." This unwelcome application, and its re-

minder that the liberated Africans were not "articles of commerce," created quite some discomfiture within the Colonial Office, who up to then
had fielded requests from rather more predictable sources: the governors
of British Honduras, British Guiana, and Trinidad. It forced an explicit debate within the Colonial Office on the moral principles that underlay the
disposal policy, and on the question of whether, in essence, the liberated
Africans of the Atlantic world were indeed free people, or were a commodity to be deployed in the service of the empire. The result was a lengthy,
somewhat soul-searching Colonial Office internal policy memorandum,
or "Minute," which aimed to arrive at a set of liberated African disposal
policies by way of an abstract moral debate about the ethics that should
guide Britain as an antislavery state with systemic responsibilities across a
complex network of linked antislavery interests.[55] It is a fascinating document. Its analysis of the challenging and uncomfortable moral trade-offs
inherent in Britain's governance of its antislavery world system offers important insights into how contemporaries understood and attempted to
navigate the issues of control, domination, responsibility, consent, and the
intervenor's self-interest—issues that have characterised discourses around
humanitarian governance ever since.

The first thing the authors of the Minute sought to do was establish
the "principle by which Government ought to guide itself in the matter" of
resettling the Havana liberated Africans—or, more accurately, to assert the
moral unassailability of Britain's motivation as the intervening state:

> The main object of Great Britain in interfering at all in the
> matter is to do good to the injured Negroes, and in doing good
> to them to proclaim her allegiance to the principles of justice
> and humanity which have been violated in their persons.

This, they were confident, "will scarcely be questioned." Yet they immediately proceeded to the question of the degree of responsibility that should
be assumed in practice:

> But tho' this be the *main* object, how far is it *paramount?* . . .
> Besides the duty which we owe to [the liberated Africans] and

to the cause which they represent, there is a duty to the Colony
into which they are to be introduced; a duty to the tax payer at
home, a duty also . . . to the country from which it is proposed
to receive them.

Above all, the crucial consideration was the question of "how much we owe
to ourselves":

It remains to consider . . . how far we are at liberty to modify
our care for the welfare of the Negroes by a care for the commercial interests of our colonies; to adopt for instance a policy
by which some good would be done to the Negroes and some
to Trinidad, in preference to one which would yield indeed a
greater benefit to the former but none at all to the latter.

The authors immediately decided that the former course of action, creating advantage for both the liberated people and the receiving colony, would
be "inconsistent" with the selfless and self-denying "policy hitherto pursued by Great Britain in dealing with slavery and the traffic in Slaves; and
cannot be adopted without a departure from the spirit of our national
policy"—a somewhat odd analysis of the British state's twenty-five year history of directly extracting unfree labour from thousands upon thousands
of enlisted and publicly apprenticed liberated Africans on both sides of the
Atlantic. Without much difficulty, the authors arrived at their conclusion
that it would be best, "in behalf of the cause for which she has already sac-
rificed so much," that Britain should "decline any profits which her exertions in behalf of these Negroes might throw in her way," and should not
seek, or perhaps not to be seen to seek, "to gain more by leaving them in a
condition better indeed than it was, but not so good as it might be." "It is
true," they judged,

that we are not called upon to load ourselves for their sakes with
any burden which we cannot fairly bear, nor are we at liberty
to do them a benefit, however great, at the risk of introducing
into our Colonies, danger, or fatal distress or moral evil. But we

are under no obligation to make a profit of our humanity; and
are therefore not entitled to make the consideration of the good
which might be done to these sufferers secondary to a consideration of any financial advantage for which their services might
be rendered available. It is assumed therefore for the purposes
of this enquiry that the single object which Government has in
view is to improve the moral and physical condition of the Africans liberated at the Havana so far as may be practicable without injury to our Colonies or seriously burdening the Nation.

Thereafter, the Minute went on to explore three possible disposal options
for the Africans liberated at Havana. The first was to leave them in Cuba,
where, the authors suggested, "the natural humanity of a Spaniard to his
Slave" meant that liberated people might well be protected from "cruelty,
neglect or wilful mismanagement" albeit they would be at risk of re-
enslavement. In the other two options lay the real conflict at the heart of
the memorandum: the option to "plac[e] them out as servants or free labourers," or to resettle them

on lands granted for the purpose of forming them into independent settlements. The former has been chiefly recommended
as relieving the Government from the expense which would
necessarily be incurred in establishing and maintaining them
during the first year or more; and also as a means of supplying
with labourers those Colonies in which labour is wanted; the
latter being more *for the happiness of the Negroes;* inasmuch as
it would exempt them from a life of regular labour to which all
of them are unaccustomed, and many unfitted by their previous
habits and would also bring them more immediately under the
care of the Government, and under the influence of moral cultivation.

The use of the word "care" is illuminating. It hints at an acknowledgement
of what had happened to the liberated Africans distributed as apprentices
in slaveholding economies since 1808, and the overwhelming evidence

documenting the harrowing experiences many had endured at the hands of private apprentice-holders.[56] Nevertheless, the Minute's authors veered away from the idea of independent settlements. In a tortuous series of arguments shot through with racialised assumptions and imaginings, yet repeatedly underscored by the stated priority of delivering "most advantage 1st to the Liberated African and 2nd to the Colonies," the authors concluded that "either way of life must be a hard one," and that the policy preference must be whichever option is likely to "train them earliest and most easily to habits of civilization"—which the authors decided was a life of regular plantation labour. At Trinidad and other plantation colonies, "a system of dependence and subjection" would be "accompanied by a habitual association with men a grade more civilized than themselves." At the Bahamas, it was implied strongly, "they should live segregated, with the power of remaining slothful and irregular, and of cherishing their old customs, having indeed the advantage of civilized superintendence but not of civilized habits or associates." Furthermore, to send the liberated Africans from Havana to the sugar colonies

> would, in promoting their commerce, most effectually serve the cause, if not of these individual Africans, *yet of the victims of the Slave Trade in general;* inasmuch as by increasing the productiveness of these Colonies it would tend to bring down the price of Sugar, consequently to diminish those profits which are now large enough to indemnify the Slave Traders in Cuba for the risk of their traffic. And this seems a fair argument (on behalf of the Negroes) for turning as large a branch of this stream into the Colonies in question as can be safely done.

The liberated African was thus framed as both an innocent and a threat: the helpless recipient of an intervention, who needed to be saved from Spanish avarice, yet also saved from themselves: "a body of Savages, [who] cannot exist in the middle of civilized community without perpetual danger to the public peace." It was the responsibility of the liberated Africans, the authors argued, to serve the new, British-led moral order by way of the empire's economic order; that is, to contribute their labour to a larger vision of post-enslavement economic prosperity, a noble sacrifice to prevent the enslavement of future generations of Africans.

The Minute is an important document not because it determined future policy—in spite of its recommendations, around nine hundred liberated Africans were transferred from Havana to the Bahamas between 1836 and 1841—but because of the insights it offers into how Colonial Office officials understood and navigated the imperatives created by Britain's "humane endeavours."[57] At the heart of the document is the persistent effort to find a logical and ethical basis for profiting from humanitarian activity. "Since the welfare of the Africans themselves [was] the primary object" of the whole antislavery undertaking, the concept of that "welfare" had to be reimagined and redefined through a protracted rationalisation in humanitarian, selfless, and paternalistic terms in order to justify the preference for control over compassion; "civilisation" over consent. The authors positioned the British state as the highest authority in a multi-tiered international moral landscape, and put forward a vision of British antislavery humanitarianism—and the essence of "Britishness" that was its bedrock— as such a self-evident good that coercing African labour to the benefit of the British empire could be fundamentally a humanitarian act. "There must be restraint" in civilised societies, the authors argued. "And unless a man can be taught to endure it, he must be compelled to do so." "It is perhaps the best thing *even for themselves* . . . that they should be placed at once under a system of merciful but steady restraint in which a moderate quantity of labour should be regularly and peremptorily enacted."[58]

Colebrooke's original request had begun from quite a different set of assumptions. First and foremost, he wanted Britain to mould the liberated Africans into "a class of devoted subjects" because that kind of devotion could reap some real practical rewards at the peripheries of empire. To his view, those "brought here after Capture . . . ought to be put down in favourable situations attended with care, and provided for till they can provide for themselves. Then indeed would our interference be a blessing to them, and call forth their gratitude." The liberated Africans were, Colebrooke argued, "peculiarly susceptible of kindness, and in a short time become reconciled & eventually a most useful and valuable people." In other words, he did not eschew the idea of instrumentalising liberated people for the benefit of the British empire; he simply had larger ambitions than replacing, individual by individual, enslaved plantation workers in the larger colonies. As a group, the liberated Africans might more usefully be made to firm up Britain's grip on the islands of the Northern Caribbean, and offer a bulwark against the ambitions of other powers seeking to jostle Britain out of its position of influence in the region. Colebrooke had a particular eye on the United States. "In a few years," he counselled, "with the help of the Moravians and other Missionaries, & the expenditure of a few thousand pounds, we could raise a rampart of [liberated Africans] in this quarter, which would enable us to bid a bold defence to our American Neighbours—and we should reap a peaceful harvest from their labours."[59]

Colebrooke was not alone in perceiving a threat on the northeastern flank of the Bahamas archipelago; throughout the 1830s, successive governors of the Bahamas drew the attention of the metropolitan government to the colony's vulnerability to American expansionism. Situated just off the Florida coast, and a short distance from the island of Cuba, the Bahamas could not afford to ignore the "anxiety already shewn by the American Government to extend their possessions in these seas, by their establishment at Key West," as Carmichael-Smyth warned the Colonial Office in 1830. Six years later, his successor reminded the Colonial Office of the ties of kinship, education, commerce, and ideology that existed between the southern United States and many of the elites of white Bahamian society, and how those bonds had only been strengthened by the recent imposition of antislavery on the colony. The foreign secretary, Lord Glenelg, concurred. As his under-secretary, James Stephen, explained in March 1838 to the military secretary at the Horse Guards, FitzRoy Somerset:

> The Western Shores of the Bahama Channel being now entirely incorporated into the United States of America, might afford shelter to Ships of war and Privateers, which would be altogether unchecked in their operations against the British homeward bound West India Trade, unless the Eastern Shores of the

same Channel should be peopled by a race of persons attached
to the British Crown and accustomed to a Maratime [*sic*] Life.
Such a population, as it appears to Lord Glenelg, might be collected by due attention to the Africans who have recently been
introduced from Portuguese & Spanish Slave Ships.[60]

The idea of shoring up unstable regions by planting outposts of grateful and loyal liberated Africans at the contested frontiers of empire was, by
the 1830s, very well established among administrators in British West Af-
rica. This had occasioned a series of experiments in the peninsula around
Freetown and a number of nearby islands from the early 1810s onwards.[61]
Governor Charles MacCarthy was the first to moot the idea of retransport-
ing liberated Africans farther afield—specifically, to the mouth of the
Gambia River to bulk out the fledgling settlement of Bathurst (present-day
Banjul) on St Mary's Island.[62] In July 1816, he wrote to Colonial Secretary
Earl Bathurst to suggest that "a part of the Captured Negroes might be use-
fully disposed of both for themselves and the Mother Country in forming
settlements in our possessions in the Gambia and on the leeward Coast."[63]
The following chapter examines the establishments that emerged on the
Gambia River and, later, on the remote southern Atlantic island of St Helena, and will consider the variables that shaped outcomes for liberated Africans across these diverse contexts of the British Atlantic.

FOUR

A Liberated African "Archipelago"

ON 19 AUGUST 1828, twenty liberated African men departed from Freetown on board the British merchant schooner *Venus*. They were bound for St Mary's Island at the mouth of the Gambia River. The assistant colonial surveyor accompanied them, carrying with him a list of the names colonial administrators had recorded for the men—among them, Degokoe, Abeowah, Mapong, Mallaw, Shallah, and Aduba—along with instructions for the commanding officer of the Royal African Corps at St Mary's, into whose custody they were to be transferred "for the purposes of being employed as Labourers." Each man carried an identical packet of "cloathing and rations": two shirts, two pairs of trousers, one blanket, one mat, a hat, a tin cup, a spoon, a tin plate, a knife, and a pair of shoes. Four kettles were sent too, one to be shared between five men. In his note to the receiving officer, the assistant superintendent of the Liberated African Department at Sierra Leone, Thomas Cole, was at pains to detail the precise amount of financial support these men had already received from government—two months of their six months' allowance of three pence per day—and the balance of what was due to them, less the cost of the provisions to sustain them on their passage north. The governor had intended to send a larger number of people, "30 or 40 lads in addition to the 20 men," but there were "none at the disposal of the Department at present suitable for the service" required by Major Findlay at the Gambia. "An arrival of at least 900 Negroes is however shortly expected," Cole assured the major. "A selection" would be made "of the number of persons you require as will be useful labourers and Apprentices."[1]

It is possible that the men chose to go. It is equally possible that they did not, and that—as the transactional tone of Thomas Cole's letter suggests—after being held for two months in the Liberated African Yard or hospital at Freetown, they were forced once again to embark aboard a European ship and to endure another ocean voyage to another unfamiliar country, all to meet the labour needs of a fledgling British colony. The papers of the Liberated African Department of Sierra Leone record many more such transfers between 1818 and 1861. As is so often the case with colonial archives, these registers obscure far more than they reveal. They document only group sizes, broken down by age and sex; few surviving records give the names of the people sent to the Gambia before 1835. The registers are often also incomplete, and it is difficult to link the groups of transferred liberated Africans to the ships on which they originally arrived.[2] As such, these documents capture only the barest glimpse of the stories of the approximately 3,500 slave-ship survivors sent north to help develop and consolidate the tiny British colonial foothold on the Gambia River between 1818 and 1861. What has not escaped the archival record, however, is the catastrophic human cost paid by many liberated Africans for this particular British experiment in imperial expansion and consolidation.

This chapter follows on directly from the preceding chapter's analysis of the liberated African establishments at Cape Colony and the British West Indies. It explores the emergence of establishments at the Gambia and St Helena—sites at which slave trade survivors suffered extraordinarily high mortality. The second part of this chapter suggests some variables that may have determined outcomes for liberated people sent to these places, together with the establishments at Cape Colony and the West Indies. Each of the British Atlantic world establishments was a distinct and unique site, yet together they formed a kind of "archipelago" of experiments in humanitarian governance and the management and control of vulnerable populations. This chapter considers the establishments in that vein, looking at the importance of governance practices and ideas imported across British imperial sites through the personages of peripatetic colonial governors and administrators. Finally, it observes the particularly carceral shared character of these sites, and how frequently, easily, and without challenge colonial governments conflated the liberated people with convicts, and crafted these "royal asylums" as a "species of prison."[3]

Bathurst and McCarthy's Island (Janjanbureh)

Liberated Africans sent from Freetown to the Gambia experienced the considerable physical and psychological stresses of a second ocean voyage, often while still weakened from the ordeal of the first. Kyle Prochnow notes the "staggering" mortality suffered by these groups: between May 1832 and December 1835 alone, of 2,468 people sent, 35 percent died, usually within weeks or months of arriving at Bathurst. One 1833 medical report described the "protracted suffering" of those who disembarked "weak and emaciated" from the transport vessels. The devastation wrought by one particularly harrowing voyage—the *Governor Campbell* in 1835, in which 108 of the 300 passengers died of smallpox on the journey or shortly after arrival—prompted an enquiry that showed culpable disregard on the part of the authorities at Sierra Leone for the welfare of the passengers, even cruelty. Many were embarked in a very weak state, some unable to walk, and a lack of blankets and other basic supplies only worsened their suffering.[4]

For many, this was a prelude to even bleaker conditions at the Gambia. In 1842, Richard Robert Madden, a Royal Commissioner conducting an enquiry into Britain's West African settlements, judged the Gambia "of all the places selected for the location" of recaptives, as "the most unfitted . . . In no place where they have been located has their condition been more unfortunate."[5] He deplored the circumstances under which "different 'cargoes' of liberated Africans" had been transported and resettled, and the "mock freedom they found here"—first at Bathurst, where

> They receive no instruction; the Governor admits there is no
> land to allot them in the settlement that would be of any benefit
> to them. A considerable number of them are kept in Bathurst,
> in the liberated African yard, as prisoners are kept in gaols, or
> slaves in barracones [*sic*]; and when they go beyond the walls it
> is as felons in a gang, to work upon the highways.

Women were distributed as "wives" in the town and its surrounding area, while men were often allocated to various public works projects, labouring alongside convicts in road building and other major infrastructure proj-ects initiated to get the new colony established.[6] The forced labour of liberated Africans was used to construct, among other things, the Govern-ment House, the military hospital, the gaol, and the dykes with sluice gates.[7] A set of experimental plantations and a brick factory were operated on the mainland from 1833. The brick factory was closed six years later, when a new governor expressed horror at the working conditions that he witnessed there: the liberated Africans were forced to endure "the most la-borious exertion—that of working the clay up to their knees in a most vio-lent manner in time to the beating of a sort of kettle."[8]

Of greater concern to Madden and others was the disastrous attempt to use liberated Africans to push out the boundaries of the colony, far up-river at Janjanbureh, known to the British as McCarthy's Island—an island some three hundred kilometres (or ten to twenty days' voyage) from Bathurst.[9] As the Sierra Leonean political theorist and historian James Af-ricanus Beale Horton observed in 1868, McCarthy's Island had been bought from the King of Calabar "for the express purpose of protecting and encouraging the trade in the upper portion of the River . . . It is well known that most of the trade in River Gambia comes from the Upper River . . . the largest quantity comes from a distance of about 175 to 200 miles further up the River [past McCarthy's Island], of which Fatta Tendah is the cen-tre."[10] The Colonial Office had shown intermittent interest in the island for some time, since it was first suggested thirty-eight years previously as a penal colony for transported British convicts. That plan had been quickly abandoned, partly because "there was an inhuman appearance in the style of the business, & it would never be received by the people of England—it was in one word an African grave."[11] Nevertheless, in 1827, the acting governor of Sierra Leone and former superintendent of liberated Afri-cans, Kenneth Macaulay, travelled to McCarthy's Island to investigate prospects for developing a settlement there. He found a small Wesleyan mis-sionary settlement already in place, along with a handful of traders from Bathurst, some government labourers, twelve liberated African men, and thirteen soldiers of the Second West India Regiment who had built the gar-rison of Fort George on the north of the island in 1823 and whose sergeant exercised authority over the island. The village about a mile from the fort had begun to attract a new indigenous population seeking "protection from the raging war in the neighbouring country." Macaulay reported that they "appear[ed] well clothed, comfortable, and contented." He concluded that he "should strongly recommend the formation of a large Liberated African establishment there" to relieve Sierra Leone of the burden of increasing numbers of arrivals.[12] In 1831, the Colonial Office issued instructions to send as many as possible to the Gambia under the now familiar model of the carefully superintended village and the temporary provision of government-sponsored rations, building materials, clothing, farming equipment, and medicines. Over the following five years, 2,582 liberated Africans were sent to the Gambia—more than five times the number that had been sent in the previous thirteen years. Kyle Prochnow and Richard Anderson estimate that at least 3,478 liberated Africans were sent to the Gambia across the period 1818 to 1861.[13]

McCarthy's Island was not selected because of any particular practical advantages for the creation and management of a new planned community, but for its potential as a commercial and "civilising" bridgehead at the frontier of untapped country.[14] The settlement that developed at McCarthy's Island thus represented a new articulation of how liberated Africans could serve the interests of the empire. The site was "developmental" and imperialistic, rather than "emergency," since all of the newly liberated Africans' basic, urgent human needs would, in theory, have been met in the Liberated African Yard and hospital at Freetown prior to transhipment. However, both in its founding motivation and in its short but tragic history, the establishment at McCarthy's Island stretches to the breaking point the idea that there was a humane purpose to that particular manifestation of disposal policy. The objective was the development of the colony; any discourse of the "improvement" and "civilisation" of the liberated Africans was markedly less prominent than in other colonial and metropolitan correspondence and decision-making processes. The transplantation of the liberated people was most likely achieved through compulsion—a disposal process that was, for those who experienced it, literally, rather than just metaphorically, "another middle passage."[15] For the period after 1832, this analogy becomes all the more acute, when Governor Findlay purchased and refitted the slave ship *Prueba* as a transport vessel to bring liberated Africans from Freetown to the Gambia. In a particularly striking act of cruelty and indifference, the first group embarked was drawn from the survivors of the *Prueba*'s last slaving voyage: a journey in which thirty-five captives had died. The question of consent was dispensed with summarily: Under-Secretary Hay's view was that "[t]o the Africans themselves, indeed, it must be an object of indifference whether they be settled in one Colony, or the other, provided a comfortable maintenance is secured to them." The *Queen Adelaide* made nine voyages in total, transporting 1,146 liberated Africans from Sierra Leone to the Gambia.[16]

From a humanitarian point of view, the experiment at McCarthy's Island was catastrophic. The first large-scale transhipment of two hundred people landed at McCarthy's Island in 1829. They arrived in the midst of the rainy season and were wholly dependent on government rations as they built huts and waited to plant their allocated plots. Overseers were ordered to provide instruction in brick-making and agricultural techniques, but the farms did not thrive. Indeed, although the liberated Africans were sent there because the land was "deemed fit for agriculture," the first comprehensive land survey was conducted only in 1836, six years after the first transfer.[17] This survey judged the agricultural prospects of the islands quite hopeless. In 1833 and 1834, two extended periods of drought killed most of the crops that were planted, and the buildings on the island were destroyed by two fires and by an attack by a local ruler, who also captured and re-enslaved many of the liberated Africans. Many more died from disease and starvation.[18] In 1835, a new barracks was built for a small garrison and also to house some new liberated Africans. A surgeon was also sent. Three years later, the Wesleyan mission took over all government land, with a view to creating a model farm and village. For a short time, the mission became the largest employer on the island, employing about seventy liberated Africans to clear the land and lay out farms, primarily for rice, corn, and groundnuts. Supplied from England with tools and seeds, the farm was relatively prosperous until 1843, when locusts ravaged the area and the island was reduced to famine conditions again for two years. At that point, the island's liberated African establishment was acknowledged to have failed and was closed down, although the Wesleyan farm remained in place until the end of the century.[19]

Some survivors remained on McCarthy's Island, while others made their own way back to Bathurst, many settling to the north and south of St Mary's Island, including on the recently ceded Barra Mile.[20] In 1843, the Liberated African Department at Bathurst was closed down, and no more liberated people were sent from Sierra Leone. Survivors were expected to fend for themselves. Of at least 1,200 people sent upriver to McCarthy's, it is estimated that about half may have died.[21] Many more escaped from the settlement into the nearby countryside, from where their fate is unknown. In 1842, Governor Huntley estimated that about half of all liberated Africans brought to the Gambia had died. Commissioner Madden concluded:

> No numerous or considerable body of them have quitted the settlement at any known period; from time to time a few of the fugitives, from the mock freedom they found here, may have escaped. They have not been kidnapped; they have not been entered as recruits into the black regiments; but they died off, and there is nothing further to be said of them . . . It was better for them no doubt to die off here than aboard the slave-ship; there was less absolute suffering and fewer horrors surrounding their dying moments; but there was sickness and privations enough to cause it to be said that the liberated Africans in this settlement . . . in colonial parlance, have "died off rapidly."[22]

Like other sites of "disposal" in the Atlantic and Indian Ocean worlds, the settlement at McCarthy's Island was a unilateral exercise of power over liberated Africans without their consent by the British antislavery state system seeking to formulate an advantageous global policy from the abolitionist imperative that had been imposed upon it by parliamentary lobbying and public opinion. What is unusual about it is that it was a tertiary site, planted deliberately at the farthest reaches of British imperial power, and indeed some distance beyond what the geographic and maritime surveys of the river had deemed practical or advisable. Its imagined value, in addition to relieving Freetown and Bathurst of responsibility, was as a trading hub and a model village: helping to consolidate British influence in the area by demonstrating to the surrounding powers the economic prosperity achievable without enslavement, and the moral "advancement" possible under British tutelage. McCarthy's Island itself offered no specific pull factors, nor was the establishment prepared to protect its inmates against adversity and physical hardship. The numbers sent from Sierra Leone were far out of proportion to the limited demand at McCarthy's Island for migrant workers and the capacity of the land to support them agriculturally, with disastrous consequences for over a thousand people.

Visiting Bathurst twenty years later, the Victorian travel writer and notorious racist Richard Burton observed the liberated Africans with his characteristic sneer. Yet his comments inadvertently hint at the community strength they had established in the area, the persistence of missionary interest in these communities, and the liberated Africans' ability advantageously to blend the resources provided by missionaries' educational programmes with their own political and cultural forms of organisation. "The liberated Africans, principally Akus and Ibos . . . have organised 'companies,'" Burton reported, "the worst of trading unions, elected head men who will become their tyrants, effected strikes, and had several serious collisions with the military. They are in missionary hands, which disciplines and makes them the more dangerous."[23] In 1864, a group of liberated Africans petitioned the colonial secretary to complain of the colonial government's neglect and failure to provide their traders with the same protection extended to European traders: "why should [we] after being liberated, settled and called British subjects, be left entirely into the hands of heathens, to be ill-treated, beaten, and wounded, without anyone to give [us] redress, for the want of protection?"[24] As this petition implies, whatever success the survivors of McCarthy's Island and of the Bathurst

Liberated African Department may have enjoyed had little to do with the support of the colonial government. For many years, the liberated people in the area around Bathurst continued to struggle to establish themselves on terms equal to other colonists (and, implicitly, in hierarchical terms, above the status they accorded to the local peoples). However, the fortunes of this group began to change from the 1840s as the group organised around their particular "liberated African" identity, and by the end of the century, the liberated Africans and their descendants formed an important elite within the colonial society of the Gambia.[25]

Commissioner Madden criticised the tendency of European observers to castigate liberated Africans for not achieving greater community prosperity, and to ascribe to them a set of group characteristics of "indolence, laziness, and depravity." The formerly enslaved were "not of one tribe, or nation, or region of Africa, but are carried away from all parts of it, and can have no characteristic qualities peculiar to them, except what belongs to their condition." In Madden's view, the group had not prospered because the colonial government had failed them, and continued to fail them through short-sighted segregationist policies like the prohibition on liberated African children attending the colony's schools. "If we look to their emancipation alone for their improvement, and locate them where there are no schools for their instruction, no fit soil for their subsistence, and no steps taken for their civilisation, we may expect to find them swarming in our gaols, or skulking about the market-places in idleness and want. My only wonder is, that being left in a state of such ignorance and destitution, their crimes are not greater and more numerous than they are."[26]

Most of all, Madden deplored the fact that the forced secondary migrations had taken place at all: "masses of men are not like bales of merchandize intended for transportation from clime to clime, unless it be intended to make merchandize of them."[27] This was no throwaway remark. He was echoing a strand of reformist discourse that had also surfaced notably in the Commission of Eastern Inquiry, which argued that the state's coercive exploitation of the labour of indigenous peoples, convicts, and other vulnerable populations constituted a kind of enslavement; that their transportation across and between imperial sites was a kind of slave trade.[28]

Madden warned the British government to see the Gambia as a cautionary tale against the secondary and tertiary transportation of liberated Africans to and within the islands of the British West Indies: "if such things have happened in the passage of so short a distance as that between Sierra Leone and the Gambia, what may not be expected to happen in the course of a little time, when the rigour of the new regulations is relaxed in longer voyages, and where the control of government officers will not exist." "Eventually," he urged "the merchant's profit must set off the sufferings of the people who are removed on freight."[29]

St Helena

Unlike the Gambia, the remote south-Atlantic island of St Helena was never planned or imagined as a resettlement outpost for liberated Africans. More than 2,200 kilometres west of Luanda and over 3,000 kilometres northwest of Cape Town, this tiny, rocky island was discovered uninhabited in 1502 by a Portuguese fleet and had served as a maritime staging post ever since. It was seized by the British in the mid-seventeenth century and had been a British colony for most of the intervening years. In 1834, it was transferred from the control of the East India Company to the Crown, although the island's four-thousand-strong population did not receive their new Crown governor until 1836.[30]

Until 1839, St Helena had played only a peripheral role in the suppression of the slave trade by supporting the resupply of the anti-slave-trade squadrons. Things changed in 1839, when Viscount Palmerston ordered the navy to stop and search Portuguese slave ships south of the equator—a whole new patrol ground for the British naval squadron.[31] New captures in a new region meant new legal cases, liberations, and disposals, and St Helena was selected as the location for the new Vice-Admiralty Court and liberated African establishment. An alarmed Governor George Middlemore was assured by the colonial secretary, Lord John Russell, that it was "highly improbable that any Africans who may be captured by Her Majesty's cruisers will be landed at St Helena." The first captured vessel arrived less than six months later with 215 enslaved people aboard, many of whom were infected with smallpox. Four more ships were brought in between mid-February and May 1841. The first groups of survivors were apprenticed according to the legislation and employed as domestics and labourers, albeit remaining a visible and consciously differentiated social grouping in an otherwise non-African population. By August 1841, however, the island had received 1,824 liberated Africans, far in excess of what its small population could absorb—and this was only the beginning. Over the lifetime of the Liberated African Department at St Helena, from 1840 to 1872, it received 450 vessels with over 25,000 liberated Africans.[32]

Having never anticipated nor sought such a population increase, the government of the island was completely unprepared. It was resourced neither for the immediate emergency welfare needs of the new arrivals nor for any long-term disposal policy adequate to these numbers. Two receiving depots were constructed hastily in Rupert's Valley and Lemon Valley, which were small self-contained and isolated locations believed to be sufficiently far removed from the capital, Jamestown, to protect the island's population from contagious diseases. A small Liberated African Department staff was cobbled together to feed and care for the new arrivals, although the degree to which they did either was, by the reports of the colony's medical officer, often not impressive.[33] Lemon Valley was designated as a quarantine site, while the larger Rupert's Valley was intended to house the able-bodied. Both locations created challenges from the outset. Both were narrow, deeply incised valleys with little room for large-scale habitation. Transporting supplies and new arrivals to Lemon Valley presented particular logistical difficulties due to its distance from Jamestown and the often very heavy surf in the bay, and this depot was abandoned in 1843.[34] Rupert's Valley was not much better. It was fewer than one hundred metres wide at its floor, with hills rising steeply on both sides. Unlike much of the rest of the island, the valley was arid, exposed, and windswept, with no natural, permanent water supply.

Nevertheless, Rupert's Valley was not an inherently unhealthy location for a settlement. St Helena's pleasant climate and the absence of diseases such as yellow fever and malaria gave it a marked advantage over some other establishment sites in the British Atlantic. During the periods where the depot was only lightly populated, contemporaries reported scenes of cleanliness, good health, and order. However, it was not uncommon for a single slave ship to arrive carrying more people than the entire capacity of the depot, and as in Sierra Leone, new arrivals at St Helena were often suffering from severe illnesses, including dysentery, yellow fever, smallpox, measles, pneumonia, diarrhoea, and various eye and skin diseases. As slave ships arrived with increasing frequency and at unpredictable times, and with little or no approved budget for foodstuffs, medicines, staff, clothing, and other necessities, the tiny establishment was periodically stretched to the breaking point and beyond. Liberated Africans, living and dead, were unloaded in the bay at Rupert's Valley. There was nowhere to house the living but a series of semi-fixed tents, with a maximum capacity of about five hundred people, and nowhere to bury the dead but in the shallow, rocky soil a short distance up the valley.[35] Many were buried only a few hundred yards away to windward. One colonial surgeon reported an "extraordinary number of rats and mice" appearing in the valley, feasting on the dead and the dying with "ferocity." It was during the particularly grim 1840s that Dr Rawlins, the establishment's medical officer, called it "a most bleak and dreary spot." Another observer called it "God-forsaken." Of the first 1,824 arrivals, 467 died at St Helena. Regardless, Rupert's Valley remained the only official liberated African depot, primarily because the governor and Collector of Customs could agree on no alternative.[36]

The establishment at St Helena protested regularly to the Foreign Office and the Admiralty that it had no capacity to manage and dispose of the volume of people arriving. Eventually, responding to pressure from both Governor Trelawney, who detested the liberated African establishment, and Lord Trevelyan at the Treasury, who detested the expense involved, the Foreign Office and the Admiralty agreed to issue naval instructions to the squadron to avoid bringing captured slave ships to St Helena from 1843 onwards. The liberated African establishment was officially decommissioned in 1843 and the island designated for use as a depot only "under exceptional circumstances" or, later, upon "unanswerable grounds of humanity." Yet within weeks, another slave ship was brought in on those very grounds, and the inward flow began again in earnest. Over 7,000 enslaved

people were captured in the area between 1858 and 1867. With the south-
ward shift of West African coastal slave trading *entrepôts* during this period, and in the aftermath of the Aberdeen Act of 1845, St Helena found
itself in the midst of an enormous traffic, notable for its much-increased
cargoes of enslaved people—on average, 450 individuals per ship, and
sometimes as many as 1,500 on a steamer.[37] Under strict instructions to
keep costs to a minimum, the establishment kept no standing stocks
of medicines or foodstuffs, and no support staff were retained on a permanent basis. The resources at Rupert's Valley—meagre at the best of
times—were frequently overwhelmed. According to an 1861 report, the
accommodation—still in that year the same twelve sheds constructed to
house around thirty people each—were "badly constructed, badly ventilated and long since condemned as unfit for habitation."[38] They had been
erected as temporary structures more than a decade previously and even
then had not been fit for purpose, nor sufficient to protect their inhabitants against the elements.

Depot life was often a harsh experience.[39] As at the yards at Freetown,
the West Indies, the Gambia, and Cape Town, liberated Africans were di-
vided into groups or "squads" under the authority of a designated overseer.[40] They were required to present themselves at muster and were
forbidden from straying any distance from the "station." The "greatest vigi-
lance and attention" was to be paid to cleanliness, with scheduled bathing
times, weekly clothing washes and changes. Mealtimes were heavily superintended. Between these times, the liberated Africans were required to
help maintain the depot, with the women washing clothes, while men
helped with cooking, overseeing, sweeping, cleaning, piling up stones, and
other "light" forms of labour. Colonial officials reported that liberated
people also occupied themselves in making and stringing glass beads,
building musical instruments, and making knives and other items both useful and decorative, as well as in activities such as singing, dancing, and
playing various games.[41] Smoking was a popular habit amongst both
children and adults. One near-contemporary wrote of a boat race organised between Europeans and liberated Africans in which the Africans won,
although to infer a depot life of cheerful camaraderie would be a serious
overstatement.

Depot staff, including the overseers and medical staff, do not seem to have acquired more than a few phrases of the diverse languages spoken by the various groups of liberated African arrivals (primarily, it would seem, languages originating in the Congo, Angola, Mozambique, and Benguela regions), and visitors passing through the island with sufficient translation skills were rare. Liberated Africans were generally kept at the depot for between one and seven months, or up to a year for the very ill. Those held for longer periods of time proved far more proficient in acquiring the English language than their overseers were in learning to communicate with them; those who stayed only briefly tended to remain confined to relationships within their own linguistic groupings. Fights between groups of men were not uncommon, and were generally understood by English-speaking observers to be the result of fractious "tribal" relationships, although the confinement, dislocation, loneliness, and boredom of life in the depots must surely have been more important factors, in addition to the immense stress and psychological trauma of their enslavement and the uncertainty of their future prospects.[42]

At St Helena, as at all other liberated African establishments in the Atlantic world, the colonial government took the opportunity to extract additional labour from those whose health permitted it. Some were employed in collecting and delivering stores; others in farming and fishing, as well as in the sort of "public works" labour common to other Atlantic-world establishments, including quarrying, road repair, clearing of gorse, and building or maintaining colonial infrastructure, such as Jamestown's wharf and drainage system. In the early 1850s, some men were employed in building a church. As at other establishments, this labour was neither voluntary nor paid, and the response from the liberated Africans was not always compliant. In 1861, colonial administrators reported "a mutinous and rebellious" few weeks, where at least one small armed uprising took place against the overseers. However in general, reported instances of violence by inmates against staff seem to have been rare. A more common form of resistance to the constraints of depot life was the "almost daily" absconding of its inmates. Dr Rawlins reported in 1847 that for the most part, once their situation was communicated adequately to the liberated Africans "and an example made of the runaways," many people tended to be content to stay within the bounds of Rupert's Valley. Amongst those who escaped, many died, although the causes of these deaths—whether from exposure, accident, illness, altercations with islanders, or suicide—were not recorded.[43]

Foreign Secretary Earl Grey wrote repeatedly to Governor Ross in the late 1840s and early 1850s of his "distress" at the depot's consistently high sickness and death rates. "I cannot too strongly impress upon you the opinion which I entertain of its being essential both to humanity, and to the honour of the British government that no pains should be spared to remedy, as far as may be possible, the cause of so extensive an evil." Stressing the urgent "necessity of using every precaution . . . for restoring the health of the Africans on their arrival," Grey requested from the governor an explanation for the mortality.[44] In response, Ross and other officers within the administration prepared detailed reports of the manner in which the liberated Africans were cared for, their accommodation, clothing, and in particular the diet schedules offered to them at different stages of illness and recovery.[45] Dr Rawlins described in 1849 how the treatment of Africans by Liberated African Department workers at Rupert's Valley was "marked with extreme kindness and attention to all their wants . . . Nothing that humanity can conceive or kindness suggest is left undone."[46]

Following the deaths of forty-six Jamaica-bound liberated African emigrants on board the *Euphrates* in September 1848, Grey expanded the scope of enquiry to include mortality on board emigrant ships. Governor Ross, now on the defensive, undertook to determine just how St Helena was performing against other liberated African establishments. He sought out mortality statistics from two other stations, Cape Colony and Sierra Leone, which he then forwarded to Grey. By Ross's somewhat dubious calculations, St Helena actually had the lowest percentage mortality, at 19 percent compared to Sierra Leone's 26 percent and the Cape of Good Hope's 39 percent.[47] Ross was not in this case comparing like with like. The three colonies' mortality statistics covered different sizes of population and different lengths of time, which meant that seasonal variations and other factors such as overcrowding were not taken into account, for example. Nonetheless, it is actually difficult to know whether St Helena was or was not a more lethal location than other liberated African establishments, such as Sierra Leone. Assuming that 5,000 of St Helena's 25,000 liberated Africans died subsequent to arriving at the depot, this was a mortality of 20 percent. By comparison, post-adjudication mortality at Sierra Leone between 1808 and 1830 was estimated by one long-serving Liberated African Department official at approximately 15 percent, with mortality in the Liberated African Hospital as high as 59 percent. Sierra Leone's Liberated African Hospital returns between 1838 and 1850 indicate that 7,147 patients died. Of these deaths, 4,003 happened between 1840 and 1849.[48]

Although even during the bleakest of times, the majority of liberated Africans who came ashore at St Helena survived their time on the island, still, the number who died at the Rupert's and Lemon Valley depots was still very substantial. Between 1842 and 1849 alone, 4,760 died, 32 percent of the Africans landed at St Helena during those years. Andy Pearson estimates that about 8,000 people died in total between 1840 and the mid-1860s; over 17,000 survived. Most of the dead were buried in mass graves at Rupert's Valley and Lemon Valley. Archaeological work led by a University of Bristol team in Rupert's Valley in recent years has identified the locations of some of the graves within the valley. In spite of the harsh weather conditions, frequent flooding, and the shallow depth of the graves, over three hundred articulated skeletons at a high degree of preservation were identified, with a "considerable volume" of disarticulated pieces of human bone scattered in the surrounding areas.[49] The archaeological team deemed the site unique: the only known burial site consisting solely of the remains of first-generation liberated Africans who died as a direct result of their capture and transportation experiences. As such, it offers an unprecedented insight into the age and medical histories of these (generally young) victims of the last decades of the transatlantic slave trade. Children between one and twelve years of age account for more than one-third of the skeletons. Children under eighteen make up 58 percent of the remains. Only 5 percent are from the oldest category represented, adults between thirty-six and forty-five.[50]

Unlike Sierra Leone, St Helena in the 1840s and 1850s was not a context in which the blended ambitions of "commerce, civilisation and

Christianity" found expression in an idealised liberated African community-building experiment, and St Helena did not become the staging ground for ambitious projects of developmental imperialism. The colony had recently been transferred to the Crown, and in the context of strict impositions of economy and restraint, there was neither demand nor desire for new settlers to augment the existing population. Quite the contrary—there was not sufficient land available to settle tens of thousands of liberated Africans as a free peasantry. As at Sierra Leone, a complex set of obligations was thrust upon the administration of St Helena before it even began to comprehend, or accept responsibility for, a task of this scale. The resulting practices were decidedly reactive rather than proactive; grudging and haphazard rather than engaged and methodical. Only around 3 percent of liberated African survivors at St Helena successfully incorporated themselves into the economic life of the island as apprentices and later settlers, or joined the British armed forces. Therefore, the establishment was almost entirely geared towards re-embarking the survivors on West-Indies-bound emigrant vessels, ideally though not necessarily voluntarily. The ramshackle tent village at Rupert's Valley was essentially a transit camp for soon-to-be indentured plantation workers.

The mass re-exportation of liberated Africans from St Helena to the sugar plantations of the British West Indies had a precedent in the Colonial Office's policy shift in Sierra Leone. Its deeper roots lie in the dramatic hardening of British public opinion against free black people after 1838—a shift that would contribute ultimately to the equalisation of the sugar duties and the opening of British markets to slave-grown sugar after 1845.[51] In total, some 36,120 liberated Africans were retransported from their place of legal liberation in the Atlantic and Indian Oceans to the British West Indies. Of these, 17,144 came from St Helena—virtually every African who survived their stay in the depots between 1841 and 1867. This large-scale transatlantic population transfer appears to have occasioned little public debate within St Helenian society. It was framed not in the language of a higher moral purpose, but of expedience—even emergency. "Any other British colony" who would agree to "pay the expense of their passage thither" was acceptable to Lord Russell as a destination for would-be liberated African emigrants. However, Russell was careful to add the stipulation that "due precautions" must be taken "for the health and comfort of the people" and that they would have consented to be removed from St Helena.[52] Subsequently, Russell's successor, Lord Stanley, responded positively to private requests from Mauritius, Jamaica, and Trinidad to obtain bonded labourers from St Helena's depots, while the governors at Cape Colony and British Guiana also petitioned the governor of St Helena eagerly, painting labour conditions within their colonies in very appealing (and misleading) terms.

In the end, almost all liberated Africans were sent to Jamaica, Trinidad, and British Guiana, with a small number also sent to Grenada, St Lucia, St Kitts, Tobago, and St Vincent. Emigrant vessels were instructed to meet basic standards of health, hygiene, and comfort. After 1846, the crew was supposed to include a staff surgeon who would certify each emigrant as healthy, and accompany every voyage, although it is clear that these standards were not always met.[53] The Colonial Office held firm to the letter if not the spirit of the rule that emigrants must demonstrate free will in leaving the island. Lord Stanley was careful to "disclaim . . . any right to compel" the liberated people "to quit that island." The governor of St Helena was

> distinctly instructed that no . . . coercion must be employed. On the other hand, as those people are unable at St Helena to find any employment profitable to themselves or the public at large, and by remaining there must continue a burden on funds . . . the legitimate influence of the local government will, of course, be employed in every fair and reasonable manner to induce them.[54]

Governor Trelawney expressed no reservations about what was being asked of him. As far as he was concerned, the export of liberated Africans as bonded workers was merely "an extension of that parental care of the British Nation by which they have been brought from slavery to freedom, and only that fatherly control that any parent would be justified in using towards his own children."[55]

Many liberated Africans responded with dismay and terror to this particular manifestation of the British state's "paternal care." Quite understandably, many refused to place their trust in Europeans ordering them onto a ship bound for the sugar plantations of the Americas. When Trinidadian recruiters came to Lemon Valley in 1842, the group of liberated Africans there—predominantly women and children—fled into the hills. For many liberated people, once aboard the westbound emigrant ships, their time at the depot at St Helena must have seemed like merely an interlude; the depot like a slave barracoon in a slightly more elaborate form. On board the ships, contemporary observers described how groups of liberated people expressed utter terror as they made landfall in the Caribbean, "men, women, and children all crying and screaming" at the prospect of what lay ahead. On at least one voyage, on the *Salzette* in December 1843, several people were subjected to violence and restraint in irons, along with a punishment diet of bread and water, because of what the captain deemed "mutinous . . . , troublesome and dangerous" behaviour. There is scant reason to believe that this episode of resistance and subjugation was an isolated incident.[56]

Commonalities, Characters, and Carceral Characteristics

The reception and "disposal" of at least 180,969 liberated Africans between 1808 and 1863 was an Atlantic-world phenomenon, and an undertaking that forged important links between different sites of British imperial power in the Atlantic world, in both conceptual and transactional senses. While it was underpinned by a shared moral vernacular, the actual practices of governance varied widely across different contexts and reflected a spectrum of attitudes towards the humanity and dignity of slave trade survivors, towards the opportunities they represented for the intervening state, and towards Britain's new "antislavery state" identity and interventionist international agenda as a whole. Several key variables shaped outcomes for liberated Africans across the diverse contexts discussed above and in the previous chapter.

It is fair to assume a reasonably equal level of desire and capacity for agency and autonomy across the liberated African populations of the Atlantic world (with a caveat that as the age profile of enslaved people in the transatlantic trade changed over time, liberated Africans in later decades were often significantly younger, with infants and small children making up a far larger proportion than previously). What varied most across the divergent contexts into which the liberated Africans arrived were the conditions that enabled some to organise and assert a group identity, to resist violence, abuse, and attempts at exploitation, to escape unwelcome constraints on their mode and manner of living, and to accumulate sufficient capital to facilitate mobility, both physical and economic. Specific local circumstances and interests at each location also shaped the kinds of opportunities available to liberated people, and how they were understood and imagined by the colonial population and the metropole. The initial disposal pathway marked out for each individual at the moment of "liberation" was a very important factor in their subsequent experiences, as were the attitudes and expectations of the communities which they joined, and the attitudes and expectations of those who assumed positions of power over those newly designated as apprentices, soldiers, wives, and more. One of the most important systemic factors was the nature of the economy to which they were brought—specifically, whether or not it was an economy based (or recently based) upon slave-worked plantation agriculture. A related variable was the presence or absence of a large or at least politically powerful white settler population.

The proximity of the colony to other territories mattered too: countless records from the liberated African establishments at Sierra Leone, the Gambia, and the British Caribbean refer to the escape or abduction of liberated Africans. This speaks to the permeability of even the most closely superintended resettlement spaces, and the ability of many liberated Africans and their nearby neighbours to subvert the state's plans. Over time, it became the perception of the British government, fuelled by the findings of a series of investigative commissions, that the greatest risk to liberated Africans was their dispersal away from the oversight of a centralised administration and into a slaveholding or formerly slaveholding white population. Simultaneously, however, the government also became increasingly anxious to reduce the cost and complexity of its establishments, and to divert labour resources towards the struggling sugar plantations.

An important factor in shaping the conditions at each site of disposal was the culture of governance created by senior figures in each colonial administration, and their understanding of how a broad antislavery policy should be interpreted and applied to a problem of local governance. A note of caution is important here: the diverse trajectories and rich cultural legacies of the liberated Africans of the British Atlantic cannot and should not be reduced to the personal ideologies or ambitions of a small group of white male governors, many of whom were but transient figures in the histories of the colonies over which they held authority for brief periods. However, to the extent that "top-down" factors influenced the trajectory of liberated people's lives, it is important to note the outsized influence these peripatetic, trans-imperial figures had in the circulation of ideas and practices that, in aggregate, comprised the first experiments in humanitarian governance. As David Lambert and Alan Lester have found in their study of imperial careers in the British empire, ideas about "race and national identity, and the governance, conversion, and "civilisation" of colonised peoples, were not simply exported from the imperial centre, nor indeed imported from the periphery." Many ideas, particularly those around slavery—itself "a profoundly mobile and contested signifier"—developed across multiple spaces, and challenged their bearers to develop different or more nuanced understandings in different contexts.[57] In the very transience of the governors' tenures lies their importance to the development and performance of the "moral vernacular" around liberated African governance. Consider some of those mentioned in this and previous chapters: Carmichael-Smyth, Colebrooke, Middlemore, Huntley, Jeremie. Each was central to the interpretation and translation of liberated African policy within particular colonial contexts at particular moments. Each also had his own set of values shaped by global careering within "the webs of Empire which traversed the vertical connections between metropole and colony" across a period of profound change in the ideas and assumptions that underpinned empire and its relations with its subject peoples.[58] To the

Bahamas, St Helena, the Gambia, and Sierra Leone, they brought understandings of slavery, antislavery, and the subaltern "other" that had been shaped and influenced by their previous postings. These values and understandings were in turn shaped and influenced by their encounters with the liberated Africans and the liberated African establishments—and not always in ways we might expect.[59]

In the mid-1820s, a few years before being appointed governor of the Bahamas, Major General James Carmichael-Smyth had been sent to the West Indies to report on the military establishments at Barbados, Berbice, Demerara, Tobago, Trinidad, Grenada, St Vincent, St Lucia, Dominica, Antigua, and St Kitts. As it happens, during this time the British Commissioners of Inquiry (including Moody and Dougan) were also moving through and between many of these colonies to investigate the treatment of liberated Africans. It is very likely that Carmichael-Smyth encountered the commission and its various reports; certainly, the things he experienced and witnessed made a powerful impression upon him. Carmichael-Smyth left the Caribbean for his next posting in Ireland nurturing strong abolitionist values. Later, during his tenure at the Bahamas, he made no secret of these abolitionist sympathies, including his plan to abolish the flogging of female slaves; to resist transporting liberated Africans to the sugar-producing colonies; and to create instead independent liberated African settlements at the Bahamas. However, when he left the Bahamas in 1833 for the very different economic context of British Guiana, his attitude towards liberated African freedom shifted markedly. As Rosanne Adderley notes, Carmichael-Smyth became rather suddenly "an aggressive advocate" for importing liberated Africans from Havana as bonded plantation labourers into British Guiana.[60]

His successor at the Bahamas was similarly peripatetic, and had also garnered experience of diverse colonial contexts before assuming the governorship. As discussed in the previous chapter, William Macbean Colebrooke brought to the Bahamas his experience as a Commissioner of Eastern Inquiry at the Cape, Mauritius, and Ceylon, where he had conducted the investigation into Charles Blair's abuse of the liberated African disposal system at Cape Colony in the mid-1820s. It is clear from his correspondence with the Colonial Office that the experience at the Cape profoundly influenced his approach to the liberated African establishment at the Bahamas. Prior to the Commission of Eastern Inquiry, between 1805 and 1818, Colebrooke had served in military campaigns in Ceylon, India, Java, and the Persian Gulf, and after governing the Bahamas between 1835 and 1837, he moved on to the governorship of the Leeward Islands, where—as at the Bahamas—he concerned himself with improving education and reforming prison discipline. He later assumed the governorship of New Brunswick and finally Barbados and the Windward Islands. There again he demonstrated a special interest in reforming the prison system and improving the system of "disposal" of recently released convicts.[61]

It is unlikely that every colonial official who attempted to protect liberated Africans from exploitation and enslavement did so out of deep abolitionist or humanitarian sympathies. There were many who were simply ordered by the Colonial Office to implement or defend a policy against planter resistance, and many more whose commitment to the cause of African freedom was rather less ardent than their desire to impress the metropolitan government with their humanitarian credentials. For this reason, and many more, it would be foolish to take at face value all expressions of humanitarian concern and heartfelt compassion that appear in official correspondence relating to liberated Africans (or indeed to any other formerly enslaved or coerced labour populations in the nineteenth-century British empire). Colebrooke's successor at the Bahamas, Francis Cockburn, is an example of a colonial administrator whose encounters with liberated Africans if anything hardened his attitudes to people of African descent.

Cockburn saw the formerly enslaved and their children as little more than labour units to be deployed and exploited, yet he recognised the importance of what would now be called "virtue signalling": the act of drenching his regressive and exploitative acts of governance in performative humanitarian zeal. Cockburn came to the governorship of the Bahamas in 1837 by way of a stint at British Honduras from 1830 to 1837. There, as governor, he had involved himself in the development of the colony's timber industry. To that end, he sought the mass importation of thousands of indentured liberated Africans, but at the lowest cost possible. He pushed to reduce even further their already austere rations of food and clothing, arguing that the liberated people were too generously supplied.[62] A couple of years later, as governor of the Bahamas, in "a lightly disguised attempt to retain for the employer class a labour force over which it could exercise a greater degree of control," Cockburn applied a similar approach, working hard to reverse the reforms Colebrooke and the Colonial Office had made to the apprenticeship system.[63] When the Colonial Office rebuffed his effort to bind over one thousand recently liberated people into indentures, Cockburn connived with the Colonial Assembly of the Bahamas in an alternative strategy to achieve the same objective: by adding to a bill extending subjecthood to liberated Africans an extraneous clause giving the governor the ultimate power of "disposal and control." Cockburn took care to couch his various schemes in the language of humanitarian concern: coerced labour, including in the arduous labour of salt raking to which free labourers refused to be bound, was "the only reasonable mode of fulfilling the benevolent views of the British government towards the liberated Africans," and of protecting them from being "enticed" away to other colonies or lapsing into "acts of Violence & Plunder."[64] While ultimately unsuccessful, Cockburn evidently believed—like many, many other colonial agents and bureaucrats in the British antislavery world system—that these self-conscious performances of humanitarian concern would impress the Colonial Office, and make partisan lobbying appear instead as "the protection of people from unfavourable conditions, from others, and from themselves."[65]

Others mentioned in this chapter had similarly mobile imperial careers which were profoundly shaped by questions of slavery, antislavery, and competing visions of a post-enslavement world order. They remind us of the importance of seeing the empire and its various projects and experiments of governance as an interconnected whole. Any reading of the official correspondence of George Middlemore—who was governor at St Helena in the crucial years of the evolution of that island's liberated African establishment from 1836 to 1842—is enriched by the awareness that he had been lieutenant-governor of Grenada in the equally critical years of 1833 to 1835. Similarly, any reading of John Jeremie's handling of liberated African emigration at Sierra Leone from 1841 must take account of his background—chief justice at St Lucia from 1824 to 1831, an ill-fated stint as advocate general at Mauritius from 1832 to 1833, and a judicial position on the Supreme Court of Ceylon from 1835 to 1840—and his prominent antislavery activities, including authoring four influential antislavery essays and participating in the World Anti-Slavery Convention of 1840.

The same is true of other colonial officials and employees, not just governors: prior to acting as Commissioner of Inquiry for the West African settlements in the early 1840s, Dr Richard Robert Madden spent a year working as a magistrate in Jamaica mediating disputes between apprentices and their former masters, after which he published the two-volume *A Twelve-Month's Residence in the West Indies During the Transition from Slavery to Apprenticeship.* An ardent abolitionist dedicated to ending not just the slave trade but the institution of slavery worldwide, Madden was subsequently appointed by Viscount Palmerston to the post of superintendent of the liberated Africans and judge arbitrator in the Mixed Commission Court at Havana, an appointment calculated to inflame the ire of Spain, particularly when he went on to publish *Address on Slavery in Cuba, Presented to the General Anti-Slavery Convention* in 1840. Madden later travelled to Egypt to advocate for a group of Jews from Damascus accused of ritual murder, and, after submitting his Commission of Inquiry report into the West African settlements, assumed a colonial secretaryship in Western Australia, where he took up the cause of indigenous rights, before returning to his home country of Ireland in 1848 to lobby for the famine-stricken peasantry. Just as the story of the liberated Africans of the British Atlantic is a story of many kinds of multidirectional mobility, both coerced and self-directed, so too is the story of many of the colonial administrators and agents through whom the antislavery world system exercised power. Each of these individuals approached his mandate through the lens of his personal experiences, values, and worldview. This perspective helped to shape how each man understood and approached the needs of the formerly enslaved and the indigenous peoples over whom he exercised power on behalf of the British empire—including the degree to which he recognised the rights, even the humanity, of the people under his control. In turn, for some of these men, the experience of this new and unusual kind of governance responsibility shaped the attitudes and beliefs they carried with them in their subsequent imperial careers.[66]

It is important to note that the liberated African establishments—the administrative hierarchies through which the antislavery world system exercised power over liberated people—frequently included at their lower levels many settled liberated Africans employed as provisioners, yard overseers, clerks, translators, village superintendents and assistants, boatmen, teachers, and more.[67] From the late 1810s, missionary organisations recruited directly from the communities of settled liberated Africans, and the department at Sierra Leone in particular came increasingly to rely upon employees drawn from the recaptive population and their children. Perhaps most importantly, settled liberated Africans also played important roles as community leaders and influential members of benefit societies.[68] Overall, these men and women represented some of the most important influences over the daily experiences of other liberated Africans and their forced transition into British colonial life, yet these influences are rendered all but invisible within the imperial archive. In surviving records relating to Sierra Leone, it is often the case that the behaviour of individual, low-ranking employees of the Liberated African Department was only noted or commented upon at moments of aberration or transgression—in particular, when specific episodes came to light of corruption, embezzlement, kidnapping, violent assault, or other forms of abuse of power.[69] In the sea of daily minutiae created by that department, it is rare to find records that describe positive relationships of support, compassionate assistance, or manifestations of humanitarian concern for vulnerable, recently liberated people. Perhaps such things can be inferred from reports that suggest regularity, routine, and the successful integration of new arrivals into colonial society and off the books of the colonial government.

To evaluate the success or otherwise of the establishments discussed in this chapter and the preceding chapter, British colonial administrators and metropolitan bureaucrats used two gauges: cost and degree of "civilisation." Like all projects of empire, particularly in the aftermath of the

French wars, the liberated African establishments of the Atlantic world were subject to a high degree of financial scrutiny and sustained metropolitan pressure for economy and parsimony. For virtually the entire duration of the slave trade suppression campaign, dialogues between the Colonial Office and each establishment were characterised by a common refrain: how much could the budget and mandate of the establishment be reduced, while still delivering the basic standards of humanity implied by its mission? An equally important measure of success was the extent to which the establishment had inculcated in its inmates "civilisation" and "habits of industry"—by which was meant submission to British cultural and economic folkways, in particular the performance of regular labour, actuated by a desire to accumulate capital and achieve social mobility; and submission to the hierarchical order of the colony, the performance of gender roles and Christian observance, and the acceptance of white supremacy. In later years, survival rates came to be an important third metric of success, particularly for the establishment at St Helena, whose creation coincided with the advent of state-sponsored emigration and the perception on the part of the British government that the suspicious eyes of its treaty partners were watching this innovation closely, searching for signs of neglect, exploitation, and a renewal of the slave trade under the British flag.

For a population so rigorously documented and over which so much ink was spilled, the archival record is frustratingly (though unsurprisingly) silent on the views of the liberated Africans themselves regarding the establishments that governed and sought to shape their lives. Some opinions can be discerned through reading against the grain of the colonial and missionary archives: for example, in sources such as the commission records of Tortola, frequent criticisms of "indolence," "sauciness," "sullenness," and "disobedience" suggest widespread, perhaps shared strategies of resistance.[70] Likewise, in the CMS records from Sierra Leone, missionaries criticised the liberated people for faking Christian conversion temporarily in order to acquire more clothing, utensils, and rations, which suggests a keen understanding of the agenda of the white intervenors, and a strong degree of pragmatism in maximising the opportunities this represented.

Direct accounts written by liberated Africans are relatively rare. Several liberated African men—including Joseph Boston May, Ali Eisami, John Wright, and Samuel Ajayi Crowther—left written accounts of their experiences of enslavement, recapture, and resettlement at Sierra Leone; however, they did so in the form of "liberation narratives," which are often heavily mediated through the lens of religious awakening and silent on the more prosaic details of resettlement and assimilation. The Reverend Joseph Boston May, for example, said almost nothing about his resettlement in Sierra Leone. The focus of his text was his experience of religious conversion; to the extent that he commented on his past life or transition, it was to express contempt for his "heathen" and "idolatrous" origins and to distance himself from those Africans around him who he felt had still not yet achieved his level of enlightenment or inclusion.[71] Liberation narratives can be immensely rich sources in many other respects, but with their apparently unquestioning acceptance of the premise of the cultural, political, religious, and moral superiority of white European folkways, such accounts give us little sense of how liberated people regarded the machine of the antislavery state and its systematic attempts to erase the pre-existing cultural and religious landscapes of its recaptive population.

Some observations can be gleaned from the work of James Africanus Beale Horton, the noted African political economist, historian, author, and army medical officer. Horton was born in 1835 in the liberated African village of Gloucester, five miles east of Freetown, to parents of Igbo origin. In his best-known work, *West African Countries and Peoples,* he portrayed the transformation of Sierra Leone as something that had happened because of the self-directed industry of the liberated people, and almost in spite of the meagre resources and structures provided by the colonial government:

> Fancy a lot of slaves—unlettered, rude, naked, possessing no knowledge of the useful arts—thrown into a wild country, to cut down the woods and build towns; fancy these ragged, wild natives under British, and, consequently, civilised influences, after a lapse of a few years, becoming large landowners, possessing large mercantile establishments and money, claiming a

> voice in the legislative government, and giving their offspring
> proper English and foreign education; and dare you tell me that
> the African . . . does not possess in himself . . . a desire of per-
> fection far surpassing many existing nations—since it cannot
> be shown in the world's history that any people with so limited
> advantages has shown such results within fifty years.[72]

Horton's suggestion was that "civilisation," and in particular, British political and economic forms of organisation, created a context in which the
immense latent talent and energy of the liberated people was able to flourish and prosper. His central purpose in writing *West African Countries and
Peoples* was to refute racist Victorian ideas about Africans—such as those
ideas being espoused by the likes of Richard Burton—and in that vein, Horton welcomed rather than challenged the full force of British cultural imperialism. In Sierra Leone, he celebrated its success in redeeming "a race
whose past generations have been in utter darkness, the mental faculty of
whose ancestors has never received any culture for nearly a thousand
years."[73] There is little suggestion in his work that he believed that something important might have been lost or erased.

In surveying the liberated African establishments in the West Indies,
Sierra Leone, the Gambia, Cape Colony, and St Helena, it is clear that in
each, and through their multidirectional linkages, unique assemblages of
governance structures and systems evolved that reflected competing pres-
sures of antislavery values and material self-interest, geopolitical ambition
and anxiety. Across all establishments, and in ways specific to the perceived
needs of the host colonies, the tension between these forces drove an imperative to instrumentalise liberated African labour for the benefit of the
empire's economic and political order, rationalised as the pathway to a
higher international moral order. This suggests a widespread shared understanding of liberated Africans not as the ultimate targets of British
antislavery interventions, but as resources accumulated during those interventions that could be subsequently deployed to help achieve Britain's
objectives. This understanding found perhaps its clearest articulation in
the words of Consul John Kirk, after the end of the transatlantic slave trade

and the eastward shift of British suppression efforts. Discussing liberated African policy at Zanzibar and on the East African mainland in March 1871, Kirk wrote, "Properly directed, a greater influence can be obtained for the abolition of slavery through those freed slaves than in any other way."[74] "We must be ready for and encourage a steady influx of freed slaves if we intend following up the wise policy laid down in the Slave Trade Report, of *making the freed slaves a means of uprooting slavery.*"[75] What was required was a "plan . . . *to dispose of and profit by* the introduction of a much larger number [of liberated Africans]."[76]

To take note of such instrumental understandings of liberated Africans is not to dismiss idealist and "progressive" imperial agendas as simply ideological legitimation for self-interested, acquisitive activities. While evidently there were plenty of colonial and imperial actors who engaged in purely performative humanitarian or philanthropic activities as a cloak for personal gain, there were also important constituencies involved in the governance of liberated Africans who understood their position of power and control in terms of a wider antislavery mission, itself a central part of an imperial mission to "effect a mutually beneficial transformation of the world and its peoples."[77] Utopian ideas about how to use the liberated Africans to serve the antislavery mission and the wider interests of empire ranged from schemes to rescue the free-labour experiment by way of the sugar plantations to the deployment of recaptive colonisers on a "civilising" crusade throughout West Africa. As we have seen from the Gambia example, such abortive schemes occasioned immense unnecessary suffering, dislocation, and trauma.

The broader effect of disposal policy was to create a slow and very incremental pathway to becoming "liberated." The moment of being declared free by the courts was, in that sense, only one step in an ongoing "middle passage," whereby putatively free people moved along a "continuum of labour exploitation."[78] And yet the results of these experiments never satisfied their framers. Over decades of "disposals," British administrators learned that they could exert physical control over individuals and small groups for periods of time, but they possessed neither the coercive power nor the cultural understanding required to prevent liberated

Africans from forming communities, resisting or adapting cultural impositions, and asserting individual and group-level autonomy, even under
severely constrained circumstances. From the very first Vice-Admiralty
Court liberations in 1808, liberated Africans consistently rewrote the
scripts written for them by the abolitionists and the British government.

In the context of this unremitting and desperately unequal power
struggle, in which even the most self-consciously reform-minded humanitarian abolitionist governors saw the freedom of formerly enslaved people
as legitimately circumscribed by a duty of obligation, it is perhaps unsur-
prising that a conceptual slippage existed from the outset between the category of "liberated African" and that of an incarcerated person, or convict.
Those liberated Africans who were enlisted at Sierra Leone into the Royal
African Corps found themselves in a regiment of white convicts "formed
principally of deserters, convicts, and men whose sentences of punishment
had been commuted for service in Africa."[79] At all sites of liberated African disposal, contemporary observers noted how liberated people were
"worked in gangs with the convicts of the place."[80] Equally, they observed
the carceral character of the establishments' physical spaces: F. Harrison
Rankin deemed the King's Yard at Freetown "a large species of prison, consisting of a central house within a square yard, surrounded by open sheds:
the whole encompassed by high walls, and secured by well-guarded gates."[81]
For R. R. Madden, the yard at Bathurst was a space where liberated Africans were held "as prisoners are kept in gaols, or slaves in barracones [sic]."

The nearby settlement of Goderich acted as another kind of holding
facility for those not apprenticed locally who were to be restored to health
before being sent to McCarthy's Island, a site which itself represented a different kind of carceral space: once thought of and dismissed as a prison
colony, it was nevertheless believed good enough for an African colonising
experiment. At St Helena, liberated Africans also laboured alongside convicts in the quarries of the island. Although there was never an incarceratory "Queen's Yard" as such on the island, the sites at Lemon Valley and
especially Rupert's Valley were specifically selected to facilitate segregation of the recaptives from the rest of the island's population. Those who
left the depots were considered to have absconded, and were punished upon

recapture; for a time, some St Helenians made a living out of capturing escaped liberated Africans for reward.[82] Richard Burton took the conflation between liberated Africans and convicts to extremes: in *Wanderings in West Africa,* he advised his readers to "ever remember that by far the greater number of the liberated [Africans] were the vilest of criminals in their own lands, and that in their case" being enslaved and trafficked was, "in fact, the African form of [convict] transportation." At Sierra Leone, these "liberated African slave-criminals" were being "allowed to loaf through a life equally harmful to themselves and others."[83] In the same vein, for Consul John Kirk at Zanzibar in 1871, it was self-evident that "the unoccupied English jail building" was perfectly appropriate for "holding more [liberated Africans] than are ever likely to be landed at any one time. For such a purpose the jail is peculiarly [well] adapted, being easily guarded, and containing within its walls a space for exercise."[84] It is not entirely clear from Kirk's remarks whether the idea was to keep liberated Africans locked in or others locked out—perhaps both.

The blurring of distinctions between liberated Africans and convicts speaks to more than the low status both groups occupied in the social hierarchies of the empire and the opportunities cash-strapped colonial governments saw to acquire coercible, low-cost labour forces. The carceral character of the British liberated African establishments was not an accidental development or a matter of administrative convenience, but a reflection of how embryonic experiments in humanitarian governance co-evolved with nineteenth-century innovations in the exploitation of penal discipline and punishment—neither of which developments can be understood independently of the shared imperial context in which they were forged. Convict regimes in the nineteenth century were central to processes of expansion and colonisation. Contrary to Foucault's representation of punishment as increasingly fixed upon the edifice of the prison in this period, the work of Clare Anderson and others demonstrates the immense mobility of the convicts of the British empire, who moved in vast flows across a global "carceral archipelago" that constituted "an expression and means of power, governmentality, discipline, and imperial expansion."[85] The liberated African establishments of the Atlantic world constituted a comparable "archipelago." They should be understood as both spaces of emergency reception or refuge, and also as spaces of carcerality, confinement, and discipline where authorities extracted marketable labour from African inmates not only on terms that resembled those applied to convicts, but with very similar justifications. The liberated African "archipelago" is an important and under-recognised dimension of the wider antislavery world system, whose foreign policy dimensions will be explored in the following chapter.

Humanitarian Governance in
International Antislavery Diplomacy

IN NOVEMBER 1855, Samuel Vines, the British consul at the Brazilian port of Belém, wrote to the British minister at Rio de Janeiro, reporting that two supposedly "free" African men by the names of Honório and Laudelino had been brought by steamer to Pará.[1] Vines suspected that they were liberated Africans who had served their terms of indenture, and that the state was now conspiring to deprive them of the liberty to which they were entitled. Under Article VII of the Anglo-Portuguese slave trade suppression treaty of 1817 and the Anglo-Brazilian treaty that replaced it in 1826, Honório and Laudelino ought to have "receive[d] from the Mixed Commission a certificate of emancipation" at the time of their arrival in Brazil, and thereafter been "employed as servants or free labourers," under the supervision of the Brazilian government, who was obliged by treaty to "guarantee the[ir] liberty." Under Brazilian law, they were allowed to be employed either by private concessionaries or public institutions ("in the navy, at the forts, in agriculture, or in the mechanical trades"), with their maximum terms of service fixed at fourteen years.[2] Vines suspected that Honório and Laudelino were instead being treated "as forced labourers," being moved up to the labour-hungry regions north of Rio de Janeiro as a way of illegally extending the duration of their service. "Knowing the deep interest Her Majesty's Government has always taken in the fate of these unfortunate beings," Vines made enquiries with local authorities to confirm that they were in fact, liberated Africans, rather than convicts, in whom the British had no interest. The inspector of the Arsenal responded "courteously," making no secret that Honório and Laudelino were indeed members of "a large body of free Africans who had been many years at Rio de Janeiro under the surveillance of the Government," who were now incarcerated (or "detain[ed] . . . in safety") in Pará pending retransportation to Amazonas, and they "would not be allowed to leave the arsenal."[3]

To Vines, these liberated Africans were "peculiar objects of sympathy, having no fixed period for the termination of their forced labour; they [were] guarded and treated with the suspicion of convicted criminals, merely allowed a miserable ration of farinha and 320 reis per day." Their situation was "infinitely worse than the slaves in Pará," who could at least "work in companies, electing from themselves a chief" and in that way, accumulate enough capital to eventually purchase their own freedom. Vines confessed his "strong conviction" that any prospect of meaningful freedom was slipping ever further from Honório and Laudelino since their removal from Rio de Janeiro: "so many slaves [had] died during the last six months of the cholera" in Pará and Amazonas, "and there [was] an increased demand for labour, with a cessation of emigration from Portugal." The consul's prediction was that the two men would soon be reported dead or fugitives, and sold privately "if not in this city [then] elsewhere in this immense province, or the adjoining one, Amazonas . . . where I am sorry to believe no conscientious scruples, and certainly no fears of detection, would prevent the purchase."[4]

Vines's report is unlikely to have caused any surprise for Minister Jerningham at Rio, or for the foreign secretary, the Earl of Clarendon. By 1855, the abolitionists and officials of the Colonial Office and the Slave Trade Department in the Foreign Office were all too familiar with the patterns of exploitation, abuse, and re-enslavement to which liberated Africans "apprenticed" in Britain's own colonial territories on both sides of the Atlantic had been subjected, and were particularly aware of the "various dangers and sufferings" of apprenticeship in the slave-holding West Indies and the Cape.[5] There was little reason to expect that the policy would result in better outcomes for people liberated in the slave-holding territories of Britain's treaty partners—in particular, Spain, Portugal, Brazil, and the Netherlands—and indeed, it did not. Accounts of the abuse, exploitation,

and re-enslavement of liberated Africans featured heavily across five decades of antislavery reportage from the consuls, ministers, ambassadors,
naval officers, traders, and missionaries stationed in the territories in which
Mixed Commission courts sat.

As early as 1824, three years after the first captured slave ship was
brought before the Anglo-Portuguese Mixed Commission Court at Rio de
Janeiro, the British commissioners, Henry Hayne and Alexander Cunningham, communicated to the foreign secretary, George Canning, their views
on the "liberation" outcomes for the *Emilia* Africans. They confirmed "the
truth of suspicions, which [they] had entertained for some time, not only
of irregularities, but actual malversation, on the part of some of those Persons who had been appointed to superintend the care and well-being" of
the liberated people. The state-appointed curator of liberated Africans
was personally enriching himself from annual payments demanded from
private apprentice-holders, under the pretence of forwarding the payments
to the Treasury. Hayne and Cunningham considered this a "fraudulent and
disgraceful" act, from which they inferred that he was capable of "committing the more heinous one" of actually selling liberated Africans into slavery. They proposed to Canning that Britain insist upon a reform of the
disposal system, conferring more rights of supervision and intervention
upon Britain, forcing the Brazilian authorities to keep a register of liberated Africans, and making the curator of liberated Africans more account-
able.[6] In July of that same year, the British commissioners of the Mixed
Commission Court in Cuba reported in similar terms about the disposal
of four hundred individuals liberated from the slave ship *María da Gloria*
by the Spanish Admiralty Court in Havana. These liberated Africans were
being sold, or "disposed of for a pecuniary consideration, without their . . .
consent," the commissioners complained. "They [were] to all intents and
purposes slaves under another name." In response, Canning directed the
British minister in Madrid to raise the matter with the Spanish government,
and "request an explanation of the intentions of the Spanish government
upon a point so essential to the welfare of the unfortunate beings."[7]

From this point onwards, British foreign policy engagement with the
question of liberated African disposal and governance in Brazil and Cuba

ran on two distinct tracks. On the one hand, there was the question of negotiating new treaty provisions for future arrivals to prevent abuses and evasions of the law.[8] On the other hand, there was the sustained effort to evaluate and monitor the continuously increasing liberated African population—whose disposal experiences were by then regarded by the British as "so little accordant with the humane views of the parties who entered into those Compacts"—and to exert diplomatic pressure to force the Brazilian and Cuban authorities (and indeed the Dutch authorities in Surinam after 1829) to protect the liberated Africans' physical welfare, financial interests, and prospects of future freedom.[9] This latter policy track itself took two forms: high-level requests for information and terse diplomatic notes—"fresh and urgent representations"—between the British commissioners at Havana and Rio de Janeiro, British ministers at Rio and Madrid, and the Brazilian, Cuban, and Spanish authorities; and the more "informal" information-gathering, lobbying, and persuasion of the British consular and sub-legation staff.[10] Mixed Commissioners were ordered to give the matter "the benefit of their superintendence" and to report regularly to the foreign secretary. The British commissioners at Rio de Janeiro duly reached out to the Brazilian government and offered to take over the responsibilities of the curator of liberated Africans, and to set up a British-run liberated African depot and disposal establishment in Brazil. This offer was rejected. Similarly, the British minister in Madrid urged in the strongest terms that Spain "institute an enquiry into the abuses said to prevail, with respect to these unfortunate persons." This request was also ignored, but nonetheless the foreign secretary, Viscount Palmerston, ordered Arthur Aston, the British minister in Madrid, to "persevere in urging it on every particular occasion, and in enforcing it by every argument in your power." Palmerston also wrote to the commissioners of the Mixed Commission Court in Havana, instructing them to "learn and to transmit" information on liberated Africans such "as can be obtained by us without appearing to interfere with the Local Authorities of the Havana, or exciting any jealousy on their part."[11]

The specific point of contention between Britain and her treaty partners was the meaning of the "liberty" liberated Africans ought to experience in the territories of Brazil, Cuba, and Surinam, and the right of Britain to insist upon her own definition of that freedom. Yet the precise lineaments of "liberty" had not been defined in the original texts of the treaties. Nor indeed was it stipulated precisely how, and by what processes, each government was expected to guarantee it (and whether, and to whom, proofs should be presented). Throughout the period after 1824, a common thread in the writings of British diplomats, consuls, and ministers was the assertion that liberated African freedom had a clear and uncontested meaning that was both self-evident and understood by all parties. Underlying the correspondence of Britain's "antislavery system" is the assumption—and frequently, in internal correspondence, the overt assertion—that Brazilian, Portuguese, Spanish, Dutch, and Cuban interlocutors consciously, cruelly, and viciously mischaracterised and subverted the meaning of freedom with the express intention of abusing, exploiting, and enslaving liberated Africans. Thirty years after the diplomatic wrangling began on this question, the precise meanings of "liberty," "freedom," and "emancipation" remained a source of conflict and friction. "Emancipação," argued Brazilian foreign minister the Visconde de Abaeté, "não é sinônimo da liberdade, significa apenas que os Africanos, alias livres, poderem sair do poder daqueles a quem tinham sidos confiados" [Emancipation is not synonymous with freedom, rather merely signifying that these Africans, as liberated people, have the right to be released from the guardianship (powers) of those to whom they have been entrusted]. From the perspective of the Brazilian government, liberated Africans were not the equals of free adult Brazilian citizens. They were not in full possession of freedom itself, but rather had the right to become free from their appointed guardian while remaining under the tutelage, control, and surveillance of the Brazilian state.[12]

Reading the liberated African disposal clauses of the 1817 and 1826 Anglo-Portuguese, Anglo-Spanish, and Anglo-Brazilian treaties against Britain's own domestic slave trade abolition legislation, it is evident that Britain demanded her treaty partners commit to a higher standard of "freedom" than that applied within British territories. Under the Abolition Act of 1807 and the revised act of 1824, slave "cargoes" were legally considered exactly that in British law—cargo—and Britain was entitled to dispose of them according to her own interest, with no reference to the agency of the liberated Africans. The word "liberated" appears several times in these texts, but only with reference to the captured ship, not its involuntary passengers.[13] In other words, British domestic legislation emphasised property, forfeiture, the opportunity to enter, enlist, and bind; and above all, the right of labour extraction by the state. By comparison, under the treaties of 1817 and 1826, Portugal, Spain, and Brazil were required to provide each individual with a certificate of emancipation, to ensure their employment as "servants or free labourers," and positively to guarantee their liberty. Later amendments to the regulatory framework underlined the assumed necessity of imposing stricter rules on non-British partners. This reflects not only a heightened British sense of antislavery righteousness in the aftermath of 1807 and especially 1833, but also a fundamental distrust of the capacity of other slave-holding states to align on a shared—and for the British, highly nuanced and outwardly contradictory—vision for post-enslavement black freedom.[14]

The Anglo-Portuguese and Anglo-Spanish treaties of 1817 and 1826 contained no positive right for the British to monitor the disposal and welfare of the Africans once they had been liberated by the Mixed Commission courts.[15] Nevertheless, Britain later opted to interpret the treaties as conferring a right of scrutiny, advocacy, and intervention. British agents then spent over five decades attempting to observe, monitor, and interfere in matters of essentially internal domestic governance in the territories of other powers, and to seek an expanded and consolidated legal right to do so.[16] The question of freedom for liberated Africans thus formed the basis of the first sustained piece of international diplomatic humanitarian advocacy, and the first engagement between Britain and another power on the subject of the humane governance of vulnerable populations. These acts of advocating for liberated Africans (and publicising this activity through published parliamentary papers infused with a tone of moral and "civilisational" superiority) amounted to a form of power projection in which Britain presented itself as the protector of the powerless and the enforcer of a vision of moral order. This narrative has helped to shape the historiography of the transatlantic slave trade and its abolition ever since, and fuelled a British self-image of benevolent and steadfast dedication to the rights of the enslaved.

"The Instrument of Which I Felt the Need": Consul Turnbull and the Emancipados of Cuba

In 1835, after years of negotiations, Britain and Spain signed a revised slave trade suppression treaty that reflected the lessons learned in the almost two decades since the preceding treaty was enacted. It included an "equipment clause" that rendered ships liable for seizure and condemnation on the basis of being fitted out for slave trading, even if they were not carrying slaves at the time when they were intercepted. The treaty also changed the provisions for administering and resettling liberated Africans. In the buildup to Britain's Emancipation Act of 1833, and anticipating a transformation of labour relations in its Caribbean colonies, the Foreign Office dropped its long-held objections to removing *emancipados* from Cuba and resettling them at British expense in British colonial territories. After 1835, all Africans liberated at the Havana Mixed Commission Court would be diverted to Trinidad, the Bahamas, Honduras, and other locations, where they would serve one-year apprenticeships before being fully free. Parallel diplomatic efforts to sign similar treaties with Portugal and Brazil (in 1817 and 1826 respectively) came to no agreement. In 1839, Britain passed a piece of legislation that became known as the "Palmerston Act," facilitating the unilateral interdiction of Portuguese slave ships; that same year, Britain also assumed the right to divert captured Brazilian slave ships to the British islands of the Caribbean and to "dispose of" the liberated Africans there.[17]

Since all liberated Africans would henceforth be "delivered over to the Government to whom belongs the Cruizer which made the Capture," some kind of British liberated African establishment was needed, first at Havana, and later Rio de Janeiro, to manage the local politics and logistics of the transfers. This was the rationale for the creation of a liberated African "depot" or receiving ship at Havana, and a new administrative post: superintendent of liberated Africans.[18] Much has been written about

Richard Robert Madden and David Turnbull, the two ardent abolitionists who were appointed successively by Lord Palmerston to the role of superintendent of liberated Africans at Havana, and the ideological (and sometimes physical) clashes that resulted from their unwelcome presence on the island of Cuba. Turnbull's time in Cuba, and in particular his role in the much-debated conspiracy and repression of the *Escalera,* have been discussed in depth elsewhere.[19] It is important for our purposes to draw attention to the political origins and purpose of Turnbull's selection for this post: Turnbull was sent out to Cuba by Lord Palmerston specifically—and at Turnbull's repeated request—to occupy two roles: as superintendent of liberated Africans and as consul-general, the latter of which was the most senior diplomatic post on the island. Turnbull's appointment was the first and only time these roles were held by the same individual. The rationale from Turnbull's perspective was that this dual role would provide him with a platform to implement his pet project: a plan to revamp the Mixed Commission Court and invest it with "inquisitorial power," allowing it to enquire into the legality of every slave contract on the island of Cuba, the majority of which everyone knew to be illegal, since the Spanish slave trade had been nominally outlawed years before. Turnbull's hope was that such inquisitorial oversight in the hands of the court would deter plantation owners from making purchases of slaves, and within a short time achieve the practical extinction not only of the slave trade, but of slavery itself.[20] Palmerston, for his part, recognised that the likelihood of successfully implementing this plan was virtually zero. Thus, in appointing Turnbull, he may have had no concrete objective beyond antagonizing the Cubans and Spanish as far as possible within the boundaries of treaty rights—an expression of frustration and pique that was entirely consistent with his personality, behaviour, and "high-handed" belief in teaching moral lessons to other, "lesser" powers who evaded and flouted their anti-slavery treaty commitments.[21]

As consul, Turnbull's primary function was "to protect and promote the lawful trade and trading interests of Great Britain by every fair and proper means," help distressed British subjects, and if ever necessary, offer refuge at the consulate.[22] In theory, all consuls had an official "information-gathering" role in the antislavery effort: to keep a watchful eye upon all undertakings for trading in slaves; and report any suspicions of British subjects or British capital "engaged or concerned in" the slave trade.[23] In practice, the consul was expected to take more initiative, actively pushing Britain's antislavery agenda where possible, and even playing an unofficial or quasi-diplomatic intervention function. The role of consul came with a degree of prestige—not equivalent to that of a diplomatic officer, but of a status that could not be ignored or sidelined as easily as the office of superintendent of liberated Africans. For Turnbull, it was the ideal platform not only to police the administration and disposal of new liberated African arrivals, but to probe the experiences and outcomes of those disposed of in Cuba since 1824.

In 1840, a man known as Gabino made contact with Turnbull via an intermediary, seeking the British consul's help in ending his illegal enslavement. Gabino was an *emancipado* who had arrived in Cuba in 1824 as a ten-year-old child, then named Dobo. He was "disposed of" at that time on a five-year contract of indenture to Luisa Aper de la Paz, a rich widow from Havana who paid substantial bribes to secure the child and then illegally to extend his term of service several times. Reporting the incident to Palmerston, Turnbull wrote in a tone of palpable excitement. "The case of Gavino [*sic*] was the first that presented itself combining all the requisites of circumstance and character to qualify him as the instrument of which I felt the need." It was "just such a case as was needed to place the iniquity of the whole system in a clear and striking light before the world," he later wrote.[24] Gabino represented an opportunity, in Turnbull's eyes: "a wedge in effecting the launch I contemplated," who seemed a suitably robust candidate for the difficulty and danger that lay ahead once his case would be thrown into the diplomatic arena by Lord Palmerston. As Turnbull remarked to the foreign secretary, "The general question of the right of the British Government to see that the existing Treaties are faithfully executed could be asserted in a more convenient and tangible form in the case of an individual like Gavino than in the case of a whole [slave ship] cargo." "In this way," Turnbull recognised that he could "strengthen your Lordship's hands" in pressing for an enquiry into the treatment of the *emancipados* and forcing the Spanish government to improve their treatment or allow them all to emigrate to British territories.[25]

In order to insulate himself from any charges of conspiring with the *emancipados* of the island, Turnbull took care not to meet Gabino personally. Instead he addressed a letter to the captain-general, the Prince of Anglona, in December 1840, acquainting him with the facts of Gabino's illegal enslavement and appealing "to the spirit of justice and philanthropy which so happily adorns Your Excellency's character." In language not written to conciliate, Turnbull wrote:

> In the name and on behalf of Gavino, I claim for him the immediate and unconditional enjoyment of that freedom which was guaranteed to him by the Treaties . . . In the name of justice, I claim for him repayment of the money he has earned during the long series of years he has been unlawfully subjected to compulsory labour.

Turnbull also informed the captain-general of his "intention to bring this matter under the cognizance of the Court of Mixed Commission."

Although Turnbull's approach initially provoked threats of expulsion from Cuba, it had the desired effect: Palmerston took up the case with the British minister in Madrid, through whom he pressed repeatedly for action to secure Gabino's freedom and to enable the Mixed Commission Court to inquire into the status of all Africans liberated at Havana since 1824. Under the tenure of Anglona's successor, Geronimo Valdés, Gabino was issued with a certificate of freedom in 1841.[26] "I obtained that man's liberty," Turnbull told a House of Lords Select Committee on the slave trade in 1850, "and then I got a good many more; in fact, it resulted in the freedom of about 2,000."[27] Although this high number is difficult to reconcile with the evidence, the consular and Mixed Commission papers show an ongoing pattern of advocacy for liberated Africans across the period of Turnbull's appointment. Primarily, he protested the corporal punishment, false imprisonment, and extortion schemes against time-expired liberated African apprentices seeking their final certificates of emancipation. Some examples include the cases of Pedro, José Maria Nunez, Felipe, Genero Alfaro, Inez, and Dionisio.[28]

In the remarkable case of one woman called Matilda, Turnbull interfered directly in a dispute with the Cuban authorities by offering sanctuary at the consulate. Matilda had been "held for fourteen years in slavery" in the home of a family named Carrillo, who had subjected her to frequent abuse and neglect. Matilda had a free-born daughter, Isabel Marina. The child was approaching an age where she could be profitably enslaved, and her mother took steps to prevent the Carillos from seizing the girl. She entrusted the child to "two white men, the one a creole of this island, named Joaquin Saguez, the other a native of the Canaries, named Francisco Abreu," who kept her safe. The Carillos—enraged by the loss of an opportunity to enrich themselves—had imprisoned, chained, and tortured Matilda "for the purpose of compelling her to disclose the place where she had concealed her daughter." At the request of Saguez and Abreu, who feared discovery by the police, Turnbull took the child into his service at the consulate. Ultimately, he was successful in negotiating the reunification of mother and daughter, and the captain-general's personal guarantee of their permanent freedom, although it is not clear whether and for how long that promise was honoured.[29]

In June 1842, Turnbull raised the case of José Jesus, apprenticed to Donna Luisa Cabrera, who had been confined to his mistress's house for three months, ever since it became known that he "had it in contemplation" to apply for his certificate of freedom. After being severely beaten in punishment for a minor infraction, José Jesus attempted to petition the captain-general for help, but was sent away. As an alternative route, "he was advised to come to the British Consul."[30] While Turnbull had kept a studied distance from Gabino, it is evident that he met with José Jesus in person at the consulate, and that Turnbull saw his injuries and heard his account firsthand. Similarly, several months earlier, Turnbull had taken twelve depositions from fourteen *emancipados,* whose stories "afford a fair average view of the actual condition of that portion of the class who reside in the city of Havana."[31] The deposition of Tranquilino Rosas is particularly noteworthy, for although heavily mediated, it nonetheless articulates explicitly what is hinted at in José Jesus's comments above: that networks of communication, advice, and counsel existed within the Cuban *emancipado* community, and that within those networks, the British consul was perceived as an important potential recourse on the pathway to emancipation:

> [Deponent states] That he has never made any formal demand for his freedom, because he is aware that when such demands have been made by others of his class, the only result has been that they were sent to some place of deposit, and detained there until applied for by some other master . . . That he has come here of his own accord, to enquire of the Consul whether he was to remain all his life a slave, or whether he was really entitled to the enjoyment of his freedom. That he . . . comes to the English Consul to ask for the protection which it would be in vain to apply for at the Government House . . . That he is acquainted with a great number of *emancipados,* and has frequently conversed with them on their common interests and condition . . . That he does not know of any *emancipado* who is really in the enjoyment of his freedom, excepting such as are physically unable to earn their livelihood; of whom there are now many, begging their bread in the streets of the Havana. That he has no doubt of his own ability to gain his livelihood if set at liberty; and if free to choose, it would be his earnest wish to emigrate to some British colony; and he has reason to believe that the same desire is entertained by a large proportion of the class of *emancipados.*[32]

In trying to evaluate how accurate a reflection of Tranquilino's opinions, mindset, and objectives this deposition represents, it is worth noting that the content, level of detail, narrative arrangement, and emphasis of the twelve depositions are quite uneven, suggesting that whatever standard questions Turnbull may have asked, the deponents may have used the opportunity to narrate in their own words the brutalizing, degrading, and dehumanizing experiences of their *emancipado* status. It is clear that the deponents sought to appeal—occasionally through overt flattery—to the antislavery zeal and sense of moral superiority of the British abolitionist consul. If we assume for a moment that Tranquilino's deposition is a reasonable reflection of his views and the themes he discussed with Turnbull, then it offers us an insight into how the British consul was perceived to have influence over the captain-general, and how the territories of the nearby British colonies were understood as sites of prospective freedom from control and exploitation. The tone of Tranquilino's closing appeal suggests that he, and perhaps other deponents, understood that their depositions would not be sent directly to the captain-general of Cuba, but to the British foreign secretary, and perhaps that their accounts might even reach a wider metropolitan abolitionist British audience.

Turnbull's tenure as consul-general and superintendent of liberated Africans was famously brief. His singular focus on the cause of abolitionism at the expense of promoting trade interests irritated British traders and, it would appear, Palmerston's successor, Lord Aberdeen. After Turnbull's removal, the superintendent and consular functions were once again separated. Aberdeen felt that Turnbull's behaviour had "not been regulated by that spirit of moderation and discretion" expected, and that "the commercial interests of HM subjects in Cuba have suffered" in the absence of "the entire and undivided attention of an individual of tact and experience."[33] Turnbull's interest in the individual narratives and group plight of the liberated Africans was not sustained by his consular successor, Joseph Crawford. While Crawford sought to maintain the impression of genuine antislavery zeal, privately he advised the judges of the Mixed Commission Court to ignore the liberated Africans he referred to them for review. In January 1854, he bragged to a colleague that he "had no more visits from those negroes."[34]

Turnbull's successful advocacy during this time on behalf of some *emancipados* should not be over-interpreted, nor should his overt prioritization of forward-leaning abolitionist policy—at the expense of good relations with the captain-general—be read as a British foreign policy position for the Americas writ large. Regardless of the often ill-tempered tone with which Turnbull conducted his relationship with the captain-general, it would be a mistake to conclude that the British state was genuinely willing to spark a major diplomatic confrontation with Spain over the plight of liberated Africans. While Turnbull may have strayed from the niceties of diplomatic discourse, it is not clear that he was ever willing to deviate seriously from the basic British line of action, or that he did more for any individual liberated Africans than what was communicated to the Cuban authorities and the Spanish government. As Turnbull described his focus in May 1842:

> I have persevered in pressing on the Captain-General's attention several cases of peculiar hardship . . . not so much because I entertain any well-founded hope that justice is thus to be obtained for the individual sufferers, but because I believe it to be desirable and necessary to convince the Spanish authorities that their iniquitous proceedings are observed, and that the constant violation of the Treaty of 1817 is still brought under the notice of Her Majesty's Government.[35]

For Turnbull, the Gabino case was not just a "wedge" to drive into the system of *emancipado* exploitation. Rather the whole liberated African cause was the "wedge": an opportunity for contesting with Spain the much larger issue of Cuba's ongoing illegal slave imports, and for pushing for a significantly expanded Mixed Commission mandate to interfere in, and ultimately to destroy, the institution of Cuban slavery. Turnbull may have developed a personal relationship with Gabino—as we might infer from Turnbull's attendance at Gabino's wedding, in which Turnbull gave away the bride, Candelaria. But it is clear that for Turnbull, Gabino was a means to an end. For Gabino, the victory was only temporary. Mere months after receiving his certificate of emancipation, he was accused by the colonial authorities of conspiracy to provoke rebellion, and he was sentenced to eight years' imprisonment, to be served in the Moroccan enclave of Ceuta. Gabino's ultimate fate—imprisonment, torture, deportation in November 1842, and death a few months later in a prison on the far side of the Atlantic—is not mentioned by Turnbull in his popular 1850 pamphlet, *The Jamaica Movement*.[36] It is unclear whether Turnbull was aware of this outcome, or whether once Gabino had served his purpose, he slipped from view.

The Limits of British Diplomacy

Both before and after Turnbull, Britain's liberated African policy in Cuba was defined by the bounds of legal and diplomatic process. Palmerston was willing to antagonise the Spanish government through the appointments of Madden and Turnbull, and after 1835, prepared to assume the cost of disposing of newly liberated Africans in British territories. But neither he nor his successors demonstrated a willingness to intervene decisively to secure the treaty-mandated rights of the settled, time-expired *emancipados* who had arrived in Cuba before 1835. As the island of Cuba destabilised into insurrection in the 1860s, even the most basic forms of antislavery pressure were pulled back in order to avoid any adverse geostrategic outcomes for Britain, such as the annexation of Cuba by the United States, or a catastrophic slave insurrection that would devastate British investments in the island. The fates of the *emancipados* of Cuba were ultimately left to the discretion of the Spanish government.[37] In practice, Britain did little to help the liberated Africans trapped unlawfully in slavelike conditions.

British policy towards the more than 10,000 *emancipados* of Brazil was similarly characterised by restraint, bilateral process, and the consideration of wider strategic and commercial interests.[38] As with Spain over Cuba, Britain engaged in a sustained and occasionally heated dialogue with Brazil, repeatedly asserting the right to be informed about the fates of Africans liberated by the Mixed Commission courts, and insisting on the fulfilment of the treaty terms. British interventions—particularly those led by various consuls—were decisive in securing the liberty of a number of individual liberated Africans. Yet as with Cuba, for the most part this rhetoric was ultimately not followed by anything more forceful. For much of the period after the passage of the Aberdeen Act of 1845, British restraint on the *emancipado* question stands in marked contrast to the aggressive-

ness of her naval interdiction strategy and the audacity of the unilateral undertaking to divert newly liberated Africans to British territories.

As in Cuba, Britain asserted throughout the nineteenth century the
right to scrutinise the liberation outcomes of Brazil's *emancipados*. After
1826, British commissioners, legation staff, and consuls sourced intelligence
that suggested that liberated Africans were being repeatedly re-indentured
through both private and government employment channels.[39] Consul
Robert Hesketh reported to the Foreign Office in 1851 on the liberated Africans' ongoing "unprotected condition" and the "unjustifiable treatment
to which a portion of them have been doomed," including the enslavement
of their children and the "barbarous," occasionally fatal, treatment meted
out by brutal indenture-holders. He concluded that "there is but too much
reason to fear that many of these liberated Africans were removed far into
the interior and sold" into "a helpless state of slavery," in clear violation of
the treaty stipulations.[40] In 1856, the Brazilian authorities issued a decree
of emancipation of all liberated Africans under private indenture. Those
in government employment were excluded from the declaration of emancipation, based on the fiction that they would be subject eventually to "re-
exportation" to Africa. The British minister, Henry Howard, reported to
the foreign secretary in 1855 that the Brazilian foreign minister "considers
the discussion to be terminated." However, the incomplete nature of the
emancipation and the failure of the Brazilian government to fulfil even its
own limited terms had resulted in "frequent applications from free Africans to Her Majesty's Legation, and the necessity of the latter interfering
in their behalf." Howard grumbled that "such interference is by no means
agreeable to Her Majesty's Legation," and expressed his surprise that "the
Brazilian Government do not avoid the humiliation which it entails upon
them by taking the matter vigorously into their own hands, and seeing that
justice is really done to those unfortunate individuals in whose welfare they
profess to interest themselves."[41]

As the future prime minister William Gladstone reminded the House
of Commons in March 1850, Britain had a right to demand the better treatment of the liberated Africans, and could follow the assertion of this right
with the exercise of real force:

> We have a treaty with Brazil, which she has broken every day
> for the last twenty years. We have tried to secure the freedom
> of the Emancipados . . . This treaty has been repeatedly bro-
> ken, and we have a perfect right to demand its fulfilment; and
> if we have the right to demand it, we have the right to do so at the
> point of the sword in case of refusal. We have now a perfect right
> to go to Brazil, and call upon her to emancipate every slave im-
> ported since 1830, and upon refusal, to make war with them
> even to extermination.

Yet, as Gladstone pointed out—approvingly—neither Palmerston nor Aberdeen had "ever entertained the idea of making or enforcing this demand upon Brazil. You would not dare to go to war upon this question with Brazil, much less with those whom you would find in the rear to support her."[42] In *The Jamaica Movement*, published in the same year, Turnbull made a similar point about British policy towards the *emancipados* of Cuba. Britain had a right to demand the observance of the treaty terms, and would have done so far more aggressively had there been some geopolitical risk or geostrategic prize at stake: "if these treaties had related to the cession of some distant island, or some petty fortress, would any of the various ad-ministrations which have succeeded each other in England since the year 1817 have sat down contentedly under the imputation?"[43]

At first glance, the suspension of diplomatic relations between Brit-ain and Brazil from 1863 to 1865 may appear to be just the sort of diplo-matic escalation on the *emancipado* question that never happened in Cuba. Triggered by the "Christie Affair," which erupted in January 1863 after a year or so of rising tensions, the breakdown of relations was the culmina-tion of long-simmering resentments relating to property seizures by the an-tislavery naval squadron and the controversial Aberdeen Act of 1845.[44] It was ostensibly precipitated by several earlier incidents—including the al-leged murder of the crew of a British ship and looting of its cargo in 1851, and the detention of the crew of another British ship in 1852—but these rea-sons are widely regarded as pretexts for the real issue: the intertwined questions of illegally imported slaves, *emancipado* rights, and the status of

Brazilian slavery itself.[45] The situation was not helped by the British minister, William Dougal Christie, who—along with the then prime minister, Lord Palmerston—seemed inclined to escalate tensions. Christie ordered the blockade of the harbour of Rio de Janeiro from 31 December 1862 until 5 January 1863; five Brazilian merchant ships were seized and detained. Palmerston subsequently defended these actions in the House of Commons, arguing that "all the efforts we have made to obtain justice for these *emancipados* have failed" because "the conduct of the Brazilian Government" with regard to them "has invariably been marked by great neglect and violation of treaty engagements." Moreover, it was the will "of the English nation, to put an end to that detestable [slave] traffic." Thus, in Palmerston's view, "the goodness of the end justified the means." "I attach so much importance to carrying out the determination of the English people," he declared, "that, much as I value the goodwill and friendship of Brazil, yet if that were put in one scale and the suppression of the slave trade in the other, I should prefer the latter."[46] William Christie's defence of his actions echoed Palmerston's. The first four chapters of his 1865 pamphlet, *Notes on Brazilian Questions,* detailed "The Story of the Free Africans," and argued that Britain gave Brazil ample opportunity to reform the system of disposal and management, but had ultimately been forced to compel the issue. "The reprisals of January 1863 and the subsequent suspension of diplomatic relations had quickened the liberation of *emancipados,*" Christie claimed. "Left to itself," the Brazilian government "did nothing . . . forgetting that treaty-stipulations gave a right to England to interfere."[47]

    The Christie Affair had much to do with the intemperate nature of William Christie and the willingness of Palmerston to gamble on an escalation against a lesser power, a move that echoed the logic of Palmerston's "Don Pacifico" dispute with Greece in 1850.[48] Regardless, even supposing one takes at face value the claim that Palmerston and Christie provoked a diplomatic crisis in defence of *emancipado* rights, the restoration of diplomatic relations several years later was not made contingent upon Brazil delivering liberated Africans into a state of meaningful freedom—quite the converse. In November 1865, after the death of Palmerston, Foreign Secretary Lord Clarendon wrote to the British minister-in-waiting Sir

Edward Thornton specifically to instruct him not to pursue the *emanci-pado* question:

> At the time of the suspension of diplomatic relations between
> this country and Brazil, a correspondence was being carried on
> between Her Majesty's Representative at Rio upon the question
> of the treatment of the [*emancipados*]. I have to acquaint you
> that it is not the wish of Her Majesty's Government that you
> should, on the resumption of diplomatic relations with Brazil,
> enter upon former matters of controversy connected with this
> question.

Thornton was merely to congratulate the Brazilian government on the Decree of 24 September 1864 granting legal emancipation to all liberated Africans in its care, and to "ask how far it has yet been carried out, and how many of these people are still waiting for the beneficial operation of the Decree."[49] The British consul, who had remained in Rio de Janeiro for the duration of the suspension of diplomatic relations, expressed low expectations. His pessimism was borne out by the lengthy, tortuous nature of the subsequent process, and by the ultimately incomplete nature of the "emancipation" conferred upon the remaining liberated Africans. In March 1865, Consul Hunt reported to the foreign secretary that the Brazilian government had disclosed the names of 8,673 liberated Africans whose indentures had expired and who were legally free. Of these, 5,099 were still in bondage. "Unless some pressure is brought to bear," Hunt advised, "they and their offspring will die in slavery."[50]

  If the Christie Affair represents a kind of "Turnbull moment" for Britain in Brazil—a disruptive, ill-tempered, and ultimately fruitless diplomatic spat—then the twenty-year career of Consul Robert Hesketh at Rio de Janeiro offers a more representative picture of the conduct of British liberated African policy in Brazil and the relatively conciliatory, perhaps unambitious approach of the British "antislavery system" on this question. Eschewing the abrasive impatience of Turnbull and Christie, Hesketh served two decades without significant conflict with the Brazilian authorities on the *emancipado* question. Although he remarked frequently on injustice towards liberated Africans, Hesketh's despatches were characterised by a tone of moderation and prudence, and an emphasis on working within the system, not railing against it from outside.[51] Born and raised in Portugal, Hesketh was a trader and British consul for nineteen years at Maranhão before his posting to Rio in 1831. His fluency in Portuguese and status as consul gave him privileged access at all levels of society. This included direct communication with local traders, naval officers, local authorities, police, harbour workers, and liberated Africans of both "new" and "settled" categories, as well as close ties with the community of Britons settled in Brazil and those with commercial interests and investments in the country. This latter group—as Joseph Mulhern's work has shown—had at best an ambivalent relationship with the British international antislavery agenda. Many in this community engaged in profitable associations with, and promotion of, race-based slavery and slave trading on an industrial scale.[52]

Hesketh's records offer us an interesting glimpse of the encounter between the British "antislavery world system" and the purported objects of its interventions. They illuminate the character of the advocacy that evolved. True to the two-track approach of the Foreign Office towards liberated Africans, Hesketh had more contact with newly liberated Africans than with the settled *emancipado* population.[53] When required, Hesketh went aboard recently captured slave ships to document the names and testimonies of both Africans and enslaved crew members.[54] He acted as emigration agent and proctor on board captured slave ships and aboard the hulk *Crescent*, witnessing firsthand the "horrible detail of the misery and suffering," and describing his own visceral reaction to being "in close contact with the wretched beings . . . men, women, children, and infants, some sinking under disease, and others disgusting from their savage apathy and brutal ferocity when fed."[55] In 1839, he provided a detailed report on the practical functioning of the adjudication and disposal system, including efforts to help malnourished liberated Africans adapt to varied diets including beef, cassava, and vegetables.[56] When the unusual circumstances of the *Flor de Luanda* seizure in 1838 allowed British agents at Rio de Janeiro to manage the disposal of several hundred liberated Africans, Hesketh worked closely with Ouseley, the British minister, to dispose of, monitor, and eventually—in a public ceremony—fully liberate the Africans and convey those who opted to emigrate to the West Indies.[57]

For those already settled in Brazil, Hesketh's interventions were more limited. As consul at Maranhão, he submitted one of the Foreign Office's earliest reports of the abuse and enslavement of liberated Africans.[58] In Rio, he acted as a confidential intermediary to help link the British commissioners of the Mixed Commission Court with "respectable residents of the country" who imparted information in confidence. When the British commissary judge arranged covertly in 1843 for a liberated African woman to be hired and placed with a private family in order to ascertain her state of education and welfare, it is very likely that Hesketh mediated the application.[59] Yet, although based in Rio for twenty years of the slave trade suppression campaign, Hesketh appears to have had little direct contact with settled *emancipados*.

This changed in September 1849, when Hesketh reported to the British minister that "a miserable-looking negro, who had suffered amputation of a leg, [had] appeared at this Consulate." Hesketh's account of the meeting implies surprise: he forgot to take the man's name, and he sent him back with a letter to the curator. The appearance of another liberated African, Estavao, at the consulate a few weeks later prompted the British minister to instruct Hesketh to track down and make a list "of the Africans who are entitled to their liberty." This "tedious process," which ultimately took Hesketh two years, was slowed by the limited knowledge he had of the settled *emancipado* population, and the indirect method of asking liberated Africans to spread the summons through their networks. "Many could only come by stealth, and some not at all."[60] In total, Hesketh collected the names of 857 liberated Africans, along with brief biographical details, the names of their purported masters and mistresses, and the nature of the treatment the deponents and their "comrades" had experienced.

Hesketh's register is an invaluable source for the study of liberated African experiences, interpersonal networks, perspectives on Brazilian society, and strategies for achieving meaningful freedom. It also offers us a

useful demonstration of the character and limits of British engagement with
liberated African rights in Brazil. In it are recorded thousands of tiny fragments of the lives and deaths of Brazil's *emancipados;* glimpses of their
family lives, their hopes, ambitions, and resilience, and the constraints and
forms of violence inflicted upon them by an overwhelmingly hostile host
society.[61] As far as we know, its underlying purpose was not to identify
people to whom refuge could be offered at the consulate, or to find *emancipados* who Britain could help escape the country (as some of Hesketh's
consular colleagues in other postings had done, such as Robert Corbett,
at São Luis in Maranhão). Nor indeed does it seem to have been intended
to support efforts to subvert Brazilian authority by unilaterally declaring
illegal indenture contracts null and void. The register's primary utility,
from the British perspective, appears to have been as a reference point upon
which to base a renewed round of the same diplomatic appeals as had been
directed at the Brazilian authorities for decades, and in particular, to identify time-expired liberated Africans from the first eighteen or so slave-ship
captures.[62]

　　That said, the process of compiling a register of liberated Africans
appears to have unexpectedly facilitated a new form of British intervention
at the individual level. From the petitions *emancipados* submitted to the
Brazilian authorities, it is clear that they viewed their compulsory service
as a period of captivity, that they were aware of the injustice and illegality
of that service being extended, and that they were prepared to fight for their
right to final emancipation and full freedom.[63] We can only speculate as to
the motivations of those who, often at great personal risk, visited the British consulate and registered their stories. Based on the number of responses
Hesketh received, it seems likely that the idea of British intercession was,
or came to be, understood amongst *emancipados* as a potential route to freedom, and that networks of liberated Africans communicated amongst
themselves the possibilities British advocacy might represent.[64] While
important work remains to be done to link the names of liberated Africans
in Hesketh's register to the second emancipation petitions submitted to the
Brazilian government after 1849, it is likely that in hearing, interrogating,
and documenting *emancipado* narratives, Hesketh—along with Westwood,

his successor as consul—became involved in the co-production of materials used in petitions later submitted to the Brazilian authorities. By the late 1840s, driven in part by the agency of liberated Africans who contributed their stories to Hesketh's register, a two-pronged British intervention evolved in the contested space surrounding the obligations of Spain, Portugal, and Brazil to "guarantee the Liberty" of liberated Africans. First, British officials seem to have helped individual liberated Africans document the petitions they later submitted to the Brazilian government. They then seem to have reinforced the claims of these petitions through dialogue at the diplomatic (ministerial) and quasi-diplomatic (consular and curatorial) levels.[65] From the British perspective, this was an opportunistic development, rather than a conscious strategy to develop new forms of intervention and advocacy. It also entailed very little risk to Britain. The risk and real effort fell to the liberated Africans. Further research may help to evaluate how beneficial British support was for individual cases, and whether this type of engagement with the British antislavery system delivered measurable value and better outcomes. Nevertheless, it is important to take note that the liberated Africans of Brazil were, at great personal risk to themselves and their loved ones, the driving energy behind a new and improvised embryonic form of state-diplomatic human rights advocacy.

The consular, legation, and Mixed Commission Court officers in Cuba and Brazil were some of the only Britons who had personal encounters with the tens of thousands of Africans liberated in the Americas under the terms of bilateral treaties. At times, the source material created by and about David Turnbull, William Christie, and other consular and legation officers implies a boldly interventionist, idealistic British pursuit of liberated African rights in Brazil and Cuba—and indeed, at times some consuls made notable efforts to assist individual *emancipados*. Nevertheless, when these examples are situated in the wider context of ongoing British antislavery diplomacy, what is most apparent is the limited and ultimately consensual nature of formal British engagement on this bilateral issue.

"The Humane Object His Lordship Has in View": Treaty Revision and Reform

Antislavery created the rationale for new kinds of British power projection across the nineteenth century. Analysis of British interventionism against the slave trade often emphasises its hard power dimensions, including naval assaults and burning barracoons on both sides of the Atlantic. Yet in the longer term, the normative implications for inter-state dialogues on humanitarian issues were in some ways more consequential. The slave trade suppression treaties created a new rationale for Britain to engage with how other powers administered, protected, and utilised the labour of vulnerable, non-native populations within their own borders. The experience of playing this role both influenced, and in turn was influenced by, Britain's evolving self-perception as a benevolent and progressive imperial power and a humane actor on the international stage.[66] While many of its interventions did little to help (and perhaps even much to harm) the liberated Africans who in these decades were the ostensible objects of British humanitarian concern, or to affect their plight of being trapped between slavery and freedom, they constituted for Britain a fifty-year foundational experience, first of designating vulnerable populations as the objects of international interest and the possessors of positive rights guaranteed by treaty, and then policing how other states respected these rights within their own territories.

What developed was a kind of "muscle memory" of conducting detailed inquiries and diplomatic representations on the circumstances and treatment of named individuals within those vulnerable populations, and attempting at least in some sense to hold the governments of those territories to account. For Britain—easily the most powerful country in the world during these decades, a global maritime empire approaching the zenith of its power—the many thousands of letters exchanged between the Foreign Office's Slave Trade Department, its worldwide agents, and its foreign interlocutors built not only a habitual discourse of international concern around appropriate and humane forms of governance, but also a platform from which to justify on moral grounds subsequent acts of violence and illegal destruction and dispossession of property. The act of lobbying on moral or humanitarian grounds was, Britain discovered, a way of accumulating power. Palmerston noted with satisfaction how "the naval operations of our squadron," sent illegally into Brazilian territorial waters in 1850, had "accomplished in a few weeks what diplomatic notes and negotiations have failed for years to accomplish." Yet it was precisely those notes and negotiations that had laid the basis for those operations, with all of their extraordinary legal and normative implications.[67] The United States did not, as the Brazilian foreign minister had hoped, respond with outrage to what was, among other things, a blatant violation of the Monroe Doctrine. France, for her part, made it "absolutely clear" to the Brazilian government "that on this issue, Brazil stood alone."[68]

A natural question that follows from all of this is just how sincere were the motives of the actors within the British "antislavery world system." Did they pursue improved conditions for the liberated Africans out of concern for them as individuals, or did they regard the liberated people as instruments available to serve the overall goal of ending the slave trade (and, in a more lukewarm fashion, the ending of global slavery)? Or, indeed, was the whole international suppression campaign merely an opportunity to consolidate global power? Surveying the individuals involved, it is clear that there is no one single answer. The archival evidence implies a spectrum of dispositions. There were the passionate risk takers, such as David Turnbull and Robert Corbett—geographically isolated and heavily outnumbered consular officers, facing down angry local authorities and crowds to intervene on behalf of specific individual *emancipados* (or at least making it sound this way for enthusiastic domestic audiences and the approval of the British government). And then there were the more obviously performative careerists, such as Consul Joseph Crawford at Havana, as well as those like Robert Hesketh: possibly sympathetic, but cautious and procedural minded individuals whose action stopped short of alienating the authorities of their host society.

But what about the British state itself, and the policymakers and diplomats who undertook to frame and pursue liberated African rights as an international issue? Some clues can be gleaned from the negotiations

Britain undertook in the 1830s and 1840s in the pursuit of a revised Portuguese treaty, and the reformed system of *emancipado* governance that it
insisted upon thereafter, particularly in the Portuguese colonial territory of
Angola. In this search for a reformed disposal process—particularly in the
specific ideas proposed and the language adopted—lie hints to how British
officials understood the relative importance of individual liberated Africans in Britain's advocacy on their behalf.

If we return to the definition of nineteenth-century humanitarian
governance put forward in the introduction to this book—namely, that
humanitarian governance should be understood as the framing of imperial
and colonial governance in the language of a higher moral purpose, the
pursuit of declared humanitarian goals through the exercise of state power,
and the design of strategies of intervention explicitly justified on the basis
of human need, articulated in a "moral vernacular," and pursued through
a purpose-built bureaucratic system—it is evident that neither in practice
nor even rhetorically did any of Britain's treaty partners meet this definition
in the arrangements they put in place to administer their *emancipados*.
The behaviour of Brazilian and Cuban authorities in particular suggests
that they were not only uninterested in abolitionist experiments regarding
the viability and profitability of post-enslavement free labour, but that they
actively resisted such innovations, and saw their treaty obligations as an
unwelcome imposition by Britain and an insult to their dignity as sovereign
powers. In such contexts, not only did liberated Africans experience exploitation; they were also regarded as an embodiment of unwelcome foreign
intrusion, as incarnations of a hostile foreign power seeking to destabilise
and undermine the institution of slavery. Liberated Africans, both as a group
and individually, became targets for resentment, hostility, and even rage
provoked by British interference.

By the late 1830s, the Vice-Admiralty courts offered Britain a more
straightforward pathway to the successful prosecution of prize cases, the
payment of head money to the capturing crews, and the management of liberated Africans in the now nominally slave-free British territories.[69] Nevertheless, to retain the legal right to stop, search, and seize foreign-flagged
ships on the high seas, Britain still had need of its web of bilateral slave

trade suppression treaties and the adjudication arrangements that these treaties conferred. As early as 1833—and in the anticipation of negotiating a new and more comprehensive antislavery enforcement treaty with the Portuguese government—Palmerston's Foreign Office began to think seriously about ways to improve governance arrangements for liberated Africans who could not be removed from the territories of bilateral treaty partners. He asked the commissioner at Rio de Janeiro, Henry Hayne, to propose a series of suggested articles for a new treaty to ensure "that [the liberated people] meet with humane and proper usage during their apprenticeships" and to "secure to them final and complete emancipation at the termination thereof."[70]

In his reply, Hayne was demonstrably eager to impress his superiors with his "cheerful" obedience and "perfect readiness and anxious desire to afford every assistance or information in [his] power to the furtherance of the humane object his Lordship has in view," and to make clear the "infinite satisfaction" it would give him to make even the slightest positive difference to the experiences of the "emancipated slaves." He laid out suggestions for a new system of safeguards against the re-enslavement and abuse of liberated people and their children. After condemnation, all of the enslaved people should be given over to the charge of the Mixed Commission Court "to be dealt with by it," rather than the host government. Any enslaved crew members found aboard the ship should also be "formally inserted in the confiscation" and handed certificates of emancipation, whether they wanted them or not.[71] Echoing advice he had given Foreign Secretary George Canning in 1825, Hayne also proposed that the Mixed Commission Court should in future have the power to select a curator of liberated Africans. Reporting directly to the court, and not the host government, the curator would be responsible for maintaining an accurate, up-to-date, and verified register, as a means of ensuring the "well being" of the liberated people and their protection from "abuses." When apprentice-holders would claim that a liberated person had died—one of "so many loopholes by which unfeeling and unprincipled men" imposed "the horrors of slavery" on *emancipados*—the curator would be responsible for ascertaining the cause of death and verifying that the body presented

was that of the named *emancipado*. The curator would also be responsible for ensuring that apprentices received training in a marketable "handi-
craft or labour by which a livelihood may be gained." Apprentice fees should
no longer be paid to the host government, but to the curator, who—with
the supervision of the court—would use the money for "the prosecution of
delinquent Masters," "the reward of some of the best conducted of the
Apprentices . . . as an encouragement to good conduct," and the "promotion of the comfort and welfare of the Apprentices." Strict time limits should
be applied to these apprenticeships too: ten years for children and a maximum of eight years for those older than thirteen, with an option to remit
part of the service. At the termination of an apprenticeship, each individual would exchange their certificate of emancipation for one of freedom.
The curator would ensure that "their enfranchisement be acknowledged
and registered according to the custom of the Country."[72]

When Lord Howard de Walden, the new British minister to Portugal, was sent to Lisbon in September 1834 to open negotiations for a new
slave trade suppression treaty, much of what Hayne had proposed was
reflected in the articles of the draft treaty with which he was furnished.[73]
Annex C of what eventually became the Anglo-Portuguese treaty of 1842—
following years of acrimonious negotiations, and by way of the serious
violation of Portuguese sovereignty that was the "Palmerston Act" of
1839—was the part of the treaty that made provision for the treatment of
liberated people.[74] Its central objectives were to ensure an educational and
vocational form of indentured labour, and to maintain the visibility of *emancipados* and the ongoing accountability of all of those notionally entrusted
with their safety and well-being. Since this new treaty opened up the high
seas south of the equator to British naval policing, a new Anglo-Portuguese
Mixed Commission Court was created in 1844 in the Portuguese colony of
Luanda. This new court oversaw the creation of a whole new system for
the disposal and management of liberated Africans, centred around a Board
of Superintendence, or *Junta da Superintendência,* consisting of the Portuguese governor and the British commissioner, through which Britain
shared powers of oversight with Portugal and, much to the irritation of the
Portuguese authorities, retained the right to intervene on Portuguese sov-

ereign territory to remove liberated people from unsuitable or abusive situations. Following Hayne's proposal, the board was empowered to appoint a curator to follow the liberated people's "progress" and report every three months.[75] Just as Hayne had suggested, those liberated Africans who made sufficient "progress" in learning a trade were to be given the right to terminate their indentures up to three years early.

In practice, the Board of Superintendence struggled to find suitable and willing hirers. Its policy in that event was to employ the liberated people as labourers on public contracts at the expense of the court until the expiry of their period of legal minority. The result was a Mixed Commission Court at Luanda that, as Samuël Coghe has observed, had the distinction of being the only one on non-British soil that "effectively attained emancipation [for liberated Africans] within the terms of the treaty."[76] It was also the only example of an officer of a Mixed Commission Court on non-British soil formally assuming some of the governance functions of a liberated African establishment, and engaging in both short-term "emergency" and medium-term "developmental" forms of intervention in the lives of liberated people, framed through humanitarian registers of governance. By contrast, discourses produced by the governments of the other territories emphasised the disorderly and dangerous potential of the liberated people, the risk they represented to the stability of the existing slave order, and the need to control their mobility and restrict their networks.

The new court at Luanda adjudicated very few cases: only 137 liberated Africans ever came under its jurisdiction.[77] Nevertheless, the process of creating the court and the experiences of the comparatively few (though no less important) liberated Africans who encountered it offer us some useful insights into how the British and Portuguese governments each conceived of the political, social, moral, and economic dimensions of the *emancipado* question, two decades on from the first successful slave-ship condemnation by an Anglo-Portuguese court. The disposal terms eventually agreed as Annex C in the 1842 treaty were not the first-choice option of Palmerston or the Foreign Office, who would have preferred a treaty arrangement similar to that enacted with Spain in 1835: to remove all liberated Africans from Angola to British territories in the Caribbean, a suggestion Portugal rejected on the grounds of national honour. Even with this compromise in mind, Annex C was still much resented by the Portuguese government and legislature as an imposition by Britain on a notionally equal treaty partner and ally. Palmerston was adamant, however. When Annex C met with vehement opposition by Portugal, and the British minister Howard de Walden "ventured beyond the limits of his instructions" and agreed in 1836 to remove it, regarding it as not essential to the suppression treaty as a whole, Palmerston insisted on its reinsertion.[78]

Gladstone was right in his observation that Britain would never have gone to war in defence of the rights of the *emancipados* of Brazil, Cuba, Surinam, Luanda, or anywhere else.[79] Yet it is nonetheless worthy of note that Palmerston—a leading politician in the most powerful state on the planet; a man who dominated foreign policy for over thirty years, first as foreign secretary and later as prime minister—would, in his years of ministerial office, repeatedly take up in diplomatic correspondence the cases of individual African men, women, and children, engaging in sustained correspondence with his networks of consuls, vice-consuls, ministers, ambassadors, and naval officers in the pursuit of the freedom to which these individuals were entitled, in interventions to keep families together, and in protest at the violence and exploitation they continued to endure.[80] Addressing the House of Commons in 1864, he spoke of the plight of the *emancipados* in Brazil, "the desolation of Africa," the "suffering and misery [slave trading brought] to hundreds of thousands of Africans," and the "importance [he attached] to carrying out the determination of the English people to put an end to the slave trade." Such was that importance, he claimed, that "much as I value the goodwill and friendship of Brazil, yet if that were put in one scale and the suppression of the slave trade in the other, I should prefer the latter."[81]

What can we infer from this? It is hard to dispute that Palmerston exhibited a sustained interest in seeing liberated Africans achieve real freedom from enslavement in the territories of foreign powers. Under his direction from the 1830s on, a variety of foreign policy and diplomatic activities and innovations sought to position Britain as the international arbiter of humane and just forms of colonial governance, with the authority to act as assessor (and at times, enforcer) of the standards it set for foreign powers. Underlying Palmerston's view of Britain's international antislavery policies was an idea of a "civilised" moral order against which Britain evaluated other states and legitimised its own use of force to police the behaviour of those states. But does this equate to a sincere and sustained personal interest in reducing or eliminating the suffering of slave trade survivors? Not exactly. In 1847, Palmerston approved a proposal by the West India Committee and the Land and Emigration Commissioners that slave ships captured on the West African coast should be diverted directly to the West Indies without ever coming ashore at Freetown—a suggestion that would have inflicted upon supposedly liberated people an extended "middle passage" scarcely distinct from the peril and trauma of a slave-ship voyage; perhaps more so, given the lengthy interlude at anchor in Freetown harbour.[82] Furthermore, during the negotiations with Portugal, he initially considered (though later rejected) a proposal to allow the Luanda authorities to transfer recently liberated people as indentured "free farmers" to the islands of São Tomé and Principe; islands notorious for the conditions under which their enslaved populations suffered, and in which no meaningful independent oversight of liberated African welfare would be possible.[83]

One way of reading Palmerston's personal engagement with the rights of liberated Africans is that the issue offered a set of positive treaty commitments against which Britain could make specific complaints in order to force other powers to submit. Palmerston remarked in 1850, "these half-civilised governments, such as those of China, Portugal, Spanish America, require a dressing every eight or ten years to keep them in order."[84] The illegal abuse and exploitation of liberated Africans certainly offered Palmerston plenty of ammunition in this respect. The importance of this point is not the motivations of a single man, but how he influenced the activities into which global agents of the British antislavery system poured their energies, often in the expectation of recognition and reward from London. It is entirely possible that Palmerston—and by extension, the organisation of British foreign policy for which he set the tone for most of the period from 1830 to 1865—was animated to pursue *emancipado* rights and freedoms primarily as an exercise of British power, selectively asserting a right of intervention in order to play the role of the enforcer of a particularly advantageous moral order.

For most liberated Africans, these high-political wranglings had little direct impact on their lives. Cast into societies that sought to deny them the protections of their legal status, those who survived their integration into the colonial societies of Cuba, Brazil, Surinam, and Angola did so through strategies of both resistance and accommodation. They endured brutal labour conditions and endemic abuse, yet fought hard to assert the rights they knew well they were entitled to. In the face of intimidation and violence, they confronted with immense courage a system that sought to render them silent, subservient labour units.[85] The final two chapters will explore in more depth the lived experience of liberated Africans under the conditions of their "disposal" as apprentices and soldiers, primarily in the British colonies of the Atlantic, and their influence on emerging discourses of humane governance and state responsibility for vulnerable populations.

Apprenticeship

TWO STRIKINGLY SIMILAR MURDER cases appeared before Sierra Leone's Chief Justice Sir John William Jeffcott in the first six months of 1831. The first was the trial of Kissiah Bacchus, accused of the murder of her liberated African apprentice, a girl ten years of age whose death had been caused "by beating her severely, rubbing pepper into her Eyes and otherwise ill using her." The second was that of a woman named Betsy Harding, whose apprentice child had suffered and died in a similar way. Chief Justice Jeffcott became convinced that "for a considerable time past, very great and wanton cruelty had been exercised towards the great mass of the Liberated African apprentices by their Masters and Mistresses." He declared his intent to prosecute more actively any apprentice holders accused of treating apprentices inhumanely. He encouraged abused and neglected apprentices to avail themselves of their right to "apply to the Judge of the Vice Admiralty" to examine their case and, if necessary, fine the master or mistress a maximum of £100 and cancel the indenture.[1]

Apprenticeship was, in its various manifestations, a central feature of the "disposal" plans for newly liberated people at Sierra Leone and throughout the British Atlantic world in the first half of the nineteenth century. The policy was conceived and built into the Abolition Act of 1807 for both ideological and practical reasons. "Freedom," under this configuration, was a state that existed either prior to enslavement or following a gradual instructional period under British-supervised tutelage, either in public works or in the homes of established colonists. While bound as an apprentice, a liberated African was not a chattel slave, but equally was not supposed to exercise true agency.[2] The stated rationale for the apprenticeship policy was that liberated people, being individuals who had experienced enslavement, needed to be "schooled" to reacquire their capacity for freedom.[3] A more prosaic function of the policy was to transfer from the colonial government to private individuals the responsibility, costs, and complexities of maintaining the safety and welfare of the formerly enslaved. The outcome was a policy that reflected the moral ambiguity of its framers on the ethics of an intervention that "liberated" by constraining individual freedom and extracting labour of marketable value.

Virtually from its implementation in 1808 until its official abolition in 1848, liberated African apprenticeship was highly controversial. Critics of the policy believed that abuse, exploitation, and re-enslavement of apprentices were endemic. European observers considered the distribution of indentured labour to have a corrosive effect on free black colonists' work ethic and on the moral fabric of society, particularly in Sierra Leone. The papers of the Liberated African Department of Sierra Leone and the reports of various colonial commissioners, missionaries, and other observers throughout the British Atlantic document countless instances of violence towards apprentices, combined with expressions of frustration on the part of colonial governments and missionaries at their inability to monitor or guarantee apprentice welfare. Yet although it followed decades of such criticism, Jeffcott's intervention in Sierra Leone in 1831 had little effect. When large numbers of apprentices tried to avail themselves of the opportunity Jeffcott had advertised, the colony's governor dismissed most complaints as opportunism and ingratitude. Apprenticeship continued to be regarded as an administrative necessity and was sustained in Sierra Leone for another seventeen years, virtually without reform. Even after its official abolition in 1848, the practice probably persisted in some capacity for at least another fifteen years. Much criticised and objected to, but nonetheless tolerated, the apprenticing of liberated Africans was one policy within a mosaic of purportedly developmental interventions by Britain during the nineteenth century in its global effort to remould the lives of colonised people.

This chapter addresses three broad questions. First, what can we know about how liberated people experienced and responded to appren-

ticeship? Second, in what ways did their experiences and responses provoke debate and reform, either towards more just and "humane" forms of
governance or towards more "pragmatic" exploitation? Finally, to what extent did critiques of apprenticeship (and indeed of other disposal policies
and practices) feed into evolving discourses of humanitarian responsibility and the duty of the British empire to provide refuge to slave trade survivors? Put another way, in what ways were discourses of governance
affected by the decades-long experience of administering, observing, and
adapting the practical implementation of the apprenticeship policy, and
what should we infer from the preservation of the policy for over forty years?

The latter two questions are more straightforward to address than the
first. Much—indeed most—of what contemporaries documented about apprenticeship was about what was being done to, or perceived to be done
to, the liberated people. The convergence of missionaries, traders, colonial officials, and travellers at Sierra Leone, and their more or less shared
disapproval of apprenticeship, resulted in the production of extensive doc-
umentation on the practice and its perceived problems, with a heavy emphasis on the cases of violence, abuse, neglect, and re-enslavement that
came to light. However firsthand narratives by liberated people of their experiences of enslavement, liberation, and lives as free people are comparatively rare. Those that do exist are often problematic sources, heavily
mediated through missionary or governmental lenses. European observers recorded in detail their impressions and opinions of apprenticeship, but
did not seek anything like the same level of firsthand reflection from liberated Africans and their children. That said, by reading against and across
the grain of the colonial archives, it is possible to recover some insights into
liberated people's voices and viewpoints.[4] Since 2013, the SHADD team
(Studies in the History of the African Diaspora—Documents) at York University's Harriet Tubman Institute has uncovered more than one thousand
narratives of formerly enslaved people.[5] These are often tiny, fragmentary
glimpses into the life of an individual, but together they form a powerful
multidimensional picture that adds greatly to our understanding of enslavement, liberation, manumission, emancipation, and post-enslavement

lives. This chapter follows a similar approach; however, its aims are modest. It makes no claim to give a full account of liberated African perspectives, but rather to assemble glimpses of possible experiences of apprenticeship and what the policy might have meant to the lives of those it touched.

The focus on Sierra Leone is in part practical: an entire book would be required for a satisfactory comparative analysis of the implementation, adaptation, and consequences of different manifestations of liberated African apprenticeship policies across the whole geography of the British Atlantic and Indian Ocean worlds (not to mention the territories of bilateral treaty partners), combined with an attempt to recover the voices and responses of those involved. The decision to focus on Sierra Leone is also due to its unique status as a colony acquired by the Crown directly to coincide with the enforcement of the Abolition Act, and the site in which the overwhelming majority of liberated Africans were resettled. While Sierra Leone was by no means ring-fenced from the forces rendering the liberation of enslaved Africans so complex throughout the wider British Atlantic world, nonetheless the process there did not provoke the kinds of social, political, and diplomatic tensions encountered in Brazil, Cuba, Angola, Surinam, Cape Town, and the British Caribbean. Discussions of liberated African disposal at Sierra Leone were often fraught, but were not the subject of four-way power struggles between the metropolitan and colonial governments, colonial legislatures, and planter elites. To a greater degree than any other site, Sierra Leone offers historians an opportunity to reflect upon the tension between the practical and the ideological elements of apprenticeship: its use as a system for "training" liberated African youth, and the way that this labour exploitation was framed in the language of a higher moral purpose—the "improvement" of Africa and the suppression of the slave trade.

The Policy of Apprenticeship

The institution of apprenticeship has deep roots. In metropolitan Britain, apprenticeship was a means of technical training that served the requirements of the pre-industrial labour market. Apprentices were often bound to masters for periods of seven to fourteen years. Masters, for their part, were contractually obliged to feed, clothe, house, and care for their apprentices as well as teach them a trade or craft. Such arrangements had a secondary function as a form of social insertion for pauper children.[6] Comparable practices appear in accounts of some West African regions, including Kru methods of training their youth for trade by bringing them on seasonal migrations as apprentices, Sierra Leonean Maroon yeomen's hiring of apprentices for husbandry of their cassava and other vegetable crops, the Yoruba *iwofa* system of pawnship (with an inherent obligation to protect), and a practice in the Mende and Temne hinterlands of sending children to Freetown to work as domestic servants—a system that shares some characteristics with the modern Haitian practice of child indenture known as *restavek*.[7]

From the late eighteenth century on, throughout the Atlantic world, ideas of apprenticeship and indenture were applied to the question of how to manage large-scale slave emancipation while still preserving white political, economic, and social control over the formally enslaved. Post-1833 British emancipation legislation is an obvious example. So too is Pennsylvania's abolition law of 1780, which stipulated terms of indenture that blurred and slowed the transition from enslavement to freedom, and held thousands in bondage for decades after the legislation.[8] The concept of apprenticeship was also deployed to support other projects of imperial expansion and consolidation in the British empire, blended with aggressive experiments in domestic social reform. Examples range from the indenture of Khoi and San "apprentice" children at the Cape to the "assignment" system for transported convicts in Australia and Van Diemen's land; from the mass transportation of thousands of impoverished children from the slums of Britain to "new lives" in colonial Canada, Australia, New Zealand, South Africa, and Rhodesia, to the apprenticeship of "free" Black Loyalists in Nova Scotia in the late eighteenth century.[9]

The policy of liberated African apprenticeship was, both in concept and execution, a highly gendered one. The framers of the Abolition Act's disposal clauses had primarily young, healthy adult males in mind. Yet on

many slave ships, the combined total of women and children equalled or
exceeded the number of adult men. In twelve of the eighteen years between
1808 and 1825, the liberated African women and children who disembarked
at Freetown outnumbered the adult men, often by a significant margin.[10]
Apprenticeship was, in theory, the only disposal option officially sanc-
tioned for female liberated Africans. Women and girls were not supposed
to be "employed in the labours of agriculture, but in domestic service,"
bound "only to such masters and mistresses as are of good repute for humanity," and only for a term "sufficient for their acquiring the knowledge
of their business as domestic servants" and to repay the master or mistress
for the cost of their instruction and support. Their age and strength were
to be considered when determining the length of the apprenticeship, and
note was also to be taken of pre-existing familial relationships between ship-
mates: "husband and wife, parent and child, or otherwise . . . shall in no
case be separated, except where the employment of either shall make such
separation indispensable." If a liberated African woman married a man who
enlisted, "the wife shall be permitted to live with her husband, or shall be
apprenticed or otherwise placed as near as possible to the place where her
husband is stationed." If the husband was instead apprenticed, preference
was to be given to a master who could take both wife and husband, and
also maintain their child or children. The legal provisions tied the term of
service to the idea of motherhood and female fertility: women who were
pregnant, had children, or were of child-bearing age could be bound involuntarily into "a longer term of [apprenticeship]," on the condition that their
children would be supported by the master (who could also extract bonded
labour from the children once they were past infancy). Such terms evidently
left the policy open to the widest of practical interpretations and facilitated
widespread abuse, particularly in the slave-holding islands of the British
Caribbean.[11]

For Sierra Leone, the policy of apprenticeship was supposed to bring
the dual benefit of removing the cost of maintenance of liberated Africans
from the colonial government and simultaneously providing a workforce
required to develop the colony and maximise its commercial potential for
its founding investors. In practice, as discussed in earlier chapters, the in-

sufficiency of apprenticeship and enlistment as the only disposal options became quickly apparent, and the colonial government had to adapt to integrate large numbers of arrivals into the economic life of the colony in ways that met some basic standards of humanity. After 1808, as numbers of arrivals surged and the colonial government shifted towards the creation of purpose-built villages, apprenticeship came to be regarded as a less desirable option for adult men and for women and girls of marriageable age. The latter were instead expected to marry established colonists as quickly as possible and support their husbands in creating stable, Christian nuclear families. As the gender imbalance of the colony became increasingly pronounced from the 1810s onwards, insufficient numbers of women soon became a major concern of the Liberated African Department. Officials sometimes went to some lengths to designate female children as "women of marriageable age" in order to put them forward for selection by men seeking wives.[12]

The arrangement of these nominally Christian marriages was, in theory, a policy distinct from apprenticeship. However, in practice, in the way the colonial government used these marriages to commoditise women's labour and reproductive capacity, and in the practices through which the Liberated African Department facilitated the advertising and distribution of available "wives," the marriage policy could be seen as an outgrowth of the apprenticeship policy and an effort to adapt its rationale to the demographic requirements of the colony of Sierra Leone.[13] As with apprenticeship, the department was motivated primarily by the imperative to reduce its own maintenance costs. Women and girls were conceived of essentially as labour units who would submit to the authority of their male masters/husbands in return for support. As the former village manager in the Liberated African Department, William Hamilton, told the 1842 Parliamentary Select Committee,

> It was necessary to do something with those women, and the men were admitted into the slave yard to make friends in the best way they could with the newly-landed women, and any man that thought proper to offer to take a woman for his wife,

provided he was thought a proper subject and could and would support a wife, was allowed to take and marry her. Our object was to provide for the women.

When asked if the women had any "discretion" in choosing partners for themselves, Hamilton replied, "No." It was merely "optional with her either to marry the man [who had selected her] or not, as she thought proper."[14]

Of more official concern were the women who refused all offers of marriage at the Liberated African Yard. Hamilton blamed this on "country-people" who approached the newly arrived women "when going to and returning from the bathing-place" and instructed them that if they rejected every male suitor, "the government would allow them to go and sit down with whomsoever they pleased." Hamilton saw this as a ploy on the part of the settled residents of the colony, who wanted the new women as "inmates of their huts" to provide "domestic services" such as caring for children, and fetching wood, food, and water. In return, the new women would be fed and clothed by their hosts. In Hamilton's characterization, Freetown's residents wished to host newly liberated African women because they knew that men would soon come seeking to marry them and would pay compensation to the host families "for her past maintenance and for the future inconvenience when they become deprived of her services." The going rate was, he claimed, 1s. 1d. for every month of a woman's residence with a host family. For these reasons, there was always a "swarm" and a "clamour" by "every proprietress in the district" to have "new women domiciled with them" in this way.[15]

In a significant divergence from policy and practice in the West Indies and elsewhere, by the mid-1820s, formal apprenticeship in Sierra Leone had come to apply primarily to unaccompanied liberated African children, and had come to mean something more akin to "involuntary child domestic labourer." Allen Howard's study of the census of 1831 suggests that almost all liberated African children were servants or apprentices: 93 percent of boys and over 94 percent of girls. The report of Commissioners Rowan and Wellington in 1827 found that the majority of apprentices were children under the age of fourteen, male and female, serving periods of indenture between three and nine years. Most were working as domestics in Freetown. The census of 1833 suggests that of the 20,420 liberated Africans living in the area around Freetown, 7,749 were children and 2,525 were apprentices, though these numbers must be taken with caution.[16]

All formal apprenticeships were supposed to operate on the basis of an indenture document. The wording of this contract captures the power relationships involved in the process. It was executed between government and master without reference to the apprentice, and endowed with the same legal force "as if" it had been voluntarily entered into by the latter. In exchange, each master or mistress undertook a positive legal obligation to treat the apprentice "humanely" or "with humanity," to provide for their basic needs, and to refrain from meting out excessive punishment.[17] In practice, however, throughout the period 1808–1848, apprentices were frequently handed out without indentures and with little oversight, mostly to work as domestic servants and agricultural labourers on small farms. Commissioners Rowan and Wellington found that of the 456 liberated Africans recorded to be apprenticed in the colony at the time of their survey, only thirty-six indenture documents were available for inspection. There is no evidence of any sustained process on the part of successive administrations to muster apprentices and monitor their health and well-being, nor evidence of the Vice-Admiralty Court taking a sustained, proactive role in enforcing the rights of apprentices and the obligations of indenture-holders. For most of the years of operation of the Liberated African Department, officials did not have a clear picture of how many liberated people were living under indenture contracts, their ages, or their occupations.[18]

"A Moral Millstone"

In the aftermath of the Bacchus and Harding murder trials, Jeffcott heard the first apprentice complaint at the Vice-Admiralty Court on 5 July 1831. It was the case of William, a liberated African boy apprenticed to an Englishman—a government employee named John Wade Miller, the surgeon to the Court of Mixed Commission. In reporting the "sickening details" to the governor, Jeffcott expressed "no ordinary feelings of pain and disgust."[19] Among the acts of violence described, the court heard how Miller flogged the child "over the back and loins" with a rope, and then rubbed salt in the boy's wounds. On three other occasions, he held William's head in a chamber pot full of urine, and on another occasion, he forced into the child's mouth a dirty sock covered with the secretions from Miller's infected leg ulcer. One of Miller's servants, Sybille, testified that he had seen the child whipped "many times" in the past; another stated that when he entered Miller's service three weeks previously, he had seen marks on William's body from previous floggings. The defence's argument was simply that the boy was a thief who had been punished appropriately, and that he had lied about the other forms of punishment. Chief Justice Jeffcott found in favour of William, ruling that Miller had "proved nothing to clear himself" of the charges, "but on the contrary the said William having given full proof of the truth thereof," Miller had "without just cause misused and ill treated the said apprentice . . . to the great damage and hurt of the said apprentice and against the form of the statute." Miller was ordered to pay a fine of £50 and to be imprisoned until such fine be paid. The child's indenture was cancelled and he was freed.[20]

A second case was heard on the same day—that of "'Quie,' alias Henry," who accused his master, John O'Connor, and his master's mother, Judith, of severe physical abuse. Like the case of William, the crux of Quie's case appears to have been the extreme violence and the torture-like nature of the beatings, rather than the fact of being flogged, which was considered an acceptable disciplinary measure by an appropriate authority. Under questioning, the young boy explained that he ran away from his master's house after being beaten with "a stick and a piece of line." Upon being apprehended by a neighbour, he was returned against his will to the home of his master's mother, where she bound him into a foetal position, passing "a stick . . . through inside the elbows and under the Knees after which his wrists, and legs above the ancles [sic] were tied." She and her son then carried him into the yard, where O'Connor flogged him "with the handle of a Country Hoe over the head and sides" while Judith used a piece of rope. The child was then taken indoors, where the O'Connors tied his wrists together and hung him from a door for a time, before putting him back out in

the yard and leaving him there, tied to a tree for the night. He described
how he untied himself gradually using his teeth, and then crawled away to
hide under the piazza of a neighbour's house, where he remained for two
days before he was noticed.[21]

William Fergusson, the West Indian doctor who would in later years
become governor of the colony, stated that, at the governor's request, he
had gone "to examine a Boy reported as almost flogged to death."[22] He
found the child almost unable to open his eyes, and covered in bruises "of
so severe a nature that he considered [his] life in very great danger." Several days later, and with the dirt cleaned from his body, Fergusson examined Quie again, and found his injuries even worse than he had previously
thought. He observed marks of ropes round the wrists, "double marks, as
if the rope had been passed round the wrists twice." Fergusson dismissed
the defence's argument that the boy's injuries had come about through an
accidental fall. "No falling on hoops, slates or sticks could have done the
injury to the eyes," nor could he "conceive that a Boy falling from a height
of 12 Feet could have marks of Cords." Rather, "such a stick as that produced [as evidence before the court] might have killed the Boy." He professed that for the first few days, he had had "serious doubts" of the child's
surviving.

Similar to John Wade Miller's defence in William's case, the
O'Connors claimed that they had flogged Quie because he was a thief.
Their neighbour, Thomas Craig, contradicted this assertion, but Thomas
Cole, assistant superintendent of the Liberated African Department,
stated that he believed it to be true. The boy had been brought in to the
department for punishment on two occasions: "once for running away and
the second time for stealing a Bottle and some eggs. He was flogged slightly
both times." He also stated that Quie had previously been accused of stealing pork from the barracks, and that on that occasion, O'Connor was
fined "for his neglect in allowing his Apprentice to go about the Town as
he liked." The O'Connors produced a character witness to back up their
denial, Dr Stormouth from the Liberated African Hospital, under whose
management Judith O'Connor had previously worked as a nurse. The court
was told that the colonial doctor considered Judith O'Connor incapable

of acts of cruelty, that she was "one of the most humane Women in the Colony." Stormouth claimed to have "seen her check her Children when [they were] about to exercise acts of cruelty towards her Servants," and he stated that "she was highly esteemed by the late [governor] Sir Charles McCarthy."[23] Nevertheless, Jeffcott found in favour of the child. He ordered that John O'Connor pay a fine of ten pounds and be imprisoned until the fine was paid. Judith O'Connor was fined half that amount. Quie's indenture was cancelled and he was freed.

The sorts of violent, abusive acts of degradation described above appear repeatedly in the writings of colonial administrators, European travellers, missionaries, and metropolitan critics of the colony of Sierra Leone. As early as 1808, Governor Thompson reported to the Colonial Secretary Lord Castlereagh the case of an eight-year-old girl who bore burn marks on her back and other evidence of abuse by her European master who, when challenged, claimed that he had "a right to do as he pleases with his own" and insisted that the girl belonged to him because he had paid money to "redeem" her.[24] *The African Herald* reported in July 1809 that a Nova Scotian woman, Susannah Caulker "did beat and evil entreat" and perpetrate "other enormous things" upon her twelve-year-old apprentice girl, including a sexual assault using a mixture of salt and pepper intended to increase the child's suffering.[25] In another case, reported in 1834, it was found that an apprentice girl had lost an eye through the physical violence of her master.[26] The surviving letterbooks of the Liberated African Department in the Public Archives of Sierra Leone contain regular, scattered references to many other such incidents that came to the attention of the administration. For example, Assistant Superintendent Thomas Cole wrote to Johnson, manager of Regent, in July 1828 that a young girl who had been apprenticed to Susan Taylor in Freetown had recently been removed from her charge due to ill treatment and was being relocated to Regent.[27] The same manager, Johnson, had been summoned to the departmental headquarters in Freetown several months earlier to explain "by whose authority" a young boy named Randolph had been put in irons. He had been found that morning "wandering about the town naked with a large shackle round his neck, and about 20 lb. weight of chain locked so tightly round his waist as to excoriate his Flesh."[28]

There is evidence that neglect and violent mistreatment of indentured liberated Africans was not confined to child victims, or to the behaviour of private inhabitants of the colony. By the mid-1820s, some groups of newly arrived liberated African adults were sent to the Ordnance Department to labour on the public works for period of several months. In 1826, Commissioners Rowan and Wellington found that supervisors had "in some instances . . . inexcusably" been "persons likely to abuse" their power, and Acting Governor Kenneth Macaulay's draft reforms of the public works in 1826 included the stipulation that "the carrying of whips as now practiced by their overseers without any authority must be discontinued."[29] Nevertheless, in their investigation into the colony in 1826, the commissioners claimed that "no instances [had] come within [their] knowledge" of apprentice children "having suffered from the neglect of [the] precaution" of a complete and binding indenture document, but advised that "the omission le[ft] an opening to abuse." They recommended a broad expansion of the practice of apprenticing liberated African adults. The commissioners had particular confidence that apprenticeships on the public works offered the chance for adults to repay the "debt" owed to their benefactors:

> For some time after the [adult] negroes are brought into the colony, they are so utterly ignorant and helpless that it is absolutely necessary, with a view to their own welfare, to treat them in some measure as children. If, during this period, their services can be made available in useful public works, it seems but just that they should in this way be made to repay a part of the expense incurred for their support.

They stressed the fact that it would be "exclusively with a view to the advantage of the negroes," the "most effectual means of attaining the end" of African "improvement."[30]

The colonial secretary, Lord Bathurst, disagreed. He expressed his view that the practice of apprenticeship had already evolved into an interminable state of "forced servitude as long as the Governor or Superintendent pleases," calculated to breed frustration and discontent, and a sense amongst the apprentices and the population generally that "the Captured

Negroes are not free, and independent . . . as the other colonists are."[31] The following year, when Dixon Denham joined the colonial administration as chief superintendent of the Liberated African Department, he called the conditions of child apprenticeship that he had personally witnessed "a servitude not a jot better than slavery itself," and he regarded the commissioners' recommendation to extend the programme of adult indentured labour as completely out of touch with the lessons of experience and current abolitionist thinking. "The giving out [of] grown men under indentures for a longer period than three years must, I should imagine, strike anyone as an evident hardship: it was tried at Tortola and Antigua and constantly failed of giving satisfaction to either party."[32] The previous year, Governor Sir Neil Campbell had closed the liberated African schools and ordered all liberated African children to be distributed as apprentices. Denham deplored this decision, and although he succeeded in having this partially reversed, he reflected on the widespread "demoralization which had taken place amongst the younger branches of the Liberated Africans" in the intervening time.[33] It had proved difficult to locate all the children who had been apprenticed and to enforce on their new masters an obligation to send them to school. Many of the elder girls, he noted, had left their adopted parents "from ill treatment or neglect" and were "now living in a state of prostitution in Freetown, generally with the soldiers."[34] In 1827, Denham entered into an agreement with the commodore of the West Africa Station to begin apprenticing groups of between four and twelve boys on board each of the naval ships, with strict instructions that they were to learn the trades of the sailmaker, ropemaker, blacksmith, shoemaker, and that of the ship's carpenter and boat builder. The regulations were very specific: that the boys were so placed in order to become "a most useful class of mechanics," and not to carry out drudge work.[35]

Almost a decade later, Governor Henry Dundas Campbell wrote to Lord Glenelg at the Colonial Office, complaining that the apprenticeship system was "nothing more than Slavery of the worst description. Any person who wanted an apprentice had one by paying 10s. In many cases, the parties receiving the unfortunate children had been but a short time in the Colony themselves."[36] He observed that, "strange as it may appear to your lordship," the inhabitants of Freetown who had once been held in slavery themselves were by no means guided by abolitionist feelings. Campbell believed that the colonists looked upon the apprentice children "in no other light than as Slaves. If you ask one of them, where did you obtain that Apprentice, the answer invariably is, I buy him in King [*sic*] Yard."[37] As soon as newly liberated Africans were located on their plot of land, Campbell claimed, "it is their first object to procure an apprentice who is obliged to do all the hard work or druggery [*sic*] for his Master; the girls are brought up much in the same way, those in Freetown too generally to prostitution, their Mistresses living by their infamy."[38] Campbell emphasised the growing social gulf between young people in the colony, since apprentice children were "obliged to do all the menial work" while "the Colony born children . . . being brought up at home in idleness" looked "with the most sovereign contempt on the poor Apprentices." It would, he claimed, "make your heart bleed to see the ill treatment some of these poor creatures receive[d]" and the department could do little to affect this; "after the child was gone" from the King's Yard, he said, "you lost sight of it."[39]

Campbell's comments hold the Liberated African Department—and by extension the colonial government—responsible not only for individual experiences and outcomes of apprenticeship, but for longer-term social stratification and its corrosive effects. These anxieties were echoed six years later by Dr William Fergusson, then governor of the colony. The continuing "importation" of liberated Africans and distribution of apprentices within Sierra Leone was, he argued, "a moral millstone round the necks of its people. By placing easily within their reach the means of obtaining gratuitous labour, idleness is engendered . . . as, at length, to become an inveterate habit." As a result, many of the free-born children of the colony were reaching adulthood "not only unaccustomed to labour, but disinclined to it, and actually incapable of working."[40] The history of Sierra Leone published in the 1870s by A. B. C. Sibthorpe—one of the earliest historians of Sierra Leone, who was likely the son of liberated African parents—says remarkably little on the subject of apprenticeship, but he does echo Campbell's and Fergusson's criticisms, saying that treating the apprentices as a servile underclass was the "beginning of ruin" of the Nova Scotians.[41] It does not appear that any Nova Scotian or Maroon masters or mistresses left detailed recollections of their experiences that might provide an alternative perspective.

Travel Writers' and Missionaries' Reports

The immediate consequence of Jeffcott's investigations in 1831 was that apprentice children began to come forward in increasing numbers to lodge official complaints. In May 1833, Governor Findlay reported to the secretary of state that "scarcely a day passes but there occurs from twenty to thirty complaints." The administration was overwhelmed, but Findlay suspected that most of these "ungovernable . . . apprentices" were lying in order to gain their freedom: selling the clothing their masters had given them and then claiming they had been deprived of clothing.[42] Most British commentators did not support Findlay's dismissive opinion. In 1816, *The British Critic* reported that apprenticeship "as it is termed" was "in reality, a state very little removed from actual slavery." Comparing "the condition of an apprentice in England and Sierra Leone," the publication found that "no two conditions can be more opposite."[43] Twenty years later, F. Harrison Rankin, author of the widely read travel narrative *The White Man's Grave,* echoed this evaluation. "Any resident in the colony," he claimed, "of any colour, may enter the King's Yard, select a boy or girl, and thereupon tie a string or piece of tape round the neck as a mark of appropriation. He then pays ten shillings; and the passive child becomes his property, under the name of apprentice, for three years. So little discrimination is exercised with respect to the purchaser, that *domestic* servants are in the habit of buying them, and of employing them in the heavier drudgery of house-work."[44] "The whites call the child so purchased from the King's Yard an apprentice," claimed Rankin, "the blacks uniformly term it a *slave.*" Rankin, who for a time served as clerk and village manager in the Liberated African Department, criticised the system that "outraged humanity" by tolerating the "prolonged tortures" inflicted on apprentices by their "daadies and maamies, as they are called." The children were, he claimed, exposed to "the caprice" of purchasers who felt "no interest in them beyond the profit of their labours, or the price of their persons, if an opportunity occurs of selling them," and he remarked upon the vulnerability of child apprentices living in a colony visited frequently by the slave dealers of the surrounding territories. So long as a master could hold a child "without at any time being called upon to account for the child, or ever to produce him," claimed Rankin, so long would "many be induced to transfer their young wards for five pounds each to the Mandingo [slave] merchant." He claimed that he could not "conceive a system better adapted to favour the slave-trade than that of apprenticeship at Sierra Leone."[45]

Two other contemporary writers, both English women of elevated social status, professed a more mixed view of apprenticeship. Like Rankin, they were writing for metropolitan British audiences. "Mary Church"—believed to be Catherine Temple, daughter of Lieutenant-Governor Octavius Temple—claimed that apprentice children were in high demand because "the Liberated Africans seem to think a servant almost necessary. I suppose this habit arises from slavery being so prevalent even amongst themselves, in their native country."[46] Church remarked that "these poor children" required all the "vigilant care and protection from the Government which is afforded them," although she later implied that such protection was indeed provided. Of "the only apprentice I have personally known," she wrote, "I was much pleased with her attachment to her mistress," a liberated African woman. "She [the apprentice girl] told me that, "her mammy was good too much," and that when her apprenticeship was over she should like to live with her. Church also mentioned witnessing "the marriage of an apprentice from her master's house" during a visit to Wellington village in 1833 or 1834, which she implies was a happy event.[47]

In the writings of another resident, Elizabeth Melville, wife of Michael Melville, the King's Advocate and Registrar of the Vice-Admiralty Court, later acting lieutenant-governor of the colony, there is an even stronger distinction between the positive personal anecdotal and the more negative general account of apprenticeship. From 1841, Melville held a succession of liberated African apprentices as domestic servants, yet she disapproved of children being sent to live with the black inhabitants of the colony. Her criticisms rested on three grounds: that apprenticeship "to the rudest and most ignorant of their country people" deprived the children of the opportunity to absorb "European" habits of "civilised life"; that free domestic labour was stunting the industry of the colony-born children, and that the apprenticed children were exposed to being abused as domestic slaves.[48] This latter point is a recurring theme in the accounts of the travel writers: suspicion that the colony's settled black population sought only to enslave apprentices, either in their own homes or through reselling them to "the Mandingo merchant," and that the priority of government ought to be to place a civilising check on such ugly inclinations.[49] By comparison, Melville claimed to teach her apprentices reading, writing, and needlework, and couched her role as apprentice mistress in terms of a broader imperialist narrative of African "improvement." She claimed that her apprentice girl, Fanyah, had been distraught on hearing of her mistress's intention to leave the colony, and claimed that the girl had been indignant at being sent to work "for black woman."[50]

Missionary observers echoed the travel writers' observations in different ways. Thomas Coke, the founder of Methodist missions, wrote that in 1811 "there [was] scarcely a family throughout the settlement, however poor, that [had] not one of these apprentices, and some [had] as many as twenty." His commentary focused not on the actions of the apprentice-masters, but on the supposed ingratitude of their charges. Instead of "acknowledging the obligation" to the British government and the colony's people for freeing them from the "horrid grasp of their tyrants . . . , some liberated Africans murmur[ed] at their condition, and [thought] themselves treated with cruelty."[51] On the other hand, the CMS missionary Samuel Abraham Walker reflected in 1847 on the great concern long felt by the missionaries for the apprentices: first, because of the "notorious" inability of "the greater number" of their masters and mistresses to fulfil their contractual duties in relation to education; second, because of the physical vulnerability of the apprentice children, particularly the girls. Walker quotes another missionary, Mr Young, who reported in June 1833 "the painful necessity" of expelling five persons from church communion, including one woman "for most cruelly treating her apprentice girl, seventeen years of age, with intent to force her to become the concubine of her own master," and a second woman for a similar offence against another apprentice girl. The victim of the former, having endured "a most cruel beating till her body was even cut with the blows as well as with the cords by which she was bound," escaped and was placed under the protection of a constable. Her case, once publicly known, prompted other apprentice girls to come forward, supposedly having not known until then that "they [were] protected." Young reported that he had of late undertaken to act on behalf of these individuals, for the masters and mistresses had up to then "had much of their own way in such deplorable acts." "It is to be feared," he continued, "that many of those poor apprentice girls fall a sacrifice to the lusts of those who ought to protect them," and whose fall into vice and sin was not by choice, but "through bodily fear."[52]

Hannah Kilham—the Quaker missionary and founder of the Charlotte school—attributed her decision to open her school to the knowledge "that grievous neglect and abuses exist with regard to the apprenticing system." "My heart was pained," she reported, "at the thought that the girls . . . might have no resource, but to be put out as apprentices." It was true, she said, that there were "some persons who conscientiously [took] care of their apprentices." Yet the Liberated African Department did not ensure this, or protect children against arbitrary acts of violence or abuse. Kilham regarded "this branch of the colonial government" as operating a system that was dangerously close to "a perfect slave trade." The department granted too many masters and mistresses a number of apprentices above what they were able to support, and then failed to enforce the terms of the indenture documents. She also believed that an unknown number of apprentices were "the helpless victims" of physical and sexual abuse, or of re-enslavement. "The system here leaves these poor children wofully [*sic*] in the power of persons who *imagine* [their] power to be almost without limit or control." She related how she once sent her messenger into a neighbouring yard to enquire why a child in there cried out so violently. The messenger found the boy "imprisoned . . . and neglected as to food," and he told the messenger "that he was left there shut up and hungry, and wanted to kill himself."[53]

So widespread was this type of neglect, and "so great" were the abuses perpetrated against apprentices, claimed Kilham, that Thomas MacFoy— one of the Liberated African Department's village managers—would not, in his village, allow an apprentice to be buried without an inquest and would not accept the usual explanations from masters and mistresses, such as "he went away and died in the bush."[54] "In many, many cases," she said, the victims of this "hard bondage" were never "fully heard or attended to." For those who did make their voices heard, she said, "there [was] often great difficulty [in acting upon the complaints] from what [was] called insuffi- ciency of evidence." Kilham's suggested remedy was simple: "an obligation laid on the masters to have the children instructed in the schools, and thus they would be kept in view." "Some account should be kept of all who are apprenticed, and there should be stated reviews of them by government au- thority." Furthermore, the governor ought to "from the apprentice fees, (which I understand are considerable) make little presents to the girls and boys who have behaved well in their places for one year," as "a stimulus to good conduct both on the part of masters and apprentices" and also to "sweeten the toils of the poor children," who likely received little else for themselves above their bare subsistence needs. Kilham's frustration at the social marginality of the substantial apprentice population is striking. "If there are in this colony four thousand five hundred apprentices," she wrote, "surely their welfare and improvement is an object of importance."[55]

An important underlying theme in British writers' critiques of ap- prenticeship is the racially hierarchical representation of "civilisation," in which white members of colonial society were presented as embodying (or being expected to embody) the highest stratum of imperial "progress." Sev- eral writers clearly construct black apprentice-holders as behaving like slave masters, in contrast to the "improving" experience of apprenticeship to a white family.[56] Excessive cruelty is also presented in explicitly racialised terms: Assistant Superintendent Cole, in his testimony before Chief Jus- tice Jeffcott in July 1831, remarked that the apprentice boy William's case against John Wade Miller was not the first in which he had heard of a mas- ter using an irritant substance to exacerbate the pain inflicted. He had previously heard on several occasions of "the Black People rubbing pepper over their apprentices' backs after flogging them," although until the Miller case he claimed he had never heard of Europeans doing so.[57] Indeed this action of rubbing cayenne pepper in the eyes, genitalia, or open wounds of a victim has appeared in other contexts, portrayed as a traditional "African" method of identifying and punishing suspected witches.[58] It was also infamous as a punishment by slave owners in the West Indies slave plantations.[59]

Another theme in British reports is an emphasis on the premature sexualisation, sexual exploitation and abuse of young female apprentices, and fears that some were subjected to extreme, even sadistic, sexually violent punishments.[60] Coerced prostitution is mentioned frequently. For example, in 1836, Lieutenant-Governor Campbell reported to Glenelg the prevalence of mistresses prostituting out their female apprentices.[61] As Barbara Bush, Ann Laura Stoler, and others have noted, an emphasis on female vulnerability to the supposedly natural brutality of non-white men was a representative trope frequently repeated in the writings of contemporary Europeans at the periphery of empire.[62] One of the earliest published critics of liberated African policy, the judge Robert Thorpe, argued that the colonial government of Sierra Leone had a duty to protect women from such brutality. Responding to an African Institution pamphlet that claimed "some of the [liberated African] females" engaged in immoral conduct—a lapse that its authors claimed would "not surprise any one at all conversant with human nature, and especially as it exists in Africa"—Thorpe launched a blistering attack on the government's active exploitation of vulnerable women and girls. He rejected the assertion that these women had been engaging voluntarily in sexual activity, arguing that "chastity is as carefully preserved in Africa as in Europe," and was "scrupulously attended to" by African women. The women, he argued, had been "debauched where they ought to have been protected, culpably neglected where they ought to have been instructed, and, on their first landing in the Colony, thrown in to a Barrack where there was a promiscuous intercourse between the sexes day and night!!" Thorpe also suggested that both the governor and the chief superintendent of liberated Africans had been in the habit of forcing liberated African girls into sexual relationships with them.[63]

Underlying these representations lay a long-running anxiety triggered by the unusual gender imbalance in the city of Freetown and its surrounding villages. Observers recognised that women were always in strong demand: some village managers even sent an escort down to the Liberated African Department to collect newly arrived women, lest they be "carried off" on the way to their new homes.[64] European writers expressed on the one hand a paternalistic desire to protect women and girls from being pounced upon, while on the other hand they expressed fear and disgust with regard to overt female sexuality and the exercise of female agency unrestrained by male influence. The need to keep the sexes in virtuous seclusion until Christian marriage was constantly reasserted. For critics and supporters of the colony alike, the ability of the colonial government and missionary organisations to enforce and normalise Christian marriage rites was considered a significant indicator of the success or failure of liberated African policy and of the European civilising mission generally.[65]

Liberated African Perspectives

Although most European observers in Sierra Leone expressed overwhelmingly negative views of the experiences of liberated African apprentices, some documented relatively positive accounts. In the mid-1820s, Commissioners Rowan and Wellington interviewed "those residents who had most improved their condition": a group of thirty-five liberated Africans. Many of the men were disbanded soldiers supported by pensions, but several of the others had risen to prosperity after starting out as apprentices in the colony.[66] The accounts of these men suggested that many of their masters had fulfilled the contractual obligations of the indenture, and that at the termination of their contracts, the government had provided some former apprentices with parcels of land for their own cultivation. One example is Richard Garrett of Freetown, who was bound as an apprentice to a mason called Robert Garrett from 1815 to 1821, and reported that he was fed and clothed by his master during this time. At the expiration of his apprenticeship, "he worked at his trade on his own account," and built himself a house with a stone cellar "on a lot of land given him by the King."[67] Similarly, Thomas Brown of Freetown was bound apprentice to a mason (also called Thomas Brown) for three years, from whom he learned his trade and, like Garrett, presumably gained his "family" name. He was then granted a lot of land in Liverpool Street, where he built a house and lived with his wife and three children. He had recently also established a public house.[68]

Several of the men interviewed had been apprenticed to the government rather than to private individuals. Sendawa of Kissy, for example, laboured on the public works for three years and now had his own cassava and rice farm, the surplus of which he sold to his country people in the village and supplied to the Liberated African Department. Samuel Williams of Freetown was apprenticed to the Engineer Department for nine years, the first two of which he spent as a servant in the house of the master mason, and the other seven of which he spent learning the trade of masonry, in which he was now employed on a contractual basis to both government and private individuals. He had received a town lot from the government seven years previously and had built his own house on it.[69] Several of the deponents by then held apprentices of their own. Malicow, a sawyer from Hastings village, had an apprentice boy who had of late become his business partner and "shares his profit."[70] George Sawyer of Wellington village, had two "country lads" whom he had been feeding since 1824 and would "continue to do so until May when he will assist in building their own houses." John Taylor of Kissy had one apprentice boy who worked with him on his three small farms.[71] All of the above sources relate to male apprentices. E. Francis White describes a rare documented example of a liberated African woman who rose from apprenticeship status to prominence: Elizabeth Coles, who was apprenticed to the Carrol family of Waterloo as a child. At the termination of her apprenticeship, Coles became housekeeper to Syble Boyle, a leading Aku merchant. With Boyle's support, she entered into a partnership with Cornelius Crowther, another wealthy merchant, and became provisioner to the garrison and to naval ships. Eventually she bought the Carrol farm where she had served as an apprentice.[72]

While caution is advised against reading too much into brief mediated narratives and depositions—Commissioners Rowan and Wellington were, after all, seeking out men to be the success stories of their report—nevertheless, taken together, these more positive examples offer at least

some counterpoint to the idea that all liberated Africans apprenticed in
Sierra Leone experienced lifelong mistreatment or exploitation as second-
class citizens. Recent work by the Studies in the History of the African
Diaspora—Documents (SHADD) project, led by Paul Lovejoy and Richard Anderson at the Harriet Tubman Institute for Research on Africa and
Its Diasporas at York University, has done much to enrich our picture of
liberated Africans' experiences of life in Sierra Leone. Probing the records
of the Church Missionary Society and Methodist Missionary Society at
Sierra Leone, Anderson and Lovejoy's team has uncovered a remarkable
number of life histories of formerly enslaved people, both firsthand accounts
written by liberated Africans themselves and accounts dictated to missionaries at various times throughout the nineteenth century. The SHADD
collection includes the largest number of firsthand accounts of enslavement anywhere in the Black Atlantic.[73] From such sources we can glean
fragments of personal experiences from the perspectives of the apprentices
themselves.

One example is that of Matthew Thomas Harding, a liberated African and "native catechist" with the Church Missionary Society. Harding
described how he was on board a slave ship captured by the Royal Navy
and "brought to Sierra Leone by the providence of God . . . at governor
Maxwell's time [between 1811 and 1814]. I was then apprenticed to a widow,
her name's Nancy Smith who I live a month, after the end of the month, I
was taken fever which carry me two month in bed by the mercy of God I
was recover six month after my recovery she was enticed by her country
man to go with him up to the country." There, Nancy sold Harding into
re-enslavement, where he was trapped for six years until he was redeemed
by "a man which was sent [from Sierra Leone] by my Ms. to find me" and
brought him back to the colony. After that, Harding was formally removed
from Nancy Smith and apprenticed to "Thos. Harding," from whom he
presumably acquired his new name, and stayed with him

for some times: at the end I was part from him, I went to the
Manager that if he should please to recommend to the Governor, to take me up to one of his village; I was then brought up

under the care of Rev. Henry Düring at Lester because there
was no house at Gloucester; only one hut in which I and some
men was to prepare a place for him; after he came he begin to
teach us how to pray, after some years I was then baptized by
Mr. Johnson at Regent in the year of our Lord 1818.[74]

Another liberated African boy, "Kealoo," liberated from the Cuban slave
ship *Veloz Pasajera*, in October 1830, gives the following account of his disposal: "We met Governor Findlay in the colony and there is no more
school in the colony for the King's boys [liberated African children] so they
bound us out as apprentices unto our country men, and other nations, but
they are the inhabitants of Sierra Leone, both boys and girls were bound
out some for seven years and some for five and they set the big men and
women at liberty." Kealoo was apprenticed for seven years to a prominent
and successful Yoruba trader known as Thomas Will, from whom he gained
a new name: "James Will." During his time in the household of Thomas
Will and his wife Nancy, James lived alongside a number of other apprentice children. He gained literacy and by the mid-1840s had established himself as a shopkeeper and Methodist preacher. He travelled to England in
1848, where he appeared before Hutt's parliamentary select committee on
the slave trade.[75]

Harding's and Kealoo's experiences stand in marked contrast to each
other: two unaccompanied children given over to the care of colonial residents, one who was sold as a slave and the other who gained a very successful livelihood, and possibly a close family network. Such narratives
offer at least a suggestive outline of the variety of possible post-liberation
trajectories for individual liberated Africans resettled in Sierra Leone, and
show the importance of the attitude and behaviour of the apprentice-holder
in establishing a foundation for the future lives of these children. Still, we
can only speculate about the real nature of the relationships forged within
these households. Most narratives offer very little information about the ordinary and the domestic, and many accounts that mention an apprentice-
holder do so very briefly, as with Harding's account of being sent "to Thos.
Harding to be with him for some times: at the end I was part from him," or

the account of another liberated African man, Peter Wilson, whose wife recalled that "He was then about 13 years of age at the period of his arrival
[in Freetown]" and he "completed the accustomed years of Apprenticeship,
under the care of a Liberated African of his Tribe or nation."[76]

It is tempting to mine these short statements for meaning: Is there a
note of loss in Harding's report of being parted from Thomas? Is there a
hint in Wilson's account that he was truly cared for and nurtured in the
home of his country people? Might we read something into the pattern of
apprentices retaining the family name of the people to whom they were indentured, when certainly not all former apprentices did this? It could be
read as an indication of affection, or perhaps it served a more pragmatic purpose, associating the former apprentice with their host family for reasons
of prestige or social integration. Perhaps it simply reflects the absence of a
more appealing alternative. Either way, apprenticeship evidently entailed
an important connection that could outlast the period of indenture. Another liberated African, the Reverend Joseph Boston May, was apprenticed as a child to an African family, but when he was subsequently adopted
by a white missionary couple, the Bostons, it was their name he retained.
In later life, he recalled the Bostons with fondness, although it is clear from
the account of his life written by his son that the relationship, affectionate
as it was, was one based on the performance of grateful servility and of charity and indebtedness, rather than unconditional familial love. In contrast
to the detailed and warm account he gave of this white family, Joseph Boston May (much like Peter Wilson) gave no details about his former apprentice life with the African family.[77]

The Limits of the Liberated African Department

A critical assessment of how the Liberated African Department managed the long-running policy of apprenticeship and its multiplicity of possible individual outcomes is important when considering the social
stratification of Sierra Leonean society and the emergence of the Krio community. In John Peterson's oft-cited *Province of Freedom*, the author's
stated priority is to rewrite the traditionally paternalistic, imperialistic nar-

rative of Sierra Leone, and attribute to the recaptive population their own primacy in the creation of a new "province of freedom" and a pathway to cultural, economic, and political pre-eminence. To this end, Peterson argues that lax Liberated African Department monitoring and ineffectual intervention—effectively, an "administrative void"—created the opportunity for the liberated African population as a whole to lead a more or less autonomous existence.[78] Yet a consideration of the experiences of the apprentices, adults and children alike, demonstrates that apprenticeship was a policy with a multiplicity of outcomes, of which the "empowered" new Krio elite was by no means the only one. The intense personal isolation evident in the testimonies of William and Quie, as documented by Jeffcott, stands in sharp relief against the picture of societal empowerment presented by *Province of Freedom*. Quie, in particular, was not protected by his neighbours. Instead he was beaten and returned forcibly to the home of Judith O'Connor. After the final beating, he did not run to friends who could shelter him. Instead, he crawled under a piazza and hid there alone for two days until he was discovered. The neighbourhoods in which these boys lived were not environments of sterile seclusion, yet it is evident from both cases that an apprentice child might have no one to turn to and no immediate means of escaping abusive treatment.

Perceptions of the prevalence of apprentice abuse were certainly influenced by the fevered anxieties of some white colonists and colonial officials, who were unable to reconcile the desire to be free of a duty of care towards liberated people with their heightened fear of what happened in the private homes of black families outside of white surveillance and "civilising" intervention. Yet there are too many specific incidents with corroborating evidence across a wide variety of sources to believe that the problem was wholly imagined by that community. To echo a point made by Padraic Scanlan, there is no reason to suppose that apprentice-holders in Sierra Leone would be any different to "nearly all people given near-absolute power over others," and that some of this cohort—like apprentice-masters in England, North America, and elsewhere where similar practices existed—"could develop a taste for sadistic violence towards their apprentices."[79]

The writings of contemporaries often lay blame on the Liberated African Department, suggesting this branch of government was either incompetent or indifferent to its duty to police the regulations surrounding apprenticeship, and that its negligence and absence of compassion had a profoundly isolating impact on apprentices. Hannah Kilham reported the story of Ninga, one of her schoolgirls, whose elder sister she knew to be in the colony but because she had "probably [been] put out as an apprentice," there was no way of finding her.[80] Elizabeth Melville related a conversation with an elderly Settler nurse, who advised her that it was no use hiring a colony-born person as a domestic servant, for they had "no love for work, all lazy too much; but King-yard child good for work." In the nurse's opinion, recently liberated children were a much better investment because, without anyone else to take care of them, they were "apt to get attached to the family to whom they were apprenticed" and "become faithful and willing servants."[81] From Chief Justice Jeffcott's transcript of William's case in 1831, it is clear that the boy initially approached the Liberated African Department complaining of ill treatment, but Assistant Superintendent Cole's response was to send him home and inform his master of the complaint.

By contrast with the apparently rare role of presenting apprentices' cases to the courts, the department had a regular role in punishing apprentices, often at the request of their masters and mistresses. Both the testimonies of Cole and the overseer, Oyoo, indicate that whipping of apprentice children took place at the Liberated African Department as a matter of standard discipline. Oyoo produced for the court "the Cat which he uses on such occasion," and explained that "to such a Boy as William he would only give a dozen lashes with 3 or 4 tails of the Cat. The flogging [was] inflicted lightly, he never cut children 'too much.'" Thomas Cole also testified in the Quie case that "in every instance where Liberated African Apprentices are brought up for trifling delinquencies he has had them flogged" but that "as they are numerous he does not keep a record of them."[82] Thus, the department played a dual role in the isolation of apprentices: passively, in apparently never implementing an effective system of checks nor fully investigating allegations of abuse, and more actively in positioning the apprentice-holder in clear priority over the apprentice. Both William's and Quie's testimonies make it clear that the boys each knew the acts perpetrated against them to be abnormally cruel and that they knew to whom they could be reported, yet as Cole's behaviour in William's case demonstrates, the departmental superintendent did not always act to investigate allegations fully. By contrast, the testimonies of both Cole and Oyoo make clear the regularity with which children were brought to the department to be whipped for minor offences.

Governor Fergusson was instructed by the Colonial Office in the mid-1840s to end all Liberated African Department involvement with, and welfare assistance to, new arrivals over the age of twelve who declined to emigrate to the West Indies. He refused to do so, arguing that this was essentially abandoning the young people to kidnapping and prostitution, and that apprenticeship was at least better than that.[83] The metropolitan government consented to the continuation, though unwillingly. Apprenticeship to private individuals was abolished finally by decree on 15 April 1848 at the behest of Acting Governor Pine, whose explanatory despatch to Grey repeated all of the old criticisms of the system and added one more: that "this pernicious system" also had the effect of providing "a large portion of the resident population" with "a direct interest in opposing [liberated African] Emigration" to the British West Indies. The decision was approved in London. It is not clear whether indentures still being served were affected by the decree: the precise wording was that the governor "deem[ed] it his duty to abstain *in future*" from supplying apprentice labour to the colony at large. It would also appear that the decree did not mean that the indentured labour of newly arrived liberated Africans to Europeans and affluent black colonists ceased. Pine explained that he would "place . . . with the missionaries, and other persons of respectability" "such of [the liberated African children] as refuse[d] to emigrate," and that these apprentices would receive "proper instruction" and "a fair amount of wages." "They [would] be distinctly told, that they [were] free to remain with, or leave their employers."[84] Employment of boys as apprentices on naval ships also continued into the 1850s and beyond. Nevertheless, the decree marked the official end of a policy that had, for thousands of recently arrived children and adults, had a profound effect upon their initial experiences of the colony of Sierra Leone.

To suggest, as John Peterson does, that the liberated Africans of Sierra Leone all enjoyed the same shared "province of freedom" is to homogenise the experience of liberated people, ignoring the social hierarchy that built up within this particular colonial context, and perpetuating a crude binary conception of power relations within the colony by reducing the complexity of that picture to a basic empire-subaltern relationship. Such a delineation between the role of the white colonial government and the black civilian population's role in resettling and integrating liberated Africans suggests that the strength or weakness of the colonial government to impose its agenda is the only gauge by which individual experiences of freedom and liberation should be measured.

Yet the power relationship within the apprenticeship system was not, for the majority of indentures, one of British colonial authority to recaptive individual. Rather, the colonial government facilitated the master-apprentice relationship for private individuals via the Liberated African Department, but did not monitor it in any meaningful way. Apprenticeship experiences and outcomes in Sierra Leone were highly uneven because the relationships created by the indenture contracts produced dramatically different kinds of social capital and hierarchies of belonging. This was an important factor in the extreme social hierarchy that developed within Freetown society.[85] Established families—those with sufficient resources to obtain an apprentice—were part of Peterson's "province of freedom"; the friendless apprentice's opportunity to exercise agency in his or her "liberation" was rather more equivocal. The indenture contracts reflect this difference: it was only ever "as if" the apprentice had entered into the contract voluntarily. Across forty years of practice, of paper reforms and real efforts alike, this essential power relationship remained constant for the thousands of liberated Africans who passed through the King's Yard and into the private homes of Sierra Leone's residents.

The final decision to stop apprenticing liberated African children in Sierra Leone was not taken because of four decades of British hand-wringing and moral condemnation, but out of an imperative to promote labour emigra-

tion to the West Indies and to address the moral "decay" of the settled colonial population at Sierra Leone.[86] When Governor Fergusson described
apprenticeship in 1842 as "a moral millstone," he meant that the practice
had cursed the colony with "idleness" such that the established population was forgetting how to provide for itself.[87] The choice of the word "millstone" is interesting. It implies a dragging effect, a sinking effect, a
prevention of "progress." It is to this decay or prevention of work ethic that
the word "moral" refers—not to the duty of care towards apprentice
children, or the supposedly endemic abuse to which Fergusson had himself borne witness in the case of Quie in July 1831.

Over a forty-year period, Britain's apprenticeship policy was a focal
point for the articulation of various anxieties about the rights and responsibilities of the intervening state in controlling and instrumentalising those
it had recaptured from the transatlantic slave trade. Documented instances
of abuse and neglect provoked outraged expressions of humanitarian concern and duty towards "the poor Apprentices."[88] Indeed, discourses of concern for apprentice welfare—particularly child welfare—had suffused
discussions about the liberated African disposal system almost from its inception. And yet the apprenticeship system was sustained for over forty
years without any meaningful improvement in its protective measures. The
justification was always that apprenticeship was a necessary evil: a cost-
effective method of integrating thousands of liberated Africans, mostly
children, into the economy of the colony and getting them off the books of
the colonial government. Apprenticeship was unpleasant, and often produced disturbing results, but, they reasoned, there was no affordable alternative system. It does not appear, however, that there was ever a sustained
interest in building even the most basic monitoring systems for the Liberated African Department to better enforce the contractual obligations of the
indentures. Compared with the vast sums spent on policing the slave trade
and rewarding prize captures, the amounts spent on Sierra Leone's liberated African apprentices were almost negligible. This lack of financing suggests a weak commitment to translating discourses of humanitarian duty
into tools of governance, and stands in marked contrast to the investment
made in developing the military and naval interventionist capabilities of
Britain's antislavery world system.

SEVEN

Enlistment

IN OCTOBER 1832, a twenty-one-year-old man from "Cosso, Africa" disembarked from a slave ship at Freetown. The officer registering him gave him the name William Blazely and sent him to the King's Yard with the other survivors. Standing five feet eight inches tall, William was evidently considered a suitable candidate by the military recruiters of the Royal African Corps, because some time after arriving at the yard—maybe hours, maybe weeks—he was attested for a lifetime of service, for a bounty of three pounds. For the next 7,615 days, or almost twenty-one years, he served as a labourer in the British military, moving between postings in Africa and the West Indies. In April 1854, he was discharged from the Third West India Regiment at Jamaica for reasons of medical unfitness, or "general debility the result of long service." William's career was eventful: he was promoted once, court martialled twice, and imprisoned twice, once with hard labour. His offences are listed as "habitual drunkenness," "striking a superior officer," and leaving his post while on sentry duty. Nevertheless, on his pension application, his superior officers recommended him as a "good soldier." He requested to be sent back to Sierra Leone, where since 1819 discharged and disbanded soldiers had had the opportunity of settling. He signed his discharge papers with a mark; William had never learned to write his name.[1]

The previous year, another liberated African man, known as "Private Charles Dickens," was discharged from the same regiment at Jamaica. Charles had been recruited just over ten years previously for the Third West India Regiment at Sierra Leone, and had served 3,709 days between Africa and the West Indies, also with the status of military labourer. Like

William, he was discharged for reasons of medical unfitness, the consequence of "two or three very severe paralytic seizures" through which he
"has almost totally lost the use of his lower extremities" and had "impaired . . . mental function," although it is not clear whether the latter was
a consequence of the seizures or had predated them. In the opinion of the
principal medical officer at Jamaica, Charles was "totally unfit not only
for the duties of a soldier, but for those of any other occupation by which
he might earn a living." The decision of the Chelsea Board is not given on
the discharge papers, however there is some reason to think they might
not have approved his pension. Charles's record was one of repeated resistance to military authority. Around two years after being enlisted, he was
court martialled for the first time for being absent from duty and was sentenced to twenty days' solitary confinement. He was soon in trouble again:
sentenced to 150 lashes in February 1845 and imprisoned again with hard
labour in December 1845, and again in October 1846, when the primary
reason given was "insubordination." Reportedly, Charles then refused to
comply with the sentence of hard labour and, for this, he received additional sentences amounting to a further 300 lashes, of which 100 lashes
were remitted. "His general character and conduct has been that of a bad
soldier," the regimental board was told, although during this time he had
also managed to gain one good conduct badge. Charles intended to retire
to Tobago. At the time of his discharge, he was twenty-eight years old.

As far as regimental paperwork was concerned, neither William Blazely nor Charles Dickens was a "liberated African." They were soldiers,
recruited in Africa to spend the remainder of their working lives in the
service of the military.[2] They and others like them were tasked with garrisoning British positions, expanding and consolidating the territorial
foothold of Britain in West Africa and the Americas, policing the sugar
islands of the Caribbean, and suppressing the various protests, revolts,
and uprisings, both before and after 1838, of both enslaved and "free"
people, that challenged the socio-racial order of the British empire.[3]
Upon enlistment, both William and Charles were no doubt recognised as
"raw" African recruits by their fellow soldiers in the regiment, yet the act
of enlisting itself entailed an important shift in the identity attributed to

them by the imperial state. If William did indeed get his wish of returning to Sierra Leone in 1854, it was with the elevated social status of a "discharged soldier." Most likely, he settled in the vicinity of Freetown or in a nearby liberated African village, and if not already married, may have been allowed to apply to the Liberated African Department for a wife.[4] Men in his position were, in theory, supposed to be provided with land, the means to build a house, and implements to tend a farm.[5] In this way, his military career would have brought him full circle back to the orbit and responsibility of the colonial government of Sierra Leone. Yet although geographically close to the site of his initial liberation from the slave ship, and perhaps even living amongst liberated people of his own country of origin, William would not simply have rejoined the "class" of liberated Africans, either in official eyes or in public opinion. The experience of military service represented a transformative experience in terms of these men's identities, prestige, and status in society.

Not all of the enlisted liberated people who were sent overseas had the opportunity to return to Africa. Many died in service, and of those who were discharged, many were forced through circumstance to remain where they found themselves. It is likely that most lived out the remainder of their lives in locations far from the places of their birth. As with apprenticeship, there was no single experience of military life, and no simple way to reconcile the experiences of enlisted liberated Africans with the "humane" overtones of the abolitionist intervention against their enslaved status. On one hand, there was the coercive nature of their recruitment, the near certainty that most had no knowledge of the true nature of the commitment, and the misery, loneliness, violence, ill health, and repeated dislocation of military life, which for many recruits involved at least one further transatlantic voyage. On the other hand, one could emphasise the elevation in status the soldiers enjoyed and the power they exercised over others. The abolitionists of the early 1800s had been careful to specify that the liberated people were to be enlisted for life with no pension; in practice, many of them were disbanded or discharged and pensioned, albeit usually once their physical health had deteriorated to an extent that they were no longer considered useful.[6] Many were promoted and rewarded during the course of their service, some rising up to the ranks of corporal and sergeant.

As David Arnold has observed, the military—the most elementary tool of colonial control—"depended on soldiers who were simultaneously coerced and coercing; who enforced the will of the elite yet made demands themselves."[7] In the case of soldiers drawn from the ranks of the enslaved or formerly enslaved, their elevation in status, and the ways they wielded power, complicate how we understand their role, both as agents within Atlantic-world societies that were still ultimately built upon slavery, and as combatants violently enacting the acquisitive appetites and rivalries of the European empires. Numerous mutinies, uprisings, and revolts occurred in British colonial territories during the first half of the nineteenth century, including Bussa's Rebellion in Barbados in 1816, the Demerara Revolution of 1823, and the mutiny of the First West India Regiment in Trinidad in 1837, which was led by a liberated African man called Dâaga, or "Donald Stewart." Many such disturbances were suppressed with the use of considerable violence and terror, and many of the soldiers tasked with that suppression had been recruited through the liberated African yards of the British Atlantic world. To echo David Lambert, any history of formerly enslaved people who served in the British armed forces in the Atlantic world must take account of their ambiguous role "as both victims and oppressors," as people coercively recruited, yet who engaged in policing functions in Caribbean slave societies that helped to preserve the institution of slavery, and who played an important role in the expansionist violence that established the British empire in West Africa.[8]

Enlistment of liberated Africans continued for six decades, with wide-ranging implications. It affected the lives of thousands of liberated Africans drawn from Sierra Leone, Cape Colony, St Helena, and the West Indies, and profoundly altered the composition of the military forces in large parts of Britain's colonial empire. Some contemporaries questioned recruiters' use of coercion and deceit, but unlike apprenticeship, the enlistment policy did not generate much debate with regard to its moral aspects. This chapter starts by examining the implementation of the enlistment policy at Sierra Leone across the period 1808–1867, seeking to situate this policy within its broader context and to understand some of the ways in which liberated people experienced and responded to military life. It further considers how the British antislavery state harnessed their labour for military purposes as a way of enhancing the force-projection capacity of the British empire. It is telling that in the soldiers' attestation documents and service records, little trace can be found of the language of humanitarianism, protective paternalism, and "civilising improvement" that was used to frame discussions of policy towards other liberated African groups. Yet overall, and particularly in dialogue with Britain's antislavery treaty partners, the enlistment policy was rationalised as a fundamentally humanitarian act that served both the needs of the "rescued" individual and the wider goals of the international antislavery effort.[9]

"A Favourable Destination for Them"

Viscount Palmerston, then secretary for war, explained to the House of Commons in June 1815 that the principle behind enlisting liberated Africans was a fortunate coincidence of obligation first and opportunity second. "As something must be done with the captured negroes, it was a favourable destination for them to be put on something like the level of a British soldier." The plan had first been proposed to government in the early 1800s by "the late member for Yorkshire," William Wilberforce.[10] Since 1795, enslaved Africans purchased by the state for the regimental service had—controversially, for white colonists—formed the backbone of British fighting forces in the Caribbean theatre of war with revolutionary France. This practice was part of a longer tradition of arming enslaved people for colonial military purposes, dating back to at least the Seven Years' War. Twelve West India Regiments were raised between 1795 and 1798, and although it was never the intention that these regiments would be primarily manned by slave soldiers purchased for service, the decimation of white troops by tropical diseases, combined with the inability of military authorities to raise troops from "patriotic" West Indian slaveholders or from the free black populations, meant that the next most feasible pathway to maintaining the regiments at fighting strength was through buying men from the slave markets. By 1808, when the Abolition Act came into force, the British state had become "perhaps the largest individual buyer of slaves" in the world. R. N. Buckley, historian of the West India Regiments, estimates that the British government spent £925,000 on a total of 13,400 slaves who were purchased and forced to enlist between 1795 and 1808.[11]

As with apprenticeship, the idea of enlisting liberated Africans therefore drew on an existing set of precedents. It also provided a ready potential success story: at no extra cost to the state, enslaved soldiers could be replaced with "liberated" ones. In September 1804, Wilberforce wrote to his friend, Prime Minister William Pitt, expressing his concerns about the enslaved men being purchased for the West India Regiments. That for an enslaved African, life as a British soldier "would be beyond comparison preferable to that of plantation slaves cannot be doubted," Wilberforce wrote, "but how can we justify buying slaves for that desirable and even humane purpose" when to do so would increase the demand for slaves and would therefore stimulate the transatlantic slave trade? It seemed to Wilberforce "extremely probable that Buonaparte will resort to this mode of obtaining a black army for the reduction of St. Domingo, and I should be sorry that we should set him the example." Immediately, though, in the same letter, Wilberforce surrendered to the inescapability of the "vicious principle": "I know not how it can be got over," he admitted. "I am sure you and I cannot differ in principle; and if you will therefore look into the matter . . . I shall be content. I should be much obliged to you at any time for a single word to satisfy my anxiety on this subject."[12]

Perhaps Wilberforce did indeed receive that single, satisfying word. Thereafter, as Buckley observes, "no written or spoken word came from the abolitionist camp to demand explanation," or publicly to hold government to account for its dominance of the world's slave purchasing.[13] If this was "inattentiveness" on the part of Wilberforce, Buckley regards it as puzzling and "highly uncharacteristic of the man." It seems more likely however that the abolitionists were embarrassed to be seen as lobbying for a policy that would diminish Britain's fighting capabilities against Napoleon, and that they were casting around for an alternative. At some point between 1804 and the finalising of the terms of what became the Abolition Act, Wilberforce and his friends connected the dots and realised that their planned naval slave trade suppression measures would produce a captive population, to be "disposed of" by the Crown. In August 1811, in response to Robert Peel's concern to find more recruits for military service, Zachary Macaulay reminded him that the navy had only to increase the number of slave captures it was making. The outright purchase of slaves as recruits was by then impossible, and voluntary enlistment of Africans was impracticable, but "no doubt can exist," Macaulay counselled, "that government have it in their [sic] power to increase that force almost indefinitely by means of [slave-ship] captures." Citing a contemporary estimate of eighty thousand enslaved people being exported annually from the African coast, he argued in favour of a strong, broadly distributed naval force with a specific mandate to capture "a very large number of slave ships . . . for adjudication [at] Sierra Leone." "If clear orders were issued on the subject to the different naval commanders in the West Indies, South America, the Cape of Good Hope and the East Indies, a still larger number would speedily come into our possession. And of every [such] cargo of slaves, half at least will be adult males, probably fit for military service." "The Negroes who should thus be captured and condemned at Sierra Leone might . . . be soon fitted from military service, and the voyage thence to Barbados is a voyage of only three weeks."[14]

In the final wording of the abolition legislation, disposal of liberated Africans by enlistment was supposed to be the priority: the first Order in Council of 16 March 1808 was unambiguous on this point. At all sites of liberation, the able-bodied men were to be enlisted into the armed forces. On receipt of a group of newly landed liberated Africans, the designated agent in each British colonial territory was instructed immediately to

> give notice to the Chief Officer of his Majesty's land forces in
> the colony . . . of the number of male Negroes fit for military
> service so received, to the intent that such officer or commander

> in chief may take any number of such Negroes, as recruits for
> West Indian or African regiments, or to form new corps, or as
> pioneers, according to such instructions as he may from time
> to time receive.

Should the number of new recruits be in excess of the needs of the military, the surplus recruits were to be handed over to the naval commanding officer, who would likewise "receive into his Majesty's naval service any number of such Negroes that the service may want."[15] Much like the provisions for apprenticeship, the order contains no language of volition or choice on the part of the Africans under discussion. In theory, enlistment was limited to men and boys over the age of eighteen. In practice, they were often much younger. Liberated African women were, strictly speaking, exempt from military duty, although as "wives," domestic servants, and prostitutes, many of them became likewise bound to the fortunes and movements of the West India Regiments, Royal African Corps, and Royal African Colonial Corps, and many were formally included in the returns as having been "enlisted," presumably with equally little regard for their consent.[16]

The precise number of liberated African men, women, and children enlisted for the military and the navy between 1808 and 1867 is not known, although for the land forces it was sufficiently high that a recruiter remarked in 1837 that "the whole of our African corps, and a great part of the West India Regiments that serve in the West Indies, are supplied from the liberated Africans at Sierra Leone."[17] Of all of the liberated African establishments in the Atlantic world, the yard at Freetown offered the largest pool of potential recruits, including those liberated not only from the Vice-Admiralty Court, but from the various Mixed Commission courts that sat in the colony. That said, had the instructions of this Order in Council been followed precisely, tens of thousands of male Africans would have been enlisted as soldiers across six decades. Most sources suggest, however, that with the exception of a few peak years, a far smaller proportion was enlisted than the recruiters had been given the right to claim. R. R. Kuczynski estimates a total of 3,147 men and boys were enlisted across the entire period.[18] While reports of contemporaries suggest that the real number was markedly higher, it was certainly not as high as all healthy males of "at least five feet three inches' height" who passed through the gates of the Liberated African Department.[19] The first 167 Africans liberated at Freetown in January 1809 included 58 adult men and 51 boys, of whom Acting Governor Ludlam claimed thirty for a "Military Corps" of labourers. Although the first Crown governor, Thomas Perronet Thompson, saw in the liberated Africans the ideal "Colonist and Soldier . . . combined" for his grandiose ambitions for the colony, recruitment in Freetown remained generally low until 1812. In that year, a former slave fort at Bunce Island in the Sierra Leone estuary was adapted as a recruiting station for the West India Regiments.[20] Between 1812 and 1814, military and naval recruitment of newly liberated Africans was proportionately at its peak: 52 percent of all arrivals were enlisted in 1812, 43 percent in 1813 and 26 percent in 1814, declining to 15 percent in 1815 and 12 percent in 1816.[21] The available records suggest that after 1816, recruitment continued to take place in small surges, from 1819 to 1821, from 1823 to 1828, and in 1832. Additionally, between 1812 and 1816, a number of women and children were recruited.[22] Of the total of 2,333 recruits in this five-year period, 6.6 percent were adult women and 8.1 percent were children. Expressing the same data another way, 2,169 or 92.97 percent of recruits were male and 164 or 7.03 percent were female.

Why were there so few recruits? In part, this was a matter of the physical health of the slave-ship survivors: those who had illnesses such as dysentery, typhoid, or severe eye infections, or who were physically injured, were not considered eligible. The severely emaciated were often not strong enough to be passed by the medical officer or selected by the recruiters.[23] A second reason is that many liberated Africans, so recently released from captivity aboard European-owned vessels and still trapped in an ambiguous form of freedom, were simply unwilling to engage themselves in an unlimited, regimented, and subservient form of labour, particularly when that service involved a transatlantic voyage to the slave-holding West Indies. It is not clear how many liberated Africans were given the opportunity to refuse, but for at least some of the period in question, successful resistance was possible and did occur. A third reason is political: some colonial governors opposed the practice of admitting military recruiters to the Liberated African Yard, particularly those from the West India

Table 2. Liberated Africans Recruited for Army and Navy Service, 1808–1833

Year	Men	Women	Boys	Girls	Total
1808	1	3	4	0	8
1809	0	1	1	0	2
1810	71	9	10	0	90
1811	66	10	31	0	107
1812	965	72	152	7	1,196
1813	144	30	41	2	217
1814	462	15	20	0	497
1815	191	4	3	0	198
1816	264	8	50	1	323
1817	0	0	0	0	0
1818	0	0	0	0	0
1819	0	0	0	0	0
1820	0	0	0	0	0
1821	0	0	0	0	0
1822	0	0	0	0	0
1823	0	0	0	0	0
1824	14	0	0	0	14
1825	7	6	13	0	26
1826	169	0	2	0	171
1827	391	11	0	0	402
1828	150	1	4	0	155
1829	23	1	5	0	29
1830	17	1	15	0	33
1831	46	0	0	0	46
1832	73	0	1	0	74
1833	17	0	3	0	20
Total	3,071	172	355	10	3,608

Source: National Archives of the United Kingdom, CO 267/127

Regiments who would remove the strongest and fittest of the new arrivals from the colony and deprive the colonial government of profitable manpower. The Commissioners of Inquiry, Rowan and Wellington, reported to Parliament in 1826 that the system of military recruitment had long "varied with the sentiments and opinions of the individual administering the government."[24]

A more pertinent question than "why so few?" might be "why such a broad recruitment mandate?" What need had the British government to make thousands of freed slaves legally available to its military recruiters—and, since liberated Africans were not yet recognised as British subjects, to go to the difficulty of arranging a special relaxation in the law preventing the enlistment of aliens into the army? For the first eight years of liberated African recruitment, the major consideration was the ongoing war with France and, related to this, the need to defend British possessions in West Africa, including the Sierra Leone colony, the Gold Coast, and (from 1819) the foothold on the Gambia river. Although more well established than in the early years of its accession as a Crown Colony, when it had been plundered repeatedly, Sierra Leone still remained vulnerable throughout the war years to aggression from regional powers more numerous, well resourced, and well organised than the colonists, as well as to attacks by the French navy and privateers. Since 1802, the Royal African Corps garrisoning Freetown had recruited Africans to replace the European officers and men killed in large numbers by disease; after 1808 the recruitment of slave trade survivors merely echoed this pattern. In the Gold Coast, hostilities with the Asante after 1806 often demanded a greater military presence than the small garrison force at the forts. In 1819 a detachment of troops was sent to Gambia to garrison a new position at Bathurst.[25] For a time, small detachments were also located at Goreé, the Isles de Los, Fernando Po, and the Banana Islands. In the mid-century, Lagos was also annexed and garrisoned.

Demand for liberated African recruits did not remain consistently high throughout the century. The end of hostilities with France led to the closure of Bunce Island. The recruitment of liberated Africans in Freetown was supposedly in abeyance from 1816 to 1824, although there is some evidence to suggest that military enlistment continued sporadically, and that as many as 724 people were recruited between 1814 and 1823.[26] This was a period of major readjustment in British land and sea forces. The decision was taken in 1818 to transfer some West India Regiments to West Africa and disband the poorly regarded Royal African Corps. In May 1819, the headquarters and five companies of the Second West India Regiment were transferred from Jamaica to Freetown. In the same year, the West India Regiments were reduced. As a result, alongside the transfer of troops in active service, an estimated total of 2,252 disbanded soldiers and their families were sent to Sierra Leone between 1818 and 1819. Those regiments that were maintained were deployed at different times across West Africa and the British Caribbean in a variety of security functions.

The postwar reductions were temporary, however. In 1819, Freetown was established as the principal naval depot on the West African coast and base of the newly constituted West Africa Squadron. From 1822, with the rise of tensions between Britain and the Asante, many of the white troops formerly of the Royal African Corps were recalled from Cape Colony and hastily reembodied into a corps "for the defence of the western coast and Gold Coast forts." The survivors of this campaign were later deposited in Freetown where, bundled together with "several drafts" of English convicts, they were formed into "the Royal African Colonial Corps," which was widely viewed as being "of the most degraded class." When a heavy death toll from disease soon depleted the ranks, recruiters turned to the Liberated African Yard. In 1824, recruitment at Sierra Leone began again in earnest, and lasted through to the 1840s.[27] In 1840, the Royal African Colonial Corps was transferred to the West Indies and reconstituted as the Third West India Regiment. The wider shift in policy in these years towards coercively removing all newly liberated Africans from Freetown to the West Indies had a substantial impact on enlistment figures in the 1840s: new arrivals of all ages were in these years given the option to enlist, emigrate, self-support, or leave the colony. Between November 1846 and May 1848, just over 55 percent of adult male arrivals at Freetown were enlisted.[28] This represented over 38 percent of the total number of Africans liberated in that period.

Enlistment Practices

Thomas Keogh, a surgeon of the Second West India Regiment, told a parliamentary select committee in 1847 that, in his experience, liberated Africans were not only willing to enlist into the regiment, but that these "very fine young men" did so "strictly [as] volunteers." "There is no difficulty at any time in getting the slaves who are brought in to volunteer in our regiments," he claimed. "They appear perfectly willing and anxious to do so." A former acting lieutenant-governor of Sierra Leone in the late 1820s, Major H. J. Ricketts, also professed a highly positive view of the enlistment procedures. In a pamphlet written in 1831, *View of the Present State of the Colony of Sierra Leone,* Ricketts claimed that recruiters were "very successful" among the liberated people. He described "villagers who voluntarily enlist, and cheerfully embark for the West Indies" and claimed that he had, during his time in Sierra Leone, "formed and cloathed [*sic*] an excellent militia," who were "well drilled, composed of the youngest of the discharged soldiers having pensions from government, and liberated Africans, who readily joined at the villages of Wellington and York."[29]

Neither source convinces. Keogh's evaluation is compromised by his racist, ethnocentric conviction of the "civilising" benefit of British leadership in a world of strict racial hierarchies. Ricketts was writing with a fevered agenda to rescue his own ailing reputation. Neither do Keogh's or Ricketts's claims find much support in the writings of their contemporaries. Commissioners of Enquiry Rowan and Wellington found in 1826 that the military was "not . . . a favourable service, either with the newly imported Africans, or with those who have been longer resident in the colony."[30] The author of *The White Man's Grave* reported ten years later that enlistment was understood by Africans as a modified form of slavery. Relating the substance of a conversation he claimed to have had with "an intelligent young Soosoo," Rankin inquired whether the man had any desire or ambition to become a soldier:

> "No, never" was his reply. Knowing him to be much attached
> to the English, I put the question whether he would refuse to

fight if the Timmanees were to make another attack upon the town. "Yes he would fight for the white men," he said, "but would not be a slave." I asked him what he meant by slave; the word had not been mentioned. "Soldiers," he answered, "are slaves; loaded with heavy arms and dress, shut up in the barracks as if it were the gaol, forced to march and labour against their will when the white men pleased"; and finally, to clench [sic] his argument, he exclaimed "they make soldiers of Captives"; that is, of the Liberated slaves. Nothing could modify his opinion, and the opinion of the Soosoo was the prevalent one.

Rankin attributed the unpopularity of military service in part to the discomfort of the military dress, of "the heating uniform of scarlet cloth, the weighty shako, the tight stiff stock, and cumbrous shoes: not to mention the weight of musket and side-arms." This sudden, forced adaptation to restrictive clothing was "no light matter" but it was not the entire explanation, in Rankin's view. "The fatigues of drill, of parade, and practice" constituted an equally severe change of lifestyle, and one "more opposed to his education and taste than the labours of a plantation."[31]

Colonial officials had previously reported on the aversion of the settlers to soldiering. In early Freetown, particularly before relatively wealthy disbanded soldiers began to return, soldiers were not perceived as an elite. Settlers reportedly considered the Militia Bill of 1811 "obnoxious," because it interrupted their personal labour and put them under the strict authority of military law, where acts of individuality were punishable as insubordination. This constant vulnerability to public flogging left the soldier, in the eyes of the population, "a degraded person."[32] Governor Macdonald reported an incident to Under-Secretary Hay in 1844 in which approximately 130 recruits were marching from the Liberated African Yard, accompanied by music, when "an Ackoo woman among the crowd assembled . . . called out something in the Ackoo language." More than half of the group ran away and could not afterwards "on any account, be prevailed upon to enlist." Before the new arrivals were allowed out of the yard, it was "customary" to permit only "officers and non-commissioned officers attended by interpreters, to have access to them."[33]

The degree of coercion exercised during this period of access may have varied; certainly, contemporaries' interpretations and representations of it did. One of former chief justice Robert Thorpe's polemic pamphlets described a scene of absolute compulsion: the "seizure" of the liberated African "the moment he landed a freeman" and his being driven "terrified . . . to the fort," not understanding "what was said to him, nor what was to become of him, and without his feelings, knowledge, or consent being in the least consulted, making him a soldier for life!!"[34] In his *Letter to William Wilberforce* in 1815, Thorpe was even more emotive:

> Here is involuntary servitude for life, established by an Act of
> Parliament purporting to abolish slavery . . . in the Colony
> founded by the most benevolent men, on the most liberal plan:
> exalted as the freest spot on earth, to enlighten benighted Africa; and displayed to the world as the finest example of British
> liberty, and British philanthropy!![35]

In a similar vein, Rankin reported in 1834 how the men chosen by the recruiters were "marched in a string, *nolentes volentes,* under strong escort to the barracks."[36] However, Dixon Denham, superintendent of the Liberated African Department and later lieutenant-governor, suggested that the dynamic was more opportunistically exploitative of the new arrivals' vulnerability than bluntly forceful. He described how, "scarcely an hour" after the transfer of several hundred newly liberated people to the department, he found in the yard "an officer, an Assistant Surgeon, and a party of the Royal African Corps" who had lined up "about 100 poor fellows perfectly naked" and were submitting them to an inspection. No mention of force is made in Denham's account, but "such of them as appeared fit were set apart, without asking them one question as to their unwillingness or not."[37] In a similar vein, Joseph Reffell, chief superintendent of the Liberated African Department since 1 April 1816, gave evidence to the Commission of Inquiry in 1826 that although "interpreters explained the intention of thus selecting them," he was of the opinion "that it was impossible they could have understood the nature of the engagement."[38] The commissioners concluded that "none" of the various recruiting parties had ever been "very successful in obtaining voluntary enlistment."[39] A report in 1840 on troop sickness, mortality, and invaliding echoed this observation: "It is only when recently landed, and ignorant of any mode of procuring a subsistence, that they can be induced to adopt a profession, of which the active duties and necessary restraints are much at variance with their habits and disposition."[40]

Governor Macdonald's description of the interference of the "Ackoo woman" above, and the impossibility of prevailing upon recruits to enlist thereafter, suggests that while enlistment was conducted under heavy enticement, it may have retained (at least sometimes) some kind of a voluntary character. A. B. Ellis's account also suggests that the recruitment efforts were persuasive rather than coercive. "A party from the garrison used to be admitted to the Liberated African Yard," he wrote, where the liberated Africans were so impressed by the "brilliant uniform," and so well "talked over by the recruiting party, who were men specially selected for this duty on account of their knowledge of African languages," that they freely "offered themselves as recruits." Those passed by the medical officer were "invariably accepted."[41] Ellis questioned the legality of the practice, however. "We have been told they did this voluntarily," he wrote of the enlistment of liberated Africans in Grenada and Dominica, "but it may be asked, if they had any will in the matter," or any real comprehension of the terms of the oath of allegiance "without which they could not, legally speaking, be considered soldiers."[42] Joseph Reffell's evidence suggests a significant degree of variation in approach and tone across the period of his employment by the Liberated African Department. Under the governorship of Charles Maxwell from 1811 to 1815—when recruiters of the West India Regiments first brought their dazzling displays of pomp and status to Freetown— Reffell told the commissioners, "the practice was for non-commissioned officers to be sent immediately on the landing of such people to select those they considered fit for his Majesty's service who were immediately marched off and if passed by the medical officer forthwith attested."[43] Under MacCarthy, from 1815 to 1820, the recruits were not to be attested until they had trained for one month to give the men time to consider their options. During this time

> the men were similarly selected and passed, considered as re-
> cruits and drilled as such, altho' not enjoying the pay or usual
> ration granted to soldiers, in place of which they had issued to
> them 2 pounds of rice and half a pound of meat per day, with a
> weekly allowance of soap and tobacco. After a few months thus
> organised and treated, they had some knowledge of the English
> language and a perfect understanding of the Nature of the
> Soldier's duties, they were then brought forward and if they
> chose to serve his Majesty, attested, but if not returned to the
> Liberated African Department to be dealt with as if they had
> never been selected.[44]

Records from the colonial government in Sierra Leone suggest high levels of desertion locally, particularly in the late 1820s and 1830s and
among recent recruits—often multiple desertions and recaptures of the
same soldier. This followed directly from a period in which Governor
Neil Campbell (1826–1828) had embarked on a programme of enlisting
all able-bodied men of his choice, and had been "vexed" by constant desertions.[45] At that time, Dixon Denham observed tartly to the commander
of the garrison that both his interests and those of "obvious justice" would
be better served by making the enlistments "perfectly voluntary." The "frequent desertions . . . often complained of" would thus be prevented.[46]
Denham later reported that following his reform of the enlistment system, "desertion from the regiment has been very trifling." Before, he
had "known twelve or fifteen [to] desert in one night, and the villages
scoured by constables to take up these poor fellows, who receive a fee for
their apprehension."[47]

Experiences and Effects of Military Life

What can we know about how liberated people felt about and responded to military life, and the effects it had upon them, physically and

psychologically? By studying the regiments into which they were enlisted, we might infer something of the character of their experiences based on the diverse locations of their postings across West Africa and the Caribbean, the quality (or otherwise) of the barracks accommodation and food, the kinds of work in which we know the soldiers and "camp followers" were employed, the proportion of time spent on garrison duty compared to active campaigning, and the proximity of their postings to wider communities with which they might have formed connections and friendships. There is another, more direct way to recover glimpses of the experiences and responses of enlisted liberated people, however: through military service records.

One particularly rich set of such sources is the "Royal Hospital Chelsea: Soldiers Service Documents" series, held at the National Archives of the United Kingdom in the War Office (WO) series.[48] Approximately eleven hundred of the extant service records relate to those of African soldiers enlisted at Sierra Leone and in the Caribbean for the Royal African Corps, the Royal African Colonial Corps, and the West India Regiments, and discharged by the West India Regiments. These papers contain important biographical data, including soldiers' names and assigned numbers, place of birth, place and date of their attestation, age and appearance at recruitment, the length of time they served, the locations and regiments in which they served, and also the place and date of their discharge from the military. The records generally give details of the reason for each soldier's discharge—usually medical unfitness, described alongside a wealth of medical observations—as well as notes on promotions, reductions, courts martial, and any other noteworthy episodes in the soldier's professional life. A range of other observations and opinions was often included, from notes on scarification, to details of each soldier's skills or trade, and, most frequently, opinions on "character and conduct," including the discharging medical officer's comments on whether a soldier's medical problems could be blamed on vice, intemperance, or "neglect."[49]

Taking a representative sample of approximately 25 percent of these service records, it is possible to make a number of observations and to offer some suggestions about aspects of life for liberated African men and boys enlisted between the years 1816 and 1857.[50] Of the soldiers in the data sample, at least 91 percent (or 266 out of 291) were born in Africa. The earliest recorded enlistment was that of "Lord Arundel," born in "Kanga, Africa," soldier number 124. He was attested at Sierra Leone on 25 December 1812, precisely when enlistment began in earnest at the Bunce Island station. Aged eighteen at the time of enlistment, he was attested for the Fourth West India Regiment of Foot and served for the next seventeen years and 250 days between Gibraltar and the West Indies. Although Lord Arundel deserted his regiment between 1821 and 1824, he still retired with a character and conduct commendation as a "very good" soldier.[51]

Only one other soldier in the data sample is listed as of "Kanga" origin. By far the most frequently mentioned ethnicities listed for the recruits were, respectively, "Ackoo" (or Yoruba) and "Eboe" (or Ibo). Other attempts at naming African places of origin, which feature routinely in the records, include "Cape Coast," "Papa," "Nango," "Hausa," "Chamba," "Bassa," "Congo," and "Cosso." The vast majority of these recruits were aged (or stated to have been aged) between seventeen and twenty-one at the time of attestation. Of the 291 records, 202 were in that age range, with 11 recruits stated to be seventeen years old, 90 given as eighteen years old, 31 nineteen years old, 51 aged twenty, and 19 aged twenty-one. The oldest recruit in the sample to be enlisted at Sierra Leone was David Bell, born in Hausa and attested in 1823 aged twenty-eight. The youngest enlisted at Freetown was a fourteen-year-old "Aku" boy named Alladay, attested in May 1825, although one younger boy also appears in this sample: Drummer Alert, born in Congo, who was attested at the age of eight in a nonspecific location in "Africa," probably Sierra Leone, on 25 September 1812. Of those soldiers whose records specify locations of service, fifteen served in West Africa alone and thirty served only in the Caribbean, while 145 served in both West Africa and the Caribbean. Fifty-eight served in more than two locations.[52] Some records give the details of campaigns fought, with specific mentions made of North America during the War of 1812, Santo Domingo during the latter half of the Napoleonic Wars, and the conflicts with the Asante that began in 1806 and led to five wars over the subsequent eight decades. Most simply record the locations of service, such as the Bahamas, Barbados, Belize, Cape Coast, Demerara, Dominica, Gambia, Gibraltar, Honduras, Jamaica, Sierra Leone, and others.

Like many of their white British counterparts, virtually all African-born soldiers were recruited for unlimited periods of service and were discharged only upon being certified medically unfit or upon the disbanding of the regiment. Most therefore served lengthy periods—over half of them serving between sixteen and twenty-five years. The shortest service length in the sample was Henry Blunt's 285 days. The longest period was William Genoo's 16,524 days—over forty-five years. The longest period served by an individual confirmed to have been recruited at Sierra Leone was 10,866 days, or almost 30 years. This was George Francis, soldier number 171, who was recruited in March 1816 at the age of eighteen and discharged at Trinidad after a career spent in the West Indies where he was distinguished by a number of good conduct awards.[53]

Individually and collectively, the records in the data sample paint a picture of the physical costs of army service in these locations in the nineteenth century, for both black and white soldiers. Only six of the 291 records in this sample do not specify a reason for their discharge. Two soldiers were discharged upon the disbanding or reduction of their regiments, while five others were discharged at their own request. The remainder of 278 were discharged as medically unfit: nine primarily for reasons of mental health or intellectual ability, and the remaining 269 deemed to be physically unfit. The specific medical reasons for these 269 discharges are varied. The most common complaints and diseases were generally attributable to climate or other environmental conditions. For example, the discharge papers for twenty-two (7.6 percent of the data sample) list asthma, bronchial, lung, or chest diseases, while fifty-eight soldiers (19.9 percent of the sample) were discharged due to debilitating rheumatism. Twenty-four (8.2 percent) were discharged due to severe eye problems, including partial or total loss of sight. Hernias and "ruptures" were also relatively common, appearing in seventeen cases, or 5.8 percent of the total dataset. One such hernia was reportedly "about the size of a child's head [of] two years old."[54] Of the eleven soldiers who served fewer than one thousand days before discharge, four (36.3 percent) were discharged primarily for debilitating rheumatic complaints, three (27.3 percent) for reasons of mental health or intellectual capability, and the remaining two for an eye and a liver complaint respectively (each 9.1 percent of the data sample). Other medical observations appear in these records, sometimes as part of the reason for discharge and sometimes as part of the soldiers' broader medical histories. These include emaciation, chronic dysentery, Guinea worm, cachexia (bodily wastage), impaired hearing or hearing loss, lameness, paralysis or paralytic seizures, epilepsy, skin diseases, syphilis, testicular diseases, tumours, ulceration, varicose veins, and the lingering effects of old injuries such as fractures and gunshot wounds. Most cases of medical unfitness in the sample (101 of the 291 soldiers) were attributed to reasons of "age" and "long service." The fourteen cases of mental illness or impairment that appear in this data sample are generally described as "defective," "weak," or "impaired" intellect; "mental imbecility," or "derangement of mind."

These findings broadly echo those of the "Statistical Report on the Sickness, Mortality and Invaliding Among the Troops in the West Indies," prepared in 1838 from the Records of the Army Medical Department and War Office Returns by Lieutenant Alexander Tulloch and the medical statistician Henry Marshall, which covers hospital admissions and mortality amongst both black and white soldiers in the Jamaica, Bahamas, Honduras, and Windward and Leeward Commands, and the all-black corps of military labourers. Overall, the report notes significant differences in the health and mortality of black and white troops. It attributes these variations to the idea that the "black troops [we]re so much less susceptible" to the climate. Across the four commands of the West Indies, the primary causes of hospital admissions were fairly consistent: "abscesses and ulcers," "fevers," "diseases of the lungs," and "diseases of the stomach and bowels." "Wounds and injuries" also feature strongly, as do "rheumatic complaints." Most fatalities of Africans in these four commands were caused by lung complaints, "diseases of the stomach and bowels," "fevers," and—in the case of the Bahamas and Honduras—a sizable number of "unknown causes." The medical conditions affecting white soldiers were also consistent across the four commands, with "fevers" and "diseases of the stomach and bowels" the main two causes of hospital admission in all regions. "Abscesses and ulcers," and "wounds and injuries" followed next in the order of prevalence. The pattern of white troop fatalities followed the pattern of hospital admissions, with "fevers" causing the vast majority of mortalities, followed by stomach and lung conditions.[55]

Tulloch and Marshall's report discusses a number of local factors believed to influence disease and mortality rates differently across the West Indies. These include local climate and temperature, rainfall, seasonal variations, prevailing winds, hurricanes and electrical storms, the ways in which troops were employed, their barracks and hospital accommodation—in particular dampness and overcrowding—and rations and diet. On the latter point, the report gives details of the diets at each command, noting some important variations. Weekly rations during the period from 1817 to 1836 at the Windward and Leeward Command consisted of "7 lbs. of bread, 2 lbs. of fresh meat, 2 lbs. of salt beef, 27 ounces of salt pork, 9 ounces of sugar, 10 ounces of rice, 5 ounces of cocoa, and 2½ pints of peas, for which the soldier pays 5d."[56] Prior to 1830, each soldier was also allowed a gill of rum, at a charge of 1d. Generally, the rations were served in two meals: a breakfast of "a pint of cocoa and his ration bread," and a dinner consisting of either "fresh meat made into a broth, with vegetables" or "salt meat boiled into soup, with the peas, and eaten with yams or potatoes." At Jamaica, from 1817 until 1835, when rations were aligned with those at the Windward and Leeward Command, each soldier received a weekly ration of "4 lbs. of fresh beef, 1 lb. of salt beef, 1½ lbs. of salt pork, 7 lbs. of flour (equivalent to 8¾ lbs. of bread) and 7 gills of rum."[57] At the Bahamas, the weekly ration for white soldiers consisted of 7 lbs. of bread, 5 lbs. of salt meat, 2 lbs. of fresh meat and a quart of rum. For black soldiers and labourers, who it was noted "suffered more" from the salt meat diet than the white troops did, their ration was adjusted to include just 1½ lbs. of salt meat, 1¾ lbs. of salt pork, 10 ounces of rice, 2½ pints of peas, 9 ounces of sugar, 5 ounces of cocoa, and 3½ gills of rum. The diet of the soldiers at Honduras was likewise very heavily dependent upon fresh and salt meat, bread, and rum.[58] Overall, a picture emerges of a generally poor diet, high in salt, fat, and protein, and low in fibre, calcium, and fresh vegetables, although as Buckley argues,

African soldiers frequently consumed less of their salt meat provisions, preferring to barter them for fresh vegetables.

Buckley identifies white soldiers' extraordinarily high consumption of low-quality rum as a cause or exacerbating factor of many of the medical conditions that afflicted them. Contemporaries believed that rum had prophylactic value against yellow fever and other illnesses. But the rum they drank often contained high concentrations of poisonous chemicals because of the lead and pewter components used in machinery for sugar-producing and distilling—chemicals now linked to diseases such as liver cirrhosis and necrosis, encephalitis, nephritis, anaemia, peripheral neuritis, and gout. It is probable that many of the deaths ascribed to yellow fever in this period were in fact caused by the combination of chronic lead and alcohol poisoning associated with the "New Rum" which soldiers drank "with a degree of desperation that is scarcely credible."[59] The symptoms of yellow fever and of alcohol-induced necrosis of the liver could be very similar: a deeply jaundiced complexion, intense thirst, and dark-coloured vomit as a result of internal haemorrhaging. Buckley notes that although rum was served in the mess and canteens of both black and white soldiers, "the problem of chronic drinking was limited almost exclusively to the white troops in the garrison."[60] For many of the African soldiers in the data sample, discharging medical officers specified that the health problems were "not associated with vice, neglect or intemperance," so as not to prejudice the soldier's chances of securing a pension.[61]

Upon discharge, soldiers were asked to formally sign or mark their discharge documents. The high proportion of marks rather than signatures for African soldiers suggests that only a handful of these soldiers achieved literacy in their period of service. Only two of the 266 African-born soldiers in this data sample signed their discharge document (while 13 of the 25 European-born men signed their forms). These two men were Charles Bate, soldier number 291, and James Ashley, soldier number 610.[62] Bate was born and attested at Cape Coast. He served 23 years and 259 days in Cape Coast, Sierra Leone, the Bahamas, and Gambia. He was commended as an "exemplary" soldier, achieving six promotions (and also three reductions). Ashley was born in "Ackoo" and attested at Sierra Leone. He served for 21 years and 331 days in Africa, the Bahamas, and the West Indies, was promoted several times and, like Bate, ultimately achieved the rank of company sergeant-major.

Of the 291 service records sampled, thirty-seven African soldiers were court martialled at one point or another in their careers, or 12.7 percent of the total. Most of the crimes related to drunkenness, occasionally accompanied by physical or verbal assaults. Only eleven of the thirty-seven court martialled soldiers were tried for desertion. Desertion is mentioned in only 3.8 percent of the records sampled, although this may reflect the nature of the source material and the profile of the men put forward for discharge and pension, and is not necessarily representative of the desertion levels of liberated African recruits across the board. As Peter Burroughs's survey of crime and punishment in the British army for the period 1815 to 1870 demonstrates, high levels of desertion, insubordination, and neglect of duty were prevalent amongst the ranks throughout the century. Dissatisfied with the "harassments," intense boredom, and monotony of army life and service—or perhaps simply ill-suited to its rigours—soldiers frequently resisted and protested through unruly behaviour, insubordination, drunkenness, absence without leave, and desertion.[63] New recruits were usually the most unsettled, struggling to adjust to the strangeness and regimentation of army life, the often oppressive treatment by superior officers, and the disappointments of their pay and daily routine. The harshness of military discipline is borne out in Tulloch's report: across the four commands in the period from 1817 to 1836, some 9,866 hospital admissions of black and white troops are recorded as a result of "punishment" (of whom 2,216, or 22.5 percent, were black soldiers). Three deaths from "punishment" are recorded in the report: all at the Windward and Leeward Command.[64]

Instances of absence without leave and desertion were also recorded frequently among troops in Britain and at overseas garrisons, particularly in British North America where "the haemorrhage of manpower through desertion was continuous, substantial, and seemingly unstaunchable." In 1843, for example, British domestic battalions lost one man in every fourteen through desertion, a total of 3,000 men in one year. In North America, 3,994 men deserted between 1816 and 1836, a loss of 5.8 percent of the average annual force under the Canada command. While mutiny in the ranks was very rare in peacetime, the crimes of disobedience and insubordination were very common; the latter offence, which could include violence, abusive language, and threatening gestures to superior officers, was three or four times as common as disobedience. Burroughs finds that "together, they constituted 12.7 percent of 31,780 offences between 1831 and 1838 and 11.2 percent of 22,020 offences between 1839 and 1843." Since many people regarded the army as a means of escape or refuge, or as a place for disposal of undesirables, it had a reputation for being filled with criminals, drunkards, bigamists, adulterers, debtors, and those who had burned their bridges with family, friends, and employers. Even in those recruits who had enlisted voluntarily, many had been deceived by recruiters working on the basis of commission, who promised high pay and an exciting life, and who won over recruits through "seduction, debauchery, and fraud." Soldiering was not a highly regarded occupation in metropolitan Britain—rather it was held in such low esteem by the population at large that Samuel Haden, secretary to the Army and Navy Pensioners Employment Society, told a royal commission on military recruiting in 1867 that he had "heard mothers solemnly declare that they would prefer to hear their sons were dead, rather than that they were enlisted."[65]

Considered in this light, the low proportion of desertions in the service records sampled bears out the nature of the source material, in that most of those soldiers applying for pension at discharge had integrated at least functionally into the military establishment and extracted from it the best terms they could. It is certainly not the case that only the records of "good" or "excellent" soldiers are reflected in this series—the files of soldiers such as Francis Cafarelli, an "Eboe" man attested at Sierra Leone in 1837 make this clear: court martialled four times and imprisoned for insubordination and absence without leave, Cafarelli was, like several others, designated a "bad soldier."[66] Similarly, some twenty-one others within this sample (7.2 percent) were designated "indifferent soldiers," with patchy records including episodes of imprisonment, court martial, demotion, hard labour, and corporal punishments of up to three hundred lashes. However, the majority of African soldiers within this dataset were never disciplined by court martial. Indeed, sixty-three of the soldiers (21.6 percent of the total) were promoted. Some had reached ranks such as corporal, sergeant, and sergeant-major at the time of their discharge. Although it is impossible to infer from their apparent integration and "good conduct" anything about these men's individual views of their enlistment and of military life, it is clear that many found ways to turn the situation to their own advantage, perhaps seeing their status as relatively better than the various alternatives, and significantly elevated by comparison with enslaved people. Of the 291 records in this sample, 239 (82.1 percent) explicitly record the soldier's general conduct or character as "good," "very good," "excellent," "most excellent," or "exemplary"—often in spite of prior recorded episodes of insubordination, misconduct, or even desertion. Many such soldiers were in receipt of good conduct pay, badges, or rings, and several had received special commendations for bravery or quality of service.[67]

The service records and discharge applications thus paint a picture of people who, across the duration of their careers, responded to the imposition of military life in complex and sometimes contradictory ways, yet who, for the most part, eventually accommodated to the demands of their role and their status as instruments of British military power. However, looking outside this sample and the part of the regimental archive it represents, it is possible to discern glimpses of the experiences and opinions of liberated Africans who responded in radically different ways. Perhaps the most dramatic example was in 1837, when a group of liberated Africans, apparently led by a man called Dâaga (or "Donald Stewart," as he had been renamed at the Liberated African Department of Freetown), rose up in mutiny against the First West India Regiment in Trinidad—the first black revolt on that island.[68]

The mutiny began early on the morning of 18 June 1837 in St Joseph, to the east of Port of Spain, when a heterogeneous and ethnolinguistically diverse group of between sixty and one hundred recruits—some of whom had joined the regiment as recently as six months previously—set fire to the barracks where the African soldiers were housed, and seized arms and ammunition from other African soldiers. One of the first casualties of the mutiny was an "older African soldier" called Charles Dixon, who was killed by Dâaga. When the commanding officer of the regiment, Colonel Bush, came out of the officers' barracks, the rebels opened fire.

Two older liberated African soldiers named Sergeant Merry and Corporal Plague provided cover for Bush and the other officers to escape.

The mutiny seems to have been premeditated, but all contemporary accounts agree that, in the execution, it was "wild and ill-planned."[69] In the absence of a clear strategy, things began to disintegrate quickly, with some mutineers dispersing into the bush while others attempted and failed to seize more weapons from the arsenal at St Joseph. Dâaga was captured. The main group of mutineers headed eastward under the leadership of Mawee of Yorubaland (also known as "Maurice Ogston"). Contemporary British observers claimed that the mutineers believed they were marching towards the Guinea coast of Africa. They were confronted by the militia at Arima in the centre of the island, where twelve of the mutineers were killed, and several more were wounded and taken prisoner. The remainder fled. Six of their number reportedly committed suicide rather than be taken prisoner again. In the aftermath of the mutiny, five of the captured men were singled out: the leaders, Dâaga and Mawee, and three others: Edward Coffin, William Satchell, and Henry Torrence. The first three were killed by firing squad on 16 August 1837. Satchell and Torrence were sentenced to transportation for life.[70]

A contemporary chronicler of Trinidadian history, Edward Joseph, marvelled that instead of taking advantage of their numbers, their arms, and the element of surprise, the mutineers had simply "howled their war notes" and fired their weapons from a distance into the walls of the officers' buildings, "a useless display of fury" that left the buildings "completely riddled" and "wasted so much ammunition" yet with "comparatively little mischief" to those inside.[71] It is difficult to know from the extant sources, including the trial records of the accused mutineers, precisely what motivated the revolt and what these men expected or hoped would happen as a result. Did they truly expect to make their way home? It is difficult to believe that these men really thought they were on a landmass contiguous with the African continent. All had endured a lengthy Middle Passage or ocean transportation from Freetown as enlisted soldiers, and all had lived at least six months in the Caribbean. Perhaps they hoped to find a secluded spot somewhere east of St Joseph to carve out a maroon community. Perhaps they hoped to commandeer a vessel.

Or perhaps they did not have a plan or any expectation of returning home, but rather had launched a mutiny and an escape from the barracks as a mass expression of rage, frustration, and despair at all that had been lost, and at the constraints, hardships, and cruelties of a life in which they were not treated as free men, and scarcely even as soldiers, but as labourers tasked with the heaviest duties. In subsequent inquiries into the causes and course of the mutiny, the personal leadership and charisma of Dâaga was foregrounded by military witnesses who were keen to downplay the wider causative factors—in particular, any suggestion of a culture of violence, excessive punishment, or other mismanagement by Colonel Bush.[72] According to Lionel Fraser, the nineteenth-century historian of Trinidad, one eyewitness at the court described Dâaga as a striking and intimidating figure of "gigantic stature," with a "voice most remarkable, being of astonishing depth and power." Fraser also relayed Dâaga's own account of himself, and his claim (which Fraser saw no reason to question) that he was a former slave trader and the adopted son of Madershee, king of the "Paupaus." He claimed that he had been tricked and overpowered by a Portuguese slave crew while loading a shipment of captives, and was thus himself enslaved alongside his "merchandise." Recaptured by the Royal Navy and brought to Sierra Leone, Dâaga "became" Donald Stewart, and was enlisted and sent to the Caribbean. According to a firsthand interview, "the seeds of mutiny were sown on the passage from Africa." He had since nurtured "a deep hatred against all white men," whom he saw as his enslavers. This was "a hatred so intense," according to Edward Joseph's account, that both during and after the mutiny, he "declared he would eat the first white man he killed." Fraser interpreted this to suggest that Dâaga's "untutored mind" was incapable of telling the difference between the Portuguese who had enslaved him and the "liberating" English, who had taken him half a world away from home for a lifetime of service as a military labourer.[73]

"Master of His Own Actions"?

The unusual nature of Dâaga's own story, and his overlapping identities of enslaver, enslaved, liberated African, and coerced military recruit, encapsulates the larger problems of trying to characterise liberated

African enlistment and its consequences. To what extent can enlisted liberated Africans (or any other non-voluntary conscripts) be held responsible
for the actions of the regiments to which they were attached? And how
much agency and volition should we read into their own individual acts of
violence and "ordering," for example during the suppression of revolts
such as Bussa's Rebellion in Barbados in 1816 or the Morant Bay Rebellion in Jamaica in 1865, or in the ongoing heavy-handed policing of enslaved and recently liberated people?[74] Was the enlisted African, as Ellis
claimed in 1885, "but a slave to the state"? Or if—as Ellis also claimed—
the liberated African soldier quartered in the West Indies considered
himself a "King's Man" and looked from a position of contemptuous superiority upon plantation slaves, should we then consider him primarily an
agent of the imperial power maintaining a race-based system of slavery
and the other forms of exploitation that followed in the wake of legal
emancipation?[75]

A further complicating factor is that as soldiers, labourers, and camp
followers, liberated Africans were the agents and instruments of the system of interventions that constituted Britain's aggressive antislavery foreign
policy in the Atlantic world. Their efforts contributed, sometimes quite directly, towards the liberation of enslaved people, and—in theory—towards
the prevention of future enslavements. For example, liberated African recruits featured heavily amongst the soldiers sent to garrison the receiving
hulks at Havana and Rio de Janeiro after 1835. As garrison troops, they
were responsible for guarding the hulks against raiding parties frequently
sent from the shore to seize and re-enslave the liberated people waiting for
retransportation to British territories in the Caribbean. They also served
some practical pastoral purposes—feeding and tending to the sick. It was
as symbols that these soldiers exerted perhaps the most power: uniformed
and armed British troops who had once been enslaved Africans, living
(some with their wives) within a stone's throw of the two last bastions of
illegal slave trading, within clear sight of their enslaved populations and
their incensed governments.[76]

When thinking about the soldiers for life they had created from the
ranks of the formerly enslaved, the British always preferred this latter

image of liberated Africans, provocatively and triumphantly wielding arms in the furious faces of the perfidious, pro-slavery Cuban and Brazilian authorities, and in pursuit of Britain's great goal of global freedom. The fury and frustration of the military labourers at Trinidad in 1837 made for a less comfortable image. Perhaps if Dâaga and his fellow recruits had been asked their opinions regarding their liberation, they might have pointed to their forced transatlantic transportation and their lifetime of strictly controlled, violently enforced heavy labour, and asked what difference it made, in truth, whether this was done in the name of slavery or freedom.

For policymakers like the Foreign Secretary Viscount Palmerston, however, it made a world of a difference—because it was Britain that had "saved" them, and Britain that had redeployed them in the interests of the system of antislavery as a whole. Three years after the Trinidad mutiny, Palmerston heard reports of a Dutch troop transport that had arrived in the Dutch colony of Surinam with fifty young African "recruits" from the West Africa coast "clothed in the dress of the military colonial corps of "Guides," each holding a certificate of their freedom.[77] For Palmerston, this was evidence of disguised slave trading, and it was not the first time the Netherlands had engaged in these practices. This kind of "pretended enlistment" was "the reverse of free and voluntary," he fumed, and the Netherlands government was engaging in "a virtual infraction of the [Anglo-Dutch antislavery] Treaties" by purchasing recruits through "slave redemption" on the West African coast.[78] Palmerston equated the behaviour of the Netherlands government to that of a plantation slave-master, exploiting the labour of men who had been "torn by violence from their houses and families, and carried off by force from their native country . . . to be sent off across the sea to a distant region, and to be there compelled by force to employ themselves in occupations not of their own choice."[79] This "was in fact Slave Trade, carried on by officers of the Dutch Government," because the recruits had had "no real and practical option as to continuing or not continuing as soldiers," and were "though under the name of soldiers, just as much slaves as if they were employed in field labour by private individuals."[80] Palmerston called the certificates of freedom "valueless pieces of paper" because they gave no right to the recruits to return to their own country or refuse to enter the Dutch service.[81]

In his outraged despatch to the British minister at The Hague, Palmerston landed upon "the essence of slavery," in his view. What mattered was not the type of day-to-day labour at the final destination, whether plantation or otherwise. Rather, it hinged upon

> the circumstance, that [the enslaved individual] is compelled to follow an employment not of his choice; that he is liable to punishment if he disobeys the orders of his employer; that he is not master of his own actions; nor free to go or to stay as he pleases . . . in short, that his existence depends upon the will of others, to whose will he has never of his own accord and free choice consented to submit.[82]

What Palmerston was objecting to was, in part, the process by which the Netherlands government was securing military recruits from the ranks of the enslaved and "recently liberated." Yet when we compare how individual Africans experienced British and Dutch enlistment processes and their military lives thereafter, there were more similarities than perhaps Palmerston might like to have acknowledged. Both sets of recruiters found the populations local to their recruiting stations unwilling to enlist, which caused recruiters to target their efforts at former slaves.[83] Both offered a bounty to potential recruits, the former to be used for the purchase of equipment, the latter for both manumission and equipment. Both establishments exported the vast majority of their recruits to overseas colonies, and both made claims to offering African recruits equal treatment with European recruits, including equal pay. For many recruits, however, the Netherlands offered substantially more generous terms of service (terms that were later resecured by the African soldiers through resistance, protest, and mutiny), including better pay, time-limited contracts, the acquisition of full Dutch nationality, and the right to choose to return to Africa or to settle in the Netherlands, as many in fact did. Dutch recruits were initially enlisted for just six years, and although later enlistments extended to unspecified periods of time, in 1844 African contracts were again constrained to fifteen years following a series of mutinies in the Netherlands East Indies.[84]

Palmerston's protests to The Hague (and, similarly, to the French government in Paris regarding its recruitment of former slaves through the *rachat* or "repurchase" system) were not objections in principle to the enlistment of Africans as soldiers for the consolidation of European overseas empires, and he had no serious qualms about the British recruitment of "free" West Africans, even in heavy-handed, coercive ways.[85] At the heart of British critiques of the morality of its neighbours' colonial enlistment practices was not a concern for the experience of the recruit, but a rejection of the idea that any other colonial power had earned the right to exploit African labour in this way. Britain conceived of its own African soldiers as part of a system of "improving" interventions, as both products and producers of its blended empire building and antislavery efforts around the world—the one justifying and legitimising the other. As Roger Anstey notes, and Richard Huzzey echoes, once "the notion that action against the slave trade on both humanitarian and commercial grounds was a good and proper concern of policy became the received conviction" of British foreign policy, it was so deeply internalised within British political culture that it did not need to be re-litigated with every rising generation of politicians and civil servants. This self-image as the world's antislavery leader brought with it implicit assumptions regarding the justice and virtue of any action taken or articulated for the purpose of ending slavery and providing "improving" opportunities to the survivors of the slave trade. Palmerston could in one despatch fulminate about the immorality of the Dutch government's recruitment policy, then in another, order the mass removal of liberated Africans from Freetown to the West Indies without obtaining their consent or allowing them onshore to recover from the gruelling experiences they had endured already. In yet another, he could order that forcibly recruited liberated African troops of the West India Regiments be posted to the HMS *Romney* at Havana as a provocation to the Cuban population—and he never had to account for the contradictions and inconsistencies of British policy, or consider whether the lifelong enlistment of slave trade survivors was an appropriate exercise of power by a state purportedly dedicated to humane forms of governance and the provision of refuge.

Prime Minister William Pitt reassured the House of Commons in February 1805 that the government "had never conceived the idea of buying slaves for their use" as soldiers of the West India Regiments, and any reports that the British government had "made a contract . . . for purchasing five or six thousand slaves" were simply not true. Rather, the army was "purchas[ing] *the redemption* of those persons from a state of slavery whom government wished to employ as soldiers. This was an idea," he claimed, "totally different from that of becoming purchasers of slaves."[86] Was this mere cynicism and hypocrisy—a claim delivered with a knowing smile to a broadly sympathetic audience? Perhaps—but it signalled the emergence of a new kind of discourse that would pervade British political culture after 1807: that of the benevolent empire's voluntary self-sacrifice and its assumption of a costly and wearisome global moral leadership on the question of free labour, in which the British imperial state had the right to demand of Africans—and particularly the recent survivors of the Middle Passage—a lifetime of unquestioning service. Or as one governor of Sierra Leone argued, it was inconceivable that the recruiters of the West India Regiments should seek the consent of the liberated Africans they wanted, and "an unnecessary waste of Public money" that the liberated people should be paid an enlistment bounty. Britain had saved them; they were therefore "at the absolute disposal of the Crown."[87] Their subsequent experiences and actions as soldiers defy simplistic categorisation of "oppressed" and "oppressor." Their years of service challenge us to think about what it meant to have survived the slave trade, and whether this was achieved at the moment of disembarkation from a slave ship, or was an ongoing process, perhaps of many years' duration.

Epilogue

3.—(1) The purpose of detention centres shall be to provide for the secure but humane accommodation of detained persons in a relaxed regime with as much freedom of movement and association as possible, consistent with maintaining a safe and secure environment, and to encourage and assist detained persons to make the most productive use of their time, whilst respecting in particular their dignity and the right to individual expression.

(2) Due recognition will be given at detention centres to the need for awareness of the particular anxieties to which detained persons may be subject and the sensitivity that this will require, especially when handling issues of cultural diversity.[1]

—Immigration: The Detention Centre Rules, 2001 (UK)

The evolution over the past two centuries of an international humanitarian order is, by any measure, a noteworthy achievement. From the small seeds of experimental charity- and state-led projects, a complex of national and international institutions and structures has emerged, underpinned by a foundation of laws, norms, and shared aspirations that together seek to end violence and deprivation, to impose on all nations a shared universal programme of human rights and human dignity, and above all to save other people from all manner of imminent perils. Surveying what has evolved in such a short space of time, it is easy to understand why many observers have been moved to interpret this as the emergence of a true international community bound together by a common humanity—a humanity defined, ultimately, by compassion for the vulnerable and desperate.

In this period of evolution, the tools of intervention have changed dramatically. The emergence of the United Nations as the cornerstone of international relief and response efforts, combined with the explosion in the number, sophistication, and professionalism of non-governmental organisations, has displaced the state from the leading role it occupied for a time in emergent systems and discourses of humanitarian governance. State-level foreign aid and development budgets are still significant elements of the more "developmental" side of humanitarian activity. Armed humanitarian and "Responsibility to Protect" interventions still in theory present possibilities for state-led emergency action that can supersede—in practice if not always in law—the inviolability of state sovereignty. However, the humanitarian sphere is now generally understood as an international space of conspicuously transnational collaboration, at least among the leading voices in international humanitarian governance, if not always fully consensual with regard to the recipient populations. Even though, as Michael Barnett acknowledges, the world's security and economic orders retain a far more prominent profile in the international system, nevertheless a blend of humanitarian and human rights values, activities, rules, and processes clearly represents a third pillar of that system. This blend of contested and constantly evolving ideas, aspirations, and endeavours is more of an incidental convergence than the product of anyone's particular design, but in many ways, it can be thought of as a kind of "international moral order."[2] Both its critics and champions alike recognise the common traits this moral order shares with security and economic orders, not least the forceful and paternalistic methods and discourses through which dominant voices in the international system seek to impose their vision of order on the rest of the world. That ongoing constructive critique is, in and of itself, a cause for some celebration.

Yet the international system of humanitarian governance, with its many agencies and arms of advocacy and intervention, is only one outcome—and perhaps not even the most direct one—of the set of imperial experiments and discourses that took shape in the nineteenth century.

Just as the British antislavery world system had both domestic and foreign policy dimensions that were conceptually quite distinct from each other, we must look in the present day to the domestic as well as the international to trace the legacies of these spheres of activity and interest. Indeed, it is in the domestic and internal imperial evolution of humanitarian governance that we find the more direct descendants of the early liberated African re-settlement experiments. It is a genealogy that leads us to the "empire" of late nineteenth-century British concentration camps, and to the ten mil-lion starving and destitute men, women, and children detained in these camps in the quarter century after 1876.[3] And it is a genealogy that leads us further, right to the present day, inside the network of razor-wire-fenced Immigration Removal Centres that form the notorious hallmark of twenty-first-century British immigration, refugee, and asylum policies.

Throughout the nineteenth century, as we have seen, Britain pursued at little effective cost to itself a policy of placing diplomatic pressure on anti-slavery treaty partners to confer meaningful forms of freedom on the sur-vivors of the slave trade. In the process, it developed a sense of moral prestige and a self-image as the defender of the vulnerable against the ex-ploitative proclivities of the primarily Catholic, slave-hungry powers of the tropics. Within its own colonial territories, however, a remarkably differ-ent tone of governance assumptions and policies emerged. It was often dif-ficult to sustain a benevolent self-image and yet enact the coercion required to control and extract value from a vulnerable, though not entirely pliant, population of survivors. While liberated African disposal policies and practices did not remain constant across the period from 1808 to the late nineteenth century, two characteristics dominated. The first was the construction of liberated Africans as requiring carceral containment, close monitoring, and restriction of their activities and relationships. The ratio-nale was that they were both threatened and a threat—or, to echo the ter-minology of both Ann Laura Stoler and Didier Fassin in relation to colonised populations sequestered in barbed-wire encampments, because they were both "at risk" and "a risk."[4] The second characteristic was the assumption that liberated people had accrued a form of debt to those who had saved them from both slavery and "barbarism"; that the state had a right to extract repayment in kind through programmes of coerced labour (generally of fixed duration), and that a routine of rigorous labour—even when it produced little value—was an "improving" intervention without which the target population might become lazy, idle, and permanently dependent on the charity of others.

As Alan Lester and Fae Dussart have shown, these themes emerged in later contexts throughout the British settler empire in the self-consciously humane endeavours of governing elites to ameliorate the condition of enslaved people and to protect Aboriginal populations from extermination while managing their systematic dispossession. From the Caribbean and British Honduras to Van Diemen's Land, New South Wales, Cape Colony, and New Zealand, colonial officials like George Arthur and George Grey invoked humanitarian registers of governance in experiments that used containment, carcerality, and coerced labour to render vulnerable and disorderly populations "safer" and more orderly within their colonial spaces; to prevent the worst excesses of settler and planter violence; and in the process, to remake enslaved, formerly enslaved, and indigenous communities as governable populations within the landscape of the expanding empire. It was a process, as Lester and Dussart's nuanced and wide-ranging study demonstrates, that provoked a range of responses from the target populations, not least—and as with the liberated Africans several decades previously—a keen understanding of the strategic and tactical opportunities made possible by this distinct strand of colonialist discourse and the evident dissentions it created amongst white colonisers.[5]

It was in the later nineteenth century, however, that the "tightly braided colonial politics of humanity and security" found their fullest expression in the creation of what Aidan Forth has termed the "empire" of concentration camps across Britain's colonial territories from 1876 to 1903. This vast network of camps emerged in response to war, famine, and plague conditions that killed and displaced millions of imperial subjects across Britain's southern African and south-Asian colonial territories in this period. They represented the convergence of a number of developments in British governance strategies up to then. In their animating purpose, the camps were humanitarian administrative reactions to various forms of conflict, disruption, and disaster unleashed or exacerbated by imperial expansion and mismanagement. Yet at their heart also lay the imperative to confine, sanitise, discipline, and extract labour from "socially, racially, or politically suspect" populations: a by-then-well-established "normative motif" of nineteenth-century British social ordering. Like the slave trade survivors held involuntarily within the walls of the many liberated African yards and enclosures of the Atlantic world in the first half of the century, the ten million starving and destitute men, women, and children encamped across India and the Cape Colony after 1876 did not stand accused of committing crimes. Still they were understood by anxious colonial administrators as potential threats to be contained and rendered safe from themselves and others.[6]

In their design and management, the network of British camps built upon previous nineteenth-century social and governmental experiments in deliberate and specific ways. They followed in the wake of the British "carceral archipelago" of workhouses, prisons, labour camps, convict settlements, prison hulks, mining compounds—and even to some extent lunatic asylums, hospitals, and factories—as well as the long history of experiments in, and discourses around, humanitarian governance across the British empire.[7] Each of these phenomena, variously found across metropolitan Britain and throughout the empire, contributed in different ways to the conceptual foundation underlying the camps of southern Africa and India. They helped to shape the institutional culture of a large-scale humanitarian relief infrastructure that was defined primarily by barbed wire and watchtowers, and by an administrative fixation on order, hygiene, and labour discipline that was militaristic in tone and in the force—even violence—of its implementation. The camps were, in this sense, the culmination of a century of what Sir Charles Trevelyan—who gained notoriety for his famously harsh oversight of relief efforts during the Irish famine of the 1840s—had celebrated as "extensive experiments in the science, if it may be so called, of relieving the destitute."[8]

Administrative techniques in the imperial concentration camps, such as the division of inmates into gangs under overseers and the daily routines of mustering, roll calls, and public inspections and punishments, directly recalled the strategies employed to monitor and control the liberated Africans disembarked at Freetown, at St Helena, and in other sites where an "emergency" infrastructure of liberated African yards, hospitals, and encampments was created to house, feed, clothe, work, and "dispose" of survivors. Half a world away, similar measures were also used to manage the Aboriginal inmates of Bruny and Flinders Islands in the 1820s and 1830s.

In their implementation of programmes of forced labour, many of the late nineteenth-century concentration camps exacted heavy physical tolls from those already weakened by disease and malnutrition. Sometimes these camp labour programmes were directed towards public works infrastructure projects, much as the liberated African establishments had sought to do at Sierra Leone, the Gambia, St Helena, Rio de Janeiro, and elsewhere in the days of the slave trade. Often, however, labour was coerced from concentration camp inmates for no measurable economic benefit, but rather to allay the anxieties of colonial administrators about creating long-term dependency through over-generous charitable support. Programmes of food provision and labour extraction were believed most advantageous to public morals when they kept camp inmates alive but not thriving; preserving life, but not without suffering, and forcing work that was "at all times" work that "no person would willingly perform . . . unless impelled thereto by want."[9]

It would be inaccurate to draw exact analogies between the liberated African and Aboriginal governance experiments, the late-century British concentration camps, and present-day domestic and international refugee relief policies. Systematised, state-run "civilising" forced labour, for example, is not a feature of formal policy in twenty-first-century UN- or Red Cross–managed refugee camps, or in the United Kingdom's network of Immigration Removal Centres, modern slavery National Referral Mechanism safehouses, and deportation holding sites through which many asylum seekers, failed asylum seekers, and foreign-born survivors of slavery and trafficking have moved in recent years.[10] The refuge-seeking adults and children pulled from the Mediterranean in the past two decades have not been herded by European governments into secure yards to be distributed without their consent as indentured labourers, conscripted soldiers for life, or wives and domestic servants by the governments in the territories of the receiving countries. British state-run facilities today do not enforce formal programmes of cultural erasure or the imposition of religious doctrines intended to remake the inmates in an imagined image of the host population. Furthermore, the popularly understood meaning of the term "concentration camp" shifted radically during the twentieth century and is now more commonly understood in terms of the political and genocidal fanaticism of the Soviet and Nazi regimes than in its original sense, such that few today would suggest that "concentration camps" remain a feature of the governance strategies of any but the most ruthless authoritarian regimes in the present—or at least few did so until the Trump administration resorted in 2017 to a policy of "brutal intimidation tactics of family separation and family detention" intended to deter those seeking asylum in the United States. This was a policy that Physicians for Human Rights (PHR) determined in a 2020 report constituted "cruel, inhuman, and degrading treatment and, in all cases evaluated by PHR experts, rises to the level of torture."[11]

Nevertheless, there are more echoes than many might like to acknowledge between these histories—including the notorious recent developments in United States immigration and homeland security policies—and the international histories of state-led humanitarian, asylum, and border security policies as a whole. The "archipelago" of British concentration camps in the late nineteenth century was not an aberration in an otherwise smooth journey from a public moral awakening towards liberal conceptions of universal human rights and global citizenship. Rather, the camps were the logical extension of the various large-scale, sustained experiments in humanitarian governance that had been enacted over decades by an expanding empire—an empire that rationalised and explained itself to its metropolitan subjects in terms of liberal values, humanitarianism, civilisation, and benevolence, but relied on violence, inequality, racism, curtailment of rights, and even overt coerced labour exploitation to enforce its vision of order on its global subjects.[12] Throughout the life span of the British empire, and even to the present day, many Britons were, and still are, shocked when confronted with the moral realities of empire—what it meant in practice to be a major world power with economic, security, and geo-strategic interests to promote and defend, and an unsentimental under-standing of who was, and who was not, likely to support those interests. The controversy surrounding the Fugitive Slave Circulars in the 1870s is a case in point.[13] The circulars were less a substantive deviation on the part of the British state from its core moral position on antislavery, and more a recognition of the "harshly realist" limits on the scope of state humanitar-ian action in the face of other strategic interests and international alliances, rivalries, and dependencies.[14] But the surprise and shock that members of the British public appear to have felt when they recognised the practical implications of that position demonstrates the discrepancy between the re-alities of national economic and security interests and a much cherished national mythology of being the international moral pioneer, rescuing in-nocents from slavery since 1807 and offering refuge to the oppressed and downtrodden of the world ever since.

That mythology is stretched to the breaking point in the present day—or rather it would be if the British public showed more interest in the human consequences of the immigration, asylum, and modern slavery pol-icies pursued in their name. The provision of refuge by the British state to foreign nationals has never been without its limits, anxieties, and racialised resentments. But this provision became increasingly constrained and politi-cised in the twentieth century, when the economic consequences of two world wars and the collapse of the British empire brought about an acute contraction of the territorial and material resources perceived to be avail-able for providing refuge to foreigners in need.[15] Although a deep vein of moral ambiguity, carcerality, and an "improving" or "civilising" view of labour coercion always featured in British systems of governance for vul-nerable imperial subjects, refugees, and stateless others, the opening of the Harmondsworth Detention Unit in 1970 heralded a new phase in the evo-lution of such governance, through the more overt criminalisation of asylum-seeking and the extreme (and racialised) emphasis on security in the state's response to those claiming refuge within its borders. Since 1970, and particularly in the aftermath of 11 September 2001 and the War on

Terror, the British state has operated an "estate" of Immigration Removal Centres (IRCs) intended to confine certain categories of "suspect" foreign nationals deemed to have no legal right to remain in the United Kingdom, pending legal review of their cases and, ultimately for many, their deportation.[16] Although this group can include visa over-stayers, undocumented people, and foreign nationals convicted of crimes in the United Kingdom, the detainees also include high numbers of failed asylum seekers, some victims of trafficking, and those whose modern slavery National Referral Mechanism claims have been denied. These are individuals who have committed no crimes and are held on administrative rather than criminal grounds but are nevertheless viewed, on the basis of their identity, as a security risk; a characteristic they share with the subjects of past British experiments in humanitarian governance.

From a total of 200 detainees in 1987, by 2014 the immigration estate was incarcerating some 3,000 people on any given day. The system still falls under the jurisdiction of the Home Office, but the majority of the day-to-day management has long been contracted out to private-sector contractors such as the GEO Group, Mitie, Serco, and G4S. According to IRC regulations published in 2001, the stated purpose of the centres is "to provide for the secure but humane accommodation of detained persons in a relaxed regime with as much freedom of movement and association as possible, consistent with maintaining a safe and secure environment." In an instruction that echoes the abhorrence felt by nineteenth-century administrators toward the destructive power of "idleness," the centres are also supposed "to encourage and assist detained persons to make the most productive use of their time, whilst respecting in particular their dignity and the right to individual expression."[17]

A report in 2016 conducted by Stephen Shaw, QC, at the request of the home secretary found that, rather than the "relaxed regime" suggested, the immigration estate had a needlessly carceral and even punitive character, such that "current policies and processes do not always distinguish the role of an IRC from that of a prison." He noted that IRCs including IRC Colnbrook, IRC Brook House, and Phase Two of IRC Harmondsworth were "all built to Category B prison security design."[18] Among other things,

Shaw drew attention to the harrowing experiences of some detainees, to reports of repeated patterns of physical and sexual abuse; to the malign effect of interminable detention on the mental health of detainees; and to the recent findings of British domestic courts that the Home Office was in breach of Article 3 of the European Convention on Human Rights (which outlaws torture and inhuman or degrading treatment). Shaw expressed surprise at the apathy of the British public toward these cases, and toward the regular failings of the system to provide for the basic welfare needs and protect the fundamental rights of its inmates. It was "simply inconceivable" that the British public would engage so little with similar news stories had they involved "children in care, hospital patients, prisoners, or anyone else equally dependent upon the state."[19] In October 2012, a thirty-one-year-old Ghanaian man called Prince Kwabena Fosu died of dehydration, malnutrition, and hypothermia in solitary confinement at the GEO Group UK–managed Harmondsworth IRC "in plain sight" of centre staff. An inquest later found that this man—who had been detained six months previously after travelling to the United Kingdom on a valid business visa which was cancelled on his arrival at Heathrow—had been subjected to gross neglect, occasioned by "serious failures by the Home Office and across all the agencies in immigration detention, as well as failures by police."[20] Between 2000 and 2019, thirty-six other people died in immigration detention facilities.

Whatever strong similarities exist between the pre-detention experiences of the most vulnerable subsection of today's immigration inmates—in particular asylum seekers and survivors of slavery and trafficking—and those of previous targets of historical British humanitarian governance projects, no one who has experienced the British immigration estate would discuss it in the same vein as international disaster relief, poverty-reduction, or food aid programmes. British policy towards the asylum seekers and slavery survivors caught up in the IRC complex does not in any meaningful sense resemble Barnett's definition of "humanitarianism," which suggests interventions invoking a duty of care towards strangers, grounded in a higher, transcendental moral purpose, with the primary objective of improving the welfare and safety of those who are unable to help themselves. Rather, immigration detention is conceptualised primarily as part of the criminal justice apparatus.[21] This essential purpose is clear from the signs posted outside IRCs: "Detention operations, part of immigration enforcement, serves the public by escorting and holding people detained under immigration law and by assisting in the removal of those not entitled to stay in the United Kingdom. Our purpose is to ensure that they are held securely and cared for with humanity." It suggests that the Home Office understands its primary duty of care to be to the domestic British public, and that its mission is to protect a social order which the detainees are assumed to threaten. These threatening others are to be held securely first, and with humanity second. A slogan adopted temporarily by the Home Office reinforces this impression: the mission was to "detain, protect, remove"—a mission that began with confinement and ended with ejection. The "protection" element was, as the Shaw report found, not delivered with the same energy as the other objectives; another trait the immigration estate shares with its antecedent experimental governance structures designed to contain and preserve the lives of vulnerable non-national populations throughout the empire over the previous two hundred years.

Human concern for the suffering of other individuals has always competed with anxieties about maintaining order and about the potential cost to the benefactor of assisting others. Ever since discourses of refuge and humanitarian governance entered the purview of the modern state, the result has been a politics of guarded humanitarianism—a tightly fused set of moral and security concerns that predates, and perhaps will outlast, the much more recent, and increasingly fragile, infrastructure of global human rights. The British empire was a crucible well suited to the articulation of new ideas about the humane management and control of those in urgent need. The experience of empire building and the encounters it generated were central to the formation of a humanitarian consciousness in the British public and a self-perception of the British state as a global force for good. In turn, the more disruptive, violent, and exploitative of these imperial encounters—from territorial conquest to slavery, forced labour, forced migration, and even extermination of indigenous populations—produced populations in "need" of British sympathy, intervention, and salvation through "civilisation" and "improvement."

As Caroline Shaw observes, and the history of nineteenth-century refuge demonstrates, power and resources have always been "in dialogue with categorical moral commitments, even if the emotional logic of those commitments constantly masks this."[22] Since the early nineteenth century, British state responses to governance challenges with humanitarian dimensions have been characterised by this close relationship between material resources and humanitarian commitments, and by the security concerns this interconnection creates. Previously, Britain's control over vast imperial territories facilitated a relatively open refuge policy, which enabled the cultivation of a national self-image of benign generosity with little material cost or disruption to the metropolitan equilibrium. Anxieties about order could be allayed by isolating the problematic, disorderly populations within the peripheries of empire, where their labour could also be turned to the benefit of imperial projects. For most states today, such opportunities no longer exist, nor would they be acceptable to domestic opinion—although Australia's "Pacific Solution" policy of offshoring asylum cases to islands such as Nauru and Papua New Guinea has strong echoes with previous policies.[23] In 2019, the chair of the House of Lords EU Home Affairs Sub-Committee, Lord Jay of Ewelme, remarked upon the United Kingdom's "long and proud history of offering sanctuary to those fleeing conflict and persecution," yet in the twelve months after June 2018 Britain received only 7 percent of the asylum applications registered in the European Union; Germany, France, Spain, Greece, and Italy all accepted more. In the United Kingdom in 2018, there were 126,720 refugees, 45,244 pending asylum cases, and 125 stateless persons. Turkey, by comparison, hosted 3.7 million refugees.[24]

Regardless of the reality of what states actually offer to those in desperate need, "humanitarian reason" continues to occupy a key position as a "powerful social imaginary" in contemporary Western understandings of international order and the ideologies and behaviours that ought to underpin it. It is embedded deeply in how many Western societies construct humanity at both individual and global levels, shaping a worldview that assumes "all lives are equally sacred and that all sufferings deserve to be relieved."[25] It is a discourse with which societies such as Britain, France,

Australia, and others engage readily as part of a confident self-image of progressive modernity, while yet sustaining—through apathy or intent— governance systems that "administer" asylum seekers and survivors of slavery and trafficking through carceral containment in austere, even brutal conditions, rife with systematic abuse and neglect. Viewing the altruistic self-image inherent in the social imaginary of "humanitarian reason" against the reality of state policy and public acquiescence in such governance systems, the evident divergence may be dispiriting, even depressing, but it is not particularly surprising. From the earliest history of states' pursuit of an international moral order—a history profoundly influenced by the British antislavery world system and its experiments in humanitarian governance—humanitarian state action has never existed independently of, or even on equal terms with, concerns about domestic order and security. In a world of increasing displacement, tightening borders, and heightening suspicion of immigration, those seeking to achieve a more just set of outcomes for vulnerable populations must keep shining the spotlight beyond "proud traditions" and onto actual practice, and thus deny both citizens and their governments the luxury of professing high normative and rhetorical standards that bear little resemblance to what happens out of sight.

Notes

Abbreviations

AHN	Archivo Histórico Nacional, Madrid
ANC	Archivo Nacional de Cuba
BL	British Library, London
BPP	British Parliamentary Papers
CMS	Church Missionary Society
DAB	Department of Archives, Commonwealth of the Bahamas
DUL	Duke University Library
HHC	Hull History Centre
LMS	London Missionary Society
MMS	Methodist Missionary Society
NLS	National Library of Scotland
PASL	Public Archives of Sierra Leone
PP	Broadlands MSS Palmerston papers, University of Southampton
SHADD	Studies in the History of the African Diaspora— Documents
TNA	The National Archives of the United Kingdom
TPT	Papers of Thomas Perronet Thompson

Introduction

1. David Eltis, Stanley L. Engerman, Seymour Drescher, and David Richardson, eds., *The Cambridge World History of Slavery,* vol. 4 (Cambridge: Cambridge University Press, 2017), 512.

2. The very first group of liberated Africans is believed to be the group of seventy captured on board the United States schooner *Nancy,* on 1 November 1807. See Sean Kelley, "Precedents: The Captured Negroes of Tortola, 1807–22," in *Liberated Africans and the Abolition of the Slave Trade,* ed.

Henry Lovejoy and Richard Anderson (Rochester: University of Rochester Press, 2020), 25–44. See also Henry Lovejoy, dir., *Liberated Africans,* http://liberatedafricans.org; Dean Rehberger, dir., *Enslaved: People of the Historic Slave Trade,* http://enslaved.org; David Eltis, dir., *Voyages: The Trans-Atlantic Slave Trade Database,* https://slavevoyages.org.

3. Padraic Scanlan, *Freedom's Debtors: British Antislavery in Sierra Leone in the Age of Revolution* (New Haven: Yale University Press, 2017), 3–4.

4. Suzanne Schwarz, "Reconstructing the Life Histories of Liberated Africans: Sierra Leone in the Early Nineteenth Century," *History in Africa* 39 (2012): 193–204.

5. Ludlam to Hamilton, 10 May 1808, PASL, Local Letters 1808–1811; Testimony of G. Caulker, 6 September 1809, TNA, CO 267/27; Thompson to Castlereagh, 2 August 1808, HHC, TPT, U DTH/1/23; Scanlan, *Freedom's Debtors,* 66–70; Schwarz, "Reconstructing the Life Histories of Liberated Africans," 195–99; J. J. Crooks, *History of Sierra Leone* (London: Browne and Nolan, 1903), 75.

6. Daniel Domingues da Silva, David Eltis, Philip Misevich, and Olatunji Ojo, "The Diaspora of Africans Liberated from Slave Ships in the Nineteenth Century," *The Journal of African History* 55, no. 3 (2014): 347, 367. Of these, Britain was responsible for capturing 1,596 ships and disembarking at least 164,333 liberated people. See also Richard Anderson, "The Diaspora of Sierra Leone's Liberated Africans: Enlistment, Forced Migration, and 'Liberation' at Freetown, 1808–1863," *African Economic History* 41 (2013): 103–40; Lovejoy and Anderson, eds., *Liberated Africans and the Abolition of the Slave Trade;* and Richard Anderson, "Liberated Africans," *Oxford Research Encyclopedia of African History,* https://oxfordre.com/africanhistory/view/10 .1093/acrefore/9780190277734.001.0001/acrefore-9780190277734-e-741, appendix 1, which contains estimates drawn from the latest scholarship on both Indian Ocean and Atlantic sites of liberation. At least 99,752 people were adjudicated by the Vice-Admiralty and Mixed Commission courts at Sierra Leone: ibid., appendix 1.

7. African Institution, *Fourth Report of the Directors of the African Institution* (London: Hatchard, 1810), 61–69.

8. Liverpool to Maxwell, 30 November 1811, PASL, Secretary of State's Despatches 3 April 1809–24 November 1812.

9. Christopher Fyfe, *A History of Sierra Leone* (Oxford: Oxford University Press, 1962), 499; Anderson, "Liberated Africans," appendix 1.

10. Ibid., appendix 1; Matthew Hopper, *Slaves of One Master: Globalization and Slavery in Arabia in the Age of Empire* (New Haven: Yale University Press, 2015), 169–70.

11. Sharla M. Fett, *Recaptured Africans: Surviving Slave Ships, Detention and Dislocation in the Final Years of the Slave Trade* (Chapel Hill: University of North Carolina Press, 2017); Ted Maris-Wolf, "'Of Blood and Treasure': Recaptive Africans and the Politics of Slave Trade Suppression," *The Journal of the Civil War Era* 4, no. 1 (2014): 53–83; Anderson, "Liberated Africans," appendix 1.

12. Only the inflows of enslaved people into Brazil and Cuba were larger in this period: Domingues da Silva et al., "The Diaspora of Africans Liberated from Slave Ships in the Nineteenth Century," 347. For a discussion of the challenges of quantifying the total liberated African population, see Lovejoy and Anderson, eds., *Liberated Africans and the Abolition of the Slave Trade,* 7–16.

13. Beatriz Mamigonian, "Out of Diverse Experiences, a Fragmentary History: A Study of the Historiography on Liberated Africans in Africa and the Americas," Paper presented at York University, July 1997: 20; Beatriz Mamigonian, *Africanos Livres: A Abolição do Tráfico de Escravos no Brasil* (São Paulo: Companhia das Letras, 2017).

14. Richard Huzzey, *Freedom Burning: Anti-Slavery and Empire in Victorian Britain* (Ithaca: Cornell University Press, 2012).

15. Ann Laura Stoler, "On Degrees of Imperial Sovereignty," *Public Culture* 18, no. 1 (2006): 134; Ann Laura Stoler, *Along the Archival Grain: Epistemic Anxieties and Colonial Common Sense* (Princeton: Princeton University Press, 2009), 66.

16. Michael Barnett, *Empire of Humanity: A History of Humanitarianism* (Ithaca: Cornell University Press, 2011).

17. Abigail Green, "Humanitarianism in Nineteenth-Century Context: Religious, Gendered, National," *The Historical Journal* 57, no. 4 (2014): 1161; Richard Ashby Wilson and Richard D. Brown, "Introduction," in *Humanitarianism and Suffering: The Mobilization of Empathy,* ed. Richard Ashby Wilson and Richard D. Brown (Cambridge: Cambridge University Press, 2008), 11.

18. Rob Skinner and Alan Lester, "Humanitarianism and Empire: New Research Agendas," *The Journal of Imperial and Commonwealth History* 40, no. 5 (2012): 733; Claire McLisky, "'Due Observance of Justice, and the Protection of Their Rights': Philanthropy, Humanitarianism, and Moral Purpose in the Aborigines Protection Society Circa 1837, and Its Portrayal in Australian Historiography, 1883–2003," *Limina: A Journal of Historical and Cultural Studies* 11 (2005): 57; David Lambert and Alan Lester, "Geographies of Colonial Philanthropy," *Progress in Human Geography* 28, no. 3 (2004): 320–41.

19. Barnett, *Empire of Humanity,* 37.

20. Alan Lester and Fae Dussart, *Colonization and the Origins of Humanitarian Governance: Protecting Aborigines Across the Nineteenth-Century British Empire* (Cambridge: Cambridge University Press, 2014), 5–6; Barnett, *Empire of Humanity,* 1–94; Skinner and Lester, "Humanitarianism and Empire: New Research Agendas"; Penelope Edmonds and Anna Johnston, "Empire, Humanitarianism, and Violence in the Colonies," *Journal of Colonialism and Colonial History* 17, no. 1 (2016).

21. Barnett, *Empire of Humanity,* 12.

22. Skinner and Lester, "Humanitarianism and Empire: New Research Agendas," 730.

23. John Peterson, *Province of Freedom: A History of Sierra Leone, 1787–1870* (London: Faber and Faber, 1969).

24. Mac Dixon-Fyle and Gibril Cole, eds., *New Perspectives on the Sierra Leone Krio* (New York: Peter Lang, 2006); Akintola J. G. Wyse, *The Krio of Sierra Leone: An Interpretive History* (London: Hurst, 1989); Christopher Fyfe, "Peter Nicholls—Old Calabar and Freetown," *Journal of the Historical Society of Nigeria* 2, no. 1 (1960): 105–14; Fyfe, *A History of Sierra Leone;* Bronwen Everill, "Bridgeheads of Empire? Liberated African Missionaries in West Africa," *Journal of Imperial and Colonial History* 40 (2012): 789–805; Jean H. Kopytoff, *A Preface to Modern Nigeria: The "Sierra Leoneans" in Yoruba, 1830–1890* (Madison: University of Wisconsin Press, 1965); Richard Anderson, "Uncovering Testimonies of Slavery and the Slave Trade in Missionary Sources: The SHADD Biographies Project and the CMS and MMS Archives for Sierra Leone, Nigeria, and the Gambia," *Slavery and Abolition* 38, no. 3 (2017): 620–44.

25. Hopper, *Slaves of One Master;* Domingues da Silva et al., "The Diaspora of Africans Liberated from Slave Ships in the Nineteenth Century," 356, 359; Mamigonian, *Africanos Livres;* Fett, *Recaptured Africans.*

26. Peterson, *Province of Freedom.*

27. Clare Anderson, "After Emancipation: Empires and Imperial Formations," in *Emancipation and the Remaking of the British Imperial World,* ed. Catherine Hall, Nick Draper, and Keith McClelland (Manchester: Manchester University Press, 2014), 113–27; Sharla Fett, "Middle Passages and Forced Migrations: Liberated Africans in Nineteenth-Century U.S. Camps and Ships," *Slavery and Abolition* 31, no. 1 (2010): 75–98; Manuel Barcia, *The Yellow Demon of Fever: Fighting Disease in the Nineteenth-Century Atlantic Slave Trade* (New Haven: Yale University Press, 2020), 125–65.

28. Skinner and Lester, "Humanitarianism and Empire," 731.

29. Lester and Dussart, *Colonization and the Origins of Humanitarian Governance,* 1–36; Edmonds and Johnston, "Empire, Humanitarianism, and Violence in the Colonies."

30. Lester and Dussart, *Colonization and the Origins of Humanitarian Governance,* 39.

31. Caroline Shaw, *Britannia's Embrace: Modern Humanitarianism and the Imperial Origins of Refugee Relief* (Oxford: Oxford University Press, 2015).

32. Michael Barnett, "International Paternalism and Humanitarian Governance," *Global Constitutionalism* 1, no. 3 (2012): 485.

33. Ibid., 486.

34. Michael Barnett, ed., *Paternalism Beyond Borders* (Cambridge: Cambridge University Press, 2016), 1. See also Didier Fassin, *Humanitarian Reason: A Moral History of the Present* (Berkeley: University of California Press, 2012); Thomas Haskell, "Capitalism and the Origins of the Humanitarian Sensibility, Part I," *American Historical Review* 90 (1985): 339–61; R. A. Wilson and R. Brown, eds., *Humanitarianism and Suffering: The Mobilization of Empathy* (Cambridge: Cambridge University Press, 2011).

35. Lauren Benton and Lisa Ford, *Rage for Order: The British Empire and the Origins of International Law, 1800–1850* (Cambridge: Harvard University Press, 2016); Lauren Benton, "Abolition and Imperial Law, 1790–1820," *Journal of Imperial and Commonwealth History* 39, no. 3 (2011): 355–74.

36. Domingues da Silva et al., "The Diaspora of Africans Liberated from Slave Ships in the Nineteenth Century," 355.

37. Lisa Ford, "Anti-Slavery and the Reconstitution of Empire," *Australian Historical Studies* 45, no. 1 (2014): 71–86; Zoë Laidlaw, *Colonial Connections, 1815–45: Patronage, the Information Revolution, and Colonial Government* (Manchester: Manchester University Press, 2005).

38. Huzzey, *Freedom Burning,* 40–74; Roger Anstey, "Capitalism and Slavery: A Critique," *Economic History Review* 21 (1968): 307–20; K. Hamilton and P. Salmon, eds., *Slavery, Diplomacy, and Empire: Britain and the Suppression of the Slave Trade, 1807–1975* (London: Sussex Academic Press, 2012).

39. Hansard House of Commons Parliamentary Debates, 1st series, 2 June 1815, vol. 31, c. 592, *House of Commons Historic Hansard Archives,* http://hansard .millbanksystems.com/. Viscount Palmerston was later home secretary, three-time foreign secretary, and twice prime minister.

40. Evidence of H. W. Macaulay, "Report from the Select Committee on Aborigines," *BPP* 1837 (425) VII.1: 34. See also A. B. Ellis, *The History of the First West India Regiment* (London: Chapman and Hall, 1885), 188, 208–12;

Ricketts to Hay, 8 December 1828, *BPP* 1830 (57) XXI.225: 33; Anderson, "The Diaspora of Sierra Leone's Liberated Africans," 105.

41. Scanlan, *Freedom's Debtors;* Padraic X. Scanlan, "The Colonial Rebirth of British Anti-Slavery: The Liberated African Villages of Sierra Leone, 1815–1824," *American Historical Review* 141, no. 4 (2016): 1085–113; Padraic Scanlan, "'The Rewards of Their Exertions': Prize Money and British Abolitionism in Sierra Leone, 1808–1823," *Past and Present* 225, no. 1 (2014): 113–42.

42. Christopher L. Brown, *Moral Capital: Foundations of British Abolitionism* (Chapel Hill: University of North Carolina Press, 2006).

43. Shaw, *Britannia's Embrace;* Caroline Shaw, "The British, Persecuted Foreigners, and the Emergence of the Refugee Category in Nineteenth-Century Britain," *Immigrants and Minorities* 30 (2012): 239–62.

44. Shaw, *Britannia's Embrace,* 2–11.

45. Act for the Abolition of the Slave Trade, 1807, 47 Geo. III, c. 36 sess. I, 25 March 1807, *The Statutes of the Kingdom of Great Britain and Ireland: 1807–1869* (London, 1807–1869), article VII.

46. Joseph C. Miller, *Way of Death: Merchant Capitalism and the Angolan Slave Trade: 1730–1830* (Madison: University of Wisconsin Press, 1988), 225; Alexander X. Byrd, "Captives and Voyagers: Black Migrants Across the Eighteenth-Century World of Olaudah Equiano" (unpublished PhD thesis, Duke University, 2001), 37–49; Fett, *Recaptured Africans,* 8; [Laura] Rosanne M. Adderley, *"New Negroes from Africa": Slave Trade Abolition and Free African Settlement in the Nineteenth-Century Caribbean* (Bloomington: Indiana University Press, 2006), 2–3, 26, 62.

Chapter 1. "Management Without Responsibility"

1. Examples include Johnson U. J. Asiegbu, *Slavery and the Politics of Liberation, 1787–1861: A Study of Liberated African Emigration and British Anti-slavery Policy* (New York: Africana Publishing Corporation, 1969), 22–23; Adderley, *New Negroes from Africa,* 3; John Flint, ed., *The Cambridge History of Africa from c. 1750 to c. 1870,* vol. 5 (Cambridge: Cambridge University Press, 1976), 179; Scanlan, *Freedom's Debtors,* 62; J. D. Hargreaves, *Prelude to the Partition of West Africa* (London: Macmillan, 1963), 26–29; Tara Helfman, "The Court of Vice Admiralty at Sierra Leone and the Abolition of the West African Slave Trade," *Yale Law Journal* 115, no. 5 (2006): 1130; L. M. Bethell, "The Mixed Commissions for the Suppression of the Transatlantic Slave Trade in the Nineteenth Century," *Journal of African History* 7, no. 1 (1966): 81.

2. Chaim D. Kaufmann and Robert E. Pape, "Explaining Costly International Moral Action: Britain's Sixty-Year Campaign Against the Slave Trade," *International Organisation* 53, no. 4 (1999): 631–68.

3. Macaulay to Ludlam, 4 November 1807, HHC, TPT, U DTH/1/2; Robert Thorpe, *A Letter to William Wilberforce,* 3rd ed. (London: Rivington, 1815), 47.

4. Macaulay to Ludlam, 26 February 1807, quoted in Fyfe, *A History of Sierra Leone,* 98; African Institution, *Fourth Report of the Directors of the African Institution,* 61–71; "Letters Patent Establishing a Court of Vice Admiralty at Sierra Leone," 2 May 1807, TNA, ADM 5/51; Robin Blackburn, *Overthrow of Colonial Slavery, 1776–1848* (London: Verso, 1988), 295–315. See also Bevan Marten, "Constitutional Irregularities in the British Imperial Courts of Vice Admiralty During the Mid-Nineteenth Century," *The Journal of Legal History* 37, no. 2 (2016): 215–43.

5. Philip Curtin, ed., *Africa Remembered: Narratives by West Africans in the Era of the Slave Trade* (Madison: University of Wisconsin Press, 1967), 123–39; Fyfe, *A History of Sierra Leone,* 93–94; "Report from the Committee on the Petition of the Court of Directors of the Sierra Leone Company," 27 February 1804, *BPP,* 1803–1804 (24) V.81: 1–129.

6. Hansard House of Commons Parliamentary Debates, 9 July 1804, vol. 2, cc. 965–69 and 29 July 1807, vol. 9, cc. 1002–5; Fyfe, *A History of Sierra Leone,* 93, 97.

7. Hansard House of Commons Parliamentary Debates, 29 July 1807, vol. 9, c. 1004.

8. See Cassandra Pybus, "'A Less Favourable Specimen': The Abolitionist Response to Self-Emancipated Slaves in Sierra Leone, 1793–1808," *Parliamentary History* 26, supp. (2007): 101–12. See also "Memorial of William Henry Gould Page to HRH the Prince Regent," 24 June 1815, TNA, FO 72/182/72-3; Wilberforce to Castlereagh, 19 January 1808, TNA, CO 267/25.

9. Macaulay to Ludlam, 4 November 1807, in Zachary Macaulay, *A Letter to His Royal Highness the Duke of Gloucester, President of the African Institution,* 2nd ed. (London: Hatchard, 1815), 22; Pybus, "The Abolitionist Response," 110–12; TNA, PC 2/175, cited in ibid., 111; Fyfe, *A History of Sierra Leone,* 105.

10. Scanlan, *Freedom's Debtors,* 21; Benton, "Abolition and Imperial Law, 1790–1820."

11. David Eltis, *Economic Growth and the Ending of the Transatlantic Slave Trade* (New York: Oxford University Press, 1987), 111; Fyfe, *A History of Sierra Leone,* 141, 191; Catherine Hall, *Macaulay and Son: Architects of Imperial Britain* (New Haven: Yale University Press, 2012); Scanlan, *Freedom's Debtors,* 97–129.

12. Siân Rees, *Sweet Water and Bitter* (London: Chatto and Windus, 2009), 35.

13. James Macqueen, *The Colonial Controversy, Containing a Refutation of the Calumnies of the Anticolonists* (Glasgow, 1825), 93; Margaret Knutsford, *Life and Letters of Zachary Macaulay* (London: Khull, Blackie, 1901), 286.

14. Diary of Thomas Perronet Thompson, 8 June 1808 quoted in L. G. Johnson, *General T. Perronet Thompson, 1783–1869: His Military, Literary, and Political Campaigns* (London: Allen and Unwin, 1957), 34.

15. Thompson to Ludlam, 27 August 1808, 1 September 1808, and 14, 16, 18 January 1809, HHC, TPT, DTH 12, 63; Scanlan, *Freedom's Debtors*, 73–74; Michael J. Turner, "The Limits of Abolition: Government, Saints, and the 'African Question,' c. 1780–1820," *The English Historical Review* 112, no. 446 (1997): 335–36; Thompson to Barker, 23 July 1808, HHC, TPT, U DTH/4/1; Thompson, "Narrative of Facts Connected with the Colony of Sierra Leone," HHC, TPT, U DTH/1/35. See also *Sierra Leone Gazette*, 7 (1 August 1808); Peterson, *Province of Freedom*, 52.

16. Journal of Thompson, 21 July–17 October 1808, HHC, TPT, U DTH/1/21; Thompson to Castlereagh, 2 August 1808, HHC, TPT, U DTH/1/23.

17. Ibid.; Thompson to Castlereagh, 2 November 1808, TNA, CO 267/24; Thompson to Barker, 23 July 1808, HHC, TPT, U DTH/4/1.

18. Thompson to Castlereagh, 7 March 1809, TNA, CO 267/25; Thompson to Castlereagh, 1 January 1810 TNA, CO 267/27.

19. *Sierra Leone Gazette*, 11 August 1808, 20 August 1808, 27 August 1808, 3 September 1808, 8 October 1808, 19 November 1808. See also *The African Herald*, 10 (11 November 1808); P. E. H. Hair, "Freetown Abused, 1809," *Durham University Journal* 28, no. 3 (June 1967): 152–60.

20. Thompson to Castlereagh, 2 August 1808, TNA, CO 267/24; Thompson to Castlereagh, 31 December 1808, TNA, CO 267/24; Affidavits dated August 1808 to January 1809, HHC, TPT, U DTH/1/65.

21. Wilberforce to Thompson, 19 October 1808, HHC, TPT, U DTH/1/61.

22. Thompson to Barker, 13 June 1810, HHC, TPT, U DTH/4/2. Emphasis in original. Thompson to Barker, 23 July 1808, HHC, TPT, U DTH/4/1.

23. Emphasis in original: Thompson to unnamed ship captain, 3 August 1809, HHC, TPT, U DTH/1/4; Turner, "The Limits of Abolition,," 345–46.

24. Quoted in Johnson, *General T. Perronet Thompson, 1783–1869*, 51.

25. Macaulay to Ludlam, 4 November 1807, HHC, TPT, U DTH/1/2; Turner, "The Limits of Abolition," 337–39.

26. Hansard House of Commons Parliamentary Debates, 28 February 1805, vol. 3, c. 673 and 17 March 1807, vol. 9, cc. 143–44; Lord Holland, "Remarks on the Objections to the Admission of Slave's Evidence" (draft), BL, Holland

House Papers, Add. MS. 51820, fols. 66–67; A. D. Kriegel, "A Convergence of Ethics: Saints and Whigs in British Antislavery," *Journal of British Studies* 26, no. 4 (1987): 441; William Wilberforce, *A Letter on the Abolition of the Slave Trade, Addressed to the Freeholders and Other Inhabitants of Yorkshire* (London: Cadell and Davies, 1807), 258–59.

27. Wilberforce to Thompson, 19 October 1808, HHC, TPT, U DTH/1/61; [Brougham], "Negro Slavery," *Edinburgh Review* 38 (February 1823): 170.

28. Stephen to Liverpool, 14 July 1811, TNA, CO 23/58. Stephen expressed concerns in a private letter about the lack of specificity in the apprenticeship clause of the Act: 11 July 1811, TNA, CO 23/85. See also George Stephen, *Anti-Slavery Recollections in a Series of Letters Addressed to Mrs. Beecher Stowe, Written by Sir George Stephen at Her Request,* 2nd ed. (London: Frank Cass, 1971), 21–22.

29. Eltis, *Economic Growth and the Ending of the Transatlantic Slave Trade,* 103.

30. Manon L. Spitzer, "The Settlement of Liberated Africans in the Mountain Villages of the Sierra Leone Colony, 1808–1841" (unpublished master's thesis, University of Wisconsin, 1969), 17; John Galbraith, "The Humanitarian Impulse to Imperialism," in *British Imperialism: Gold, God, Glory,* ed. Robin Winks (New York, 1963), 72.

31. William Wilberforce, *A Practical View of the Prevailing Religious System of Professed Christians in the Higher and Middle Classes in This Country; Contrasted with Real Christianity* (London: Cadell and Davies, 1834), 302.

32. Spitzer, "The Settlement of Liberated Africans," 20.

33. Suzanne Schwarz, "Commerce, Civilization, and Christianity: The Development of the Sierra Leone Company," in *Liverpool and Transatlantic Slavery,* ed. David Richardson, Suzanne Schwarz, and Anthony J. Tibbles (Liverpool: Liverpool University Press, 2007), 254; Pybus, "The Abolitionist Response," 111; Christopher L. Brown, *Moral Capital: Foundations of British Abolitionism* (Chapel Hill: University of North Carolina Press, 2006), chapter 6; Seymour Drescher, *The Mighty Experiment: Free Labour Versus Slavery in British Emancipation* (Oxford: Oxford University Press, 2004); Andrea Downing, "Contested Freedoms: British Images of Sierra Leone, 1780–1850" (unpublished PhD thesis, University of Liverpool, 1998).

34. [Sierra Leone Company], *A Substance of the Report delivered by the Court of Directors of the Sierra Leone Company . . . 27th of March 1794* (London: J. Phillips, 1794), 59–60; Wilberforce to Dundas, 1 April 1800, BL, Add. MS 41085; Pybus, "The Abolitionist Response," 109. See also Hall, *Macaulay and Son,* 1–92.

35. Catherine Hall, "White Visions, Black Lives: The Free Villages of Jamaica," *History Workshop,* no. 36 (Autumn 1993): 102–3.

36. "Sierra Leone. Report of the Commissioners of Inquiry into the State of the Colony of Sierra Leone. First part," *BPP,* 1826–1827 (312), VII.267: 54; Thorpe, *Letter to William Wilberforce,* 23–26.

37. [African Institution], *Rules and Regulations of the African Institution Formed on the 14th of April 1807* (London: Phillips, 1807), 27–28.

38. Eltis, *Economic Growth and the Ending of the Transatlantic Slave Trade,* 111.

39. Lester and Dussart, *Colonization and the Origins of Humanitarian Governance,* 275.

40. Scanlan, *Freedom's Debtors,* 96.

Chapter 2. "With a View to Their Own Welfare"

1. James T. Boyle, *A Practical Medico-Historical Account of the Western Coast of Africa* (London: Highley, 1831), 399–400; Barcia, *The Yellow Demon of Fever,* 1–6, 62–124; Mary Wills, "The Royal Navy and the Suppression of the Atlantic Slave Trade, c. 1807–1867: Anti-Slavery, Empire, and Identity" (unpublished PhD thesis, University of Hull, 2012), 153–59; Mary Wills, *Envoys of Abolition: British Naval Officers and the Campaign Against the Slave Trade in West Africa* (Liverpool: Liverpool University Press, 2019); Hannah Kilham, *Present State of the Colony of Sierra Leone,* 2nd ed. (London: Lindfield, 1832), 20–23; Robert Clarke, *Sierra Leone: A Description of the Manners and Customs of the Liberated Africans* (London: James Ridgway, 1843), 83–85; Richard Anderson, *Abolition in Sierra Leone: Rebuilding Lives and Identities in Nineteenth-Century West Africa* (Cambridge: Cambridge University Press, 2020), 66–95. See also Denham to Hay, 25 February 1827, TNA, CO 323/148.

2. William Hamilton, "Sierra Leone and the Liberated Africans," *The Colonial Magazine and Commercial Maritime Journal* 6 (September–December 1841): 328, 334; Clarke, *Sierra Leone: A Description of the Manners and Customs of the Liberated Africans,* 84–85. See also Barcia, *The Yellow Demon of Fever,* 142, 158–59; Peterson, *Province of Freedom,* 256–58; Maria Louisa Charlesworth, *Africa's Mountain Valley, or The Church of Regent's Town, West Africa* (London: Seeley, Jackson, and Halliday, 1856), 13; F. W. Butt-Thompson, *Sierra Leone in History and Tradition* (London: Witherby, 1926), 160. For a comparison with St Helena, see George McHenry, "An Account of the Liberated African Establishment at St Helena," *Simmond's Colonial Magazine and Foreign Miscellany* 6 (September–December 1845): 253, 262–63.

3. "Total Africans Liberated and Disposed of at Sierra Leone, 1808–1833," TNA, CO 267/127; Peterson, *Province of Freedom,* 60; Spitzer, "The Settlement of Liberated Africans," appendix 1; Stiv Jakobsson, *Am I Not a Man and a Brother? British Missions and the Abolition of the Slave Trade and Slavery in West Africa and the West Indies, 1786–1838* (Uppsala: Gleerup, 1972), 173.

4. Nyländer to Pratt, 7 December 1810, CMS, CA1/E2/42; Jakobsson, *Am I Not a Man and a Brother?,* 176; R. R. Kuczynski, *Demographic Survey of the British Colonial Empire,* 2 vols. (London, 1948), vol. 1, 126–32; Fyfe, *A History of Sierra Leone,* 115, 183–84, 270–72; Daniel Augustine Vonque Stephen, "A History of the Settlement of Liberated Africans in the Colony of Sierra Leone During the First Half of the Nineteenth Century" (unpublished master's thesis, University of Durham, 1963), 31. Numerous cases of escaping and kidnapping also appear in the volumes of Local Letters, Court Records, Liberated African Department Letterbooks and Governors' Despatches from 1808 to mid-century, held at PASL and partially digitised by the British Library: BL, EAP443/1, https://eap.bl.uk/project/EAP443. See also Schwarz, "Reconstructing the Life Histories of Liberated Africans," 195–99, 203–4.

5. Anderson, *Abolition in Sierra Leone: Rebuilding Lives and Identities in Nineteenth-Century West Africa,* 96–126; Fyfe, *A History of Sierra Leone,* 138; Scanlan, *Freedom's Debtors,* 167–209.

6. Maxwell to Liverpool, 7 May 1812, TNA, CO 267/34; Fyfe, *History of Sierra Leone,* 115.

7. Maxwell to Goulbourn, undated, TNA, CO 267/40; Scanlan, *Freedom's Debtors,* 139–44.

8. Maxwell to Liverpool, 13 September 1812, TNA, CO 267/34; Scanlan, *Freedom's Debtors,* 96, 142–43, 150, 166.

9. Bathurst to Maxwell, 26 October 1812, TNA, CO 267/30; "Papers Relating to Captured Negroes at Sierra Leone," *BPP,* 1813–1814 (354) XII. 337; "Finance Accounts of Great Britain, for the Year Ended 5 January 1814," *BPP,* 1813–1814 (77) X.225. Nevertheless, by the end of Maxwell's tenure in 1814, bills drawn "for the Subsistence and Maintenance, &c. of Captured Negroes" of over £11,000 were being reimbursed to colonial officers by a special Treasury grant. See also "General Return of Slaves Received into the Colony of Sierra Leone . . . 1808 to 1825," TNA, CO 267/91, appendix A12 and "Census of Population and Liberated Africans," 1832–1834, TNA CO 267/127.

10. Bruce Mouser, "Origins of Church Missionary Society Accommodation to Imperial Policy: The Sierra Leone Quagmire and the Closing of the Susu

Mission, 1804–17," *Journal of Religion in Africa* 39, no. 4 (2009): 375–402; T. R. Birks, ed., *Memoir of the Rev. Edward Bickersteth, Late Rector of Watton, Herts.,* 2 vols. (New York: Harper, 1851).

11. *Royal Gazette and Sierra Leone Advertizer,* 13 September 1823; Spitzer, "The Settlement of Liberated Africans," 37–38.

12. MacCarthy to Pratt and Bickersteth, 26 November 1819, BL, CMS, CA1/ E8/74.

13. Quoted in The Reverend Samuel Walker, *The Church of England Mission in Sierra Leone, Including an Introductory Account of That Colony and a Comprehensive Sketch of the Niger Expedition in the Year 1841* (London: Seeley, Burnside, and Seeley, 1847), 3–4.

14. MacCarthy to Bathurst, 31 May 1816, TNA, CO 267/42.

15. Scanlan, *Freedom's Debtors,* 167–209.

16. "Sierra Leone: Report of the Commissioners of Inquiry into the State of the Colony of Sierra Leone. First Part," *BPP,* 1826–1827 (312) VII.267: 27, 56–58; William Hamilton, "Sierra Leone and the Liberated Africans," *The Colonial Magazine and Commercial Maritime Journal* 7 (September 1841–June 1842): 218. See also Fyfe, *A History of Sierra Leone,* 167–68.

17. "General Return of Slaves Received into the Colony of Sierra Leone from 5 January 1814 to 4 January 1824," 10 January 1825, TNA, CO 267/65.

18. "Sierra Leone: Report of the Commissioners of Inquiry into the State of the Colony of Sierra Leone. First Part," *BPP,* 1826–1827 (312) VII.267: 27–28; Reffell to Superintendents, 15 August 1822, PASL, Liberated African Department Letterbook, 1820–1826.

19. "Abstract Statement of the Expenditure in the Colony of Sierra Leone from the Year 1812 to 1825," TNA, CO 267/91; TNA, CO 267/46; Jakobsson, *Am I Not a Man and a Brother?,* 206; "Abstract Statement of Expenditure in Sierra Leone, 1812–1815, Commission of Inquiry, 1827, Evidence no. 1A," TNA, CO 267/91.

20. "Sierra Leone: Report of the Commissioners of Inquiry into the State of the Colony of Sierra Leone. First Part," *BPP,* 1826–1827 (312) VII.267: 63–64; Fyfe, *A History of Sierra Leone,* 154.

21. Nyländer to Bickersteth, 3 March 1819, BL, CMS, CA1/E7A/30; Nyländer report, 6 June 1819, Quarterly Meeting, BL, CMS, CA1/E8/16. Emphasis in original.

22. Wenzel to Pratt, 22 July 1816, BL, CMS, CA1/E5/144; Wenzel to Pratt, 17 October 1816, BL, CMS, CA1/E5A/6; Haensel to Pearson, 24 November 1831, BL, CMS, CA1/O108a/49. See also MacCarthy to Pratt, 29 June 1817, BL, CMS, CA1/E6; MacCarthy to Bickersteth, 20 June 1818, BL, CMS, CA1/E7;

MacCarthy to Bathurst, 1 April 1817, TNA, CO 267/45; MacCarthy to Bathurst, 14 January 1822, TNA, CO 267/56; "Leopold Report," 26 December 1820, BL, CMS, CA1/M1.

23. Hall, "White Visions, Black Lives," 128–29.

24. David Northrup, "Becoming African: Identity Formation Among Liberated Slaves in Nineteenth-Century Sierra Leone," *Slavery and Abolition* 27, no. 1 (2006): 7.

25. "Sierra Leone. Report of the Commissioners of Inquiry into the State of the Colony of Sierra Leone. First part," *BPP*, 1826–1827 (312), VII.267: 54; Peterson, *Province of Freedom*, 258.

26. Fyfe, *A History of Sierra Leone*, 167–69, 170–71, 186, 234–35; Coker to Ricketts, 12 August 1829, PASL, Local Letters Received 1823–1829; Cole to Jones, 27 May 1830 and Cole to Gerber, 4 November 1830, PASL, Liberated African Department Letterbook 1830–1831; Peterson, *Province of Freedom*, 102–3, 234–37.

27. Bathurst to Pratt, 9 June 1824, TNA, CO 268/20.

28. Turner to Bathurst, 25 January 1826, "Sierra Leone. Return to an address . . . 19th May 1829," *BPP*, 1830 (57), XXI.225: 6; Bathurst to Denham, 20 November 1826, ibid., 11. See also Christopher Fyfe, "Denham, Dixon (1786–1828)," *Oxford Dictionary of National Biography* (Oxford: Oxford University Press, 2004), online ed., January 2008, www.oxforddnb.com/view/article/7476; Fyfe, *A History of Sierra Leone*, 155.

29. Bathurst to Campbell, 25 November 1826, "Sierra Leone. Return to an address . . . 19th May 1829," *BPP*, 1830 (57), XXI.225: 9; "Sierra Leone. Report of the Commissioners of Inquiry into the State of the Colony of Sierra Leone. First part," *BPP*, 1826–1827 (312), VII.267: 11.

30. Emphasis in original. This description of an unnamed friend is quoted in H. M. Stephens, "Campbell, Sir Neil (1776–1827)," rev. Stewart M. Fraser, *Oxford Dictionary of National Biography* (Oxford: Oxford University Press, 2004) online ed., January 2008, www.oxforddnb.com/view/article/7476.

31. Fyfe, *A History of Sierra Leone*, 155.

32. "An Extract of the Minutes and Instructions by Major General Sir Neil Campbell, for the Superintendent of the Liberated African Department, and the Managers of the Villages," 1 December 1826, enclosed in Campbell to Bathurst, 19 January 1827, "Sierra Leone. Return to an address . . . 19th May 1829," *BPP*, 1830 (57), XXI.225: 11–14; Walker, *The Church of England Mission in Sierra Leone*, 275.

33. Denham to Hay, 21 January 1827, TNA, CO 323/148; Denham to Hay, 13 February 1827, TNA, CO 323/148; Denham to Hay, 4 April 1827, TNA, CO

323/148; Denham to Hay, 14 May 1828, "Sierra Leone. Return to an
address . . . 19th May 1829," *BPP,* 1830 (57), XXI.225: 25–26; Denham to
Bathurst, 21 May 1827, "Sierra Leone. Return to an address . . . 19th May
1829," *BPP,* 1830 (57), XXI.225: 15–18; Denham to Hay, 20 September 1827,
TNA, CO 323/148.

34. Denham to Hay, 13 February 1827, TNA, CO 323/148.
35. Denham to Hay, 4 April 1827 and Campbell to Hay, 24 February 1827, TNA,
    CO 323/148.
36. Denham to Hay, 20 September 1827, TNA, CO 323/148.
37. Denham to Hay, 4 April 1827, TNA, CO 323/148.
38. Denham to Hay, 6 October 1827 and Denham to Hay, 25 February 1827,
    TNA, CO 323/148; Denham to Hay, 16 May 1828, TNA, CO 323/151.
39. "Report from the Select Committee on the West Coast of Africa. Part I—
    Report and Evidence," *BPP,* 1842 (551), XI.1, XII.1, appendix 15: 252;
    Kenneth Macaulay, *The Colony of Sierra Leone Vindicated from the
    Misrepresentations of Mr MacQueen* (London: Hatchard, 1827), 5–6.
40. "Return of the Establishment of the Liberated African Department at Sierra
    Leone from 1 July to 31 December 1841," PASL, Liberated African Depart-
    ment Misc. Returns, 1839–1844. See also "Report of the Commission of In-
    quiry into the State of Sierra Leone 1826–1827," appendix B 22, "Return of
    Persons Employed in Lib. Afr. Department," TNA, CO 267/92.
41. Terry to Doherty, 3 November 1838, PASL, Liberated African Department
    Letterbook, 1837–1842.
42. Stanley to Macdonald, 5 June 1843, "Emigration: West Indies and Mauri-
    tius," *BPP,* 1844 (530), XXXV.297: 120–22. See also "Report from the Select
    Committee on the West Coast of Africa . . . Part II," *BPP,* 1842 (551), XI.1,
    XII.1, appendix 15: 250; Maeve Ryan, "A 'Very Extensive System of Pecula-
    tion and Jobbing': The Liberated African Department of Sierra Leone,
    Humanitarian Governance and the Fraud Inquiry of 1848," *Journal of Co-
    lonialism and Colonial History* 17, no. 3 (2016).
43. "Report from the Select Committee on the West Coast of Africa . . . Part II,"
    BPP, 1842 (551), XI.1, XII.1, appendix 17: 365; "Instructions for the Guid-
    ance of Managers or Assistant Managers in the Districts or Villages," "Re-
    port from the Select Committee on the West Coast of Africa . . . Part II," *BPP,*
    1842 (551), XI.1, XII.1, appendix 17: 372–73.
44. "Return of the Establishment of the Liberated African Department at Sierra
    Leone from 1 January to 30 June 1846," PASL, Liberated African Department
    Miscellaneous Returns, 1845–1861; "Return of the Establishment of the
    [Liberated African Department] at Sierra Leone from 1 July to 31 Decem-

ber 1841," PASL, Liberated African Department Miscellaneous Returns, 1839–1844.

45. Stanley to Macdonald, 5 June 1843, "Emigration: West Indies and Mauritius," *BPP,* 1844 (530), XXXV.297: 120–22.

46. "Report from the Select Committee on Colonial Accounts," *BPP,* 1845 (520), VIII.1, appendix 5: 586–87, 594–95.

47. The last condemnation was a nameless, flagless slave ship carrying equipment but no slaves, which ran aground and was burned at the Compani River, north of the Rio Nunez in late 1864: Blackall to Russell, 13 July 1864, "Return of Vessels Captured on Suspicion of Being Engaged in the Slave Trade," *BPP,* 1865 (3503), LVI.1: 5–6; "Civil Services and Revenue Departments: Appropriation Accounts, 1874–75," *BPP,* 1876 (45), L.1: 278.

48. The fifty-two surviving pensioners (thirty men, twenty-two women) received 2d. per day: Fyfe, *A History of Sierra Leone,* 499.

49. Stanley to Macdonald, 5 June 1843, "Emigration: West Indies and Mauritius," *BPP,* 1844 (530), XXXV.297: 120–22. See also "Report from the Select Committee on the West Coast of Africa . . . Part II," *BPP,* 1842 (551), XI.1, XII.1, appendix 15: 250.

50. Evidence of H. D. Campbell, "Report from the Select Committee on the West Coast of Africa . . . Part I," *BPP,* 1842 (551 551-II), XI.1, XII.1: 552–70.

51. Hall, "White Visions, Black Lives," 111; Glenelg to Gipps, 31 January 1838 plus enclosures, *BPP,* 1839 (526), XXXIV.391: 4–21; Lester and Dussart, *Colonization and the Origins of Humanitarian Governance,* 71–78, 114–72; N. J. B. Plomley, *Weep in Silence: A History of the Flinders Island Aboriginal Settlement* (Hobart: Blubber Head Press, 1987); Lyndall Ryan, *The Aboriginal Tasmanians,* 1st ed. (St Lucia: University of Queensland Press, 1981); Henry Reynolds, *Fate of a Free People* (Hawthorn: Penguin Books Australia, 1995); Benjamin Madley, "From Terror to Genocide: Britain's Tasmanian Penal Colony and Australia's History Wars," *Journal of British Studies* 47 (2008): 77–106; Tom Lawson, "'The Only Thing to Be Deplored Is the Extraordinary Mortality': Flinders Island and the Imagination of the British Empire," in *Monstrous Geographies: Places and Spaces of the Monstrous,* ed. Sarah Montin and Evelyn Tsitas (Freeland: Interdisciplinary Press, 2013), 1–9.

52. *The Antislavery Reporter* 16 (29 July 1840) in *The British and Foreign Antislavery Reporter,* vol. 1 (London: Kraus reprint, 1969), 188; Hall, "White Visions, Black Lives," 113–17.

53. James Mursell Phillippo, *Jamaica, Its Past and Present State* (London: John Snow, 1843), cited in Hall, "White Visions, Black Lives," 117–19.

54. Alan Lester, "Personifying Colonial Governance: George Arthur and the Transition from Humanitarian to Development Discourse," *Annals of the Association of American Geographers* 102, no. 6 (2012): 1468–88; Anna Johnston, "George Augustus Robinson, the 'Great Conciliator': Colonial Celebrity and Its Postcolonial Aftermath," *Postcolonial Studies* 12, no. 2 (2009): 153–72. See also Katherine Ann Roscoe, "Island Chains: Carceral Islands and the Colonisation of Australia, 1824–1903" (unpublished PhD thesis, University of Leicester, 2018), 46–48, 86–96, 204; Tom Lawson, *The Last Man: A British Genocide in Tasmania* (London: I.B. Tauris, 2014), 261–313.

55. Lester and Dussart, *Colonization and the Origins of Humanitarian Governance*, 66–67.

56. Ryan, *The Aboriginal Tasmanians*, 182–93.

57. Ibid., 182, 186, 193.

58. Lester and Dussart, *Colonization and the Origins of Humanitarian Governance*, 74.

59. Reynolds, *Fate of a Free People*, 159–89.

60. For examples of how contemporaries constructed sites of intervention and social engineering as "refuges" or "asylums," see Thorpe, *A Letter to William Wilberforce*, 25; "Mary Church," *Sierra Leone; Or, the Liberated Africans*, 32. The inscription over the main gate of the Liberated African Yard survives in modern-day Freetown, and reads: "Royal Hospital and Asylum for Africans Rescued from Slavery by British Valour and Philanthropy." See also Shaw, *Britannia's Embrace*, 113–23; Arthur to Goderich, quoted in Lester and Dussart, *Colonization and the Origins of Humanitarian Governance*, 74; Huzzey, *Freedom Burning*, 21–39.

61. Shaw, *Britannia's Embrace*, 6, 46, 77–82, 100–123.

62. *Hansard Parliamentary Debates*, 25 February 1845, vol. 77 c. 1174.

63. Barnett, ed., *Paternalism Beyond Borders*.

64. Evidence of H. W. Macaulay, "Report from the Select Committee on the West Coast of Africa . . . Part I," *BPP*, 1842 (551 551-II), XI.1, XII.1: 326–27.

65. "Slave Trade. Papers Relating to Captured Negroes," *BPP*, 1826 (81), XXVII.1: 85.

Chapter 3. Seeking Freedom in a Slave Society

1. Walter Hawthorne, "'Being Now, as It Were, One Family': Shipmate Bonding on the Slave Vessel *Emilia*, in Rio de Janeiro and Throughout the Atlantic World," *Luso-Brazilian Review* 45, no. 1 (2008): 53–77.

2. Huzzey, *Freedom Burning*, 43, 51. See also Huzzey and Burroughs, eds., *Suppression of the Atlantic Slave Trade;* K. Hamilton and P. Salmon, eds., *Slavery, Diplomacy and Empire: Britain and the Suppression of the Slave Trade, 1807–1975* (London: Sussex Academic Press, 2012), 20; Maeve Ryan, "The Price of Legitimacy in Humanitarian Intervention: Britain, the Right of Search, and the Abolition of the West African Slave Trade, 1807–1867," in *Humanitarian Intervention: A History*, ed. Brendan Simms and D. J. B. Trim (Cambridge: Cambridge University Press, 2011), 231–56.

3. David Lambert and Alan Lester, eds., *Colonial Lives Across the British Empire: Imperial Careering in the Nineteenth Century* (Cambridge: Cambridge University Press, 2006); Kirsten McKenzie, *Imperial Underworld: An Escaped Convict and the Transformation of the British Colonial Order* (Cambridge: Cambridge University Press, 2016), 11.

4. Kate Boehme, Peter Mitchell, and Alan Lester, "Reforming Everywhere and All at Once: Transitioning to Free Labor Across the British Empire, 1837–1838," *Comparative Studies in Society and History* 60, no. 3 (2018): 688–718.

5. "Minute on the Condition and Disposal of the Captured Africans at the Havana," 24 October 1835, TNA, CO 318/123.

6. Lovejoy and Anderson, eds., *Liberated Africans and the Abolition of the Slave Trade;* Christopher Saunders, "Liberated Africans in Cape Colony in the First Half of the Nineteenth Century," *International Journal of African Historical Studies* 18, no. 2 (1985): 223–39; Christopher Saunders, "'Free, Yet Slaves': Prize Negroes at the Cape Revisited," in *Breaking the Chains: Slavery and Its Legacy in the 19th Century Cape Colony*, ed. Nigel Worden and Clifton Crais (Johannesburg: Witwatersrand University Press, 1994), 99–115; Christopher Saunders, "Liberated Africans in the Western Cape: My Work and After," *Bulletin of the National Library of South Africa* 70, no. 1 (2016): 21–34; Patrick Harries, "The Hobgoblins of the Middle Passage: The Cape and the Trans-Atlantic Slave Trade," in *The End of Slavery in Africa and the Americas: A Comparative Approach*, ed. U. Schmieder et al. (Berlin: LitVerlag, 2011), 27–50; Patrick Harries, "Negotiating Abolition: Cape Town and the Trans-Atlantic Slave Trade," *Slavery and Abolition* 34, no. 4 (2013): 579–97; Patrick Harries, "Middle Passages of the Southwest Indian Ocean: A Century of Forced Immigration from Africa to the Cape of Good Hope," *Journal of African History* 55, no. 2 (2014): 173–90; Patrick Harries, "Slavery, Indenture, and Migrant Labour: Maritime Immigration from Mozambique to the Cape, c. 1780–1880," *African Studies* (2014): 323–40; Hopper, *Slaves of One Master;* Michael Reidy, "The Admission of Slaves and 'Prize Slaves' into the Cape Colony, 1797–1818" (unpublished master's thesis, University of Cape Town, 1997).

7. Saunders, "Liberated Africans in Cape Colony in the First Half of the Nineteenth Century," 224–33; Harries, "Hobgoblins of the Middle Passage"; McKenzie, *Imperial Underworld,* 111.

8. Ibid., 4.

9. Chris Saunders, "Liberated Africans at the Cape," in *Liberated Africans and the Abolition of the Slave Trade,* ed. Lovejoy and Anderson; Clare Anderson, "Convicts, Carcerality, and Cape Colony Connections in the 19th Century," *Journal of Southern African Studies* 42, no. 3 (2016): 431.

10. "Slaves, Cape of Good Hope: (Prize Slaves)," *BPP,* 1826–1827 (42), XXI.1; Saunders, "Liberated Africans in Cape Colony in the First Half of the Nineteenth Century," 234; "Journal of Proceedings of the Commissioners of Enquiry at Capetown, Commenced 28 July 1823," TNA, CO 414/1; Saunders, "Liberated Africans at the Cape: Some Reconsiderations"; Jake Richards, "Anti-Slave-Trade Law, 'Liberated Africans' and the State in the South Atlantic World, c. 1839–1852," *Past and Present* 241, no. 1 (2018): 180–82; McKenzie, *Imperial Underworld,* 116; Patrick Harries "'Ideas of Liberty and Freedom': Servile Labour at the Cape Colony Before and After Emancipation," in *Travail et culture dans un monde globalisé: De l'Afrique à l'Amérique Latine,* ed. Babacar Fall, Ineke Phaf-Rheinberger, and Andreas Eckert (Paris: Karthala; Berlin: Humboldt-Universität zu Berlin, 2015), 173–94; R. L. Watson, "'Prize Negroes' and the Development of Racial Attitudes in the Cape Colony," *South African Historical Journal* 43, no. 1 (2000): 138–62.

11. "Journal of Proceedings of the Commissioners of Enquiry at Capetown, Commenced 28 July 1823," TNA, CO 414/1; "Prize Negroes and Free Blacks," TNA, CO 414/6; Anderson, "Convicts, Carcerality, and Cape Colony Connections," 431.

12. Richards, "Anti-Slave-Trade Law, 'Liberated Africans,' and the State in the South Atlantic World," 202, 183.

13. Saunders, "Liberated Africans at the Cape: Some Reconsiderations," 306.

14. Saunders, "Liberated Africans in Cape Colony in the First Half of the Nineteenth Century," 231–35.

15. "Prize Negroes and Free Blacks," TNA, CO 414/6; "Journal of Proceedings of the Commissioners of Enquiry at Capetown, Commenced 28 July 1823," TNA, CO 414/1.

16. McKenzie, *Imperial Underworld,* 105, 110; Saunders, "Liberated Africans in Cape Colony in the First Half of the Nineteenth Century," 227; Saunders, "Free Yet Slaves," 104–6; Craig Iannani, "Contracted Chattel: Indentured and Apprenticed Labour in Cape Town, c. 1808–1840" (unpublished master's thesis, University of Cape Town, 1995), 131–72.

17. McKenzie, *Imperial Underworld,* 103–58.

18. "Slaves, Cape of Good Hope: (Prize Slaves)," *BPP*, 1826–1827 (42), XXI.1: 15; Charles Blair, "Return of Slaves Imported into This Colony Since the 1st January 1808," in George McCall Theal, *Records of the Cape Colony*, vol. 15 (London: Clowes, 1903), 212–13.

19. McKenzie, *Imperial Underworld*, 124; "Slaves, Cape of Good Hope: (Prize Slaves)," *BPP*, 1826–1827 (42) XXI.1: 15.

20. An exception can be found in the evidence of a formerly enslaved woman, Wilhelmina Rosina Hendrikson: "Slaves, Cape of Good Hope: (Prize Slaves)," *BPP*, 1826–1827 (42), XXI.1: 157–58, 169; Iannini, "Contracted Chattel," 11, 131–72.

21. Reidy, "The Admission of Slaves and 'Prize Slaves,'" 82. Blair retained his post until 1826.

22. "Replies of Mr. Blair and Mr. Wilberforce Bird, Dated 21 June 1825," "Slaves, Cape of Good Hope: (Prize Slaves)," *BPP*, 1826–1827 (42), XXI.1: 107–10. Emphasis added.

23. Ibid., 107–10; Blair to Somerset, 14 July 1823 ibid., 116; Evidence of Samboo and Malamo, ibid., 169–70.

24. For echoes of these arguments in another misconduct investigation, see Dixon to Grey, 26 December 1848, TNA, CO 267/10; Ryan, "A 'Very Extensive System of Peculation and Jobbing.'"

25. "Report of the Commissioners of Inquiry, 22 July 1825," "Slaves, Cape of Good Hope: (Prize Slaves)," *BPP*, 1826–1827 (42), XXI.1: 11–22.

26. Adderley, *New Negroes from Africa;* [Laura] Rosanne Marion Adderley, "'A Most Useful and Valuable People?' Cultural, Moral and Practical Dilemmas in the Use of Liberated African Labour in the Nineteenth-Century Caribbean," *Slavery and Abolition* 20, no. 1 (1999): 59–80; Anita Rupprecht, "'When He Gets Among His Countrymen, They Tell Him That He Is Free': Slave Trade Abolition, Indentured Africans, and a Royal Commission," *Slavery and Abolition* 33, no. 3 (2012); Monica Schuler, *Alas, Alas Kongo: A Social History of Indentured African Immigration to Jamaica* (Baltimore: Johns Hopkins University Press, 1980); Howard Johnson, "The Liberated Africans in the Bahamas, 1811–1860," *Immigrants and Minorities* 7, no. 1 (1988): 16–40; Johnson Asiegbu, "The Dynamics of Freedom: A Study of Liberated African Emigration and British Antislavery Policy," *Journal of Black Studies* 7, no. 1 (1976): 95–106; Asiegbu, *Slavery and the Politics of Liberation;* Fett, *Recaptured Africans;* K. O. Laurence, *A Question of Labour: Immigration into the West Indies in the Nineteenth Century* (St. Lawrence: Caribbean Universities Press, 1971).

27. Adderley, *New Negroes from Africa,* 3–4; Domingues da Silva et al., "The Diaspora of Africans Liberated from Slave Ships in the Nineteenth Century,"

369; Grace Turner, "In His Own Words: Abul Keli, a Liberated African Apprentice," *Journal of the Bahamas Historical Society* 29 (October 2007): 27–31.

28. Adderley, *New Negroes from Africa*, 2–14; "Minute on the Condition and Disposal of the Captured Africans," TNA, CO 318/123.

29. See "The Colonial Hospital, Southern View," in "Sierra Leone and Gambia Photographs, 1870s–1920s," TNA, CO 1069/88. See also lithographs by Auguste François Laby, c. 1850, Yale Center for British Art, Paul Mellon Collection in Scanlan, "The Colonial Rebirth of British Anti-Slavery," 1084.

30. Colebrooke to Glenelg, 18 July 1836, TNA, CO 23/97/15; Colebrooke to Glenelg, 30 August 1836, TNA, CO 23/97/34. See also Hunter to Glenelg, "Proposed Enlistment of Liberated Africans to West India Regiment," 10 December 1836, DAB Governors' Despatches, fol. 1256.

31. Adderley, *New Negroes from Africa*, 41; Richards, "Anti-Slave-Trade Law, 'Liberated Africans,' and the State in the South Atlantic World," 196.

32. Michael Craton and Gail Saunders, *Islanders in the Stream: A History of the Bahamian People*, 2 vols. (Athens: University of Georgia Press, 2004), vol. 2, 38. See also "Reports by Commissioners of Inquiry into State of Africans Apprenticed in West Indies. (I) Papers Relating to Captured Negroes" *BPP*, 1825 (114), XXV.193: 56; "Commissioners of Enquiry into the State of the 'Captured Negroes' in the West Indies," TNA, CO 318/82–98; Rupprecht, "When He Gets Among His Countrymen," 435–55; Anita Rupprecht, "From Slavery to Indenture: Scripts for Slavery's Endings," in *Emancipation and the Remaking of the British Imperial World*, ed. Hall, Draper, and McClelland, 77–97; Kelley, "Precedents: The Captured Negroes of Tortola, 1807–1822"; Alvin O. Thompson, *Unprofitable Servants: Crown Slaves in Berbice, Guyana, 1803–1831* (Kingston, Barbados: University of the West Indies Press, 2002), 113–14. On commissions of enquiry in the empire more broadly, see Zoë Laidlaw, "Investigating Empire: Humanitarians, Reform and the Commission of Eastern Inquiry," *The Journal of Imperial and Commonwealth History* 40, no. 5 (2012): 749–68; McKenzie, *Imperial Underworld*, 5–6; Oz Frankel, *States of Inquiry: Social Investigation and Print Culture in Nineteenth-Century Britain and the United States* (Baltimore: Johns Hopkins University Press, 2006), 139–72.

33. Adderley, *New Negroes from Africa*, 38, 58.

34. Johnson, "The Liberated Africans in the Bahamas," 92–93.

35. Craton and Saunders, *Islanders in the Stream*, vol. 2, 6.

36. There is some disagreement over the location of Head Quarters. Located seven miles from Nassau, the settlement later known as Carmichael seems

most likely. See Whittington B. Johnson, *Race Relations in the Bahamas: The Nonviolent Transformation from a Slave to a Free Society* (Fayetteville: University of Arkansas Press, 2000), 114. See also "Land Bought by Charles Poitier to Serve as a Place for Freed African Apprentices," 4 May 1825, DAB, Registrar General Department, Indentures Book V3, 257.

37. Poitier to Bathurst, 8 February 1825, TNA, CO 23/74.

38. Carmichael-Smyth to Murray, 13 March 1830, "Reports from Slave Colonies of State, Treatment and Employment of Africans Captured and Apprenticed Since Abolition of Slave Trade," *BPP*, 1831 (304), XIX.261: 10–11.

39. This appeared in the *Dublin Morning Post* on 28 July 1830 with the subheading, "Noble Conduct of the Governor of the Bahama Islands."

40. Carmichael-Smyth to Goderich, 5 February 1832, TNA, CO 23/86; Johnson, *Race Relations in the Bahamas,* 116; Johnson, "The Liberated Africans in the Bahamas," 23. See also *The Bahamas Argus,* 11 November 1835, "School Built at Adelaide Village for Africans," DAB.

41. *West Indian Slave-Holders' Lust of Cruelty, the Same Now as Ever,* BL, 1879.c.5.(14.), 1.

42. Carmichael-Smyth to Goderich, 5 February 1832, TNA, CO 23/86.

43. Adderley, *New Negroes from Africa,* 241–43; Johnson, "The Liberated Africans in the Bahamas," 24; Craton and Saunders, *Islanders in the Stream* vol. 2, 8; Hunter to Glenelg, 18 February 1837, TNA, CO 23/99/71–72; Patrice Williams, *A Guide to African Villages in the Bahamas* (Nassau: Bahamas Department of Archives, 1979), 8–10; Johnson, *Race Relations in the Bahamas,* 115.

44. Hunter to Glenelg, 18 February 1837, TNA, CO 23/99/71–72; Williams, *A Guide to African Villages,* 9; Colebrooke to Glenelg, 18 July 1836, TNA, CO 23/97/77; "Minute on the Condition and Disposal of the Captured Africans at the Havana," 24 October 1835, TNA, CO 318/123.

45. Twiss to Stewart, 31 August 1830, "Reports from Slave Colonies of State, Treatment and Employment of Africans Captured and Apprenticed Since Abolition of Slave Trade," *BPP*, 1831 (304), XIX.261: 12; Adderley, "A Most Useful and Valuable People," 66; Carmichael-Smyth to Goderich, 22 July 1831, TNA, CO 23/84; Adderley, *New Negroes from Africa,* 54–56. See also Nesbitt to Stanley, "Squatting on Crown Land of Liberated Africans; Fox Hill as Possible Site," 12 July 1842, DAB, Governors' Despatches, fol. 1613.

46. Craton and Saunders, *Islanders in the Stream* vol. 2, 7; "Minute on the Condition and Disposal of the Captured Africans at the Havana," 24 October 1835, TNA, CO 318/123.

47. Rigby to Nisbitt, 8 April 1833, TNA, CO 23/89.

48. Craton and Saunders, *Islanders in the Stream* vol. 2, 6–8; *Royal Gazette,* 26 November 1836.

49. Colebrooke to Aberdeen, 2 June 1835, TNA, CO 23/93; Williams, *A Guide to African Villages,* 2–17.

50. "Minute on the Condition and Disposal of the Captured Africans at the Havana," 24 October 1835, TNA, CO 318/123.

51. Boehme et al., "Reforming Everywhere and All at Once," 688–94.

52. Huzzey, *Freedom Burning;* Boehme et al., "Reforming Everywhere and All at Once," 700–708. See also Alan Lester, Kate Boehme, and Peter Mitchell, *Ruling the World: Freedom, Civilisation, and Liberalism in the Nineteenth-Century British Empire* (Cambridge: Cambridge University Press, 2021).

53. Stephen to Stanley, 3 November 1841, TNA, CO 295/135; Thomas Clarkson, *Thoughts on the Necessity of Improving the Condition of Slaves in the British Colonies with a View to Their Ultimate Emancipation* (New York, 1823); William A. Green, "The West Indies and British West African Policy in the Nineteenth Century: A Corrective Comment," *Journal of African History* 15, no. 2 (1974): 252; Adderley, "A Most Useful and Valuable People?" 65–66.

54. David Murray, *Odious Commerce: Britain, Spain, and the Abolition of the Cuban Slave Trade* (Cambridge: Cambridge University Press, 1980), 120–22; Leslie M. Bethell, *The Abolition of the Brazilian Slave Trade: Britain, Brazil, and the Slave Trade Question, 1807–1869* (Cambridge: Cambridge University Press, 1970), 380–83; Foreign Office to the Colonial Office, 17 August 1832, TNA, FO 84/133, discussed in Murray, *Odious Commerce,* 279.

55. "Minute on the Condition and Disposal of the Captured Africans at the Havana," 24 October 1835, TNA, CO 318/123.

56. Adderley, *New Negroes from Africa,* 49.

57. Ibid., appendix I, 241–43.

58. "Minute on the Condition and Disposal of the Captured Africans at the Havana," 24 October 1835, TNA, CO 318/123. Emphasis added.

59. Colebrooke to Stephen, 19 August 1835, TNA, CO 23/94; Johnson, "The Liberated Africans in the Bahamas," 26–27.

60. Stephen to Somerset, 10 March 1836, TNA, CO 23/109, quoted in Johnson, "The Liberated Africans in the Bahamas," 27.

61. Peterson, *Province of Freedom;* Scanlan, *Freedom's Debtors.*

62. Florence Mahoney, *Creole Saga: The Gambia's Liberated African Community in the Nineteenth Century* (Banjul: privately published, 2006), 19.

63. Anderson, "The Diaspora of Sierra Leone's Liberated Africans," 114.

Chapter 4. A Liberated African "Archipelago"

1. Cole to Findlay, 19 August 1828, PASL, Liberated African Department Letterbook 1826–1827.

2. On using the Liberated African Registers to trace individuals and reconstruct narratives, see Richard Anderson, Alex Borucki, Daniel Domingues da Silva, David Eltis, Paul Lachance, Philip Misevich, and Olatunji Ojo, "Using African Names to Identify the Origins of Captives in the Trans-Atlantic Slave Trade: Crowd Sourcing and the Registers of Liberated Africans, 1808–1862," *History in Africa* 40 (2013): 165–91; G. Ugo Nwokeji and David Eltis, "The Roots of the African Diaspora: Methodological Considerations in the Analysis of Names in the Liberated African Registers of Sierra Leone and Havana," *History in Africa* 29 (2002): 365–79; Suzanne Schwarz, "Extending the African Names Database: New Evidence from Sierra Leone," *African Economic History* 38 (2010): 137–63; Schwarz, "Reconstructing the Life Histories of Liberated Africans." See also Henry Lovejoy, "The Registers of Liberated Africans of the Havana Slave Trade Commission: Implementation and Policy, 1824–1841," *Slavery and Abolition* 37, no. 1 (2016): 23–44; Henry Lovejoy, "The Registers of Liberated Africans of the Havana Slave Trade Commission: Transcription Methodology and Statistical Analysis," *African Economic History* 38 (2010): 107–35; Hawthorne, "Being Now, as It Were, One Family," 54.

3. F. H. Rankin, *The White Man's Grave,* vol. 2 (London: Richard Bentley, 1836), 106. On the short-lived establishment created by Captain William Fitzwilliam Owen at Fernando Po, see Robert T. Brown, "Fernando Po and the Anti-Sierra Leonean Campaign: 1826–1854," *International Journal of African Historical Studies* 6, no. 2 (1973): 249–64.

4. Kyle Prochnow, "'Perpetual Expatriation': Forced Migration and Liberated African Apprenticeship in the Gambia," in *Liberated Africans and the Abolition of the Slave Trade,* ed. Lovejoy and Anderson, 352; "Medical Report on the General State of Health and Quarters of the Liberated Africans at Bathurst, River Gambia," 31 December 1833 in Rendall to Hay, 9 April 1834, TNA, CO 87/10; Rendall to Glenelg, 11 January 1836, TNA, CO 87/14.

5. "Report from the Select Committee on the West Coast of Africa . . . Part II," *BPP,* 1842 (551), XI.1, XII.1, appendix 8: 187–88.

6. Ibid., 187–88; Mahoney, *Creole Saga,* 39; Rendall to Hay, 16 October 1834, TNA, CO 87/10; Maeve Ryan, "'It Was Necessary to Do Something with Those Women': Colonial Governance and the 'Disposal' of Women and Girls in Early Nineteenth-Century Sierra Leone," *Gender and History* (forthcoming,

2021); "Report from the Select Committee on the West Coast of Africa. Part I—Report and Evidence," *BPP*, 1842 (551), XI.1, XII.1: 261. See also "The Liberated African Yard, Bathurst" in "Sierra Leone and Gambia Photographs, 1870s–1920s," TNA, CO 1069/88.

7. Mahoney, *Creole Saga*, 31; Francis Bisset Archer, *The Gambia Colony and Protectorate: An Official Handbook* (London: Frank Cass, 1967), 36–37. See also Colebrooke to Glenelg, 18 July 1836, TNA, CO/23/97/12, for a comparable example of liberated Africans employed at cutting canals in the salt ponds on Long Island in the Bahamas.

8. Mahoney, *Creole Saga*, 37; Prochnow, "Perpetual Expatriation," 359.

9. Janjanbure is a name that predates the British colonization, and may refer to a "place of refuge": John Miller Gray, *A History of the Gambia*, 335.

10. James Africanus Beale Horton, *West African Countries and Peoples* (London: W. J. Johnson, 1868), 237–38.

11. Diary of Edward Thompson, 3 January 1785, quoted in Emma Christopher, *A Merciless Place: The Fate of Britain's Convicts After the American Revolution* (New York: Oxford University Press, 2010), 312. See also Patrick Webb, "Guests of the Crown: Convicts and Liberated Slaves on McCarthy Island, the Gambia," *The Geographical Journal* 160, no. 2 (1994): 136–38; Cassandra Pybus, "Bound for Botany Bay: John Martin's Voyage to Australia," in *Many Middle Passages: Forced Migration and the Making of the Modern World*, ed. Emma Christopher, Cassandra Pybus and Markus Rediker (Berkeley: University of California Press, 2007), 97.

12. Macaulay to Bathurst, 28 June 1826, TNA, CO 267/72; Mahoney, *Creole Saga*, 19. See also Brown, "Fernando Po and the Anti-Sierra Leonean Campaign," 249–64.

13. Anderson, "The Diaspora of Sierra Leone's Liberated Africans," 115–16, 127; Prochnow, "Perpetual Expatriation," 349; "Returns of Liberated Africans (Gambia)," 1835–1836, TNA, CO 87/16.

14. Evidence of Matthew Forster, "Report from the Select Committee on the West Coast of Africa . . . Part I," *BPP*, 1842 (551 551-II), XI.1, XII.1: 710; Goderich to Campbell, 25 August 1827, "Sierra Leone . . . Correspondence on the Treatment of Captured Negroes and Liberated Africans," *BPP*, 1830 (57), XXI.225: 21.

15. Fett, "Middle Passages and Forced Migrations," 75–98; Christopher et al., *Many Middle Passages*, 1–15; Paul E. Lovejoy, "The African Diaspora: Revisionist Interpretations of Ethnicity, Culture and Religion Under Slavery," *Studies in the World History of Slavery, Abolition, and Emancipation* 2, no. 1 (1997).

16. "Returns of Liberated Africans (Gambia)," 1835–1836, TNA, CO 87/16; Hay to Stewart, 10 December 1832, TNA, T 1/3774. See also Russell to Jeremie, 20 March 1841, "Emigration. Return to an Address . . . 9 March 1842," *BPP,* 1842 (301), XXXI.49: 447–49.

17. "Sierra Leone. Report of the Commissioners of Inquiry into the State of the Colony of Sierra Leone. Second Part," *BPP,* 1826–1827 (552), VII.379: 4.

18. "Returns of Liberated Africans (Gambia)," 1835–1836, TNA, CO 87/16; "Report from the Select Committee on the West Coast of Africa; Part II," appendix 8: 179–80; Mahoney, *Creole Saga,* 39.

19. "Report from the Select Committee on the West Coast of Africa; Part II," appendix 8: 212–14; Kuczynski, *Demographic Survey of the British Colonial Empire,* vol. 1, 126.

20. Mahoney, *Creole Saga,* 37; Webb, "Guests of the Crown," 140; James Edward Alexander, *Excursions in Western Africa* (London: Henry Colburn, 1840), vol. 1, 74–77.

21. Anderson, "The Diaspora of Sierra Leone's Liberated Africans," 115–16; Murray to Ricketts, 15 May 1829, "Sierra Leone . . . Correspondence on the Treatment of Captured Negroes and Liberated Africans," *BPP,* 1830 (57), XXI.225: 35–36; Hay to Rendall, 29 November 1831, "Liberated Africans. Correspondence Respecting the Treatment of Liberated Africans," *BPP,* 1840 (224), XXXIV.365: 5; "Report from the Select Committee on the West Coast of Africa . . . Part II," appendix 8: 187; Webb, "Guests of the Crown," 139; "Liberated African Population at McCarthy's Island" and "List of Liberated Africans Under the Superintendence of the Government at MacCarthy's Island on the 30th June 1835," TNA, CO 87/16.

22. "Report from the Select Committee on the West Coast of Africa; Part II," appendix 8: 187–88.

23. Richard F. Burton, *Wanderings in West Africa: From Liverpool to Fernando Po* (London: Tinsley Brothers, 1863), 155.

24. Quoted in Florence Mahoney, "Government and Opinion in the Gambia, 1815–1901" (unpublished PhD thesis, School of Oriental and African Studies, 1963), 128–29.

25. Liza Gijanto, "Serving Status on the Gambia River Before and After Abolition," *Current Anthropology* 61, supplement 22 (October 2020): 263–64; Arnold Hughes and David Perfect, *A Political History of the Gambia, 1816–1994* (Rochester: University of Rochester Press, 2006), 55–77; John Miller Gray, *A History of the Gambia* (London: Frank Cass, 1966), 320.

26. "Report from the Select Committee on the West Coast of Africa; Part II," appendix 8: 187–88.

27. Ibid., 187–88.

28. Anderson, "Convicts, Carcerality, and Cape Colony Connections," 430.

29. "Report from the Select Committee on the West Coast of Africa; Part II," appendix 8: 188.

30. Andrew Pearson, *Distant Freedom: St Helena and the Abolition of the Slave Trade, 1840–1872* (Liverpool: Liverpool University Press, 2016), 13–16.

31. Ibid., 16; Leslie M. Bethell, "Britain, Portugal, and the Suppression of the Brazilian Slave Trade: The Origins of Lord Palmerston's Act of 1839," *The English Historical Review* 80, no. 317 (1965): 761–84; Christopher Lloyd, *The Navy and the Slave Trade: The Suppression of the African Slave Trade in the Nineteenth Century* (London: Routledge, 1968); Wills, *Envoys of Abolition*.

32. Russell to Middlemore, 12 July 1840 and "Ordinance for the Protection and Care of Such Liberated Africans as Shall Become Servants or Apprentices in the Island of St Helena," no. 3, 27 July 1842, quoted in Andrew Pearson, Ben Jeffs, Annsofie Witkin, and Helen McQuarrie, *Infernal Traffic: Excavation of a Liberated African Graveyard in Rupert's Valley, St. Helena* (York: Council for British Archaeology, 2011), 12, 34; 3.

33. George McHenry, "Account of the Liberated African Establishment at St Helena," *Simmond's Colonial Magazine and Foreign Miscellany,* vols. 5–7 (London, 1845–46); Pearson, *Distant Freedom,* 115–16.

34. Pearson et al., *Infernal Traffic,* 31; Young to Pennell, 29 December 1845, "Emigration . . . of Labourers from Sierra Leone and St. Helena to the West Indies," *BPP,* 1850 (643), XL.271: 87–88.

35. McHenry, "Account of the Liberated African Establishment at St Helena"; Pearson, *Distant Freedom,* 106–53; Barcia, *The Yellow Demon of Fever,* 125–27, 135–36. The Sandy Bay Lunatics Asylum was established on the south side of the island to treat those suffering from psychological trauma: ibid., 142.

36. "Dr Vowell's Report," "Emigration . . . of Labourers from Sierra Leone and St. Helena to the West Indies," *BPP,* 1850 (643), XL.271: 73, 86; "Extracts from a Report of Dr Rawlins," 25 May 1849, "Emigration . . . of Labourers from Sierra Leone and St. Helena to the West Indies," *BPP,* 1850 (643), XL.271: 91; Pearson et al., *Infernal Traffic,* 23.

37. Ibid., 16–22; Pearson, *Distant Freedom,* 106–200. Under the controversial "Aberdeen Act," or Slave Trade Brazil Act of 1845, Britain applied a new interpretation of the Anglo-Brazilian slave trade suppression treaty of 1826 in order to declare the Brazilian transatlantic slave trade piracy. See Leslie Bethell, *Brazil: Essays on History and Politics* (London: University of London School of Advanced Study Institute of Latin American Studies, 2018), 67–71 at https://sas-space.sas.ac.uk/6915/1/Bethell.pdf.

38. "Dr Vowell's Report," "Emigration . . . of Labourers from Sierra Leone and St. Helena to the West Indies," *BPP*, 1850 (643) XL.271: 91–97; Pearson, *Distant Freedom*, 106–53.

39. Barcia, *The Yellow Demon of Fever*, 125–65.

40. "Extract from Instructions to the Superintendent [of the] Liberated African Establishment, dated 26 December 1845 and 6 July 1848," "Emigration . . . of Labourers from Sierra Leone and St. Helena to the West Indies," *BPP*, 1850 (643) XL.271: 91.

41. "Dr Vowell's Report," ibid., 78.

42. Pearson et al., *Infernal Traffic*, 34; Pearson, *Distant Freedom*, 137–43.

43. Ibid., 129–31.

44. Grey to Ross, 22 November 1849, "Emigration . . . of Labourers from Sierra Leone and St. Helena to the West Indies," *BPP*, 1850 (643), XL.271: 110, 120–22.

45. Ross to Grey, 26 July 1848 and Ross to Grey 14 August 1849, ibid., 65, 101–2; "Dr Vowell's Report," ibid., 82–83, 90.

46. Rawlins to Young, 7 August 1849, ibid., 104.

47. "Comparative Statement Showing the Total Number of Liberated Africans Which Have Died Prior to Their Disposal from the African Depots at the Undermentioned Colonies," enclosed in Ross to Grey, 1 September 1848, ibid., 68. See also ibid., 67–70, 89, 97–101, 111, 120.

48. The assistant superintendent of the Liberated African Department, Thomas Cole, described to the colony's governor in 1830 the "frightful number of deaths which had occurred during the last year." In late 1831, the colonial secretary, Viscount Goderich, noted Cole's report that of the 33,595 liberated Africans who survived the transit to Freetown and had settled in the colony between 1808 and 1830, one fifth had died; 5,039 of the deaths had occurred within four months of their arrival: Cole to Findlay, 24 May 1830, PASL, Liberated African Department Letterbook 1830–31; Goderich to Findlay, 18 January 1832, quoted in Kuczynski, *Demographic Survey of the British Colonial Empire*, vol. 1, 108. In 1839, 1,635 deaths were recorded at the Liberated African Hospital of a total of 2,773 admissions: ibid., 109. Mortality returns for Sierra Leone are incomplete. Furthermore, those who were kidnapped, absconded, or otherwise "disappeared" were sometimes returned as deceased. Beatriz Mamigonian, "To Be a Liberated African in Brazil: Labour and Citizenship in the Nineteenth Century" (unpublished PhD thesis, University of Waterloo, Canada, 2002), 108–10 compares post-adjudication mortality statistics for seventeen ships adjudicated at Rio between 1821 and 1841 and finds a range of mortalities between 0% and 52.63%. Mortality totals for the Cape Colony are unknown. See "Return of Vessels . . . Adjudicated by

the Vice-Admiralty Court at the Cape," "Class A . . . April 1, 1849, to March 31, 1850," *BPP*, 1850 (1290), LV.111: 221–25 for pre-adjudication death statistics at Cape Colony between August 1839 and September 1849.

49. Ross to Grey, 26 July 1848 and Ross to Grey, 12 June 1849, "Emigration . . . of Labourers from Sierra Leone and St. Helena to the West Indies," *BPP*, 1850 (643) XL.271: 65–66, 70–71.

50. Pearson et al., *Infernal Traffic*, xviii–xix; MacQuarrie and Pearson, "Prize Possessions: Transported Material Culture of the Post-Abolition Enslaved— New Evidence from St Helena," *Slavery and Abolition* 37, no. 1 (2016): 45–72; Ewen Callaway, "What DNA Reveals About St Helena's Freed Slaves," *Nature* 540 (2016): 184–87.

51. *Hansard House of Commons Parliamentary Debates*, 3rd series, 16 June 1848, vol. 99 c. 732; 29 June 1848, vol. 99 cc. 1341–42; Green, "Corrective Comment," 252; Richard Huzzey, "Free Trade, Free Labour, and Slave Sugar in Victorian Britain," *The Historical Journal* 53, no. 2 (2010): 359–79; Thomas C. Holt, *The Problem of Freedom: Race, Labor, and Politics in Jamaica and Britain, 1832–1938* (Baltimore: Johns Hopkins University Press, 1992), xxiv; Catherine Hall, *Civilising Subjects: Metropole and Colony in the English Imagination, 1830–1867* (Chicago: University of Chicago Press, 2006), 379. See also Catherine Hall, "Going a-Trolloping: Imperial Man Travels the Empire," in *Gender and Imperialism,* ed. Clare Midgley (Manchester: Manchester University Press, 1998), 180–99.

52. Russell to Middlemore, 8 May 1841, TNA, CO 247/55; Pearson, *Distant Freedom*, 215–17, 284–87.

53. Hope to Burge, 27 January 1842, "Emigration. Return to an Address . . . 9 March 1842," *BPP*, 1842 (301) XXXI: 482–83.

54. Trelawney to Stanley, 3 March 1842, TNA, CO 247/57; Pearson, *Distant Freedom*, 225.

55. Emily Jackson, *St Helena: The Historic Island* (London, 1903), 266.

56. Lambert and Lester, eds., *Colonial Lives Across the British Empire*, 25.

57. Catherine Hall, "Of Gender and Empire: Reflections in the Nineteenth Century," in *Gender and Empire,* ed. Philippa Levine (Oxford: Oxford University Press, 2004), 65.

58. Zoë Laidlaw, "Richard Bourke: Irish Liberalism Tempered by Empire," in *Colonial Lives Across the British Empire,* ed. Lambert and Lester, 113–44.

59. R. H. Vetch, "Smyth, Sir James Carmichael-, First Baronet (1779–1838), Army Officer and Colonial Governor," *Oxford Dictionary of National Biography* (Oxford University Press, 2008); Adderley, *New Negroes from Africa*, 56.

60. C. A. Harris, "Colebrooke, Sir William Macbean George (1787–1870)," *Oxford Dictionary of National Biography;* Sean MacConville, *A History of English Prison Administration* (New York: Routledge, 2016), 390.

61. Tim Soriano, "Promoting the Industry of Liberated Africans: Liberated Africans in British Honduras: 1824–1841," in *Liberated Africans and the Abolition of the Slave Trade,* ed. Lovejoy and Anderson, 365–83.

62. Johnson, "The Liberated Africans in the Bahamas," 32–34.

63. Cockburn to Glenelg, 19 May 1838, TNA, CO 23/102.

64. Barnett, *Paternalism Beyond Borders,* 1.

65. H. M. Chichester, "Middlemore, George (d. 1850)," *Oxford Dictionary of National Biography;* Alexandra Franklin, "Jeremie, Sir John (1795–1841)," ibid.; Rigg, "Madden, Richard Robert (1798–1886)," ibid.

66. "Return of the Establishment of the Liberated African Department at Sierra Leone from 1 July to 31 December 1841," PASL, Liberated African Department Misc. Returns, 1839–1844; "Return of Persons Employed in Lib. Afr. Department," TNA, CO 267/92, "Report of the Commission of Inquiry into the State of Sierra Leone 1826–1827," appendix B 22; Anderson, *Abolition in Sierra Leone,* 167–91; Peterson, *Province of Freedom.*

67. Ryan, "A 'Very Extensive System of Peculation and Jobbing'"; "Report of Commission of Enquiry into the Conduct of Mr. Dixon," 1848–1849, TNA, CO 267/210, appendix 1.

68. Anderson, *Abolition in Sierra Leone,* 167–91; Peterson, *Province of Freedom.*

69. "Reports by Commissioners of Inquiry into State of Africans Apprenticed in West Indies. (I) Papers Relating to Captured Negroes" *BPP,* 1825 (114) XXV.193: 56; "Commissioners of Enquiry into the State of the 'Captured Negroes' in the West Indies," TNA, CO 318/82–98; Rupprecht, "When He Gets Among His Countrymen," 435–55.

70. J. Claudius May, *A Brief Sketch of the Life of the Reverend Joseph May* [Freetown, 1896]; Joseph Boston May, "Autobiographical: His Conversion" (1838). I would like to thank Professor Leo Spitzer for very kindly sharing with me his copies of these texts. See also Paul E. Lovejoy, "'Freedom Narratives' of Transatlantic Slavery," *Slavery and Abolition* 32, no. 1 (2011): 91–107; Curtin, ed., *Africa Remembered;* Sandra Rowoldt Shell, *Children of Hope: The Odyssey of the Oromo Slaves from Ethiopia to South Africa* (Athens: Ohio University Press, 2018).

71. May, "Autobiographical: His Conversion," 8–10; May, *A Brief Sketch of the Life of the Reverend Joseph May.*

72. Horton, *West African Countries and Peoples,* 25–26.

73. Ibid., ii.

74. Kirk to Granville, 20 March 1871, "Class B. East Coast of Africa," *BPP,* 1872 (C.657) LIV.765: 32.

75. Kirk to Granville, 5 September 1871, ibid., 54–55. Emphasis added.

76. Kirk to Granville, 22 September 1871, ibid., 59. Emphasis added. See also Vivian to Kirk, 12 December 1871, National Library of Scotland (NLS), Acc 9942/6.

77. Lambert and Lester, "Geographies of Colonial Philanthropy," 321–23.

78. Anderson, "After Emancipation: Empires and Imperial Formations," 113–27.

79. Crooks, *A History of the Colony of Sierra Leone,* 84–86.

80. Evidence of H. D. Campbell, "Report from the Select Committee on the West Coast of Africa . . . Part I," *BPP,* 1842 (551 551-II), XI.1, XII.1: 552–70.

81. F. H. Rankin, *The White Man's Grave,* vol. 2 (London: Richard Bentley, 1836), 106.

82. Pearson, *Distant Freedom,* 131.

83. Burton, *Wanderings in West Africa,* 220, 265.

84. Kirk to Granville, 22 September 1871, "Class B. East Coast of Africa," *BPP,* 1872 (C.657) LIV.765: 59.

85. Clare Anderson, "Introduction: A Global History of Convicts and Penal Colonies," in *A Global History of Convicts and Penal Colonies,* ed. Clare Anderson (London: Bloomsbury Academic, 2018), 1–36.

Chapter 5. Humanitarian Governance in International
Antislavery Diplomacy

1. This chapter is partly derived from Maeve Ryan, "British Antislavery Diplomacy and Liberated African Rights as an International Issue," in *Liberated Africans and the Abolition of the Slave Trade,* ed. Lovejoy and Anderson, 215–37.

2. Mamigonian, "To Be a Liberated African in Brazil," 49.

3. Vines to Jerningham, 29 November 1855, *BPP,* 1856 (o.2), LXII.167: 230–32.

4. Ibid, 230.

5. Hansard House of Commons Parliamentary Debates, 28 June 1821 vol. 5 c. 1445; Hudson to Palmerston, 17 November 1846, TNA, FO 84/634.

6. Hayne and Cunningham to Canning, 30 December 1825, *BPP,* 1826–1827 (010), XXVI: 152.

7. Kilbee to Captain-General, 12 September, 1824, TNA, FO 84/29; Kilbee to Canning, 20 September 1824, TNA, FO 84/29; Lovejoy, "The Registers of Liberated Africans of the Havana Slave Trade Commission," 27–29; Bosanquet to de Zea Bermudez, 10 February 1825, *BPP,* 1824–1825 (012), XXVII.463: 14.

8. Beatriz Mamigonian, "In the Name of Freedom: Slave Trade Abolition, the Law and the Brazilian Branch of the African Emigration Scheme," *Slavery and Abolition* 30, no. 1 (2009): 41–66.

9. Palmerston to Aston, 1 November 1831, *BPP*, 1831–1832 (010), XLVII.533, 681: 108–9; Pieter C. Emmer, "Abolition of the Abolished: The Illegal Dutch Slave Trade and the Mixed Courts," in *The Abolition of the Atlantic Slave Trade: Origins and Effects in Europe, Africa, and the Americas,* ed. David Eltis, James Walvin, and Stanley Engerman (London, 1981), 177–92; Lance and Dalrymple to Aberdeen, 14 September 1830, *BPP,* 1831 (004), XIX.321, 463: 134.

10. Palmerston to Aston, 1 November 1831, *BPP*, 1831–1832 (010), XLVII.533, 681: 108–9; Pennell to Palmerston, 12 February 1831, ibid., 113–14; Pennell to Palmerston, 12 January 1831, ibid., 95–96; Aberdeen to H.M. Commissioners, 28 June 1830 and Lance and Dalrymple to Aberdeen, *BPP*, 1831 (004), XIX.321, 463: 132–34.

11. Palmerston to Aston, 1 November 1831, *BPP,* 1831–1832 (010), XLVII.533, 681: 108; Macleay and Mackenzie to Palmerston, 29 March 1832, *BPP,* 1833 (007), XLIII: 52.

12. Abaeté to Howard, 8 May 1854, quoted in Daryle Williams, "'A Necessária Distinção Entre Liberdade e Emancipação': African, English, and Brazilian Notions of Being 'Emancipado,'" in *Instituições Nefandas: O fim da escravidão e da servidão no Brasil, nos Estados Unidos e na Rússia,* ed. Daniel Aarão Reis Filho, Keila Grinberg, and Ivana Stolze Lima (Rio de Janeiro: Fundação Casa Rui Barbosa, 2018), 151–70. With thanks to Daryle Williams for his generous assistance and expert guidance on many aspects of Brazilian and Anglo-Brazilian history and archival material.

13. 47° Georgii III, Session 1, cap. XXXVI (1807) and 5° Georgii IV, cap. XVII (1824), http://web.archive.org/web/20210714012931/https://www.pdavis.nl/SlaverBackground.htm.

14. "An Act for Carrying into Effect a Treaty made between His Majesty and the Queen Regent of Spain for the Abolition of the Slave Trade," 6 Gulielmi Cap. VI, 30 March 1836, *The Statutes of the United Kingdom of Great Britain and Ireland* 14 (London: Eyre and Spottiswoode, 1838), 6–18.

15. Britain also chafed against the constraints of the Anglo-Dutch treaty of 1818. In 1829, the British commissioners at Surinam investigated the fates of the 49 survivors of the slave ship *La Nueve of Snauw* "delivered over" to Dutch authorities in 1823. Governor-General Cantz'laar replied that the commissioners had no right to the information. Cooperating with the investigation would be "inconsistent with the independence and dignity of any government that would allow it." The jurisdiction of the court was "only of a judicial

nature," limited to adjudicating slave-ship captures. Cantz'laar to Lance and Dalrymple, 4 July 1829, *BPP*, 1830 (014), XXXIII.23: 173–74.

16. Valdés to Turnbull, 24 June 1841, *BPP*, 1843 (483), LVIII.347: 80–81.

17. Adderley, "A Most Useful and Valuable People," 61–62; "Minute on the Condition and Disposal of the Captured Africans at the Havana," 24 October 1835, TNA, CO 318/123; Murray, *Odious Commerce*, 120, 271–81; Bethell, *The Abolition of the Brazilian Slave Trade*, 111–21, 380–83.

18. "An Act for Carrying into Effect a Treaty made between His Majesty and the Queen Regent of Spain for the Abolition of the Slave Trade," 6 Gulielmi Cap. VI, 30 March 1836, *The Statutes of the United Kingdom of Great Britain and Ireland,* Annex C: "Good Treatment of Liberated Negroes." See also Jennifer Nelson, "Liberated Africans in the Atlantic World: The Courts of Mixed Commission in Havana and Rio de Janeiro, 1819–1871" (unpublished PhD thesis, University of Leeds, 2015); Jennifer Nelson, "Slavery, Race, and Conspiracy: The HMS Romney in Nineteenth-Century Cuba," *Atlantic Studies* 14, no. 2 (2017): 174–95.

19. Murray, *Odious Commerce*, 92–158; Nelson, "Slavery, Race, and Conspiracy"; Aisha K. Finch, *Rethinking Slave Rebellion in Cuba: La Escalera and the Insurgencies of 1841–1844* (Chapel Hill: University of North Carolina Press, 2015); Robert Paquette, *Sugar Is Made with Blood: The Conspiracy of* La Escalera *and the Conflict Between Empires over Slavery in Cuba* (Middletown, Conn.: Wesleyan University Press, 1988); J. Curry-Machado, "How Cuba Burned with the Ghosts of British Slavers: Race, Abolition, and the 'Escalera,'" *Slavery and Abolition* 25, no. 2 (2004): 71–93; David R. Murray, "Richard Robert Madden: His Career as a Slavery Abolitionist," *Studies: An Irish Quarterly Review* 61, no. 241 (1972): 41–53; R. R. Madden, *The Island of Cuba: Its Resources, Progress, and Prospects* (London: Charles Gilpin, 1849).

20. David Turnbull, *The Jamaica Movement for Promoting the Enforcement of the Slave Trade Treaties* (London: Gilpin, 1850), 16–37, 133; "Select Committee on Consular Service and Appointments," *BPP,* 1857–1858 (482), VIII.1: 74.

21. Murray, *Odious Commerce*, 137; Palmerston to De Walden, private, 24 January 1839, PP, GC/HO/830; Palmerston to Baring, 3 September 1850, PP, GC/BA/310.

22. "Select Committee on Consular Service and Appointments," *BPP,* 1857–1858 (482), VIII.1: 362–64.

23. "Select Committee on the Consular Establishment," *BPP,* 1835 (499), VI.149: 101–5.

24. Turnbull to Palmerston, 30 December 1840, TNA, CO 318/151; Turnbull, *Jamaica Movement,* 135; Inés Roldán de Montaud, "Origen, Evolución, y

Supresión del Grupo de Negros 'Emancipados' en Cuba, 1817–1870," *Revista de Indias* 42, no. 169–70 (1982): 559–641; Inés Roldán de Montaud, "En Los Borrosos Confines de la Libertad: El Caso de Los Negros Emancipados en Cuba, 1817–1870," *Revista de Indias* 71, no. 251 (2011): 195–92.

25. Turnbull to Palmerston, 30 December 1840, *BPP,* 1842 (403), XLIII.1: 210–12.

26. Valdés to British Consul, 23 June 1841, AHN, Estado, Esclavitud, Legajo 8019/39/10. See also Oscar Grandio-Moraguez, "Dobo: a Liberated African in Nineteenth-Century Havana," http://web.archive.org/web/20210712130619 /https://www.slavevoyages.org/voyage/essays.

27. "Report from the Select Committee of the House of Lords Appointed to Consider the Best Means Which Great Britain Can Adopt for the Final Extinction of the African Slave Trade," *BPP,* 1850 (590), IX.585: 73–76.

28. Commissioners to Aberdeen, *BPP,* 1842 (482), LVIII.17: 160–63, 170–73; Turnbull to Aberdeen, 24 December 1841, *BPP,* 1843 (483), LVIII.347: 85–93; Kennedy and Dalrymple to Aberdeen, 13 June 1842, *BPP,* 1842 (482), LVIII.17: 169; Turnbull to Aberdeen, 14 December 1841, *BPP,* 1843 (483), LVIII.347: 52–55; Turnbull to Aberdeen, 25 November 1841, *BPP,* 1842 (403), XLIII.1: 424–26; Jenny S. Martinez, *The Slave Trade and the Origins of International Human Rights Law* (Oxford University Press, 2012), 102–7.

29. Turnbull to Aberdeen, 25 November 1841, *BPP,* 1842 (403), XLIII.1: 424–25; Turnbull to Aberdeen, 14 December 1841, *BPP,* 1842 (403), XLIII.1: 52–55; Turnbull to Commissioners, 16 May 1842, *BPP,* 1843 (482), LVIII.17: 162; Kennedy and Dalrymple to Aberdeen, 31 May 1842, *BPP,* 1843 (482), LVIII.17: 161–64; Martinez, *The Slave Trade and the Origins of International Human Rights Law,* 102–7.

30. Deposition of José Jesus, 3 June 1842, *BPP,* 1842 (482), LVIII.17: 172.

31. Turnbull to Aberdeen, 24 December 1841, *BPP,* 1843 (483), LVIII.347: 85–93.

32. "Declaration of Tranquilino Rosas," 9 November 1831 in Turnbull to Aberdeen, 24 December 1841, ibid., 88; Kennedy and Dalrymple to Aberdeen, 13 June 1842, *BPP,* 1843 (482), LVIII.17: 169–72.

33. Aberdeen to Turnbull, 10 February 1842, TNA, FO 72/608.

34. Luis Martínez-Fernández, *Fighting Slavery in the Caribbean: The Life and Times of a British Family in Nineteenth-Century Havana* (New York: Sharpe, 1998), 55.

35. Turnbull to Commissioners, 25 May 1842, *BPP,* 1842 (482), LVIII.17: 163–64.

36. Grandio-Moraguez, "Dobo: A Liberated African in Nineteenth-Century Havana."

37. Dunlop to Granville, 19 November 1870, *BPP*, 1871 (C.341), LXII.785: 64.

38. Robert Conrad, "Neither Slave nor Free: The Emancipados of Brazil, 1818–1868," *The Hispanic American Historical Review* 53, no. 1 (1973): 51.

39. Commissioners to Aberdeen, 22 December 1843, *BPP*, 1845 (632), XLIX.1: 177–79.

40. Quoted in W. D. Christie, *Notes on Brazilian Questions* (London: Macmillan, 1865), 37; Hesketh to Hudson, 30 September 1850, *BPP*, 1852–1853 (0.3), CIII Pt.II.1: 325–26.

41. Howard to Clarendon, 28 May, 30 May 1855, *BPP*, 1856 (0.2), LXII: 138–42; Howard to Abaeté, 9 April 1855, ibid., 142.

42. Hansard House of Commons Parliamentary Debates, 19 March 1850 vol. 109 c.1170.

43. Turnbull, *The Jamaica Movement,* 14.

44. Alan Manchester, *British Preëminence in Brazil: Its Rise and Decline; A Study in European Expansion* (Chapel Hill: University of North Carolina Press, 1933), 265.

45. Richard Graham, *Britain and the Onset of Modernization in Brazil* (Cambridge: Cambridge University Press, 2008), 168–69; Richard Graham, "Os Fundamentos da Ruptura de Relações Diplomáticas entre o Brasil e a Grã-Bretanha em 1863: 'a Questão Christie,'" *Revista de História* 24 (1962): 117; Beatriz Mamigonian, "Building the Nation, Selecting Memories: Vitor Meireles, the Christie Affair and Brazilian Slavery in the 1860s" (Gilder Lehrman Center 12th Annual International Conference, Yale University, 2010).

46. Hansard House of Commons Parliamentary Debates, 12 July 1864, vol. 176 c. 1377.

47. Christie, *Notes on Brazilian Questions,* 33, xxxv.

48. Geoffrey Hicks, "Don Pacifico, Democracy, and Danger: The Protectionist Party Critique of British Foreign Policy, 1850–1852," *International History Review* 26, no. 3 (2004): 518–19.

49. Clarendon to Thornton, 25 November 1865, *BPP,* 1866 (3635-I), LXXV.115: 12.

50. Hunt to Russell, 10 March 1865, *BPP*, 1865 (3503-I), LVI: 71–86, 287–319.

51. Hesketh to Ouseley, 31 May 1839, *BPP*, 1840 (265), XLVI: 286–92.

52. Joseph Mulhern, "After 1833: British Entanglement with Brazilian Slavery" (unpublished PhD thesis, Durham University, 2018), http://etheses.dur.ac.uk /13071/; William Hamilton to John Backhouse Snr., 25 February 1837, DUL, Backhouse Papers, Box 9; William Hamilton to John Backhouse Snr., 6 September 1841, DUL, Backhouse Papers, Box 12. See also Mamigonian, "To Be a Liberated African in Brazil," 195–257.

53. Hesketh to Palmerston, 14 February 1850, *BPP,* 1850 (1291), LV: 164.

54. Hudson to Palmerston, 15 March 1851, *BPP,* 1852–1853 (0.5), CIII II.1: 151–52.

55. Hesketh to Ouseley, 31 May 1839, *BPP,* 1840 (265), XLVI: 285, 291; "Select Committee on Consular Service," *BPP,* 1857–1858 (482), VIII.1: 362; Hesketh to Palmerston, 20 April 1839, ibid., 378; Hesketh to Palmerston, 19 June 1839, ibid., 379–80.

56. Hesketh to Ouseley, 31 May 1839, *BPP,* 1840 (265), XLVI: 289.

57. Mamigonian, "In the Name of Freedom," 49–52.

58. Conrad, "Neither Slave nor Free," 59–60.

59. Commissioners to Aberdeen, 22 December 1843, *BPP,* 1845 (632), XLIX.1: 177–79.

60. Hesketh to Hudson, 30 September 1849, *BPP,* 1852–1853 (0.3) CIII Pt.II.1: 325–26.

61. Hesketh's return, "Slave Trade, Mixed Commission, etc., Miscellaneous Papers," TNA, FO 131/7. I am very grateful to Daryle Williams for sharing valuable insights on the implications of Hesketh's return and the wider context within which this source was created. See also Southern to Malmsbury, 14 July 1852, *BPP,* 1853 (0.5), CIII Pt.III.201: 136–37.

62. For the examples of Robert Corbett, "Black Will," Fernando, and John Freeman, see Dale Graden, "'Meu Coração Me Dictou de Fugir Porque Somos Forros': Microhistória, Macrohistória, e o Fim do Tráfico dos Escravos Transatlântico Para o Brasil," in *Corpos, Africanos, Medicina e Escravidão,* ed. Talga Salgado Pimenta and Flávio dos Santos Gomes (São Paulo: Editora Hucitec, 2019).

63. Mamigonian, "To Be a Liberated African in Brazil," 196; Mamigonian, *Africanos Livres;* Daryle Williams, *The Broken Paths of Freedom,* web.archive.org /web/20210628130228/https://web.stanford.edu/group/spatialhistory/cgi -bin/site/project.php?id=1069; Daniela Carvalho Cavalheiro, "Africanos Livres No Brasil: Tráfico Ilegal, Vidas Tuteladas e Experiências Coletivas no Século XIX" (unpublished master's thesis, UFRRJ, Brazil, 2015), https:// tede.ufrrj.br/jspui/bitstream/jspui/3137/2/2015%20Daniela%20Carvalho %20Cavalheiro.pdf; Daniela Carvalho Cavalheiro, "Caminhos Negros: Vida e Trabalho dos Africanos Livres na Construção da Estrada de Magé a Sapucaia (c. 1836–1864)," *Revista Ars Histórica* 7 (2014): 41–59.

64. Williams, "A Necessária Distinção."

65. Hesketh to Hudson, 30 September 1851, *BPP,* 1852 (0.3), CIII Pt.II.1: 325–26; Christie, *Notes on Brazilian Questions,* 206, 224.

66. Lester and Dussart, *Colonization and the Origins of Humanitarian Governance;* Samuel Furphy and Amanda Nettelbeck, eds., *Aboriginal Protection*

and Its Intermediaries in Britain's Antipodean Colonies (New York: Routledge, 2019). On Britain making recognition of Brazilian independence conditional on anti-slave-trade cooperation, see Nelson, "Liberated Africans in the Atlantic World: The Courts of Mixed Commission in Havana and Rio de Janeiro," 13.

67. Palmerston to Baring, 3 September 1850, PP, GC/BA/310.

68. Bethell, *The Abolition of the Brazilian Slave Trade,* 333, n. 2; Heitor Lyra, *Historia de Dom Pedro II,* vol. 1 (São Paulo: Editora da Universidade de São Paulo, 1977), 321–22.

69. Although see Marten, "Constitutional Irregularities in the British Imperial Courts of Vice Admiralty During the Mid-Nineteenth Century" on the wider issues created by this court system.

70. George Shee to Henry Hayne, 12 November 1833, TNA, FO 84/138. Hayne had made previous recommendations in 1825: Hayne and Cunningham to Canning, 30 December 1825, *BPP,* 1826–1827 (010), XXVI: 152–53.

71. "Regulations for the Care and Protection of Negroes Emancipated Under Sentence of the Mixed Commission," enclosed in Henry Hayne to George Shee, 28 November 1833, TNA, FO 84/138. On the subject of enslaved crew members who rejected liberated African status, see Walter Hawthorne, "Gorge: An African Seaman and His Flights from 'Freedom' Back to 'Slavery' in the Early Nineteenth Century," *Slavery and Abolition* 31, no. 3 (2010): 411–28; Nelson, "Liberated Africans in the Atlantic World: The Courts of Mixed Commission in Havana and Rio de Janeiro," 70–71.

72. "Regulations for the Care and Protection of Negroes Emancipated Under Sentence of the Mixed Commission," enclosed in Henry Hayne to George Shee, 28 November 1833, TNA, FO 84/138; Hayne and Cunningham to Canning, 30 December 1825, *BPP,* 1826–1827 (010), XXVI: 152–53.

73. Palmerston to Howard de Walden, no. 3, 8 September 1834, TNA, FO 84/155; Bethell, "Britain, Portugal, and the Suppression of the Brazilian Slave Trade," 769–71.

74. Samuël Coghe, "Apprenticeship and the Negotiation of Freedom: The Liberated Africans of the Anglo-Portuguese Mixed Commission in Luanda (1844–1870)," *Africana Studia* 14 (2010): 258–62.

75. Annex C: "Regulations in Respect to the Treatment of Liberated Negroes," "Treaty Between Her Majesty and the Queen of Portugal for the Suppression of the Traffick in Slaves," 3 March 1842, *BPP,* 1843 (414), XLV.143: 27–41.

76. Samuël Coghe, "The Problem of Freedom in a Mid Nineteenth-Century Atlantic Slave Society: The Liberated Africans of the Anglo-Portuguese Mixed Commission in Luanda (1844–1870)," *Slavery and Abolition* 33, no. 3 (2012):

493. However, for information on the use of branding to mark the skin of liberated Africans at Luanda, see ibid., 485–87; Guilherme Demony, "Reports of the Curator," 31 March 1851 and 5 April 1851, *BPP*, 1852–1853 (0.2), 57.748–52: 131–32; Gabriel to Aberdeen, 9 June 1845, *BPP*, 1846 (723), L.3: 724; "Regulations for the Care and Protection of Negroes Emancipated Under Sentence of the Mixed Commission," enclosed in Henry Hayne to George Shee, 28 November 1833, TNA FO 84/138. For the implications of this practice, see Katrina Keefer, "Marked by Fire: Brands, Slavery, and Identity," *Slavery and Abolition* 40, no. 4 (2019): 660–62.

77. Coghe, "The Problem of Freedom in a Mid Nineteenth-Century Atlantic Slave Society," 482. See also José C. Curto, "Producing 'Liberated' Africans in Mid-Ninteenth-Century Angola," in *Liberated Africans and the Abolition of the Slave Trade,* ed. Anderson and Lovejoy, 238–56; Vanessa Oliveira, "Between Freedom and Captivity: Experiences of Liberated Africans in Luanda," Paper presented at "Liberated Africans and the Abolition of the Slave Trade" conference, Toronto, June 2017; Mário António de Oliveira, "Os 'Libertos' em Luanda No Terceiro Quartel do Séc. XIX," in *Actas da I Reunão Internacional de História da África: Relação Europa-África no 30 Quartel do Séc. XIX,* ed. Maria Emília Madeira Santos (Lisbon: Instituto de Investigação Científica Tropical, 1999), 258–61.

78. Howard de Walden to Palmerston, 24 April 1838, TNA, FO 84/248; Palmerston to Howard de Walden, 19 May 1838, TNA, FO 84/249; Palmerston to Jerningham, 23 July 1838, TNA, FO 84/250; Bethell, "Britain, Portugal and the Suppression of the Brazilian Slave Trade," 772–74.

79. Hansard House of Commons Parliamentary Debates, 19 March 1850 vol. 109 c.1170.

80. For example, Palmerston to Commissioners, 13 August 1846, *BPP*, 1847 (854), LXVII.85: 141; Palmerston to Aston, 23 August 1841, *BPP*, 1842 (403), XLIII.1: 147.

81. Hansard House of Commons Parliamentary Debates, 12 July 1864, vol. 176 cc. 1377–86.

82. Colin Newbury, *British Policy Towards West Africa: Select Documents, 1786–1874* (New York: Oxford University Press, 1965), 181, 210; Stanley to Merivale, 18 November 1847, TNA, CO 267/201. It is doubtful that this was ever implemented on a routine basis. Green, "Corrective Comment," 256–57.

83. Coghe, "Apprenticeship and the Negotiation of Freedom," 266.

84. Palmerston annotation dated 29 September 1850 on Foreign Office memorandum, 28 September 1850, TNA, FO 17/173/129.

85. Mamigonian, *Africanos Livres,* 322–23, 360–61.

Chapter 6. Apprenticeship

1. Jeffcott to Findlay, 11 July 1831, TNA, CO 267/109. See also Saunders, "Liberated Africans in Cape Colony," 227–29; Marina Carter, *The Last Slaves: Liberated Africans in Nineteenth-Century Mauritius* (Port Louis, Mauritius: CRIOS, 2003); Indenture of Pompey Dala, TNA, CO 23/94/6; Kuczynski, *Demographic Survey of the British Colonial Empire,* vol. 1, 110–12. This chapter is derived in part from Maeve Ryan, "'A Moral Millstone'? British Humanitarian Governance and the Policy of Liberated African Apprenticeship, 1808–1848," *Slavery and Abolition* 37, no. 2 (2016): 399–422.

2. Scanlan, "The Rewards of Their Exertions," 116.

3. See Coghe, "Apprenticeship and the Negotiation of Freedom," 262.

4. Anderson, "Uncovering Testimonies of Slavery and the Slave Trade in Missionary Sources."

5. SHADD: Studies in the History of the African Diaspora—Documents, https://web.archive.org/save/https://tubman.info.yorku.ca/publications/shadd/.

6. Mamigonian, "To Be a Liberated African in Brazil," 50; Joan Lane, *Apprenticeship in England, 1600–1914* (London: UCL Press, 1996).

7. Stephen, "A History of the Settlement of Liberated Africans," 24; "Sierra Leone. Report of the Commissioners of Inquiry into the State of the Colony of Sierra Leone. First part," *BPP,* 1826–1827 (312), VII.267: 17; Thomas Coke, *An Interesting Narrative of a Mission Sent to Sierra Leone, in Africa, by the Methodists, in 1811* (London: Paris and Son, 1812), 46; Evidence of Captain T. Midgely, "Report from the Select Committee on the West Coast of Africa . . . Part I," *BPP,* 1842 (551 551-II), XI.1, XII.1: 239. See also Monica Schuler, "Kru Emigration to British and French Guiana, 1841–1857," in *Africans in Bondage: Studies in Slavery and the Slave Trade,* ed. Paul Lovejoy (African Studies Program, University of Wisconsin–Madison, 1986), 162; E. Adeniyi Oroge, "Iwofa: An Historical Survey of the Yoruba Institution of Indenture," *African Economic History* 14 (1985): 75–106; James Walker, *The Black Loyalists: The Search for a Promised Land in Nova Scotia and Sierra Leone, 1783–1870* (Toronto: University of Toronto Press, 1992), 252–53; Gwyn Campbell, Suzanne Miers, and Joseph C. Miller, eds., *Children in Slavery Through the Ages* (Athens: Ohio University Press, 2009); Fyfe, *A History of Sierra Leone,* 192; Érika Melek-Delgado, "Liberated African 'Children' in Sierra Leone: Colonial Classifications of 'Child' and 'Childhood,' 1808–1819," in *Liberated Africans and the Abolition of the Slave Trade,* ed. Lovejoy and Anderson, 81–100; Christine Whyte, "'Freedom but Nothing Else': The Legacies of

Slavery and Abolition in Post-Slavery Sierra Leone, 1928–1956," *The International Journal of African Historical Studies* 48, no. 2 (2015): 231–50.

8. Erica Dunbar, *A Fragile Freedom: African American Women and Emancipation in the Antebellum City* (New Haven: Yale University Press, 2008), 28–30.

9. Paul E. Lovejoy, *Transformations in Slavery: A History of Slavery in Africa* (Cambridge: Cambridge University Press, 2000), 239–40; Rebecca Swartz, "Child Apprenticeship in the Cape Colony: The Case of the Children's Friend Society Emigration Scheme, 1833–1841," *Slavery and Abolition* (2020); Tom Dunning and Hamish Maxwell-Stewart, "Mutiny at Deloraine: Ganging and Convict Resistance in 1840s Van Diemen's Land," *Labour History* 82 (2002): 38–40; Walker, *The Black Loyalists,* 43–50; Iannani, "Contracted Chattel"; Roger Kershaw and Janet Sacks, *New Lives for Old* (Richmond: The National Archives, 2008); Hamish Maxwell-Stewart, "Convict Transportation from Britain and Ireland, 1615–1870," *History Compass* 8, no. 11 (2010): 1231–34; A. P. Kup, "John Clarkson and the Sierra Leone Company," *The International Journal of African Historical Studies* 5, no. 2 (1972): 203–20.

10. "General Return of Slaves Received into the Colony of Sierra Leone . . . 1808 to 1825," TNA, CO 267/91; "Census of Population and Liberated Africans," 1832–1834, TNA, CO 267/127. See also "Return of Africans Received into the Liberated African Department from the 2nd of November 1846 to 31st May 1848," TNA, CO 267/210.

11. African Institution, *Fourth Report,* 65–66; Rupprecht, "When He Gets Among His Countrymen," 6–13; Adderley, *New Negroes from Africa,* 126–52; Macaulay to Peel, 22 August 1811, TNA, CO 267/31.

12. "Sierra Leone. Report of the Commissioners of Inquiry into the State of the Colony of Sierra Leone. First part," *BPP,* 1826–1827 (312), VII.267: 52 suggests that liberated African girls could be married at 13 or 14. See also Rankin, *The White Man's Grave,* vol. 2, 108; Melek-Delgado, "Liberated African 'Children' in Sierra Leone."

13. Ryan, "'It Was Necessary to Do Something with Those Women': Colonial Governance and the 'Disposal' of Women and Girls in Early Nineteenth-Century Sierra Leone."

14. Evidence of William Hamilton, "Report from the Select Committee on the West Coast of Africa . . . Part I," *BPP,* 1842 (551 551-II), XI.1, XII.1: 261.

15. William Hamilton, "Sierra Leone and the Liberated Africans," *The Colonial Magazine and Commercial Maritime Journal* 7 (January–April 1842): 38–43.

16. Allen M. Howard, "New Insights on Liberated Africans: The 1831 Freetown Census," in *Liberated Africans and the Abolition of the Slave Trade,*

ed. Lovejoy and Anderson, 101–26; PASL, Liberated African Department Miscellaneous Return Book 1826–1834, 331–32; PASL, Liberated African Department Miscellaneous Return Book 1834–1838, 165. See also Domingues da Silva et al., "The Diaspora of Africans Liberated from Slave Ships in the Nineteenth Century."

17. Act for the Abolition of the Slave Trade, 1807, 47 Geo. III, c. 36 sess. I, 25 March 1807, *The Statutes of the Kingdom of Great Britain and Ireland: 1807–1869* (London, 1807–1869).

18. "Sierra Leone. Report of the Commissioners of Inquiry into the State of the Colony of Sierra Leone. First part," *BPP*, 1826–1827 (312), VII.267: 52–54; Sarah Biller, ed., *Memoir of the Late Hannah Kilham* (London: Darton and Harvey 1837), 454; "Report of the Commission of Inquiry into the State of Sierra Leone 1826–1827," appendix A 4–9, TNA, CO 267/91; Evidence of William Hamilton, "Report from the Select Committee on the West Coast of Africa . . . Part I," *BPP*, 1842 (551 551-II), XI.1, XII.1: 272.

19. Jeffcott to Findlay, 11 July 1831, TNA, CO 267/109.

20. Ibid.

21. Ibid.

22. Ibid.

23. Ibid.

24. Turner, "The Limits of Abolition," 336; Schwarz, "Reconstructing the Life Histories," 202–3.

25. *The African Herald,* 29 July 1809.

26. "Return Books," 10 November 1834, quoted in Stephen, "A History of the Settlement of Liberated Africans," 31. See also Schwarz, "Reconstructing the Life Histories," 202.

27. Cole to Johnson, 12 July 1828, PASL, Liberated African Department Letterbook 1827–1828.

28. Cleugh to Johnson, 14 April 1828, ibid.

29. "Sierra Leone. Report of the Commissioners of Inquiry into the State of the Colony of Sierra Leone. First part," *BPP*, 1826–1827 (312), VII.267: 55; Crooks, *A History of the Colony of Sierra Leone,* 118; Kenneth Macaulay instructions, 22 March 1826, PASL, Liberated African Department Letterbook 1820–1826.

30. "Sierra Leone. Report of the Commissioners of Inquiry into the State of the Colony of Sierra Leone. First part," *BPP*, 1826–1827 (312), VII.267: 54. Henry Dundas Campbell later gave evidence that after adjudication, "the [liberated African] men were put into gangs, and sent to labour on the public works, with the convicts, for three months," Evidence of Henry Dundas Campbell, *Proceedings of the General Antislavery Convention Called by the Committee*

of the British and Foreign Antislavery Society (London: British and Foreign Antislavery Society, 1841), 502.

31. Bathurst to Macaulay, 11 July 1826, quoted in Claude George, *The Rise of British West Africa* (London: Frank Cass, 1967), 280.

32. Denham to Hay, 13 February 1827, TNA, CO 323/148; Denham to Hay, 20 September 1827, TNA, CO 323/148.

33. Denham to Hay, 27 August 1827, PASL, Liberated African Department Letterbook 1827–1828; Denham to Hay, 4 July 1827, TNA, CO 267/83. See also Denham instructions to managers, 25 March 1827, TNA, CO 323/148; *The Missionary Register for MDCCCXXVIII* (London: Seeley, 1828), 16–17.

34. Denham to Hay, 4 July 1827, TNA, CO 267/83; Denham to Hay, 27 August 1827, PASL, Liberated African Department Letterbook 1827–1828.

35. Denham to Hay, 5 February 1828, TNA, CO 323/151. See also Evidence of Captain William Jardin Purchase, "Report from the Select Committee on the Settlements of Sierra Leone and Fernando Po," *BPP*, 1830 (661), X.405: 30. See also PASL, Liberated African Department Statement of Disposals 1821–1833, disposal of 2 liberated African men from the "Teresa" who were "placed on board the Redwing to learn the art of Seamanship" (undated entry; likely 1825).

36. Dundas Campbell to Glenelg, 5 September 1836, TNA, CO 267/133.

37. Dundas Campbell to Glenelg, 8 August 1836, ibid.

38. Dundas Campbell to Glenelg, 5 September 1836, ibid.

39. Evidence of H. D. Campbell, "Report from the Select Committee on the West Coast of Africa . . . Part I," *BPP*, 1842 (551 551-II), XI.1, XII.1: 553.

40. Fergusson to Stanley, 30 January 1842, TNA, CO 267/175, quoted in Robert W. July, *The Origins of Modern African Thought* (Trenton: Africa World Press, 2004), 136.

41. A. B. C. Sibthorpe, *The History of Sierra Leone,* 28; Christopher Fyfe, "A. B. C. Sibthorpe: A Tribute," *History in Africa* 19 (1992): 327; Howard, "New Insights on Liberated Africans: The 1831 Freetown Census."

42. Findlay to Goderich, 15 May 1833, quoted in Stephen, "A History of the Settlement of Liberated Africans," 31.

43. *The British Critic for 1816* 5 (April 1816): 366.

44. Rankin, *The White Man's Grave,* vol. 2, 108–9. See also Downing, "Contested Freedoms," 195–367; Fyfe, *A History of Sierra Leone,* 264.

45. Rankin, *The White Man's Grave,* vol. 2, 92, 109–10 (emphasis in original).

46. Fyfe, *A History of Sierra Leone,* 264.

47. A Young Lady/"Mary Church," *Sierra Leone; Or, the Liberated Africans* (London: Longman, 1835), 31–36.

48. [Elizabeth Melville], *A Residence at Sierra Leone, by a Lady* (London: John Murray, 1849), 32, 73–74, 123–24, 126, 241, 252.

49. "Mary Church," *Sierra Leone*, 31–32; Downing, "Contested Freedoms," 352.

50. [Melville], *A Residence at Sierra Leone*, 309.

51. Coke, *An Interesting Narrative of a Mission*, 39–40.

52. Walker, *The Church of England Mission in Sierra Leone*, 302, 328.

53. Kilham, *Present State of the Colony of Sierra Leone*, 4, 22.

54. Ibid., 13, 22. Emphasis in original. See also Katrina H. Keefer, *Children, Education, and Empire in Early Colonial Sierra Leone* (London: Routledge, 2018).

55. Biller, *Memoir of the Late Hannah Kilham*, 419–21, 454.

56. [Melville], *A Residence at Sierra Leone*, 32; Rankin, *The White Man's Grave*, vol. 2, 133; "Report from the Select Committee on the West Coast of Africa . . . Part I," appendix 17, *BPP*, 1842 (551 551-II), XI.1, XII.1: 389.

57. Jeffcott to Findlay, 11 July 1831, TNA, CO 267/109. See also Rankin, *The White Man's Grave*, vol. 2, 109.

58. Peterson, *Province of Freedom*, 203; Evidence of Dundas Campbell, "Report from the Select Committee on the West Coast of Africa . . . Part I," *BPP*, 1842 (551 551-II), XI.1, XII.1: 553; Evidence of Dundas Campbell, *Proceedings of the General Antislavery Convention Called by the Committee of the British and Foreign Antislavery Society* (London: Ward, 1841), 502; Russell to Maclean, 14 July 1841, "Report from the Select Committee on the West Coast of Africa . . . Part I," appendix 4, *BPP*, 1842 (551 551-II), XI.1, XII.1: 139–40.

59. Darius Rejali, *Torture and Democracy* (Princeton: Princeton University Press, 2007), 233.

60. Evidence of R. R. Madden, "Report from the Select Committee on the West Coast of Africa . . . Part I," *BPP*, 1842 (551 551-II), XI.1, XII.1: 646; Walker, *The Church of England Mission;* Dundas Campbell to Glenelg, 5 September 1836, TNA, CO 267/133.

61. For example, Dundas Campbell to Glenelg, 5 September 1836, TNA, CO 267/133; Prince Manna to Denman, 28 November 1840, "Report from the Select Committee on the West Coast of Africa . . . Part I," appendix 22, *BPP*, 1842 (551 551-II), XI.1, XII.1: 458.

62. Barbara Bush, "'Daughters of Injur'd Africk': African Women and the Transatlantic Slave Trade," *Women's History Review* 17, no. 5 (2008): 673–98; Ann Laura Stoler, "On Degrees of Imperial Sovereignty," *Public Culture* 18, no. 1 (2006): 132.

63. African Institution, *Ninth Report of the Directors of the African Institution* (London: African Institution, 1815), 62; Robert Thorpe, *Postscript to the Reply "Point by Point": Containing an Exposure of the Misrepresentation of the Treatment of the Captured Negroes at Sierra Leone* (London, 1815), 29.

64. Journal of Johnson, 21 May 1821, BL, CMS, CAI/O126; Fyfe, *A History of Sierra Leone,* 138.

65. Downing, "Contested Freedoms," 37–41; Cole to Jones, 11 June 1836, PASL, Colonial Secretary's Letter Book 1835–1836, quoted in part in Silke Strickrodt, "African Girls' Samplers from Mission Schools in Sierra Leone, 1820s to 1840s," *History in Africa* 37 (2010): 203.

66. "Sierra Leone. Report of the Commissioners of Inquiry into the State of the Colony of Sierra Leone. First part," *BPP,* 1826–1827 (312), VII.267: 32.

67. Deposition of Richard Garrett, "Report of the Commission of Inquiry into the State of Sierra Leone 1826–1827," appendix A 11, TNA, CO 267/91.

68. Deposition of Thomas Brown, ibid. See also Deposition of James Maggan of Kissy, ibid.

69. See also Depositions of Jem Joe, John Spencer, Matthew Mason, and Robert Gray, ibid.

70. Deposition of Malicow, ibid.

71. Deposition of John Taylor, ibid.

72. E. Francis White, *Sierra Leone's Settler Women Traders: Women on the Afri-European Frontier* (Ann Arbor: University of Michigan Press, 1987), 33. See also Suzanne Schwarz, "Adaptation in the Aftermath of Slavery: Women, Trade, and Property in Sierra Leone, c. 1790–1812," in *African Women in the Atlantic World,* ed. Mariana P. Candido and Adam Jones (Rochester: James Currey, 2019), 19–37.

73. Anderson, "Uncovering Testimonies of Slavery and the Slave Trade in Missionary Sources," 621; SHADD: Studies in the History of the African Diaspora—Documents, https://web.archive.org/save/https://tubman.info .yorku.ca/publications/shadd/. See also Shell, *Children of Hope: The Odyssey of the Oromo Slaves from Ethiopia to South Africa,* appendix B.

74. "Narratives of Three Liberated Negroes," *Church Missionary Record,* no. 10, vol. 8 (October 1837), BL, CMS, Sierra Leone, CA1/O112/2.

75. Richard Anderson and Maria Clara Sales Carneiro Sampaio, "From Kealoo to James Will: Slavery and Liberation in Yorubaland and Sierra Leone," available at SSRN: https://ssrn.com/abstract=2252236. I am very grateful to Richard Anderson for kindly sharing his research on James Will, including transcriptions of his and other liberated Africans' narratives, and the draft of his article co-authored with Maria Clara Sales Carneiro Sampaio. See also "Third Report from the Select Committee on the Slave Trade; Together with the Minutes of Evidence, and appendix," *BPP,* 1847–1848 (536), XXII.467: 184.

76. Eliza Wilson, "A Brief Memoir of the Late Peter Wilson, Member of Kissy Road Church, By His Wife Eliza" (1860), BL, CMS, Sierra Leone, CA1/

O6/53. See also narratives of Samuel Ajayi Crowther, Joseph Wright, and Ali Eisami: Curtin, *Africa Remembered*, and Lovejoy, "'Freedom Narratives' of Transatlantic Slavery," 91–107.

77. BL, CMS, CAI/059, Journal of Frederick Bulman, 9 March 1842; May, *A Brief Sketch of the Life of the Reverend Joseph May*; Leo Spitzer, *Lives in Between: Assimilation and Marginality in Austria, Brazil, West Africa, 1780–1945* (Cambridge: Cambridge University Press, 1989), 61–63. Elizabeth Melville gave an account of Peter Wilson working in her household after his apprenticeship: [Melville], *A Residence at Sierra Leone*, 23–24.

78. Peterson, *Province of Freedom*, 300.

79. Scanlan, *Freedom's Debtors*, 73.

80. Biller, *Memoir of the Late Hannah Kilham*, 425.

81. [Melville], *A Residence at Sierra Leone*, 32.

82. Jeffcott to Findlay, 11 July 1831, TNA, CO 267/109. See also "Mary Church," *Sierra Leone*, 31.

83. Fyfe, *A History of Sierra Leone*, 230.

84. Pine to Grey, 26 April 1848, TNA, CO 267/204.

85. See Bronwen Everill, *Abolition and Empire in Sierra Leone and Liberia* (Basingstoke: Palgrave, 2012); Nemata Blyden, "'We Have the Cause of Africa at Heart': West Indians and African-Americans in 19th Century Freetown," in *New Perspectives on the Sierra Leone Krio*, ed. Mac Dixon-Fyle and Gibril Cole (New York: Peter Lang, 2006), 91–105.

86. Pine to Grey, 26 April 1848, TNA, CO 267/204; Hansard House of Commons Parliamentary Debates, 3rd series, 25 February 1845, vol. 77, cc. 1173–203; "Memorandum on the Condition and Method of Disposal of Captured Africans at Sierra Leone, by Sir George Barrow," 1847, TNA, CO 879/1/29. See also Fyfe, *A History of Sierra Leone*, 230 and [Melville], *A Residence at Sierra Leone*, 124.

87. Fergusson to Stanley, 30 January 1842, TNA, CO 267/175, quoted in July, *Origins of Modern African Thought*, 136.

88. Evidence of H. D. Campbell, "Report from the Select Committee on the West Coast of Africa . . . Part I," *BPP*, 1842 (551 551-II), XI.1, XII.1: 553.

Chapter 7. Enlistment

1. Service Record of William Blazely, TNA, WO 97/1155.

2. Service Record of Charles Dickens, TNA, WO 97/1157.

3. David Lambert, "'[A] Mere Cloak for Their Proud Contempt and Antipathy Towards the African Race': Imagining Britain's West India Regiments in the

Caribbean, 1795–1838," *The Journal of Imperial and Commonwealth History* 46, no. 4 (2018): 627–50.

4. "Report of the Commission of Inquiry into the State of Sierra Leone 1826–1827," appendix A 11, TNA, CO 267/91; Missionary Journal of Johnson, 21 May 1821, BL, CMS, CAI/O126; Fyfe, *A History of Sierra Leone,* 138; Ryan, "'It Was Necessary to Do Something with Those Women': Colonial Governance and the 'Disposal' of Women and Girls in Early Nineteenth-Century Sierra Leone."

5. "Sierra Leone. Report of the Commissioners of Inquiry into the State of the Colony of Sierra Leone. First part," *BPP,* 1826–1827 (312), VII.267: 25; Carl Campbell, "Jonas Mohammed Bath and the Free Mandingos in Trinidad: The Question of Their Repatriation to Africa, 1831–8," *Journal of African Studies* 2, no. 4 (1975–1976): 485.

6. Charlotte Macdonald and Rebecca Lenihan, "Paper Soldiers: The Life, Death, and Reincarnation of Nineteenth-Century Military Files Across the British Empire," *Rethinking History* 22, no. 3 (2018): 382.

7. Quoted in Frederick Cooper and Ann L. Stoler, "Introduction—Tensions of Empire: Colonial Control and Visions of Rule," *American Ethnologist* 16, no. 4 (1989): 613.

8. Lambert, "[A] Mere Cloak," 631–32.

9. There has been a recent resurgence of interest in British military recruitment of Africans. Regimental historians offered some of the earliest studies: A. B. Ellis, *History of the First West India Regiment* (1885); Roger Norman Buckley, *Slaves in Red Coats: The British West India Regiments, 1795–1815* (New Haven: Yale University Press, 1979), 130–34; Roger Norman Buckley, *The British Army in the West Indies: Society and the Military in the Revolutionary Age* (Gainesville: University Press of Florida, 1998). See also Brian Dyde, *The Empty Sleeve: The Story of the West India Regiments of the British Army* (St John's, Antigua: Hansib, 1997), and Kuczynski, *Demographic Survey of the British Colonial Empire,* vol. 1, 117–25. Christopher Leslie Brown and Philip D. Morgan, eds., *Arming Slaves: From Classical Times to the Modern Age* (New Haven: Yale University Press, 2006), broke important new ground in demonstrating the global dimensions of the phenomenon of enslaved soldiers, and highlighting the experiences of the enslaved and the impact of these practices on slavery as an institution. The recent Africa's Sons Under Arms project produced important scholarly contributions from David Lambert, Tim Lockley, Elizabeth Cooper, Melissa Bennett, Rosalyn Narayan, Manuel Barcia, Gary Sellick, Sarah Davis Westwood, Michelle Moyd, and Anna Maguire. See David Lambert and Tim Lockley, eds., Africa's Sons Under

Arms, special issue, *Slavery and Abolition* 39, no. 3 (2018); Tim Lockley, *Military Medicine and the Making of Race: Life and Death in the West India Regiments 1795–1874* (Cambridge: Cambridge University Press, 2020). See also S. C. Ukpabi, "Recruiting for the British Colonial Forces in West Africa in the Nineteenth Century," *Odù: Journal of Yoruba and Related Studies* 10 (1974): 77–97; Paul Mmegha Mbaeyi, *British Military and Naval Forces in West African History, 1807–1874* (New York: NOK, 1978), 41, 67; Ineke Van Kessel, "African Mutinies in the Netherlands East Indies: A Nineteenth Century Colonial Paradox," in *Rethinking Resistance: Revolt and Violence in African History,* ed. Jon Abbink, Mirjam de Bruijn, and Klaas van Walraven (Leiden: Brill, 2003), 141–69; Ineke Van Kessel, "'Courageous but Insolent': African Soldiers in the Dutch East Indies as Seen by Dutch Officials and Indonesian Neighbours," *Transforming Cultures eJournal* 4, no. 2 (2009). Most recently, Matthew Dziennik and Kyle Prochnow have done much to illuminate the wider picture of British recruitment of Africans for the West India Regiments throughout the Atlantic world: Kyle Prochnow, "'Saving an Extraordinary Expense to the Nation': African Recruitment for the West India Regiments in British Atlantic World," *Atlantic Studies* 18, no. 2 (2020): 149–71; Matthew Dziennik, *Colonial Recruitment and the Making of the British Empire, c. 1756–1857* (forthcoming). I am very grateful to Matthew for kindly sharing insights from his forthcoming book.

10. Hansard House of Commons Parliamentary Debates, 1st series, 2 June 1815, vol. 31, c. 592.

11. Brown and Morgan, eds., *Arming Slaves;* Buckley, *Slaves in Red Coats,* 55–56, 82–105. See also Maria Alessandra Bollettino, "'Of Equal or of More Service': Black Soldiers and the British Empire in the Mid-Eighteenth-Century Caribbean," *Slavery and Abolition* 38, no. 3 (2017): 510–33.

12. Wilberforce to Pitt, 14 September 1804, Robert and Samuel Wilberforce, eds., *The Correspondence of William Wilberforce,* vol. 1 (London: John Murray, 1840), 309–11.

13. Buckley, *Slaves in Red Coats,* 57.

14. Macaulay to Peel, 22 August 1811, TNA, CO 267/31.

15. African Institution, *Fourth Report,* 57–66; Fyfe, *A History of Sierra Leone,* 135–36. See also "Instructions to Naval Commanders and Privateers," TNA, WO 1/742; "Treaty Between His Britannic Majesty and His Catholic Majesty," *BPP,* 1818 (001) XVIII.9: 11; Bethell, "The Mixed Commissions," 79.

16. Buckley, *Slaves in Red Coats,* 125–26; Prochnow, "Saving an Extraordinary Expense to the Nation," 10–11.

17. Evidence of H. W. Macaulay, "Report from the Select Committee on Aborigines" *BPP,* 1837 (425), VII.1: 34. See also A. B. Ellis, *The History of the First*

West India Regiment (London: Chapman and Hall, 1885), 188, 208–12; Ricketts to Hay, 8 December 1828, *BPP,* 1830 (57), XXI.225: 33; Anderson, "The Diaspora of Sierra Leone's Liberated Africans," 105.

18. Kuczynski, *Demographic Survey of the British Colonial Empire,* vol. 1, 112–13, 117–21.

19. Dyde, *The Empty Sleeve,* 30.

20. Thompson to the Directors of the African Institution, 2 November 1808, HHC, DTH 1/27; "Papers Relating to a Recruiting Depot on the Coast of Africa, for the West India Regiments," *BPP,* 1812 (370), X.301: 1–9.

21. Maeve Ryan, "The Human Consequences of Slave Trade Abolition: The Liberated African Department and the Administration of Liberated Africans at Sierra Leone, 1808–1863" (unpublished PhD thesis, Trinity College Dublin, 2014), appendix 1, table 3, based on TNA, CO 267/127. See also African Institution, *Ninth Report,* 54. Maxwell to Liverpool, 10 December 1811, TNA, CO 267/30; Frederick to Bathurst, 8 December 1814, TNA, CO 267/32. Different enlistment figures for 1812 and 1813 are suggested in "Slave Trade: Further Papers Relating to Captured Negroes Enlisted, and to the Recruiting of Negro Soldiers in Africa, for the West India Regiments," *BPP,* 1813–1814 (356), XII.345.

22. Buckley, *The British Army in the West Indies,* 141–51.

23. Robert Burroughs, "Eyes on the Prize: Journeys in Slave Ships Taken as Prizes by the Royal Navy," *Slavery and Abolition* 31, no. 1 (2010): 99–115.

24. "Sierra Leone. Report of the Commissioners of Inquiry into the State of the Colony of Sierra Leone. First part," *BPP,* 1826–1827 (312), VII.267: 54.

25. Mbaeyi, *British Military and Naval Forces,* 40–41.

26. Ryan, "The Human Consequences of Slave Trade Abolition," appendix 1, table 3, based on TNA, CO 267/127.

27. Buckley, *Slaves in Red Coats,* 135–43; Kuczynski, *Demographic Survey of the British Colonial Empire,* 122–25; Taylor to Sutherland, 6 May 1824, TNA, CO 267/62 quoted in Prochnow, "Saving an Extraordinary Expense to the Nation," 17.

28. "Report of Commission of Enquiry into the Conduct of Mr. Dixon," 1848–1849, TNA, CO 267/210, appendix 1.

29. H. J. Ricketts, *Narrative of the Ashantee War* (London: Simpkin and Marshall, 1831), 187–88; Evidence of Thomas Keogh, M.D., "First Report from the Select Committee on Slave Trade," *BPP,* 1847–1848 (272), XXII.1, 146.

30. "Sierra Leone. Report of the Commissioners of Inquiry into the State of the Colony of Sierra Leone. First part," *BPP,* 1826–1827 (312), VII.267: 26.

31. Rankin, *The White Man's Grave,* vol. 2, 111–12.

32. Crooks, *A History of the Colony of Sierra Leone,* 86.

33. Macdonald to Stanley, 10 October 1843, quoted in Kuczynski, *Demographic Survey of the British Colonial Empire,* vol. 1, 121; "Sierra Leone. Report of the Commissioners of Inquiry into the State of the Colony of Sierra Leone. First part," *BPP,* 1826–1827 (312), VII.267: 26.

34. Robert Thorpe, *A Reply "Point by Point" to the Special Report of the Directors of the African Institution* (London: Rivington, 1815), 84.

35. Thorpe, *A Letter to William Wilberforce,* 46–47, 23–24, 50–51.

36. Rankin, *The White Man's Grave,* vol. 2, 107.

37. Denham to Hay, 14 May 1828, *BPP,* 1830 (57), XXI.225: 25–26.

38. Reffell evidence to the 1826–1827 Commission of Inquiry, Questions 28–31, TNA, CO 267/92, appendix B, 10.

39. "Sierra Leone. Report of the Commissioners of Inquiry into the State of the Colony of Sierra Leone. First part," *BPP,* 1826–1827 (312), VII.267: 26.

40. "Statistical Reports on the Sickness, Mortality, & Invaliding, Among the Troops in Western Africa, St. Helena, the Cape of Good Hope, and the Mauritius," *BPP,* 1840 (228), XXX.135: 15.

41. Ellis, *The History of the First West India Regiment,* 16; Cole to Morgan (undated; likely June 1826), PASL, Liberated African Department Letterbook 1820–1826.

42. Ellis, *The History of the First West India Regiment,* 192–93.

43. Reffell evidence to the 1826–1827 Commission of Inquiry, Questions 28–31, TNA, CO 267/92, appendix B 10. See also Scanlan, *Freedom's Debtors,* 130–53.

44. Reffell evidence to the 1826–1827 Commission of Inquiry, Questions 28–31, TNA, CO 267/92, appendix B 10; Fyfe, *A History of Sierra Leone,* 178.

45. Denham to Hay, 14 May 1828, "Sierra Leone. Return to an address of the Honourable House of Commons, dated 19th May 1829," *BPP,* 1830 (57), XXI.225: 25–26; Ukpabi, "Recruiting for the British Colonial Forces in West Africa in the Nineteenth Century," 82–85; Denham to Hay, 14 May 1828, *BPP,* 1830 (57), XXI.225: 25–26; African Colonial Corps Muster Books and Pay Lists, January 1829–December 1830, TNA, WO 12/10356; Cleugh to McFoy, Pierce and Campbell, 26 June 1827, PASL, Liberated African Department Letterbook 1827–1828.

46. Denham to Lumley, 30 September 1827, PASL, Liberated African Department Letterbook 1827–1828.

47. Denham to Hay, 14 May 1828, *BPP,* 1830 (57), XXI.225: 26.

48. "Royal Hospital Chelsea: Soldiers Service Documents" series, TNA, WO 97/1155–62. See also WO 97/1171–72.

49. Macdonald and Lenihan, "Paper Soldiers," 375–89.

50. This year range reflects the findings of the sample set, not the full year range of all records within TNA, WO 97/1155–62. See Maeve Ryan, "The Human Consequences of Slave Trade Abolition," appendix 7.

51. Service Record of Lord Arundel, TNA, WO 97/1155.

52. Sixteen of the records did not specify age at attestation. Sixty-five records do not specify locations of service.

53. Service Record of Henry Blunt, TNA, WO 97/1155; Service Records of William Genoo and George Francis, TNA, WO 97/1158.

54. Service Record of Nicholas Raven, TNA, WO 97/1161.

55. [Tulloch and Marshall], *Statistical Report on the Sickness, Mortality, and Invaliding Among the Troops in the West Indies* (London: Clowes and Sons, 1838), 3–96. See also Lockley, *Military Medicine and the Making of Race,* 84–138; Philip D. Curtin, *Disease and Empire: The Health of European Troops in the Conquest of Africa* (Cambridge: Cambridge University Press, 1998); Peter Burroughs, "An Unreformed Army? 1815–1868," in *The Oxford History of the British Army,* ed. David G. Chandler and Ian Beckett (Oxford: Oxford University Press, 2003).

56. [Tulloch and Marshall], *Statistical Report on the Sickness, Mortality, and Invaliding Among the Troops in the West Indies,* 5.

57. Ibid., 43.

58. Ibid., 72–76.

59. Buckley, *The British Army in the West Indies,* 281–95; Buckley, *Slaves in Red Coats,* 100–105; Dr. T. Gordon's Observations, enclosed in "General Return of the Sick and Wounded . . . to January 1803," TNA, CO 318/32.

60. Buckley, "The Destruction of the British Army in the West Indies, 1793–1815: A Medical History," *Journal of the Society for Army Historical Research* 56, no. 226 (1978): 79–92; Buckley, *The British Army in the West Indies,* 281–95.

61. "Royal Hospital Chelsea: Soldiers Service Documents" series, TNA, WO 97/1155–62.

62. Service Records of Charles Bate and James Ashley, TNA, WO 97/1155.

63. Peter Burroughs, "Crime and Punishment in the British Army, 1815–1870," *The English Historical Review* 100, no. 396 (1985): 545–71.

64. [Tulloch and Marshall], *Statistical Report on the Sickness, Mortality, and Invaliding Among the Troops in the West Indies,* 7, 12, 45, 50, 74, 77.

65. Burroughs, "Crime and Punishment in the British Army, 1815–1870," 549–53. See also Buckley, *The British Army in the West Indies,* 217. Matthew Dziennik's important forthcoming study situates the recruitment and experiences of African soldiers in its global context, with a close examination of the experiences and treatment of black and white recruits of the lowest ranks.

Dziennik's findings to date demonstrate the importance of coercion and deceit in the recruitment and impressment process, and suggest a much greater degree of commonality of experience in this regard than we might have expected between black and white soldiers of the West India Regiments. Dziennik, *Colonial Recruitment and the Making of the British Empire.*

66. Service Record of Francis Cafarelli, TNA, WO 97/1156. See also Court Martial of William Grant, TNA, WO 71/298; Thomas August, "Rebels with a Cause: The St. Joseph Mutiny of 1837," *Slavery and Abolition* 12, no. 2 (1991): 82–84.

67. See also Fyfe, "Peter Nicholls—Old Calabar and Freetown," 105–9.

68. Papers relating to the "Mutiny of the 'Black Troops,'" TNA, CO 295/118; Hill to Glenelg, 20 June 1837, TNA, CO 295/114.

69. E. L. Joseph, *History of Trinidad* (Trinidad: Mills, 1839), 265.

70. See also Duffield, "From Slave Colonies to Penal Colonies: The West Indian Convict Transportees to Australia," *Slavery and Abolition* 7, no. 1 (1986): 25–45.

71. Joseph, *History of Trinidad,* 265.

72. Evidence of Colonel Bush, quoted in Lionel Mordaunt Fraser, *History of Trinidad, 1814–1839* (London, 1891), vol. 2, 348–50; Hill to Glenelg, 10 November 1837, TNA, CO 295/114.

73. Joseph, *History of Trinidad,* 261; Fraser, *History of Trinidad,* vol. 2, 345.

74. See Private letter, 27 April 1816, St Ann's, Barbados, TNA, CO 28/85 for a brief account of the behaviour of the African soldiers of the West India Regiment during the suppression of Bussa's Rebellion.

75. Ellis, *The History of the First West India Regiment,* 193. However, see also "Remarks on the Establishment of the West India Regiments," enclosed in Hislop to the Duke of York, 22 July 1804, TNA, WO 1/95.

76. "Class B. Correspondence with Spain . . . January 1 to December 31 1841," *BPP,* 1842 (403), XLIII.1: 8, 117–39, 142, 159, 286; Commissioners to Palmerston, 23 September 1837, *BPP,* 1837–1838 (124), L.1: 135–36. See Dale Graden, *Disease, Resistance, and Lies: The Demise of the Transatlantic Slave Trade to Brazil and Cuba* (Baton Rouge: Louisiana State University Press, 2014), 159; Nelson, "Liberated Africans in the Atlantic World: The Courts of Mixed Commission in Havana and Rio de Janeiro 1819–1871," 105–39; Nelson, "Slavery, Race, and Conspiracy: The HMS *Romney* in Nineteenth-Century Cuba," 174–95.

77. Samo to Palmerston, 29 June 1840, *BPP,* 1841 Session 1 (330), XXX.1: 360.

78. Palmerston to Disbrowe, 25 November 1836, *BPP,* 1837 (002), LIV.377: 52–53.

79. Palmerston to Disbrowe, 10 September 1840, *BPP,* 1841 Session 1 (331), XXX.373: 240–41.

80. Palmerston to Dedel, 7 September 1840, ibid., 239–40; Palmerston to Disbrowe, 8 December 1840, ibid., 252–53.

81. Palmerston to Disbrowe, 10 September 1840, ibid., 240–41.

82. Palmerston to Disbrowe, 8 December 1840, ibid., 252–53.

83. See Pine to Labouchere, 10 February 1858, TNA, CO 96/43. See also Ukpabi, "Recruiting for the British Colonial Forces in West Africa," 84–85.

84. Van Kessel, "African Mutinies in the Netherlands East Indies," 143–44, 164.

85. Bourqueney to Palmerston, 17 December 1840 (plus six enclosures), *BPP,* 1842 (404), XLIV: 16–31. See also "Class C. Correspondence with Foreign Powers . . . May 11 to Dec. 31 1840," *BPP,* 1841 Session 1 (332), XXX.645: 1–41; Myron Echenburg, *Colonial Conscripts: The Tirailleurs Sénégalais in French West Africa, 1857–1960* (Portsmouth: Heinemann, 1991), 8–9; Echenberg, "Slaves into Soldiers: Social Origins of the *Tirailleurs Sénégalais,*" in *Africans in Bondage,* ed. Lovejoy, 311–34; Doherty and Lewis to Palmerston, 6 May 1840, *BPP,* 1841 (330), XXX.1: 4–5.

86. Hansard House of Commons Parliamentary Debates, 28 February 1805, vol. 3, c. 668.

87. Maxwell to Bathurst, 13 September 1812, TNA, CO 267/34.

Epilogue

1. Immigration: The Detention Centre Rules 2001, Statutory Instrument 2001/238, www.legislation.gov.uk/uksi/2001/238/pdfs/uksi_20010238_en .pdf. Under the Nationality, Immigration and Asylum Act 2002, these centres were renamed "Immigration Removal Centres."

2. Barnett, "Humanitarian Governance," 380.

3. Aidan Forth, *Barbed-Wire Imperialism: Britain's Empire of Camps, 1876–1903* (Oakland: University of California Press, 2017).

4. Ann Laura Stoler, "Colony," *Political Concepts: A Critical Lexicon* 1, www .politicalconcepts.org/colony-stoler/; Didier Fassin, "Compassion and Repression: The Moral Economy of Immigration Policies in France," *Cultural Anthropology* 20, no. 3 (2005): 381.

5. Lester and Dussart, *Colonization and the Origins of Humanitarian Governance.* See also Lester, Boehme, and Mitchell, *Ruling the World: Freedom, Civilisation, and Liberalism in the Nineteenth-Century British Empire.*

6. Forth, *Barbed-Wire Imperialism,* 3–5.

7. Ibid., 6, 14; Michel Foucault, *Discipline and Punish: The Birth of the Prison* (London: Penguin, 1977), 297–302; Anderson, *A Global History of Convicts and Penal Colonies;* Katherine Roscoe, "A Natural Hulk: Australia's Carceral Islands in the Colonial Period, 1788–1901," *International Review of Social History* 63 (2018): 45–63.

8. Charles Trevelyan, *The Irish Crisis* (London: Longman, Brown and Green, 1848), 185; Tehila Sasson and James Vernon, "Practising the British Way of Famine: Technologies of Relief, 1770–1985," *European Review of History* 22, no. 6 (2015): 861–63. Charles Trevelyan was the assistant secretary to the Treasury. He was also the son-in-law of Zachary Macaulay.

9. Quoted in Forth, *Barbed-Wire Imperialism,* 64–68.

10. Although the policy of paying immigration detainees in the United Kingdom very low wages for work has attracted some accusations of exploitation. See Karen McVeigh, "Yarl's Wood Detainees 'Paid 50p an Hour,'" *The Guardian,* 2 January 2011, www.theguardian.com/uk/2011/jan/02/yarls-wood-detainees -paid-50p-hour. On UN cash assistance and conditional cash transfer policies, see United Nations High Commissioner for Refugees (UNHCR), "Policy on Cash-Based Interventions," 13 October 2016, UNHCR/HCP/2016/3; UNHCR, "Operational Guidelines for Cash-Based Interventions in Displacement Settings," 6 February 2015, https://reliefweb.int/report/world/operational -guidelines-cash-based-interventions-displacement-settings.

11. Physicians for Human Rights, "You Will Never See Your Child Again: The Persistent Psychological Effects of Family Separation," February 2020, https:// phr.org/our-work/resources/you-will-never-see-your-child-again-the -persistent-psychological-effects-of-family-separation/.

12. Lester, Boehme, and Mitchell, *Ruling the World: Freedom, Civilisation, and Liberalism in the Nineteenth-Century British Empire,* 7–12, 336–39.

13. William Mulligan, "The Fugitive Slave Circulars, 1875–76," *The Journal of Imperial and Commonwealth History* 37, no. 2 (2009): 183–205.

14. Shaw, *Britannia's Embrace,* 178.

15. Ibid., 207–41.

16. Mary Bosworth, *Inside Immigration Detention* (Oxford: Oxford University Press, 2014), 22.

17. "Purpose of Detention Centres," Immigration: The Detention Centre Rules 2001, Statutory Instrument 2001/238, www.legislation.gov.uk/uksi/2001/238 /pdfs/uksi_20010238_en.pdf. A report in 2020 noted that the number of detainees had fallen steeply following the onset of the COVID-19 pandemic in early 2020: Migration Observatory, "Briefing: Immigration Detention in the UK," 7th revision (20 May 2020), 3–9.

18. Stephen Shaw, "Review into the Welfare in Detention of Vulnerable Persons: A Report to the Home Office by Stephen Shaw," Cm 9186 (January 2016), https://assets.publishing.service.gov.uk/government/uploads/system /uploads/attachment_data/file/490783/52532_Shaw_Review_Print_Ready .pdf. The physical form of the IRCs has varied over time, and has included a floating detention centre, adapted from a decommissioned commercial ferry: Bosworth, *Inside Immigration Detention,* 26. On the history of "hulks" or floating prisons, see Anna McKay, "Private Contracting to State Control: The British Prison Hulk Establishment, 1776–1820," Economic History Society Annual Conference, Queen's University Belfast, April 2019; Charles Campbell, *The Intolerable Hulks: British Shipboard Confinement, 1776–1857,* 3rd ed. (Tucson: Fenestra, 2001). On private sector involvement, see Christine Bacon, "The Evolution of Immigration Detention in the UK: The Involvement of Private Prison Companies," RSC Working Paper (Oxford, Refugee Studies Centre), 1–36.

19. Shaw, "Review into the Welfare in Detention of Vulnerable Persons," 7.

20. Lucy McKay, "Jury Concludes Neglect and Gross Failures Contributed to the Death of Prince Fosu in Immigration Detention," 2 March 2020, http:// web.archive.org/web/20210714025355/https://www.inquest.org.uk/prince -fosu-inquest-conclusion.

21. Bosworth, *Inside Immigration Detention,* 19. See also "The Report of the Inquiry into the Use of Immigration Detention in the United Kingdom: A Joint Inquiry by the All Party Parliamentary Group on Refugees & the All Party Parliamentary Group on Migration," 40–42. See also detailed firsthand accounts of the experiences of detainees: Written evidence to the All-Party Inquiry, https://web.archive.org/save/https://detentioninquiry.com/submitted -evidence/written-evidence/.

22. Shaw, *Britannia's Embrace,* 238–40.

23. Janet Phillips and Harriet Spinks (Department of Parliamentary Services, Parliament of Australia), "Immigration Detention in Australia" (2013), http:// web.archive.org/web/20210714025816/https://parlinfo.aph.gov.au/parlInfo /download/%20library/prspub/1311498/upload_binary/1311498.pdf; Janet Phillips, "The 'Pacific Solution' Revisited: A Statistical Guide to the Asylum Seeker Caseloads on Nauru and Manus Island" (2012), http://web.archive .org/web/20210709204008/https://parlinfo.aph.gov.au/parlInfo/download /library/prspub/1893669/upload_binary/1893669.pdf;fileType=application /pdf.

24. "Asylum Policy After Brexit Considered in New Report," 11 October 2019, www.parliament.uk/business/committees/committees-a-z/lords-select/eu

-home-affairs-subcommittee/news-parliament-2017/brexit-asylum-report/; UNHCR, "Asylum in the UK," undated, https://web.archive.org/web /20200319172511/https://www.unhcr.org/uk/asylum-in-the-uk.html; UK Home Office, "How Many People Do We Grant Asylum or Protection To?" 22 August 2019, https://web.archive.org/web/20200319172644/https://www.gov .uk/government/publications/immigration-statistics-year-ending-june-2019 /how-many-people-do-we-grant-asylum-or-protection-to; UNHCR, "Global Trends in Forced Displacement in 2018" (20 June 2019): 3.

25. Fassin, *Humanitarian Reason,* 247–48.

Index

abduction, of liberated Africans, 47, 119, 193, 269n48; re-enslavement, 134, 188

Aberdeen, Lord, 72, 145, 149

Aberdeen Act (1845), 112, 147, 149, 268n37

abolition: in British empire, 9, 73, 77, 91, 139, 169; gradualism, 20, 40, 169; interpretation of policy, 74

Abolition Act. *See* Slavery Abolition Act (Emancipation Act, 1833); Slave Trade Abolition Act (1807)

abolitionists, 9; Anti-Slavery Society, 91; attacks on hypocrisy of, 37; Central Negro Emancipation Committee, 91; grand narrative of, 62–63; humanitarianism and, 10; motivations of, 3, 10, 16–17, 41; objectives of, 24–25; self-interest of, 7, 10, 27, 30–31, 33, 44; shareholders in Sierra Leone Company, 3; support for apprenticeships and enlistments, 40–41

Aboriginal peoples: resettlement programme, 64, 66–69, 234; rights of, 124

abuse, 11, 36; in Bahamas, 89; in Brazil, 148; in Cape Colony, 78–81; in Cuba, 142; of detainees, 238; protection from, 159; resistance to, 119

Adderley, Laura Rosanne, 86, 121

Address on Slavery in Cuba, Presented to the General Anti-Slavery Convention (Madden), 124

advocacy for liberated Africans, 138, 158; British self-image and, 139; driving

energy behind, 155; *emancipados* of Cuba and, 139–47; as exercise of power, 163–64; Hesketh's, 151–55; motivations of, 157–64; Turnbull's, 140–47

Africa, West. *See* Sierra Leone

African Herald, The, 176

African Institution, 15, 31, 34, 37, 38, 43–44, 62–63

agency, of liberated Africans, 70–71, 119, 186, 210, 224

agriculture, 67, 105–6, 173, 187

Anderson, Clare, 13, 131

Anderson, Richard, 104, 188

Angola, 158, 164. *See also* Luanda

Anstey, Roger, 18, 227

Anti-Slavery Society, 91

antislavery state, 18–19, 118

antislavery world system, 6, 231, 241; British self-image and, 227; encounters with objects of, 152; grand narrative of, 62–63; liberated African archipelago in, 132; moral order and, 163; power and, 17–19; sincerity of motives in, 157–64; using liberated Africans to serve, 129, 224

apprentice fees, 3, 35, 160

apprentices, 181; abuse of, 79–81, 91, 134, 173–79, 185, 191; escaped, 35; expenditures on, 195; hiring out of, 83; isolation of, 191, 192–93, 194; masters' obligations to, 169; murder of, 165, 173; names of, 190; number of, 172–73; obtained by liberated Africans, 179–80; official complaints by, 180; sexual exploitation of, 185